The Social Roots of Delusions

International Perspectives in Philosophy and Psychiatry

Series editors: Bill (K.W.M.) Fulford, Lisa Bortolotti, Matthew Broome, Katherine Morris, John Z. Sadler, and Giovanni Stanghellini

VOLUMES IN THE SERIES:

Maladapting Minds: Philosophy, Psychiatry, and Evolutionary Theory
Adriaens and De Block

Portrait of the Psychiatrist as a Young Man: The Early Writing and Work of R.D. Laing, 1927–1960
Beveridge

Mind, Meaning, and Mental Disorder 2e
Bolton and Hill

What is Mental Disorder?
Bolton

Delusions and Other Irrational Beliefs
Bortolotti

Postpsychiatry
Bracken and Thomas

Philosophy, Psychoanalysis, and the A-Rational Mind
Brakel

Unconscious Knowing and Other Essays in Psycho-Philosophical Analysis
Brakel

Psychiatry as Cognitive Neuroscience
Broome and Bortolotti (eds.)

Free Will and Responsibility: A Guide for Practitioners
Callender

Reconceiving Schizophrenia
Chung, Fulford, and Graham (eds.)

Psychiatry Reborn: Biopsychosocial psychiatry in modern medicine
Davies, Savulescu, Roache, and Loebel

Darwin and Psychiatry
De Block and Adriaens (eds.)

The Oxford Handbook of Philosophy and Psychiatry
Fulford, Davies, Gipps, Graham, Sadler, Stanghellini, and Thornton

Nature and Narrative: An Introduction to the New Philosophy of Psychiatry
Fulford, Morris, Sadler, and Stanghellini (eds.)

The Oxford Textbook of Philosophy and Psychiatry
Fulford, Thornton, and Graham

The Mind and its Discontents
Gillett

Psychiatric Neuroethics: Studies in Research and Practice
Glannon

The Abraham Dilemma
Graham

Is evidence-based psychiatry ethical?
Gupta

Thinking Through Dementia
Hughes

Thomas Szasz: An Appraisal of his Legacy
Haldipur, Knoll, and Luft (eds.)

Dementia: Mind, Meaning, and the Person
Hughes, Louw, and Sabat (eds.)

Talking Cures and Placebo Effects
Jopling

Vagueness in Psychiatry
Keil, Keuck, and Hauswald

Philosophical Issues in Psychiatry II: Nosology
Kendler and Parnas (eds.)

Philosophical Issues in Psychiatry III: The Nature and Sources of Historical Change
Kendler and Parnas (eds.)

Philosophical Issues in Psychiatry IV: Classification of Psychiatric Illness
Kendler and Parnas (eds.)

Philosophy of Psychedelics
Letheby

Discursive Perspectives in Therapeutic Practice
Lock and Strong (ed.)

Schizophrenia and the Fate of the Self
Lopez-Silva & McClelland

Intruders in the Mind: Interdisciplinary Perspectives on Thought Insertion
Lysaker and Lysaker

Embodied Selves and Divided Minds
Maiese

Responsibility and Psychopathy
Malatesti and McMillan

Body-Subjects and Disordered Minds
Matthews

Rationality and Compulsion: Applying action theory to psychiatry
Nordenfelt

Diagnostic Dilemmas in Child and Adolescent Psychiatry
Perring and Wells (eds.)

Philosophical Perspectives on Technology and Psychiatry
Phillips (ed.)

The Metaphor of Mental Illness
Pickering

Mapping the Edges and the In-between
Potter

Trauma, Truth, and Reconciliation: Healing Damaged Relationships
Potter (ed.)

The Philosophy of Psychiatry: A Companion
Radden

The Virtuous Psychiatrist
Radden and Sadler

Addiction and Weakness of Will
Radoilska

Autonomy and Mental Disorder
Radoilska (ed.)

Madness and the Demand for Recognition
Rashed

Feelings of Being: Phenomenology, psychiatry and the sense of reality
Ratcliffe

Experiences of Depression: A study in phenomenology
Ratcliffe

Recovery of People with Mental Illness: Philosophical and Related Perspectives
Rudnick (ed.)

Values and Psychiatric Diagnosis
Sadler

The Oxford Handbook of Psychiatric Ethics
Sadler, Van Staden, and Fulford

Madness and Modernism: Insanity in the light of modern art, literature, and thought
Sass

Disembodied Spirits and Deanimated Bodies: The Psychopathology of Common Sense
Stanghellini

Lost in Dialogue: Anthropology, Psychopathology, and Care
Stanghellini

One Century of Karl Jaspers Psychopathology
Stanghellini and Fuchs

Emotions and Personhood
Stanghellini and Rosfort

Essential Philosophy of Psychiatry
Thornton

The Oxford Handbook of Psychotherapy Ethics
Trachsel, (eds)

Naturalism, Hermeneutics, and Mental Disorder
Varga

The Healing Virtues: Character Ethics in Psychotherapy
Waring

Empirical Ethics in Psychiatry
Widdershoven, McMillan, Hope and Van der Scheer (eds.)

The Sublime Object of Psychiatry: Schizophrenia in Clinical and Cultural Theory
Woods

Alternate Perspectives on Psychiatric Validation: DSM, ICD, RDoC, and Beyond
Zachar, St. Stoyanov, Aragona, and Jablensky (eds.)

Intruders in the Mind: Interdisciplinary Perspectives on Thought Insertion
Lopez-Silva and McClelland

Vice and Psychiatric Diagnosis
Sadler

Philosophical Perspectives on Psychedelic Psychiatry
Letheby, Gerrans

Anatomy of an Avatar: The virtual self in pathologies of self awareness
Philip Gerrans

How Psychiatrists Make Decisions: The Science of Clinical Reasoning
Douglas W. Heinrichs

The Social Roots of Delusions

DANIEL WILLIAMS
SAM WILKINSON
KENGO MIYAZONO

OXFORD
UNIVERSITY PRESS

OXFORD
UNIVERSITY PRESS

Great Clarendon Street, Oxford, OX2 6DP,
United Kingdom

Oxford University Press is a department of the University of Oxford.
It furthers the University's objective of excellence in research, scholarship,
and education by publishing worldwide. Oxford is a registered trade mark of
Oxford University Press in the UK and in certain other countries.

Published in the United States of America by Oxford University Press
546 Fifth Avenue, New York, NY 10036, United States of America.

British Library Cataloguing in Publication Data
Data available

Library of Congress Control Number: 2026937328

ISBN 9780192874177

DOI: 10.1093/9780191976360.001.0001

Printed and bound by
CPI Group (UK) Ltd., Croydon, CR0 4YY

The manufacturer's authorized representative in the EU for product safety is
Oxford University Press España S.A. of Parque Empresarial San Fernando de Henares,
Avenida de Castilla, 2 - 28830 Madrid (www.oup.es/en or product.safety@oup.com).
OUP España S.A. also acts as importer into Spain of products made by the manufacturer.

FSC
www.fsc.org
MIX
Paper | Supporting responsible forestry
FSC® C013604

Contents

Preface

It is unusual in academic philosophy for a book to be co-authored. It is especially unusual for it to be co-authored by three people. Nevertheless, it is all the more fitting that a book that is fundamentally about human sociality and the capacity of humans to shape and influence each other's views should be written in this collaborative manner. One could say that this book is a product of the very phenomenon that it is fundamentally about: human sociality and collaboration. But this book is also about delusion. Hopefully there is not too much in what follows that people would consider delusional.

The very idea for the book was born from a series of blog posts that the three authors wrote for the *Imperfect Cognitions* blog (imperfectcognitions.blogspot.com) in May 2021. The first, written by Kengo Miyazono, published on 11th May, presented "The Social Epistemological Conception of Delusion", drawing closely on ideas from his co-authored paper with Alessandro Salice (Miyazono & Salice, 2021). The second, written by Daniel Williams, with his co-author Marcella Montagnese, published on 18th May, presented the core ideas from their paper "Bayesian Psychiatry and the Social Focus of Delusions" (Williams & Montagnese, 2023). And the third, written by Sam Wilkinson, presented the central ideas behind his paper "Expressivism about Delusion Attribution" (Wilkinson, 2020). Kengo reached out to both Sam and Dan and pointed out that the three contributions were saying very different, and yet highly complementary things. Conversations began over Zoom, and the rest, as they say, is history.

Although we have all contributed to every chapter and have endeavoured to make the book feel as coherent as possible, different authors had different responsibilities in the writing process. Daniel Williams is primarily responsible for Chapter 1, Part 2 (Chapters 3–5), and Chapters 7 and 8. Sam Wilkinson is primarily responsible for Chapter 2. Kengo Miyazono is primarily responsible for Chapter 9. All authors contributed equally to Chapter 6. Early parts of Chapter 2 are based on elements of Wilkinson (2020) and Wilkinson (2025). Chapter 9 is partly based on Miyazono & Salice (2021).

We would like to thank Lisa Bortolotti for starting the *Imperfect Cognitions* blog and for inviting us to contribute. Kengo and Sam had an opportunity for valuable discussion at the workshop "Are Conspiratorial Beliefs Pathological?" on 24 and 25 April at the University of Birmingham, and we would like to thank Ema Sullivan-Bissett for organising that. At numerous junctures, people have acted as valuable sounding boards for our ideas, including Lisa Bortolotti, Ema Sullivan-Bissett, Phil Corlett, and Ryan McKay. Dan Williams in particular would like to thank Stephen Gadsby, Marcella Montagnese, and Eric Funkhouser for helpful discussions. Sam Wilkinson would like to thank, on the topic of delusion attribution in particular, Tom Roberts, Victor Fernandez-Castro, Miguel Nunez de Prado Gordillo, and Marko Jurjako, as well as audiences at the University of Granada, Spain, and the University of Rijeka, Croatia. Kengo Miyazono would like to thank Alessandro Salice for research collaboration on group identification, which greatly informed the discussions in Chapter 9. He is also grateful to Alexandre Billon for hosting his productive research visit to Université de Lille in March 2023, during which he presented some of the ideas in this book at invited seminars. He acknowledges the financial support of JSPS KAKENHI (Grant Numbers: 21H00464 and 24H00076).

We would like to thank Lucy Jarman and Oxford University Press for their helpfulness and patience. And finally, we would like to thank our better halves, Marcella, Felicity, and Mie, for putting up with us through what must have felt at times like a never-ending process.

During the preparation of this work, the authors used Grammarly Premium and Claude Pro for limited proofreading (spelling/grammar/clarity). The authors take full responsibility for the content of the publication.

Introduction

The Social Roots of Delusions

1. The Many Puzzles of Delusions

Consider John. The year is 1959. He is thirty years old. Last year, he was appointed a tenured professor at the Massachusetts Institute of Technology (MIT). He has already achieved astonishing academic success, including a doctoral thesis that revolutionised the field of economics and would later earn him a Nobel Prize. He is widely recognised as a genius. And yet, his loved ones and colleagues are growing increasingly concerned about his behaviour. He has started reporting and acting on bizarre beliefs. He thinks that the Pope and the CIA are spying on him, and that people wearing red ties are part of a communist plot. His lectures stop making sense. At one point, he abandons his classes and flees. His paranoia eventually grows so intense that he attempts to give up his citizenship.

Now consider Marjorie. The year is 2020. She is in her mid-forties. As a proud American and successful businesswoman, she is running for Congress. Like John, she also seems to endorse several beliefs that strike many people as paranoid and bizarre. For example, she seems to think that there is a global cabal of Satan-worshipping, cannibalistic paedophiles that includes prominent Democrats, celebrities, and business elites, and that this conspiracy is being exposed in cryptic online messages by an anonymous figure known as "Q". But unlike John, she is not alone in these convictions. Millions of Americans claim to share these beliefs. In November, she is elected to Congress in a landslide.

To many who encounter these two cases, the beliefs might be described as "crazy", "mad", or "insane". There is a temptation to think that the individuals have "lost contact with reality" or even "lost their minds". The beliefs do not merely seem false or mildly irrational. They are, one might say, "delusional".

And yet, the two cases clearly differ in crucial respects. The first case, that of the mathematical genius John Nash, involved beliefs that emerged in isolation as Nash retreated into a private world that baffled and frightened those

The Social Roots of Delusions. Daniel Williams, Sam Wilkinson, and Kengo Miyazono, Oxford University Press.
 DOI: 10.1093/9780191976360.003.0001

around him (Capps, 2004; Nasar, 1998). They were associated with significant psychological distress and life difficulties. Like many people who develop such persecutory ideas, Nash was eventually diagnosed with schizophrenia and prescribed anti-psychotic medication and other treatments. When doctors classified his persecutory beliefs as "delusions", they were using a technical term in psychiatry. So understood, delusions are a common psychotic symptom associated with schizophrenia and many other psychiatric and neurological conditions, including bipolar disorder, delusional disorder, and dementia.

The second case involves the prominent American politician, Marjorie Taylor Greene, the first open supporter of the conspiracy theory "QAnon" to be elected to Congress (Wu et al., 2022). To many people, QAnon seems no less strange or irrational than the persecutory delusions reported by Nash. And yet, widespread endorsement of the conspiracy theory does not seem to be associated with any form of mental illness or psychological dysfunction. Instead, many advocates of QAnon, including Greene herself, appear to be highly functional and successful individuals who show no signs of needing medical attention or psychiatric treatment. Given this, although some are inclined to call such beliefs "mad", "crazy", or "delusional"—indeed, a *New York Times* article is titled "The QAnon Delusion Has Not Loosened Its Grip" (Edsall, 2021)—they would not qualify as delusions in modern psychiatry. They are examples of what Charles Mackay (1841) famously termed "extraordinary popular delusions and the madness of crowds" (henceforth just "popular delusions"). From witchcraft accusations to bizarre conspiracy theories, cult-based fanaticism to mass panics, human history is replete with similar examples of popular delusions that strike many observers as absurd.

These contrasting cases highlight fundamental questions that have puzzled researchers across a wide range of academic disciplines.

Perhaps most fundamentally, what *are* delusions? What properties must a belief or other mental state possess to qualify as delusional? What distinguishes delusions from other beliefs? Many scientists, clinicians, and philosophers working on such questions today assume that only clinical cases, such as Nash's, qualify as *real* delusions, delusions in the literal sense of the term. For example, most modern psychiatric manuals explicitly define the concept to exclude beliefs held by other members of a person's culture or subculture, regardless of how strange or irrational the beliefs in question might be (American Psychiatric Association, 2013, p.819). This makes "popular delusion" a contradiction in terms. However, not only does this stipulation conflict with common usage, but it has also seemed highly arbitrary to many theorists (see Bortolotti, 2022; Coltheart, 2007; Murphy, 2013). Why should the mere number of people who believe something be relevant to whether it is delusional? How many people must someone convince of their delusions before they cease to be delusional? What properties do clinical delusions possess that bizarre collective beliefs like QAnon lack?

In addition to these conceptual issues, delusions also raise a more important set of explanatory questions. Whatever we decide to call them, what gives rise to such strange beliefs? Why do human minds, equipped with sophisticated psychological capacities for navigating reality, sometimes produce beliefs that appear so radically disconnected from it? What drives otherwise rational people to embrace highly irrational beliefs, or at least beliefs that seem highly irrational? And why do some strange beliefs emerge in isolated cases while others seem to spread through entire communities?

These issues matter. Philosophically, delusions engage with fundamental questions concerning the nature of belief, mental illness, and the basic categories with which we understand and evaluate human minds and behaviour. They force us to explore the boundaries of human sanity and rationality, as well as the conditions under which our individual and collective belief-forming practices succeed or fail.

Scientifically, clinical and popular delusions are some of the most complex and mysterious manifestations of human psychology. They challenge and inform our understanding of how the mind works and provide a unique window into the psychological processes underlying "normal" belief formation. Clinical delusions can reveal what happens when such processes malfunction or are disturbed. Popular delusions can reveal their complex and often fragile connections to truth and norms of rationality.

Most importantly, understanding these beliefs is important for practical reasons. Clinical delusions often cause profound distress for those who hold them and those who care for those who hold them. They are frequently associated with an increased risk of suicide, social isolation, and functional impairment (Freeman, 2016). In contrast, the dangerous consequences of popular delusions typically lie at the societal level. They can destabilise democracy, fuel polarisation and violence, and undermine collective responses to shared challenges that depend on accurate models of problems and available solutions. These individual and collective harms make it critical to understand the psychological and social processes through which such beliefs are formed and maintained.

2. The Social Roots of Delusions

The central thesis of this book is that human "sociality" in the broadest sense of this term—the fact that we are intensely social animals navigating intensely social environments—is crucial for understanding delusions and addressing many of the questions that they raise.

This thesis can be situated in the context of a growing interdisciplinary awareness of the extent to which our species' "ultra-social" nature shapes almost every aspect of our psychology and behaviour (Boehm, 2012; Henrich & Muthukrishna, 2021; Tomasello, 2014b; Raihani, 2021; Wrangham, 2019). In recent decades, this social perspective has transformed our understanding of human evolution and psychology. It has revealed that most of the distinctive features of our species, including our enlarged brains, sophisticated capacities for reasoning and belief, and ecological dominance, are closely connected to the challenges and opportunities of navigating complex, fluid social groups (Mercier & Sperber, 2011; 2017; Tetlock, 2002; Tomasello, 2014a, 2014b; Simler & Hanson, 2016). Instead of treating humans simply as individually smarter versions of other animals, this work has emphasised how our intelligence, motivations, and emotions function to help us navigate dynamic social worlds involving highly complex forms of cooperation, cultural transmission, and competition. According to this perspective, human minds are fundamentally social minds.

This social orientation has also increasingly transformed the field of epistemology. Where much traditional philosophical theorising on the nature of knowledge focused on individual thinkers, often confronting sceptical scenarios in isolation, the growing influence of social epistemology has highlighted the degree to which most forms of human knowledge and ignorance are produced and acquired through complex social practices (Fricker, 2007; Goldman, 1999a; Longino, 2002; Mills, 2017). We learn about reality not primarily through direct experience and individual reasoning but through testimony, cultural transmission, and a complex division of cognitive labour (Henrich, 2015; Levy, 2021; Sterelny, 2021). Our beliefs, including misbeliefs, are shaped by whom we trust and mistrust, the cultures and communities we belong to, and how such groups are organised. According to some philosophers, even the concept of knowledge itself cannot be understood outside its role in social practices of epistemic cooperation (Craig, 1990).

Nevertheless, much research into delusions has remained surprisingly divorced from this social context, especially within the areas of philosophy, psychology, and neuroscience with which we are most familiar. Traditionally, theorising about delusions has focused overwhelmingly on psychological or biological factors that bear no essential relation to human sociality, such as cognitive biases, chemical imbalances, strange experiences, and abnormal reasoning. Although we agree that such factors are often critical for understanding delusions, this book argues that an individualistic focus overlooks delusions' complex connections to, and roots in, human ultra-sociality. Specifically, we argue that this ultra-sociality is relevant for addressing three big-picture topics: (i) the practice of classifying people and their beliefs as delusional (Part 1, and Chapter 2 in particular); (ii) the characteristics and causes of popular delusions (Part 2); and (iii) the characteristics and causes of clinical delusions (Part 3).

First, when it comes to the most basic question of what delusions *are* (i.e., what makes a belief delusional and distinguishes delusions from other beliefs), we criticise a dominant framework that treats "delusion" as a purely descriptive label that tracks objective features of beliefs or believers. In its place, we advocate an approach that begins by asking what role the attribution of delusional status (i.e., calling people or their beliefs "delusional") plays in human social life. In this context, we argue that many aspects of delusion attribution can fruitfully be understood as a social practice of epistemic flagging and gatekeeping. When people call beliefs or believers "delusional" (or, in more colloquial language, "mad", "crazy", or "insane"), they are typically expressing folk-epistemic bafflement and flagging to others that the believer in question is a "rational lost cause", someone who falls beyond the reach of rational engagement, at least concerning the specific belief in question.

This approach has many important implications. For example, it opens up the possibility that beliefs treated as delusional might be extremely heterogeneous in their causes and characteristics. It also undercuts the widespread assumption that delusions are essentially tied to individual pathology, which makes room for the recognition of popular delusions as *bona fide* instances of the category, not merely a metaphorical extension of clinical terminology. Although delusion attribution may be most formally regimented in modern psychiatry, and individual pathology often gives rise to beliefs that trigger this social response, we argue that the core social practice of delusion attribution is much older than modern psychiatry and not restricted to clinical cases.

Second, we argue that many popular belief systems that seem "delusional" or "mad" to outsiders are rooted in complex social motivations and practices. Against individualistic explanations of such beliefs that focus primarily on cognitive biases or motivations to believe things that produce emotional comfort, we trace popular delusions to interactions between what we call "socially motivated cognition" (i.e., cognitive processes biased by social motivations of persuasion, advocacy, and reputation management) and subtle forms of social coordination involving epistemic norms, status competition, and a complex division of cognitive labour organised around the promotion and protection of shared ignorance and misbeliefs.

This framework reveals a strategic but hidden social rationality underlying many popular delusions. Specifically, although such beliefs are highly epistemically irrational (i.e., very poorly supported by available evidence and resistant to rational correction), they typically serve social functions for those who embrace and advocate them. For example, we argue that the bizarre supernatural convictions associated with many sects and cults function as signals of community commitment and cooperation, and that outlandish conspiracy theories often result not from simple cognitive mistakes but from coordinated forms of unconscious "propaganda" aimed at demonising target groups.

Finally, we argue that the nature and complexities of human sociality play critical roles in the character and causes of clinical delusions. Although we agree with traditional explanatory approaches that such beliefs are typically connected to perceptual and cognitive abnormalities related to individual pathology or dysfunction of some kind, we argue that these approaches fail to explain three of delusions' most striking social features: their predominant, cross-cultural focus on social themes such as persecution, surveillance, and status; their social determinants in experiences such as abuse and marginalisation; and their stubborn resistance to social correction.

As with our analysis of popular delusions, our approach to clinical delusions acknowledges the role of individual psychological factors, including anomalous experiences and domain-general disturbances to thought and reasoning. Nevertheless, we argue that the social focus and determinants of clinical delusions cannot be understood without locating these factors in the context of our intense drives for status and belonging, our strong preoccupation with social threats, and the unique complexity and opacity of the social environment. Moreover, we argue that the puzzling resistance of clinical delusions to social correction emerges from disturbances to fragile psychological processes of "epistemic vigilance" (Sperber et al., 2010) that normally help us benefit from social learning while protecting us from manipulation and misinformation.

In our approach to popular and clinical delusions, we grapple with a fundamental tension captured in quotations from Nietzsche and Keynes. On the one hand, Nietzsche's (2002 [1886], p.70) famous observation that "madness is rare in the individual—but in groups, parties, peoples, and ages it is the rule" highlights the extent to which the most spectacular forms of epistemic irrationality often arise at the collective level. This was the lesson that Mackay (1841) drew from his exploration of extraordinary popular delusions. "Men", he wrote, "think in herds; it will be seen that they go mad in herds, while they only recover their senses slowly, one by one" (Mackay, 1841, p.3). This perspective paints human sociality as the most potent source of delusion.

On the other hand, Keynes's (1936, p.vii) observation that "it is astonishing what foolish things one can temporarily believe if one thinks too long alone" highlights something very different: our complete dependence on other people to acquire knowledge, and the dangers that arise when we lose access to their testimony and corrective feedback. According to this perspective, which is the foundational idea of much research in social epistemology (Goldman, 1999a), cultural evolution (Sterelny, 2021), and the study of reasoning (Mercier & Sperber, 2017), human sociality is our species' epistemic superpower, the source of our ability to acquire and accumulate knowledge and to navigate our environments effectively.

Our book aims to reconcile these perspectives. Our species is uniquely reliant on social learning and cultural transmission to know and navigate the environment. When this reliance breaks down due to illness, dysfunction, or psychological disturbances of various kinds, delusions often emerge. This is Keynes's insight. But Nietzsche's observation also captures something crucial. Just as our most spectacular epistemic achievements rely on social learning and epistemic cooperation, so do our most spectacular epistemic failures. Hence, the very social forces that function to prevent individuals from developing delusions by the lights of their community can drive entire communities to embrace highly irrational belief systems that strike outsiders as delusional. Understanding delusions, then, requires an understanding of how these two faces of human sociality, its epistemic benefits and dangers, interact with individual psychology and the social environment to produce these beliefs.

3. Delusions Research and the "Social Turn"

There is a complex academic literature on delusions spanning multiple disciplines, including philosophy, psychology, psychiatry, and the social sciences. For example, philosophers have explored fundamental questions about how to define delusions, the mental states they involve, their relationship to concepts like rationality, and the ethical and political questions they raise (see

Bortolotti, 2022; Sullivan-Bissett, 2024c). They have also engaged extensively with empirical research into the causes of both clinical and popular delusions. In the former case, this empirical research involves a vast body of work across the psychological, brain, and medical sciences, much of which is concerned with developing sophisticated models of the aetiology of delusions across different psychiatric conditions (Garety & Freeman, 2013; Sterzer et al., 2018). In the case of popular delusions, there is a similarly vast empirical literature across disciplines like social psychology, cognitive science, anthropology, and political science studying the characteristics and causes of beliefs like conspiracy theories (Douglas et al., 2017), religious convictions (Boyer, 2001), moral panics (Cohen, 2011), and ideological extremism (Iannaccone & Berman, 2006).

This book can be situated within this interdisciplinary literature, although we depart from much theorising in our attempt to correct an individualistic bias in existing research. As we have already noted, research into both popular and clinical delusions often focuses overwhelmingly on individual factors, such as cognitive biases, perceptual abnormalities, reasoning deficits, or neurochemical imbalances, with an overarching emphasis on what goes "wrong" within individual minds (Douglas et al., 2017; Garety & Freeman, 2013; Kapur, 2003; Maher, 1974). When human sociality is integrated into such work, it is often treated as a secondary influence. For example, research might explore how social isolation affects psychosis or how social media algorithms facilitate the viral spread of conspiracy theories.

In contrast, our approach places human sociality at the centre of analysis from the outset. Although we acknowledge the critical role of non-social psychological factors, such as perceptual experiences and domain-general cognitive biases, in many delusions, we argue that such factors should be situated within a broader explanatory approach that recognises the deeply social nature of human minds and worlds.

This approach aligns with a growing but still minority "social turn" in delusions research (see Bell et al., 2021; Gold & Gold, 2015; McKay & Mercier, 2023; Miyazono & Salice, 2021; Raihani, 2021; Williams, 2024a). For example, in research into clinical delusions, several philosophers and social scientists have recently argued that abnormal social cognition and social learning play underappreciated roles in their formation (Bell et al., 2021; Gold & Gold, 2015; McKay & Mercier, 2023). Similarly, a growing chorus of researchers has argued that what we are calling "popular delusions" can only be understood either by locating individual cognition in distinctive social environments (Levy, 2021) or by understanding how individual cognition is systematically biased by social goals distinct from the pursuit of truth (Funkhouser, 2017, 2022; van Leeuwen, 2023).

Admittedly, talk of a "social turn" is somewhat artificial. Many researchers have long acknowledged the role of social factors in delusions, including their associations with social experiences (e.g., abuse and marginalisation) and subtle disturbances to social cognition (e.g., Bentall, 2004; Frith, 2004; Luhrmann, 2007). Nevertheless, even those who oppose the social turn have recognised that it represents a genuine shift in the extent to which theorists have sought to make human sociality more central to delusions research (Corlett et al., 2025).

Our book is part of this social turn. However, there are two respects in which we diverge from most other prominent examples of research within it. Most obviously, there is the range of phenomena we focus on. We argue that human sociality is relevant not only to the characteristics and causes of popular and clinical delusions but also to the prior conceptual question of what delusions *are*. This is the sense in which the roots of delusions are fundamentally social. It is not just that delusional beliefs emerge and develop in ways richly connected to our social psychology and environment. In our framework, to *be* delusional is fundamentally to have a certain social-epistemic status.

Second, we aim to expand our understanding of how human sociality can be relevant to delusional phenomena. In most existing social approaches, this relevance is understood in terms of relatively narrow features of human social cognition. For example, researchers have sought to trace clinical delusions to abnormalities in dedicated sociocognitive processes, including processes concerned with inferring mental states (Frith, 2004), detecting and managing social threats (Gold & Gold, 2015), or navigating the complex dynamics of human coalitions (Bell et al., 2021). Similarly, in the case of popular delusions, researchers have traced specific kinds of beliefs (e.g., conspiracy theories or religious convictions) to distinctive social functions of beliefs (Funkhouser, 2017; 2022; Kurzban, 2011; Mercier, 2020; van Leeuwen, 2023) or cognitive processes (Trivers, 2011).

There are significant insights in many of these proposals, which our book builds upon. Nevertheless, our approach also goes beyond these contributions in several ways.

When it comes to popular delusions, we do not just focus on how social goals unconsciously bias individual-level cognitive processes. We also argue that such cognitive processes are scaffolded through complex social-epistemic practices. In these practices, agents coordinate both to discourage co-believers from sharing evidence that contradicts collectively valued beliefs and to encourage those who affirm, enforce, and rationalise them. It is only through such collective processes that community members can become convinced of beliefs that strike many outsiders as delusional. In other words, we view popular delusions as collective "achievements" that must be understood by moving beyond individual social cognition to examine the social-epistemic environment in which people think, reason, and communicate.

Similarly, our approach to clinical delusions aims to expand our understanding of how human sociality can be relevant to their characteristics and causes. Although we do not rule out the possibility that localised disturbances to social cognition play a role in delusion formation in some cases, we emphasise how even seemingly individualistic delusion-promoting factors, such as strange experiences or cognitive biases, operate within deeply social minds confronting uniquely complex, high-stakes social environments. And although we think that human minds are specialised for navigating uniquely human threats and opportunities, we agree with prominent critics of the "social turn" that such specialisations are unlikely to involve encapsulated, special-purpose modules that break down or malfunction as part of the delusion formation process (see Corlett et al., 2025). Indeed, one of our central aims is to showcase how human sociality can be highly relevant to understanding delusions, even if this relevance does not take the form of malfunctioning social modules.

For example, we argue that the devastating impacts of social adversity (e.g., childhood abuse, marginalisation, and social isolation) on delusions cannot be understood merely as stressors that "break" specific sociocognitive processes. Instead, such experiences disrupt basic expectations about social threats and safety, dysregulate stress physiology, undermine general coping abilities, and threaten the formation and maintenance of trusting relationships necessary for social support and epistemic regulation, all of which, in turn, exacerbate perceptual abnormalities or undermine people's ability to interpret and explain them. Similarly, we argue that the overwhelming social focus of clinical delusions results not from their origins in localised dysfunctions in social cognition, but from the way strange experiences and subtle cognitive biases emerge in minds for which navigating the social world is the most consequential and complex challenge they face.

This perspective leads us to emphasise the multifactorial, dynamic complexity of delusions. Rather than seeking simple causal stories of delusions or replacing one set of individualistic factors with another set of social ones, we aim to show how multiple influences spanning different levels of analysis (e.g., perceptual anomalies, cognitive biases, affective disturbances, social stressors, and cultural forces) interact within the minds and environments of an ultra-social species that evolved to navigate a social world characterised by highly complex forms of cooperation, culture, and competition.

Importantly, whereas much research on delusions is primarily concerned with what is unique about delusional individuals, our project is equally concerned with those features of human psychology and social environments shared between delusional and non-delusional individuals. Independent of delusions, humans are obsessively interested in social phenomena, rely on fragile processes of social and epistemic vigilance, confront the unique complexity and opacity of social environments, and are vulnerable to self-reinforcing cycles of social withdrawal, isolation, and suspicion. It is only by attending to these shared features of human beings that we can grasp why delusions take the forms they do.

4. Our Methodological Approach

As philosophers undertaking a highly ambitious project that spans multiple disciplines and questions, we should be explicit about our methodological approach, its benefits, and its limitations and risks.

Most obviously, our approach is philosophically naturalistic. That is, we take for granted that intellectual inquiry should be conducted in ways continuous with and informed by our best scientific evidence and research, even if we sometimes have strong views about what constitutes our best scientific research. Relatedly, our approach is synthetic, not analytic (Schliesser, 2019). Our goal is to understand complex natural phenomena in ways that synthesise insights, knowledge, and arguments from the special sciences. Even when considering conceptual questions about delusions, we do not attempt to provide a precise definition that can be tested against intuitions or potential counterexamples. Instead, we aim to understand how delusion attribution fits into the functions of specific social-epistemic practices within human social life. In these respects, we view our project similarly to Kim Sterelny's characterisation of his approach in *The Evolved Apprentice*,

> The essay is an essay in philosophy in part because it depends primarily on the cognitive toolbox of philosophers: it is a work of synthesis and argument, integrating ideas and suggestions from many different research traditions. No one science monopolizes this broad project though many contribute to it. So I exploit and depend on data, but do not provide new data. (Sterelny, 2012, p.xi)

As should be clear already, our project is also highly ambitious. We do not restrict ourselves to narrow puzzles or questions but aim to develop a general theoretical approach applicable to a wide range of delusional phenomena, including not only delusion attribution but also the characteristics and causes of clinical and popular delusions. It is also explicitly speculative and programmatic. Given the sheer scope and complexity of the phenomena we focus on, we cannot hope and do not try to provide definitive answers to all the questions we raise or decisive evidence for the hypotheses we advance. Instead, our goal is to develop a promising theoretical approach, generate fruitful speculations and ideas, and, most importantly, demonstrate the explanatory potential of making human sociality central in delusions research.

We believe that this big-picture, synthetic, and highly ambitious approach has significant theoretical advantages. It allows us to step back and synthesise insights across otherwise disparate disciplines, identify novel connections and patterns, and develop frameworks that would not emerge from more narrowly focused philosophical or empirical investigations. Such an approach, we believe, can play a significant role in intellectual progress by reframing existing debates, suggesting new research directions, and highlighting overlooked phenomena.

At the same time, we are also aware of the significant limitations and risks associated with this type of work. Most obviously, such a broad focus necessarily involves a degree of coarse-graining that may obscure important details and nuances. We cannot engage with all the relevant empirical and philosophical literature in the depth that many researchers might prefer, and we do not provide the kind of detailed mechanistic accounts that many researchers in the cognitive and neural sciences might expect. In the long and complex process of drafting and re-drafting this book, we have repeatedly removed detailed engagements with specific scientific hypotheses and philosophical views to maintain our core focus and ensure that the book did not become even longer than it already is. We have attempted to be explicit about these limitations, and we revisit some of the most critical omissions in our concluding chapter, where we set out future research directions. However, we are acutely aware that some researchers will feel that the book does not adequately address their preferred theoretical perspective, and that some empirical researchers may regard our conjectures as insufficiently detailed and excessively speculative. Although we believe that the advantages of our big-picture, synthetic, and speculative approach outweigh these limitations, it is ultimately up to readers to judge whether this assessment is accurate.

5. How the Book Hangs Together

One unusual feature of this book is that it is divided into three relatively independent parts. Part 1 establishes a theoretical foundation, examining the nature of human ultra-sociality and how practices of delusion attribution fit into human social life. Part 2 examines "popular delusions", providing an account of why and how groups produce, maintain, and protect shared beliefs and narratives that strike outsiders as extremely irrational and incorrigible. Part 3 then turns to clinical delusions, identifying their underappreciated social characteristics and advancing a theoretical framework for understanding and explaining them.

These parts are independent in the sense that one could, in principle, be persuaded by our claims in any one of these parts without endorsing those advanced in the others. For example, one could accept our account of delusion attribution in Part 1 but reject the explanatory frameworks that we develop in Parts 2 and 3, or embrace our account of popular delusions in Part 2 but reject our analysis of delusion attribution in Part 1 and our treatment of clinical delusions in Part 3.

This independence of parts has some advantages. It means that readers interested in only one of the topics that we explore can focus exclusively on that part of the book, and that one need not be persuaded by every claim that we advance to be persuaded by some of them. Nevertheless, given this logical independence, one might reasonably ask why we have presented our arguments and conjectures together in a single volume rather than as separate works.

Our answer lies in several forms of unity that run through the book. Most fundamentally, the book is unified by our commitment to placing human sociality at the centre of analysis. That is, our approaches to delusion attribution, popular delusions, and clinical delusions share a core commitment to the underappreciated relevance of human sociality to all these topics. Moreover, this understanding of human sociality goes beyond the bland recognition that humans are highly social animals. As we outline in our foundational Chapter 1, humans are a very specific kind of social animal. We are intensely cooperative, navigating complex, interdependent social worlds regulated by norms, reputations, surveillance, and "partner choice," in which people choose and exclude cooperation partners based on their perceived traits. We are also epistemically interdependent, cultural animals who come to know and navigate the environment in ways reliant on the information we acquire from others. And we are fiercely competitive, producing complex and often brutal forms of status competition and conflict that demand highly attuned vigilance against social threats and exploitation. These features of human sociality and their complex interactions recur throughout our treatment of different questions and phenomena in the book, providing an underlying picture and explanatory approach that ties together its disparate elements.

In addition, several core themes run throughout the book, providing overall theoretical coherence. One such theme is the interplay between heterogeneity and unity. From the beginning of our analysis, we emphasise that delusions are not a monolithic category reducible to one kind of explanation. Precisely because there are many causal pathways through which people can end up embracing and holding onto beliefs that mark them as "rational lost causes" to others, delusions are highly diverse in their characteristics and causes. At the same time, we recognise core features of human sociality that emerge across otherwise very diverse cases, including the unique challenges and complexity of social cognition, our obsessive social interests, and our dependence on social support to regulate our beliefs and acquire knowledge.

A related unifying theme is our rejection of what might be called "pathocentrism", the tendency to treat delusions as essentially pathological states. We argue that this pathocentric analysis misunderstands the core practice of delusion attribution, which is not essentially tied to pathology and can be triggered by beliefs that arise in non-clinical contexts, including the popular delusions we explore in Part 2. However, even our framework for understanding clinical delusions in Part 3 stresses the continuities between clinical delusions and "normal" cognition, as well as the explanatory importance of non-pathological features and dynamics for understanding why and how clinical delusions emerge and persist. A central feature of our explanatory approach here, which we will return to in more depth in our concluding chapter once all the ingredients of our framework have been introduced, is the fragility of human knowledge. Once it is appreciated how being in "contact with reality" is rarely the default state of human minds but a precarious achievement of social cooperation and scaffolding, the epistemic failures characteristic of delusions come to seem less aberrant and mysterious.

Finally, we adopt a fundamentally *interactional* framework for understanding delusions. Delusions are not simply states inside individual heads. They emerge from complex, dynamic interactions between individuals and their social environments. This is true in the sense that social experience and interactions, or the lack thereof, often trigger and reinforce delusional beliefs, but also in the more fundamental sense that what it is to *be* delusional is itself determined through social negotiation and evaluation.

By developing such themes against the backdrop of our core understanding of human ultra-sociality, we aim to construct a more cohesive and illuminating explanatory approach than would be possible by addressing any single aspect of delusional phenomena in isolation. In this way, we hope that the whole becomes more than the sum of its parts, offering insights that would remain invisible if delusion attribution, popular delusions, and clinical delusions were treated separately. Given this, although readers can certainly focus on those parts of the book most relevant to their specific interests, we believe that the most illuminating perspective comes from engaging with the book as a whole, seeing how different aspects of delusional phenomena connect when viewed through a unified theoretical lens.

6. Roadmap

The rest of the book proceeds as follows.

Part 1: Theoretical Foundations establishes the empirical and conceptual groundwork for the book's arguments.

Chapter 1: A New Kind of Social Animal examines what makes humans distinctive in terms of social psychology and organisation. Drawing on evolutionary psychology, anthropology, and cognitive science, we identify three key features of human sociality: intense cooperation structured by norms, reputation, and partner choice; epistemic interdependence and cumulative culture, which enable extensive information sharing and collective knowledge production; and competition for power and prestige. We demonstrate how these features and their complex interactions have shaped our psychology and environments, creating minds that are exquisitely attuned to social information, feedback, and threats, and deeply embedded in networks of shared beliefs and practices.

Chapter 2: Why Do We Call People Delusional? turns to the concept of delusion itself. After exploring traditional approaches to defining this concept, we argue that it is more fruitful to set aside questions of definitions and counterexamples and instead examine how the practice of delusion attribution fits into human social life. In our account, this practice involves marking certain beliefs as violations of shared epistemic norms and signalling that ordinary processes of rational argument and persuasion have become impossible. This perspective opens up space for significant heterogeneity in the causes of beliefs that trigger this social response, explains the true relationship between delusion and pathology and how it is not as tight as many have supposed, and illuminates why the boundaries of what counts as delusional shift across cultural and historical contexts.

Part 2: The Social Roots of Popular Delusions explores cases of widespread irrational beliefs in non-clinical populations.

Chapter 3: The Puzzle of Popular Delusions introduces what we call the "functional delusions puzzle": why healthy, otherwise rational communities often embrace beliefs that outsiders view as bafflingly and incorrigibly irrational. After documenting several examples of such beliefs, we identify five of their recurrent features that demand explanation: (i) their unusual epistemic irrationality, (ii) the selectivity of this irrationality, (iii) their compartmentalisation, (iv) people's attachment to the relevant beliefs, and (v) the social practices that sustain them. We review individualistic explanations of such beliefs that appeal to cognitive biases and motivated reasoning, and argue that while these factors likely play important roles, they cannot fully account for the distinctive features and complexities of popular delusions.

Chapter 4: The Social Roots of Popular Delusions begins developing our positive account of popular delusions. We introduce the concepts of "socially adaptive belief" and "socially motivated cognition", which arise when beliefs are adopted not to track reality or to regulate individual emotions, but in the process of achieving strategic, social objectives. The two most important forms of socially motivated cognition that we identify are *propagandistic cognition*, in which people internalise beliefs that they are motivated to propagate, and *social signalling*, in which people internalise beliefs acquired to signal their positive qualities and group allegiances. We show how these processes play highly consequential roles in canonical examples of popular delusions.

Chapter 5: The Social Scaffolding of Popular Delusions completes our social framework by exploring how socially motivated cognition interacts with collective dynamics in which communities coordinate to promote, protect, and rationalise shared delusions. Specifically, the chapter examines how distributed motivations to spread or embrace unfounded beliefs create "epistemic reward systems", social norms and incentives that regulate community behaviour in ways that hide contradictory evidence and encourage supporting evidence, enabling forms of collective epistemic irrationality that would be impossible for individuals to achieve alone.

Part 3: The Social Roots of Clinical Delusions turns to the topic of clinical delusions.

Chapter 6: Individualistic Accounts of Clinical Delusions reviews traditional explanatory approaches to clinical delusions, including cognition-based, experience-based, two-factor, and predictive processing accounts.

Although we acknowledge that these approaches often contain important insights, we identify three underappreciated social dimensions of clinical delusions that pose explanatory challenges for them: the challenge of social determinants (the causal relevance of factors like abuse and marginalisation to delusions); the challenge of social focus (the predominant, cross-cultural social focus of delusional content); and the challenge of social evidence (the peculiar role of social evidence in the delusion formation process).

Chapter 7: Existing Social Accounts of Clinical Delusions reviews attempts to replace traditional accounts of delusions with explanatory approaches that trace clinical delusions to localised abnormalities in social cognition. Focusing primarily on Gold and Gold's (2015) conjecture that clinical delusions result from a disordered "suspicion system" tasked with identifying and managing social threats, we argue that, although this theory has several promising features, it rests on implausible assumptions about the cognitive architecture of social threat management and struggles to explain the characteristics and heterogeneity of clinical delusions.

Chapter 8: The Social Determinants and Focus of Clinical Delusions addresses the challenges of social determinants and social focus. We argue that clinical delusions typically arise from complex, dynamic interactions between anomalous experiences, domain-general cognitive biases, emotions, behaviours, and social environment. In this explanatory context, the social determinants of clinical delusions increase delusion risk via multiple pathways, including by heightening social vigilance, disrupting mood regulation, undermining generalised coping abilities, and creating social withdrawal. The predominant social themes of delusions then emerge not because of dysfunctions in dedicated social modules, but because delusion-producing factors arise in ultra-social minds that are biased towards interpreting ambiguous events in terms of agency and social meaning.

Chapter 9: The Social Insensitivity of Clinical Delusions extends the pluralist, social-cognitive framework developed in Chapter 8 by addressing the challenge of social evidence: why clinical delusions appear remarkably unaffected by what other people tell the individual, even when the testimonial evidence seems overwhelming. We argue that the asymmetry with which delusional people treat social and non-social evidence can be understood in terms of two related "testimonial failures": testimonial isolation, in which factors like social withdrawal, stigma, or communication breakdown prevents the person from encountering corrective testimony; and testimonial discount, in which testimony is discounted in favour of experientially grounded beliefs, both because of general features of epistemic vigilance and because of various processes through which such vigilance becomes amplified in delusional contexts.

Finally, the concluding chapter steps back and summarises what we take to be the book's main contributions, identifies some of its most significant limitations and omissions, and sets out an agenda for future work.

PART 1

1
A New Kind of Social Animal

1. Introduction

Humans are social animals. So are bees. To understand why human sociality is relevant to delusions, it is important to move beyond nebulous statements of our social nature to a richer and more detailed account of human psychology and social behaviour. This chapter takes up this task and reviews the scientific literature relevant to the ideas we will develop in later chapters.

After clarifying the role of evolutionary psychology in our theoretical approach (Section 2), the first half of the chapter focuses on two distinctive features of human sociality: our reliance on cooperation (Section 3) and culture (Section 4). Section 5 then focuses on the character of competition and conflict in human social life. As we hope to establish in this book, these domains and their complex interactions are relevant to understanding many aspects of delusions. For example, in Chapter 2, we will explore how classifying people as delusional is best understood in the context of cooperative, norm-governed, social-epistemic practices. In Part 2 (Chapters 3, 4, and 5), we will explore how popular delusions emerge when such practices are distorted by social goals of propaganda and signalling. Finally, in Part 3 (Chapters 6, 7, 8, and 9), we will explore how our interdependence and social vulnerability illuminate the social determinants of clinical delusions, their common focus on social themes, and their resistance to social correction.

2. Evolution and Cognitive Architecture

This book will draw on findings and ideas from many fields, including cognitive science, social psychology, anthropology, psychiatry, and sociology. One of these fields is *evolutionary psychology* in the broadest sense, which draws on evolutionary theory and hypotheses about the selection forces that shaped human evolution to understand our minds and behaviour (Del Giudice, 2018; Nesse, 2023; Nettle & Scott-Phillips, 2023). Because evolutionary psychology

The Social Roots of Delusions. Daniel Williams, Sam Wilkinson, and Kengo Miyazono, Oxford University Press.
 DOI: 10.1093/9780191976360.003.0002

is controversial, it is important to begin with some remarks on its role within the book.

First, some critics claim that evolutionary psychology involves speculative "just-so stories" about the adaptive problems confronted by our ancestors, plausible-sounding narratives of the evolution of psychological traits that lack any independent basis in evidence (Gould & Lewontin, 1979). This criticism is often reasonable when targeted at specific applications of evolutionary psychology. Given this, in what follows we will draw only on evolutionary ideas that meet very high standards of plausibility and evidential support, and we will not rely on speculative theorising about the fine-grained ecological conditions our ancestors confronted. Nevertheless, we assume that the human mind evolved through natural selection and that we are not completely ignorant of the general selection pressures our ancestors confronted (Boehm, 2012; Del Giudice, 2018; Sterelny, 2021).

Second, another criticism of evolutionary psychology is that it involves an insufficient appreciation of the importance of development, learning, and cultural variation in understanding human minds and behaviour (Buller, 2006; Heyes, 2018; Prinz, 2014). According to this view, evolutionary psychology too readily assumes that psychological traits are genetically inherited adaptations (i.e., traits that evolved because they conferred a fitness advantage on our ancestors), neglecting complex interactions between genetics, development, and culture, and non-adaptive evolutionary processes like genetic drift (i.e., changes in the frequency of gene variants due to random chance).

Again, this criticism is often reasonable when directed at specific applications of evolutionary ideas. Many psychological traits are not adaptations, human psychology is extremely flexible, and people rely on a massive amount of learning to acquire information and capacities advantageous within local cultural contexts (see Section 4 below). Nevertheless, as with other scholars who emphasise our status as cultural animals, we assume that our ancestors faced recurrent problems and opportunities that favoured the evolution of species-universal psychological traits (Henrich, 2015; Richerson & Boyd, 2005; Sperber, 1996). For example, because all humans depend on social learning, we have evolved motivations and abilities specialised for acquiring useful information from others whilst protecting us from misinformation and manipulation (Mercier, 2020; Sperber et al., 2010). Similarly, although there is significant cultural variation in the character of social norms, status hierarchies, and social threats, all human beings navigate norm-governed social worlds characterised by status competition and complex social dangers

(Boehm, 2012; Boyd, 2017; Sterelny, 2021). As we will argue in Parts 2 and 3, these and other universal features of human sociality are relevant to understanding cross-cultural patterns in popular and clinical delusions, including their recurrent themes and the psychological and social processes that give rise to them.

Finally, some critics target *massive modularity*, a hypothesis according to which our cognitive architecture (i.e., the structure and organisation of the human mind) consists of many specialised, autonomous modules that evolved to solve specific adaptive problems, such as mate choice, social exchange, and threat detection (Gold & Gold, 2015; Stokes & Bergeron, 2015; Tooby & Cosmides, 1992). There remains significant controversy over how to understand this hypothesis, but most proponents endorse at least three claims. First, modules are highly specialised for solving specific adaptive problems, which means that different modules operate according to different principles. Second, modules are informationally encapsulated, meaning they are highly restricted in the information they can access. This explains why modules can generate rapid, automatic inferences and decisions and why their behaviour is largely isolated from other cognitive systems. Finally, modules are functionally dissociable, meaning they can become selectively disordered in ways that have little effect on other modules (and hence the mind more broadly).

The hypothesis of massive modularity is controversial. Among many objections, critics argue that: its model of our cognitive architecture is not supported by neuroscientific evidence (Anderson, 2010; Zerilli, 2020); it ignores the power of domain-general learning and inference mechanisms (such as hierarchical Bayesian inference) (Lake et al., 2017; Reed et al., 2020; see Chapters 6 and 7); human cognition exhibits too much flexibility and adaptability to be subserved by specialised, compartmentalised modules (Sterelny, 2012); and many of our psychological capacities are underpinned by mechanisms that are neither informationally encapsulated nor functionally dissociable (Prinz, 2014).

We aim to remain largely neutral on these controversies throughout this book. Although in Part 3 we will criticise specific conjectures about the role of a highly modular system for detecting and managing social threats, the general perspective on delusion attribution and formation that we will develop is consistent with many different views of cognitive architecture, except where we explicitly indicate otherwise. Given this, we assume that much can be said about human psychology without settling controversies concerning the structure of the human brain's information-processing mechanisms.

Importantly, this does not mean that we reject evolutionary psychology's assumption that our minds are specialised for coping with distinctive challenges and opportunities. Rather, we assume that this commitment is distinct from and does not imply massive modularity, which is just one hypothesis about how minds are specialised to perform specific functions and achieve specific goals (Anderson & Finlay, 2014; Barrett, 2014; Sterelny, 2012). Moreover, when it comes to sophisticated, flexible psychological capacities that integrate large bodies of information across diverse domains, it is not an especially plausible one (Barrett, 2014; Cantlon & Piantadosi, 2024; Sterelny, 2018). It is one thing to claim (as we will assume) that humans are endowed with capacities and motivations specialised for navigating social worlds characterised by distinctive forms of cooperation, culture, and competition. It is another thing to conjecture that such capacities are subserved by special-purpose, informationally encapsulated, functionally dissociable cognitive systems vulnerable to selective impairment.

With these preliminary clarifications out of the way, we will now turn to the main business of this chapter.

3. Cooperative Animals

Human beings are extremely cooperative. We depend on complex networks of social support, mutual aid, and the collective provision of public goods to satisfy even our most basic survival requirements, and this dependence goes back very far in our lineage (Raihani, 2021; Sterelny, 2021). Given that the scale and complexity of this cooperation exceed anything found in other animals, many theorists characterise our species as uniquely "*ultrasocial*" (Henrich & Muthukrishna, 2021; Tomasello, 2014b).

From an evolutionary standpoint, this ultrasociality is puzzling. Cooperation involves coordinating to achieve goals that could not be achieved (or achieved as easily) by individual means. This is challenging because natural selection is a competitive process. Very roughly, it favours traits that enhance individual animals' long-term reproductive success (Del Giudice, 2018; Raihani, 2021).[1] Given this, the interests of evolved animals are rarely perfectly aligned, which threatens cooperation. Not only can dominant animals steal the profits of cooperation with force and coercion (Boehm, 2012; Wrangham, 2019), but cooperation is vulnerable to free riders who reap its

[1] For a more precise overview of what is selected for in evolution, see Del Giudice (2018).

benefits without paying their share of the costs required to produce them (Henrich, 2006; Olson, 1965; Raihani, 2021).

These challenges explain why cooperation is inherently fragile and difficult to achieve. Nevertheless, many animals do cooperate, in some cases in spectacular ways. Evolutionary theorists have developed various explanations for this (see Raihani, 2021). The simplest such explanation appeals to kin selection, a form of natural selection favouring the evolution of altruism when it benefits an organism's genetic relatives (Hamilton, 1964). This process is not evolutionarily puzzling—genes that promote kin-based helping proliferate because they benefit organisms with the same genes—and it explains most extraordinary forms of self-sacrifice and altruism in non-human animals. Kin-based altruism is also central to human social life, from parents and relatives who invest substantially in raising children to broader kinship networks that provide the dominant form of social organisation throughout most societies (Henrich, 2020; Hrdy, 2009). Nevertheless, our species is labelled "ultrasocial" because we routinely achieve complex, large-scale cooperation involving non-relatives. What explains this capacity?

3.1 Interdependence and Reciprocity

First, some cooperation rests on interdependence (Aktipis et al., 2018; Barclay et al., 2021; Tomasello, 2016). Although cooperation is often fragile because of misaligned interests, in some cases, agents are interdependent in such a way that they can benefit themselves by benefiting each other. Some theorists propose that ecological and social changes forced our ancestors into situations of greater interdependence, which played a significant role in the evolution of our unique cooperative tendencies (Tomasello, 2016). Whatever the merits of this hypothesis, interdependence is pervasive in human relationships, and people carefully assess their degree of interdependence with others and adjust their tendencies to cooperate accordingly (Aktipis et al., 2018; Barclay et al., 2021).

Second, much of human cooperation involves reciprocity, whereby individuals help others in exchange for help in return (Trivers, 1971). This structures everything from the simple repayment of favours to long-term relationships in which trust is built over long periods. Given this, people are highly sensitive to reciprocity in social interactions and are likelier to confer benefits on others when they expect them to be reciprocated (Nowak, 2006; Raihani, 2021). Although reciprocity is distinct from interdependence, reciprocal relationships create interdependence (we come to depend on those we form relationships with), and interdependence fosters reciprocity (we are more likely to cooperate with those with whom we are interdependent) (Barclay, 2020; Pinsof et al., 2023).

Reciprocal cooperation typically involves both *partner control*, whereby individuals encourage others to maintain cooperative relationships through rewards or punishments, and *partner choice*, whereby individuals selectively form relationships with those judged to be valuable cooperators, which depends on a person's perceived competence (i.e., their ability to help others) and trustworthiness (i.e., their willingness to help others) (Sterelny, 2012). For this reason, humans inhabit a *partner-choice ecology* in which survival and success depend on attracting cooperation partners by cultivating and displaying socially valued traits (Barclay, 2013; Baumard et al., 2013; Sperber & Baumard, 2012). Nevertheless, there are many forms of cooperation that reciprocity involving simple two-person relationships cannot explain. For example, mutual aid and collaboration often occur within broader units of social organisation, including bands, tribes, chiefdoms, gangs, subcultures, cliques, unions, political parties, nation-states, and more. To understand such community-level cooperation, it is necessary to turn to indirect reciprocity (Alexander, 1987; Boehm, 2012; Sterelny, 2021).

3.2 Indirect Reciprocity: Norms, Reputations, and Gossip

With direct reciprocity, cooperation or failure to cooperate only influences the agents directly affected. With indirect reciprocity, such behaviours influence how unaffected third parties within a broader cooperative community act towards you. As Schmid and colleagues put it, "Direct reciprocity means that my behaviour towards you depends on what you have done to me. Indirect reciprocity means that my behaviour towards you also depends on what you have done to others" (Schmid et al., 2021, p.1292). Indirect reciprocity supports efficient forms of group-based cooperation and is central to human social life: people constantly evaluate and respond to others in their cooperative community according to their general cooperative dispositions (their niceness, friendliness, generosity, and so on), not just the effects of such dispositions on themselves (Boehm, 2012; Origgi, 2017). Given this, people must be extremely sensitive to how their actions might influence the judgements of anybody in the relevant community, not just individuals directly affected by the actions (Alexander, 1987).

Indirect reciprocity is typically mediated by the interlocking social technologies of norms, surveillance, reputations, and gossip (Boehm, 2012; Pan et al., 2024; Simler & Hanson, 2016; Sterelny, 2021). Most abstractly, social norms are standards of behaviour enforced by a community (Chudek & Henrich, 2011; Young, 2015). In addition to directly promoting cooperation (e.g., norms against uncooperative behaviours such as selfishness, lying, and physical aggression), they also solve coordination problems of various kinds, both directly (e.g., rules about which side of the road to drive on) and indirectly, by reducing ambiguity about what constitutes cooperation (Sterelny, 2021). However, norms can encourage or discourage any pattern of behaviour, not just cooperative ones. Therefore, some norms exist solely to differentiate groups from each other, and others function not to promote mutually beneficial coordination but to support exploitative and hierarchical relationships. This fact will be important when we turn to the role of norms in supporting popular delusions in Chapter 5.

In some cases, norm enforcement involves imposing direct material costs on norm violators (e.g., physical punishment). However, enforcement is often indirectly achieved simply by social disapproval and reputational damage (Boehm, 2012; Origgi, 2017; Sperber & Baumard, 2012). In norm-governed social worlds, a reputation for norm conformity determines an individual's access to social support. Given this, norms are often enforced simply by removing or reducing a willingness to cooperate with norm violators (Boehm, 2012; Heath, 2022), including by abandoning or reducing motivations to protect such violators from being manipulated and exploited by others (Bhui et al., 2019).

With reputations comes gossip, the social exchange of information about people's traits and behaviours (Dunbar, 2004; Pan et al., 2024). Because gossip is indispensable for evaluating potential partners and whether they are norm-abiding community members, people are highly motivated to share and consume gossip, which greatly increases the potential reputational consequences of norm-violating behaviours. Moreover, because gossip is so useful, people are often motivated to acquire gossip and investigate people's behaviours so they can share the information with others, encouraging intense social scrutiny and surveillance (i.e., "nosiness").

In these ways, norms, reputations, and gossip constitute the basic social technologies with which our species scaffolds complex cooperation, and there are good reasons to believe that they have played a significant role in shaping the evolution of human psychology and social behaviour in many ways (Alexander, 1987; Boehm, 2012; Raihani, 2021; Tomasello, 2016).

3.3 Cooperation, Mentalising, and Beyond

When studying human social cognition, many theorists focus on abilities that underpin the attribution of mental states. These abilities are often referred to as "theory of mind", "mindreading", or—the term that we will use—"mentalising" (Frith & Frith, 2021). According to this perspective, the most important aspect of human social cognition is the capacity to explain and predict other people's behaviour by attributing mental states like beliefs, desires, and intentions. Sophisticated mentalising abilities like this are essential for the complex forms of coordination that underlie much of human cooperation. Moreover, because reputation management is so important in human social life, we also rely on sophisticated mentalising when we engage in "social self-monitoring", deliberately regulating behaviour in response to its anticipated effects on the evaluations—and hence mental states—of others (Tomasello, 2014a).

Nevertheless, human cooperation relies on many other capacities beyond mentalising in this narrow sense (Boehm, 2012; Henrich, 2015; Sterelny, 2021; Tomasello, 2014a). For example, because human social worlds are structured around complex webs of norms, we must possess abilities for identifying, learning, and responding to such norms (Chudek & Henrich, 2011). This is not trivial: many norms are implicit, instantiated only in patterns of community enforcement, which often manifests in purely reputational ways (i.e., in the altered evaluations that others make of you). Moreover, social norms demand the normative regulation of one's thoughts and behaviour, including abilities to justify one's actions and attitudes to others. Human reasoning is often dedicated to such tasks (Haidt, 2013; Mercier & Sperber, 2011, 2017; Tetlock, 2002). Although it was traditionally assumed that reasoning capacities exist primarily to enhance individual cognition by facilitating more rational judgements and decisions, there is a growing recognition that reasoning often functions to help people navigate dense webs of social accountability that norms, reputations, and gossip create (Mercier & Sperber, 2017; Williams, 2021b). In such social worlds, there are strong pressures to play an active role in managing one's reputation through producing and sharing reasons that highlight one's conformity to community standards. As a result, reasoning has a well-documented lawyerly character, such that its chief function in many contexts is "not to motivate or guide us in reaching conclusions but to explain and justify after the fact the conclusions we have reached" (Mercier & Sperber, 2017, p.112).

Further, our dependence on cooperation meant that throughout most of our evolutionary history, the loss of access to social support was a death sentence, and even today, social exclusion always brings a range of negative material consequences. Given this, losing access to the cooperation of others (e.g., through ostracism, exploitation, or social isolation) is extremely psychologically aversive and tends to produce a panoply of insidious health effects, including disturbed sleep, anxiety, reduced immune function, and a significantly increased risk of death (Eisenberger et al., 2017; Holt-Lunstad et al., 2015; Manning, 2020; Slavich, 2020). Correspondingly, human beings have intense motivations to belong and win social acceptance and approval (Baumeister & Leary, 1995; Raihani, 2021; Wrangham, 2019). Indeed, many people claim they would rather die than suffer a terrible reputation in their community (Vonasch et al., 2018).

More generally, the pressures of a norm-governed partner choice ecology in which individuals depend on cultivating a good reputation and attracting cooperation partners have shaped many facets of human psychology and motivation (Baumard et al., 2013; Boehm, 2012; Hoffman & Yoeli, 2021; Origgi, 2017). People are highly attentive to social attention and scrutiny, which they frequently overestimate (Gilovich et al., 2000; Leary & Kowalski, 1990). They are also extremely responsive to real or imagined social evaluations from a young age, consciously and unconsciously regulating their behaviour in response to social feedback (Tomasello, 2014a, 2016). As we will explore in Part 2 of this book, such motivations run extremely deep. They do not just shape people's outward behaviours; they shape the very contents of people's minds, including what they believe. They will also be central when we explore the social determinants and themes of clinical delusions in Part 3.

4. Cultural Animals

The term "culture" is used in many ways. In describing us as cultural animals, we are adopting what Sterelny (2021, p.50) refers to as the "mundane" sense of the term, capturing the following fact about our species:

> What we know, what we believe, what we can do and even to a considerable extent what we want, is learned from other hominins. Over the approximately seven million years of hominin history, cultural learning has had an increasing imprint on hominin minds. In that sense, we have become increasingly encultured. (ibid.)

As with cooperation, the scale and complexity of this enculturation go far beyond anything found in other animals (Boyd, 2017; Richerson & Boyd, 2005; Sperber, 1996; Tomasello, 2014a). First, although many species engage in social learning, this almost always involves acquiring information and abilities that they could, in principle, learn on their own. In contrast, we acquire an enormous amount of information far beyond what we could learn individually. This fact is obvious today, where people use a vast range of cognitive and social tools accumulated over many successive generations, including a complex language, many technical concepts and mental skills, and numerous technologies and institutions. However, the intergenerational accumulation of skills and information—*cumulative cultural evolution*—is ancient and has plausibly shaped human evolution in many ways (Richerson & Boyd, 2005).

Second, we do not just benefit from social learning; we depend on it (Sterelny, 2021). Humans have rapidly adapted to and transformed an unprecedentedly diverse range of environments, not primarily through environment-specific genetic adaptations or individual-level learning but through technologies, inherited knowledge, and social customs and institutions (Henrich, 2015). Such knowledge is typically extremely difficult to acquire via individual learning and problem-solving or even through intense social cooperation within short timeframes, a fact demonstrated by the large number of European explorers who quickly perished in ecological conditions in which local indigenous groups flourished with the aid of culturally accumulated knowledge and skills (Boyd, 2017).

In summary, we are beneficiaries and sometimes victims of two distinct lines of inheritance: a genetic inheritance of a sort that all animals possess and a unique cultural inheritance through which we acquire an enormous set of concepts, skills, habits, ideas, beliefs, preferences, and more from those around us (Henrich & McElreath, 2007). In this section, we focus on the basic psychological capacities with which we navigate this cultural dependence via social learning (Section 4.1) and epistemic vigilance (Section 4.2), and identify some of the complex interactions between human culture and cooperation (Section 4.3).

4.1 Social Learning

The basic challenge of social learning is to acquire useful information from others whilst minimising the dangers of misinformation and manipulation. People possess sophisticated capacities specialised for addressing this challenge that emerge early in childhood and appear cross-culturally universal (Henrich, 2015; Mercier, 2020; Sperber et al., 2010).

First, social learning is sensitive to how common beliefs, traits, and behaviours are within a population. However, against a popular image of human beings as mindless conformists, people respond to the prevalence of cultural traits in sophisticated ways that factor in their own informational situation, the likely sources of cultural popularity, the relevant cultural trait in question (e.g., beliefs, skills, norms, rituals, etc.), and the social costs of nonconformity (Mercier, 2020; Morin, 2016). For example, people intuitively distinguish between social pressure to conform to things like community norms and rituals (*normative conformity*) and cases in which other people's beliefs constitute evidence about what is true *(informational conformity)*. And in the latter case, they typically factor in the source and strength of majority opinion, the degree to which group opinions were formed independently, and the competence and benevolence of relevant group members (Mercier & Morin, 2019).

Second, people evaluate the characteristics of models (i.e., potential agents to learn from) in social learning and preferentially attend to and learn from models likely to have useful information. For example, people use cues of success, skill, competence, and prestige to guide social learning, and they tend to be disproportionately influenced by similar individuals and fellow group members because they are more likely to possess information useful to them in their specific situation (Henrich, 2015).

4.2 Epistemic Vigilance

As with much research on this topic, this description of social learning biases assumes that social learning is directed at agents who are largely passive in the process (see André et al., 2023). However, other agents frequently attempt to influence which information we acquire from them. Such intentional communication amplifies the potential volume and benefits of social learning. It also increases its risks. Not only might communicators unintentionally spread misinformation, but they might also deliberately deceive or manipulate others. To cope with this challenge, humans possess sophisticated capacities for *epistemic vigilance* that emerge early in childhood and appear to be cross-culturally universal (Mercier, 2017, 2020; Sperber et al., 2010).

First, epistemic vigilance involves plausibility checking, whereby people compare communicated messages against their pre-existing beliefs. All else equal, people are much less likely to accept messages that conflict with their own intuitions. For this reason, people rarely shift their beliefs in response to even unanimous opinions of others if their own contrary beliefs are strong enough, although they will often pretend to do so under reputational pressure (Mercier, 2020). By filtering social learning through prior beliefs in this way, plausibility checking protects against manipulation. However, it also creates an inherent conservatism in social learning.

Second, when people lack prior beliefs on a topic or hold beliefs at odds with a communicator's message, they often insist on persuasive arguments (Mercier & Sperber, 2017). Indeed, just as much of reasoning is specialised for reputation management (see Section 3.2), reasoning plays a significant role in interactive processes of communication more broadly. Given this, people tend to reason differently when producing and evaluating reasons. In producing reasons, we are lawyerly and subject to a "myside bias": we are disposed to generate one-sided evidence and arguments that help us to persuade others (Haidt, 2013; Mercier & Sperber, 2017). However, when evaluating other people's arguments, we are biased in the opposite direction, subjecting their claims to significant scrutiny in ways that protect against manipulation (Mercier, 2020).

Third, epistemic vigilance involves evaluating communicators' competence. Once again, contrary to the popular impression that people are easily swayed by the opinions of prestigious or authoritative figures, people evaluate competence in sophisticated and domain-specific ways (Morin, 2016). For example, they estimate whether communicators are likely to have reliable access to the information they transmit, and they factor in people's track record of accuracy in the relevant domain about which they communicate (Mercier, 2020).

Finally, epistemic vigilance involves evaluating communicators' honesty and diligence in communicating useful information. These evaluations factor in people's general trustworthiness, but personality and moral tendencies are typically insufficient on their own. You should temporarily abandon trust in even highly trustworthy people if playing poker against them, and it can be rational to trust extremely untrustworthy people if it is in their self-interest to be honest. Therefore, honesty assessments are highly sensitive to assessments of the degree to which it is in a communicator's interests to be honest (Mercier, 2017). As we return to shortly (Section 4.3), this alignment of incentives is often supported by the same processes that underlie human cooperation more broadly.

Before turning to the rich connections between culture and cooperation, it is worth briefly stepping back to extract a general lesson about epistemic vigilance. An influential intellectual tradition paints humans as a conformist and gullible species (Brennan, 2016; Gilbert et al., 1993). For many theorists, this analysis is supported by commonsense observation of what they see around them, including the popular delusions that we explore in Part 2, and by superficially plausible arguments that our dependence on social learning makes it adaptive to be credulous (Boyd, 2017). Research on epistemic vigilance demonstrates that this tradition is mistaken. Adaptive credulity is only plausible if you focus exclusively on the benefits of social learning. Social learning also brings risks, however. Whenever agents without perfectly aligned interests communicate, those sending the message will often be incentivised to manipulate its recipient to their advantage. Gullibility therefore cannot be evolutionarily stable. If people were credulous, they would be easy to manipulate, and credulity would cease to be adaptive. Therefore, on evolutionary grounds, we should strongly expect people to be vigilant and sophisticated social learners (Mercier, 2020). They are (Mercier, 2017; Sperber et al., 2010). Indeed, if anything, this research shows that humans are naturally *pig-headed*, systematically assigning excessive weight to their own beliefs over those of others (Mercier, 2020; Morin et al., 2021). This feature of epistemic vigilance will be important when we turn to clinical delusions in Part 3.

4.3 Culture and Cooperation

In addition to epistemic vigilance, cooperative communication is scaffolded by the same processes that underlie human cooperation more broadly. This includes kin selection, interdependence, direct reciprocity, and partner choice, as well as the social scaffolding of norms, reputations, and gossip (Pinker, 2010; Mercier, 2020; Mercier & Sperber, 2017). For example, groups uphold and enforce social-epistemic norms that regulate people's communicative conduct. In addition to obvious examples (e.g., against lying), communities almost always enforce many subtler epistemic norms (e.g., concerning when it is appropriate to make assertions, which information should and should not be shared, etc.), compliance with which influences people's reputations. These norm-governed, social-epistemic practices will be central to our explanation of delusion attribution in Chapter 2. Moreover, although social practices often support diligent and honest communication, Part 2's analysis of popular delusions will explore how they sometimes function not to promote collective knowledge but to undermine it.

5. Competition and Conflict in Human Social Life

Evolution by natural selection is an inherently competitive process. Roughly, it selects for the evolution of traits that help individual organisms survive and reproduce in competition with other organisms. Given this, competition and conflicts of interest are endemic to the lives of social animals, except for eusocial species in which genetic similarities and reproductive strategies foreclose intra-group competition (Raihani, 2021). We are not eusocial. Hence, competition is also central to human social life (Boehm, 2012; Heath, 2022; Raihani, 2021; Wrangham, 2019).

Although humans are spectacularly cooperative, even a basic familiarity with the facts of human societies and histories reveals that mutually beneficial cooperation is not universal. People often seek to benefit themselves by acting in ways that impose costs on others. There are many examples of such competition and conflict, including intergroup violence involved in raids, battles, and wars; group-based domination involved in phenomena such as slavery, caste-based social hierarchies, and patriarchy; violence, bullying, and domination between individuals within societies; and everyday occurrences of selfishness and free riding. In this section, we will focus on status, a crucial locus of competition and conflict in human social life (Section 5.1), and then identify some important ways that competition and conflict have shaped human psychology that will be relevant to the ideas developed in later chapters (Section 5.2).

5.1 Status

Social animals typically have status hierarchies that determine their relative social influence and access to goods such as mates, security, and resources. Humans are no exception. However, the forms that human status takes and how humans understand and navigate status hierarchies are exceptional. This subsection reviews the two major forms of human status: dominance (Section 5.1.1) and prestige (Section 5.1.2).

5.1.1 Dominance

Group-living animals typically compete with fellow group members for fitness-relevant goods such as food, territory, and mates. However, competition is costly. Dominance hierarchies commonly emerge to reduce such costs (Tibbetts et al., 2022). They consist of stable social rankings in which subordinate animals yield goods and resources to dominant ones. Of course, such stability is only ever partial—dominance can be contested, and the results of such contests can alter the group's dominance ranking—but their partial stability is rooted in the fact that animals benefit from the avoidance of recurrent conflict in favour of a stable recognition of their relative power and formidability. However, from the perspective of subordinate animals, this stability is rooted entirely in fear and the avoidance of harm. That is, dominance status is always *coerced*: dominant animals force submission from those lower down through aggression and intimidation, and subordinates only ever submit to avoid the costs inflicted on them if they resist.

Our species has dominance hierarchies (Chen Zeng et al., 2022; Cheng et al., 2013). However, several important features distinguish human dominance from dominance in other animals. First, as we return to below (Section 5.2.2), people use far more sophisticated cognitive and social tools to achieve and resist dominance, including species-unique capacities for complex planning, social coordination, deception, and tool use. For example, many small-scale, hunter-gatherer groups are far more egalitarian than similarly sized groups among other great apes because they can coordinate to sanction domineering individuals (Boehm, 2012; Wrangham, 2019).

Second, dominance hierarchies in our species are often organised around groups (Sidanius & Pratto, 2001). In general, human social worlds are typically organised around coalitions of multiple kinds and sizes, ranging from small-scale fleeting alliances to more stable friendship circles, bands, tribes, chiefdoms, ethnic groups, gangs, unions, political parties, religions, cults, sects, nation-states, and more. For this reason, competition for dominance and relations of domination and subordination often occur at the level of such coalitions.

Third, there is a sharp tension between dominance hierarchies in human social life and our reliance on cooperation. As we have seen in Section 3, the human environment is structured around interdependence, reciprocity, partner choice, norms, reputations, surveillance, and gossip. Given this, people typically benefit from being seen as cooperative, prosocial, trustworthy, and non-aggressive (Leary & Kowalski, 1990; Origgi, 2017). As Chen Zeng and colleagues put it, this means that our dominance psychology has "had to adapt to a norm-governed world where manipulative use of coercive incentives had to be accomplished more subtly, within the context of social rule and third-party monitoring" (Chen Zeng et al., 2022, p.3). For this reason, most people obfuscate or deny attempts to dominate others, either by framing dominance as a form of benevolence (e.g., the narrative of the "white man's burden" that accompanied British Imperialism) or through the imagination of inherent differences between groups that justifies their relative social position (Sidanius & Pratto, 2001). This fact will be important when we turn to certain examples of popular delusions in Chapter 4.

5.1.2 Prestige

Unlike most other social animals, our species has another form of social status: prestige (Cheng et al., 2013; Henrich & Gil-White, 2001; Ridgeway, 2019; Storr, 2021). Prestige rests on the perception of merit and excellence rather than force and the imposition of costs; it promotes admiration and respect rather than fear; and people strive to be near and observe those that they regard as prestigious, in contrast with dominant individuals, whom subordinates strive to avoid. Most fundamentally, whereas dominance is coerced, deference to prestigious individuals is freely conferred. However, like dominance, prestige is also a form of social rank, and it determines influence and access to a range of goods, services, and opportunities (Henrich & Gil-White, 2001; Ridgeway, 2019).

It is easy to understand why people would submit to formidable individuals out of fear and intimidation, but why would they freely bestow prestige on others? First, people tend to respect, admire, and defer to other agents when such agents appear to possess *instrumental social value*, characteristics that help those who defer to them achieve their goals (Leary et al., 2014). For this reason, acts of virtue and sacrifice that promote other people's interests and advance a group's goals are frequently rewarded with respect and admiration. In this way, prestige competition channels the self-interested pursuit of status into acts that benefit others (Brennan & Pettit, 2004; Ridgeway, 2019; Storr, 2021; Willer, 2009).

Second, prestige hierarchies play an important role in facilitating the cultural transmission of information and skills (Henrich, 2015; Henrich & Gil-White, 2001; Mercier, 2022). Because we are so dependent on social learning, we naturally seek out opportunities to learn from individuals who demonstrate success and excellence in domains that are socially valued in our current context. That is, we seek contact with impressive people, and we offer them deference and admiration in return for access to learning opportunities.

Just as prestige competition facilitates unique forms of human cooperation, channelling self-interest into self-sacrifice and altruism, it is also central to social learning and the division of cognitive labour, producing an economy of esteem in which individuals admire and defer to successful and competent individuals in exchange for access to their information and skills (Brennan & Pettit, 2004). This fact will be important when we turn to social practices that sustain popular delusions in Chapter 5.

As with dominance, prestige hierarchies often arise between groups, not just individuals. Think, for example, of teenagers desperate to join the cool clique in their high school or, for a more sinister example, the relative prestige accorded to different races, ethnic groups, and castes in different societies worldwide. Further, because the pursuit of prestige involves social competition, it similarly conflicts with the intensely cooperative nature of most human societies. Therefore, people rarely describe their behaviour in terms of the pursuit of prestige, which often involves what Raihani (2021) calls a "reputation tightrope", a complex balancing act in which people compete for prestige without being seen to do so (Storr, 2021).

5.2 Competition, Conflict, and the Mind

Status and social competition more broadly shape human psychology in many ways. Here, we will highlight only two important influences: the impact of status on human motivations, feelings, and health (Section 5.2.1) and capacities for managing and avoiding social threats (Section 5.2.2).

5.2.1 Motivations, Feelings, and Health

Status is profoundly relevant to people's motivations, feelings, and health. As with all social animals that navigate dominance hierarchies, people strongly resist being dominated, and those lower in such hierarchies experience not only the concrete negative consequences of reduced influence but also heightened stress, anxiety, and many negative health effects (Marmot, 2005; Sapolsky, 2004, 2005). However, evidence suggests that the pursuit of dominance over others is not a human universal but varies among individuals (Anderson et al., 2015).

Prestige is different. There is strong evidence that the desire for prestige is what Anderson and colleagues (2015) call a "fundamental motive" that shapes human psychology and behaviour in many important ways. In this respect, prestige introduces another way social evaluations determine our individual success. For example, in discussing cooperation (Section 3), we noted that our dependence on cooperation creates fundamental motives to be accepted, trusted, and liked by others and ensures that the loss of such approval is psychologically and even physically devastating. This is the fundamental *need to belong* (Baumeister & Leary, 1995). Prestige is different. It is not merely a matter of being liked, trusted, and welcomed into communities; it is about one's relative esteem. Nevertheless, prestige is also a fundamental, universal motive that drives many behaviours across multiple timescales, from developing long-term plans and deep-rooted passions to adjusting tastes in light of fast-changing social fashions (Hoffman & Yoeli, 2021; Ridgeway, 2019; Storr, 2021). Moreover, achieving and losing prestige have powerful hedonic consequences and shape longer-term psychological adjustment, well-being, and health (Anderson et al., 2015; Leary & Baumeister, 2000). For example, health and happiness relate to the degree to which people feel they are respected and deferred to by others, and low prestige and the precipitous loss of prestige are strongly associated with a range of negative health outcomes and are common causes of suicide (Manning, 2020; Sapolsky, 2004; Storr, 2021; Wilkinson, 1999).

5.2.2 Threat Detection

To navigate human environments successfully, people require sophisticated capacities for detecting, managing, and avoiding social threats. "Social threat" is a heterogeneous category that encompasses any case in which agents act individually or collectively in ways that impose costs on an individual, ranging from everyday forms of selfishness and free riding to brutal forms of domination and violence. Humans are obviously not unique in our vulnerability to social threats, which are endemic to the lives of all social animals, but we are unique in the kinds of threats people pose and in the motivations and capacities required to detect, manage, and avoid them.

People pose unique threats because of their unique abilities. Unlike other threats (predators, falling objects, viral diseases, etc.), humans possess sophisticated capacities for reasoning, planning, deception, and coordination. To appreciate the difficulties such capacities pose, consider two examples from anthropology. First, Wrangham (2019, pp.417–8) describes a case in which a group of hunter-gardener Yanomamö men became frustrated with an arrogant and domineering group member. Unable to end his behaviour directly, they coordinated to trick the man into climbing a tree to extract honey. Once the man laid down his weapons to climb the tree, the others executed him. As Chagnon (2013) notes, such treachery is sufficiently common among the

Yanomamö that they have a specific word for it: "nomohori", which roughly translates as *dastardly trick*.

Second, Hayden (2018) and other anthropologists have documented the independent emergence of secret societies across complex ("trans-egalitarian") hunter-gatherer groups, horticulturalists, and agriculturalists throughout the world, including in Melanesia, the Amazon, and West Africa. Such societies typically involve high-status coalitions of older men within the relevant communities who claim to possess secret ritual knowledge that confers supernatural powers, such as the ability to control spirits, exorcise the possessed, and resurrect the dead. As Hayden documents, such secret societies typically bolstered these claims through dramatic rituals and ruthless enforcement in which anybody who questioned or challenged the society and its claim to supernatural knowledge would be punished.

These examples might seem far removed from the circumstances of readers of this book. However, the social dynamics they manifest are not far removed from the conditions our ancestors navigated, and they illustrate several lessons that apply to social threats across all human contexts. First, such threats often originate in complex planning and coordination over extended time scales. Second, they can involve not just direct physical confrontations (e.g., being executed) but the very structure and organisation of complex social institutions, the functions of which are explicitly denied by those who run them. This is evident in technologically advanced societies where military, surveillance, and bureaucratic mechanisms are often exploited in the service of domination. However, the independent emergence of secret societies across diverse societies, even among complex hunter-gatherer groups, shows that the threats posed by conspiring elites and coercive institutions are not a uniquely modern problem. Finally, and relatedly, social threats rarely announce themselves. They are often facilitated by sophisticated deception and shrouded in self-justifying rationalisations that obscure their functions and effects.

For these reasons, navigating a world of possible social threats requires distinctive capacities and motivations (Gold & Gold, 2015; Raihani & Bell, 2019; Singh, 2021). In later chapters of Parts 2 and 3, we will explore such capacities and motivations in much greater depth as they are relevant to understanding both popular and clinical delusions. However, several general implications are worth briefly identifying here. First, people's sensitivity to social threats is calibrated to the variable costs of false alarms and false negatives across different contexts (Raihani & Bell, 2019). Moreover, as with most psychological processes, this calibration is especially influenced during sensitive periods such as childhood and adolescence, such that early and recurrent exposure to social exploitation has long-lasting effects on social vigilance in ways that are difficult to unlearn (Del Giudice, 2018).

Second, as with most threats, lack of evidence does not equal evidence of absence. However, this problem is greatly exacerbated in the case of social threats because they originate with agents who have the capacity and motivation to conceal their plans and intentions. Given this, once people become suspicious of other people's motives, it becomes difficult to assuage the suspicion because such vigilance puts people on guard against the risk of deception.

Finally, social threat detection must integrate both fast, automatic detection of social threats in the immediate context with motivations and capacities for ruminating and reflecting on possible threat-related scenarios involving complex, future-oriented, and deliberately concealed intentions (see Gold & Gold, 2015). For this reason, people cannot be solely preoccupied with detecting threats in their immediate environment; they must also be capable of anticipating future threats and explore how other agents might exploit them. All these features will be highly relevant when we explore popular and clinical delusions in Parts 2 and 3.

6. Chapter Summary

The human "Umwelt" (Uexküll, 1992)—the world as it exists insofar as it bears on our contingent goals and interests—is fundamentally a social world. It is a world largely composed of other people, the complex effects of their behaviours and interactions at multiple timescales, and their many subtle cooperative and competitive relationships. We navigate such worlds with correspondingly social minds. We spend much of our lives inside the minds of others; we are highly attuned to individual and group identities, reputations, norms, social pressures, and status relations; we deploy complex communicative and reasoning abilities in persuasion, argument, and reputation management; and we are social learners, acquiring from other people most of the concepts, beliefs, preferences, skills, and abilities with which we navigate the world. Through intense needs to belong and be respected, we adjust our traits, lives, and behaviours to win social approval and admiration. When we succeed, we typically experience happiness, health, and the feeling that our lives have meaning and importance. When we fail, the effects are catastrophic (Storr, 2021).

Our overarching thesis in this book is that this intense sociality is highly relevant to the project of understanding delusions. We will briefly conclude this chapter by anticipating the nature of this relevance.

In Chapter 2, we will explore various questions about delusions and delusion classification, such as: What are delusions? And what makes a belief or person delusional? Whereas most attempts to answer such questions treat *being delusional* as an objective property and typically define the concept either in terms of a belief's objective connection to pathology or epistemic irrationality, we advocate a very different approach. In our social function-based approach, delusion attribution is understood as a social act undertaken within the context of norm-governed, social-epistemic practices of the sort that we have described in this chapter. In such practices, to treat somebody as delusional is not to describe a fact about them but to express a kind of folk-epistemic bafflement and flag them as a rational lost cause—that is, as somebody not amenable to rational persuasion. In addition to exploring the functions and aetiology of this social-epistemic practice, we identify the theoretical and practical advantages of this approach over traditional alternatives.

In Part 2 (Chapters 3–5), we turn to what we call "popular delusions", widespread beliefs that arise in non-clinical populations often flagged as delusional by outsiders in the sense that we explicate in Chapter 2. Whereas much research on popular delusions identifies individualistic factors such as cognitive biases and motivated irrationality, we argue that they arise from a combination of distinctively social goals and the ways these goals shape norm-governed, social-epistemic practices that promote collective ignorance and misperceptions. In this explanatory framework, the intensely cooperative, cultural, and competitive aspects of human sociality reviewed in this chapter are all central. Specifically, we argue that there is often a strategic social rationality underlying the appearance of widespread irrationality and the "madness of crowds". This social rationality can only be understood once one understands how much of human psychology and behaviour is specialised for influencing other people, winning approval and esteem, and enforcing and conforming to local norms.

In Part 3 (Chapters 6–9), we then turn to clinical delusions. After reviewing traditional explanatory approaches to clinical delusions, we identify three under-appreciated social features of such delusions that must be explained: their frequent social focus (e.g., on themes such as persecution, surveillance, and status), their social determinants (e.g., in abuse and discrimination), and—perhaps most surprisingly, given our dependence on social learning—their resistance to social correction (Chapter 6). Chapter 7 reviews existing social accounts of clinical delusions, most of which attempt to link delusions to selective dysfunctions in specialised sociocognitive modules, before we develop our alternative theoretical framework in Chapters 8 and 9. The features of human sociality reviewed in this chapter are central to this framework. When it comes to the social focus and determinants of clinical delusions, we argue that they emerge from complex interactions between our powerful drives for status and belonging, our resistance to social threats, and the unique complexity and opacity of the social world (Chapter 8). When it comes to understanding the resistance of clinical delusions to social correction, we argue that it arises from features of epistemic vigilance and the ways in which this vigilance is modulated by various factors, as well as from biases in human reasoning that arise when people are isolated from social processes of communication and persuasion (Chapter 9).

2
Why Do We Call People Delusional?

1. Introduction

In the previous chapter, we examined the depth and variety of human sociality. We are intensely cooperative creatures, navigating interdependent social worlds organised around systems of norms, gossip, reputation, punishment, and partner choice. We are also cultural animals harnessing extensive communication, argument, and social learning to regulate our beliefs and acquire knowledge. To navigate the benefits and risks associated with this cultural dependence, we exercise sophisticated psychological capacities of "epistemic vigilance", evaluating the plausibility of testimony, the competence and honesty of testifiers, and the quality of their arguments. But epistemic vigilance is also a collective achievement involving the same social machinery of norms, reputations, and partner choice that regulates human cooperation more broadly. Finally, as with other social primates, we are profoundly competitive. This competition poses many of the problems that systems of cooperation aim to solve, yet competition also relies on such systems. We cooperate to compete, forming cohesive alliances and coalitions to outcompete other groups. And in competition for prestige, we compete to cooperate—to be more helpful, generous, and informative than others.

What does all of this have to do with delusions? One might think that an obvious question that needs to be answered, early on, in a book about delusions is: What are delusions? We will argue that a more fruitful question to ask is: Given that humans are the way they are, as described in Chapter 1, why might they need a concept of delusion? In other words, *why do we call people delusional?* And once we answer this question, we will ask what our answer tells us about the concept of delusion, and what we are doing when we apply it. What does it mean to treat people as delusional, and when is doing so appropriate? In subsequent chapters in Parts 2 and 3, we will then look at why people fall into states worthy of being called delusions, but these conceptual issues, which delineate the territory, must come first.

We begin by presenting some standard approaches to the concept of delusion, which aim to define it, either in psychiatric or epistemic terms (Section

The Social Roots of Delusions. Daniel Williams, Sam Wilkinson, and Kengo Miyazono, Oxford University Press.
 DOI: 10.1093/9780191976360.003.0003

2). After seeing that both approaches seem problematic, we explore what definitions of delusions might be answerable to, and argue that the concept does not seem to track a natural kind or phenomenon of theoretical importance (Section 3). Given this, we propose an alternative approach. Instead of asking, "What does the concept of delusion *mean* or *refer to*?" and trying to answer that question by definition and stipulation, we ask, "What is the concept of delusion *for*?" This leads us to present a *genealogy* of delusion attribution (Section 4), tracing the emergence of a beneficial social-epistemic practice that eventually came to encompass the practice of calling people delusional as it is widely understood today. In this analysis, delusion attribution expresses a kind of bafflement at people's beliefs and functions to flag them as "rational lost causes". In Section 5, we then examine what individual instances of delusion attribution look like, and what norms they are subject to, leading to a picture of when delusion attribution is sincere and appropriate. With appropriate caveats, this gives us an understanding of the concept of delusion. We conclude with three important lessons from this discussion concerning the heterogeneity of delusions, their contingent relation to pathology, and the inherently perspectival nature of delusion attribution (Section 6).

2. The Standard, Definitional Approaches

In this section, we present standard analyses of the concept of delusion, which we might call "definitional" for reasons that will become clear. Although this group of definitional approaches is so broad as to encompass most existing views in the literature, we do not aim to provide an exhaustive overview of this literature. We also do not assume that the objections we raise are decisive. Our goal in Sections 2 and 3 is rather to identify significant challenges to a dominant approach to understanding the concept of delusion, thereby motivating the very different approach that we will advocate in Sections 4–6. Theory choice is always comparative. It is only once our rival approach has been introduced and clarified that the challenges for existing views identified in these early sections can be fully contextualised and evaluated.

2.1 Definitional Approaches

Put simply, definitional approaches take delusions to be the set of things that fit a certain definition, that fit certain criteria. Different versions of this approach are, therefore, generated by the proposal of different criteria, and indeed of different *types* of criteria. And disagreement arises over these proposed criteria. Since something qualifies as a delusion in virtue of meeting specific criteria on this approach, it treats delusion attribution as *appropriate* when it involves accurately detecting those criteria in the target phenomenon, namely, a person and their beliefs.

This is clearly seen in diagnostic practice in general, including in the Diagnostic and Statistical Manual of Mental Disorders' (DSM) definition of delusion. The purpose of this definition is to enable a clinician to *identify* and hence *attribute* delusion to a potential patient. The definition of delusion in the glossary of DSM-5, which is almost the same as the one in DSM-IV, is as follows:

> Delusion. A false belief based on incorrect inference about external reality that is firmly sustained despite what almost everyone else believes and despite what constitutes incontrovertible and obvious proof or evidence to the contrary. The belief is not one ordinarily accepted by other members of the person's culture or subculture (e.g., it is not an article of religious faith). When a false belief involves a value judgment, it is regarded as a delusion only when the judgment is so extreme as to defy credibility. (American Psychiatric Association, 2013, p.819)

The DSM definition is problematic if it is viewed as a strict definition. For example, Coltheart (2007) puts into question more or less every statement contained within it:

> 1. Couldn't a true belief be a delusion, as long as the believer had no good reason for holding the belief? 2. Do delusions really have to be beliefs—might they not instead be imaginings that are mistaken for beliefs by the imaginer? 3. Must all delusions be based on inference? 4. Aren't there delusions that are not about external reality? "I have no bodily organs" or "my thoughts are not mine but are inserted into my mind by others" are beliefs expressed by some people with schizophrenia, yet are not about external reality; aren't these nevertheless still delusional beliefs? 5. Couldn't a belief held by all members of one's community still be delusional? (Coltheart, 2007, p.1043)

It must be said, however, that several theorists (e.g., Cooper 2007, Bortolotti 2009, Murphy 2013) have suggested that the DSM "definition" should not be viewed as a strict definition that delineates necessary and sufficient conditions.

Instead, it points to a prototype, or provides clinical guidelines for canonical cases. This is important because it means that counterexamples are not as damaging if a definition is not intended to be strict.

Another thing to note is that while this definition features in the DSM, and so implies that we are talking about a pathological phenomenon, a phenomenon of clinical interest, it is laden with epistemic notions (false belief, evidence, credibility). This points to two different approaches to the criteria: psychiatric approaches, and epistemic approaches.

2.2 Psychiatric Definitional Approaches

It is often assumed that delusion is, by definition, pathological. Indeed, one approach may be to *define* delusion as *pathological belief*, and then to reflect on what it is for a belief to be pathological. For example, following Wakefield (1992), one might understand pathology in terms of harmful dysfunction, and then define a delusion as a belief that is pathological in this sense, namely, the belief is not doing what beliefs are supposed to do (e.g., "aim at truth"), and it is harmful.[1] This may have the merit of enabling us to distinguish false beliefs that are not delusions from those that are. Thus, one might think that many false beliefs are not delusions because they do not involve harmful dysfunction, either because they are not harmful enough or because their falsity does not involve any dysfunction; it is rather a "misfunction" (see Miyazono, 2015, 2018; Sullivan-Bissett, 2024a).

Another way of tying delusion closely to pathology is not so much through tying pathology directly to belief, via the theoretically abstract notion of a pathological belief, but through the idea that delusions necessarily arise as an upshot of pathology. This more indirect, but still conceptually tight, view is fairly mainstream among clinicians, although it is typically implied or assumed rather than explicitly stated. Thus, consider a leading neuropsychiatrist, Tony David (David, 1999), who cites as obstacles to standard definitions of "delusion" that some of the proposed definitional features are found in the non-clinical population. For example, he observes that "the irrationality seen in 'normal' reasoning, undermines the specificity of these characteristics for delusions" (p.17), and that "maladaptiveness ... [is] sometimes equally applicable to other beliefs held by non-psychotic fanatics of one sort or another" (p.18). The fact that these non-clinical cases are treated as counterexamples,

[1] There is then a challenge of articulating what we mean by "harm" and to whom.

rather than admitted as cases of delusion, suggests that something occurring in a healthy, non-pathological mind cannot be a "delusion". Either way, whether delusion is conceptually tied to pathology directly, via the notion of pathological belief, or indirectly, as a hallmark of pathological cognition, the upshot is that "non-pathological delusion" is a contradiction in terms.

In stark contrast, some philosophers have argued that the relationship between delusion and pathology, though potentially causally tight, is not conceptual (Miyazono, 2015, 2018). On such a view, delusion is an indicator, but crucially not a guaranteed one, of underlying pathology. Belief formation tends not to give rise to delusion, and when it does, it might be an indicator of underlying pathology interfering with that. But, in principle, other things besides pathology could interfere with that. As a result, there is no *conceptual contradiction* in non-pathological delusions, or in a "healthy" person having a delusion.

As we will see in Part 2, there are certainly examples of strange, false, and seemingly highly irrational beliefs in the non-clinical population that are plausible candidates for delusional status, and which are classified as such by many people (Edsall, 2021; Mackay, 1841). Moreover, there are also examples of false beliefs produced by underlying pathology that do not qualify as delusions (e.g., a colourblind person's inaccurate beliefs about an object's colour), presumably because they lack distinguishing properties of delusions that can be identified independently of pathology. Such observations pose a problem for views that draw an essential connection between delusion and pathology and provide some support for thinking that the concept of delusion should be defined in epistemic terms, not psychiatric terms. Indeed, one way of thinking of delusion is as diametrically opposed to knowledge. Just as many philosophers assume that knowledge is constituted by holding beliefs that are epistemically good in a certain way or to a certain extent (e.g., true, justified, reliable, etc.), perhaps delusions are simply beliefs that are epistemically bad in a certain way or to a certain extent. As Dominic Murphy summarises this view,

> A delusion is a false belief, just as knowledge is true belief, but, as with knowledge, philosophers do not rest there. Knowledge is true belief plus something else. So too, philosophers try to find *that extra property* of the false belief that converts it from a mere false belief into a delusion (Murphy, 2013, p.115, emphasis added).

What might that extra property be?

2.3 Epistemic Definitional Approaches

Epistemic definitional approaches take delusions to be defined in terms of violating epistemic norms. But which ones? As we have seen, falsity is not sufficient to make a belief delusional. And although Murphy's central point is well taken, most theorists acknowledge that a delusion could be accidentally true (Coltheart, 2007). Given this, perhaps the extra property that makes a belief delusional might come from fleshing out this sense of "accidentally"? This seems to be about whether beliefs are formed, retained, and revised in ways that are *epistemically rational*. Roughly speaking, while practical rationality consists in acting in ways that help you to achieve your practical goals, epistemic rationality consists in thinking and acting in ways that will help you to achieve your epistemic goals, chief among which is the acquisition of knowledge or true beliefs. At a minimum, this includes conformity to commonsense epistemic norms such as basing beliefs on adequate evidence, giving due weight to evidence that might cause you to *revise* your belief, preventing motivational influences from derailing your tracking of, or concern for, the truth (i.e., wishful thinking), and maintaining consistency among your beliefs.

Defining the concept of delusion in terms of epistemic irrationality seems far more promising than mere falsehood. While a delusion might be accidentally true, it does not seem that it could be the result of a truth-*conducive* process. However, there are obstacles to such a view. Some have noted (including one of us, in Wilkinson, 2020) that epistemic irrationality seems neither sufficient nor necessary for something to count as a delusion.

First, if epistemic irrationality is *sufficient* for delusionality, one would expect that the more epistemically irrational you are, the more delusional you should be. The worry is that this correlation may not hold. Stated plainly, Person A might be *more* epistemically irrational than Person B, but be *less delusional*. Consider, for example, a mother whose son has been convicted of murder (from Nozick, 1993, cited in Murphy, 2012). We can understand that she will be *highly* resistant to evidence suggesting that he is guilty. But even if she is more epistemically irrational than a delusional individual, we may not be tempted to call her delusional. In Section 5, we will see how our view explains why we are not intuitively drawn to calling her delusional, as well as how this intuition might change in response to possible variations in the case.

Of course, one response to this example is to insist that delusional individuals always exhibit a degree of epistemic irrationality far beyond non-clinical cases of self-deception or denial. It is far from obvious that this is true, however. Indeed, it is not even obvious that epistemic irrationality is *necessary* for delusionality. As we will see in Chapter 6, advancements in cognitive neuropsychiatry and other disciplines have provided increasing theoretical and experimental support for the view that at least some delusions are formed based on strange or anomalous experiences. For example, a highly influential account of Capgras delusion (i.e., the belief that a loved one has been replaced by an impostor) proposes that brain injury disrupts the delusional individual's emotional responses to familiar faces in such cases, causing a disturbing sense of unfamiliarity when they encounter their loved one. This experience is then interpreted as evidence that it is not their loved one, after all. It is an impostor.

According to some versions of this hypothesis, this anomalous experience is sufficient to give rise to Capgras delusion even in the absence of any irrational cognition or reasoning. As Brendan Maher characterises this kind of view, "The delusional belief is not being held 'in the face of evidence strong enough to destroy it', but is being held because evidence is strong enough to support it" (1974, p.99). If so, this would mean that at least some delusions arise from broadly *rational* use of very bizarre and misleading evidential inputs rather than from the *misuse* of normal evidential inputs. Of course, such a belief would *look* highly resistant to counter-evidence among those who do not share the relevant experiences. However, if the private experiential evidence on which the belief is based is strong enough, this resistance to publicly available counter-evidence, including testimonial counter-evidence (see Chapter 9), might be perfectly epistemically rational from the delusional person's subjective vantage point. Put simply, they might be thinking and reasoning in ways that would ordinarily be truth-conducive. The problem lies not with any unusual epistemic irrationality on their part; it lies with the misleading data they are exposed to.

It is a complex empirical question whether this hypothesis is correct for any specific case of delusion (see Chapter 6). But our question here is conceptual: If there were people who believed bizarre things on fully adequate private grounds, and hence were epistemically rational (or at least *as* epistemically rational as "normal" people), *would* we still be right to consider them delusional? Interestingly, Jennifer Radden (2010) thinks not. As "reasonable inferences from misleading perceptual experiences, 'perceptual delusions' are *not epistemic lapses of the sort by which delusional states are identified*" (2010, p.28, emphasis added). This would amount to us retrospectively retracting our delusion attributions in light of a *stipulation* that delusions are tied to epistemic irrationality. In other words, it may turn out that some utterly paradigmatic cases of delusion (e.g., Capgras delusion) are not delusional after all.

A contrasting approach asks: *Granting* that these subjects are delusional, how can we explain their delusional status? On this view, a discovery that beliefs thought to be paradigm examples of delusions are epistemically rational should not cause us to abandon their classification as delusions. It would rather demonstrate that delusions need not be epistemically irrational, and that our concept of delusion ought to accommodate that.

3. The Issue of "Answerability"

When we theorise about the concept of delusion, a lot of what guides our theorising, when we test out our views on the matter, is our intuitions about whether a given case counts as a delusion. But suppose that two theorists disagree about whether and why a given case should count as a delusion. How do we adjudicate between them? How do we decide who is right?

As we have seen, Radden (2010) proposes to retrospectively retract our delusion attributions in light of the stipulation that delusions must be epistemically irrational. This approach is revisionary in the sense that, if Capgras delusion turns out to be an epistemically rational response to anomalous experience, we should no longer regard it as a delusion. If someone objects, insisting that Capgras delusion is a delusion *even if it is epistemically rational*, how should we decide who is right?

3.1 Conceptual Conservatism and Revisionism

This raises the issue of "answerability": when we are trying to define a concept or characterise a phenomenon, what is our theorising *answerable* to, outside of the terminological stipulations that we make? In many cases, the answer is: not much. As a result, people talk past each other until they clarify their terminology, and it becomes clear that they are disagreeing about the meaning of words rather than about facts. They are making different terminological stipulations. What is more, there may be nothing better about one terminological stipulation over another. You can sometimes define a term in one way or another, with no clear benefit either way.

However, there are at least two contexts in which there is particularly clear answerability. In the first, the concept is one of central theoretical importance (as Marcus (1990) suggests about the concept of belief). If you do not define a term in the right way, then there are many other things you cannot do, theoretically speaking. In the second, the phenomenon you are theorising about is a "natural kind", an objective kind of "stuff" that exists in the world, like gold or water. In that case, your theorising about the concept is constrained by how things actually stand in the world, by the actual nature of the kind in question.

Is the concept of delusion either one of fundamental theoretical importance or one that denotes a natural kind? If so, our theorising can *revise* our intuitions about usage and applicability—for example, in light of discoveries about the natural kind, or arguments about the revised concept's theoretical importance. In the absence of this answerability, we should typically aim to capture and reflect (and perhaps better understand) current usage. We should be *conservative* rather than *revisionary.*

3.2 Is "Delusion" Theoretically Important?

Is there a concept of delusion that wields a strong degree of theoretical importance, such that revisionism is warranted? It does not seem obvious that there is. In a manner that prefigures the next section, we can ask: What would be lost, *theoretically* speaking, if we could not use the concept of delusion? We could still, after all, talk about a Capgras patient in terms of *what* they believe (e.g., that their loved one has been replaced by an impostor), and *how* they believe it (e.g., tenaciously and with little apparent regard to counter-evidence), and miss out on very little, if anything, *theoretically* speaking. Indeed, we can easily imagine that we simply called it "the Capgras belief" or reverted to the somewhat old-fashioned terminology of "Capgras syndrome".

Perhaps there is another way that you might defend its theoretical importance as a concept. Perhaps it adds nothing to our understanding of *specific* delusions, but is instead important for tying together the various cases that we call delusions? So you might think that, in calling *two* people delusional, you are classifying them based on some theoretically important property or set of properties that they have in common. Although this seems more promising, it runs up against a problem that we will return to in much greater depth in Part 3 (especially Chapters 6 and 7): the category of things that we count as delusions is highly heterogeneous, in content, degree of conviction, clinical presentation, aetiology, diagnostic context, and more. The florid and elaborate delusional systems of someone with a diagnosis of paranoid schizophrenia are radically different from the circumscribed delusional misidentifications that sometimes arise in the context of brain injury, which in turn are quite unlike the grandiose delusions often found in bipolar disorder. The viable treatment options also frequently differ for different examples of delusional beliefs. In other words, even if we restrict our attention to clinical delusions, there is extreme heterogeneity in their manifestations, correlates, and aetiology. As we have already noted, however, the term "delusion" is also often used in non-clinical contexts, which introduces even more heterogeneity. Such immense heterogeneity speaks against the idea that the concept of delusion carries deep theoretical significance. From a purely theoretical perspective, the concept seems to bundle together phenomena that are profoundly different in their characteristics and causes.

Of course, this is not to say that there cannot be scientific research on those phenomena that we call delusional. For example, you can examine the neuroscience of person identification in delusional misidentification disorders (e.g., Ellis & Young, 1990), the information-processing aberrations associated with psychosis in conditions such as schizophrenia (Kapur, 2003), or the psychological and social dynamics implicated in "extraordinary popular delusions and the madness of crowds" (Mackay, 1841). However, such research will tell you how a particular kind of belief or belief system arises. Given the immense heterogeneity in such belief systems, it is far from obvious that the "delusionality" of the phenomenon should be understood as an additional property that science can uncover.

3.3 Is Delusion a Natural Kind?

Alternatively, one might argue that the concept of delusion denotes a natural kind (Samuels, 2009). It is a kind of thing that is "out there", like water or gold. Although there are different accounts of what natural kinds are, including essentialist accounts (which are considered the strictest), "homeostatic property cluster" accounts (Boyd 1991), and simple causal theory accounts (Craver 2009), the precise details do not matter for our purposes.[2]

If you couple the natural kind view with an influential view about the meaning of natural kind concepts, it amounts to an anti-definitional view, but of a very different sort to the one that we will defend. This view states that natural kind concepts refer *directly* and not in virtue of fitting a particular description

[2] Although some accounts make the thesis that delusions are natural kinds more plausible than others (as Samuels 2025 points out). Our concern with the natural kind view runs too deep for any particular account to avoid.

or definition (Putnam 1975). For example, "gold" refers to whatever the thing in the world gold is.[3] Through scientific investigation, we can discover gold's objective properties, such as its atomic number 79. And with such discoveries, we can learn that previous attempts at understanding gold were mistaken (e.g., definitions in terms of superficial properties like being a heavy, yellow, shiny metal), and that things previously considered gold are in fact not gold (e.g., metals like pyrite, "Fool's Gold", which superficially resemble gold but lack the atomic number 79). The reason that these constitute discoveries *about gold*, and not the introduction of a new concept, is that the concept does not refer to whatever thing happens to satisfy proposed definitions. It refers directly to gold, the objective natural kind to which our definitions are answerable.

Similarly, one might argue that the concept of delusion refers directly to the natural kind, *delusion*. If so, the question "What is a delusion?" would not be a surface-level, conceptual question to be adjudicated by people's intuitions, and much less a matter of arbitrary stipulation. It would be settled by scientific investigation answerable to the world itself. Through such investigation, we might discover that delusions involve, say, a specific kind of neurobiological dysfunction, which might, in turn, lead us to revise our initial beliefs about delusions and which mental states qualify as delusions. For example, just as we have discovered that pyrite ("Fool's Gold") is not *really* gold, we might learn that the mental states involved in some apparent examples of delusions are not *really* delusions because they do not involve the relevant kind of neurobiological dysfunction.

Although this view is *coherent*, we do not find it *appealing*.[4] There does not seem to be an objective "joint" in nature separating the delusional from the non-delusional. For example, the immense heterogeneity of delusional phenomena and their causal aetiologies is just as much in tension with the existence of a unitary natural kind as it is with the idea that the concept is one of theoretical importance. Moreover, whereas things are either water or gold, it seems clear that beliefs can be more or less delusional.[5] And in a related

[3] And in a related manner are "rigid designators", referring to the same things in all possible worlds where said things exist. In this respect, natural kind terms are a bit like a general (kind) version of the singular proper name. In this same tradition, names are also directly referring rigid designators that refer to the same individual in all possible worlds where that individual exists.

[4] Interestingly, Hilary Kornblith (2002) has suggested that knowledge is a natural kind, based on the pivotal role that it plays in the scientific study of the mind. This merges the natural kind and theoretical centrality considerations for answerability in ways that seem more plausible for knowledge than for delusion, but it would take us too far afield to elaborate on this.

[5] It is worth noting, without digressing too far, that some theorists believe that natural kinds can come in degrees while still having an essence. An example of this is temperature (defined, for example, as the kinetic energy of the particles in an object). But notice that the having of temperature, per se, is binary: either something has a temperature or it does not, even though a particular temperature reading may come in degrees.

manner, since evaluations are typically scalar, a concept that is as evaluatively laden as "delusion" is a strange candidate for a natural kind. It is somewhat like claiming that "goodness" or "beauty" are natural kinds. Natural kinds are supposed to be the brute, neutral furniture of mind-independent reality. They are not inflected with value and valence. Delusion, in contrast, seems to be so inflected.

Indeed, to return to the question of what is added to a description of the Capgras patients by using the word "delusion", one might say: nothing factual or descriptive, but rather something evaluative and prescriptive. It is a belief that this person *should not* have. To say that something has the *status* of being a delusion is to evaluate it as *bad* in a particular way.

3.4 What Is the Concept of Delusion for?

Although these considerations are certainly not dispositive, they put pressure on the assumption that analyses of the concept of delusion have the kind of "answerability" to theory construction or nature that would justify a revisionary definition. Nevertheless, we will now suggest that if we look at the world, there *is* a phenomenon in nature (though not a natural kind) that tells us a great deal about the concept of delusion. It is a phenomenon among human beings as characterised in Chapter 1—as cultural, testimonial creatures who police their informational ecosystems and flag to members of their epistemic communities which sources of information are good, and which are bad. Indeed, as the positive flipside of this practice indicates, this approach could apply not only to the attribution of delusion but also to the attribution of knowledge. Within such a framework, knowledge and delusion are not objective *things* to which our concepts are answerable. They are social statuses conferred on beliefs when epistemic communities flag people as good or bad sources of information.

A very similar treatment of knowledge can be found in Edward Craig's book, *Knowledge and the State of Nature* (1990), and our approach bears many similarities to his. Craig is sceptical of attempts to cleanly define knowledge via "conceptual analysis", favouring instead "conceptual synthesis". This means that instead of asking the static question: "Under what conditions does the concept of knowledge apply?" he asks a more dynamic, practical, functional question: "Why did the concept of knowledge emerge, and what purpose did it serve?" His answer to this question is that the concept of knowledge, and its application, serve to flag good sources of information.

Although Craig himself does not use the terminology, we agree with Matthieu Queloz (2021) that this story of the emergence of the concept of knowledge is a *genealogy*. A genealogy is a story about where a concept or practice comes from, and one that sheds valuable light on certain features of that concept or practice. Famous examples of genealogies are Nietzsche's genealogy of Western, post-Christian morality (2008 [1887]), and Foucault's genealogies of psychiatry (1961), medicine (1963), and the modern penal system (1975). A genealogy can draw on different posits (e.g., forces, motives, power dynamics, material conditions, etc.) to make its story convincing. For example, while Nietzsche appealed to drives and motives, Craig appeals to the practical needs of a social species. His account is processual: over time, humans progressed from basic information seeking and sharing to recommending certain informants in specific contexts to eventually developing a more stable, "objectivised" way of doing so that functioned across contexts. As Craig puts it, the concept of knowledge "lies at the objectivised end of the process" (Craig, 1990, p.91).

Just as Craig is sceptical of attempts to define knowledge ("conceptual analysis"), our approach is sceptical of similar attempts to define "delusion", whether these be strict attempts to provide necessary and sufficient conditions, or something looser. Developing a function-first epistemology inspired by Craig (and, more recently, Michael Hannon (2019)), we will argue that the function of the concept of delusion is similar to the concept of knowledge insofar as it flags sources of information, but that it has the opposite valence: bad sources of information. Another similarity is that, like Craig, we put attribution first: the concept of delusion is whatever we can read off our practices of calling people delusional. It is not that we explain delusion attribution as those instances where we detect a thing in the world called "delusion", whether that be something that fits a definition, loose or strict, or is a natural kind.

4. A Genealogy of Delusion Attribution

What is the concept of delusion for? And what would we lose if we could not apply it?

Our strategy is as follows. We will present a genealogical account of the emergence of delusion attribution. This is a dynamic story over time that will shed light on the kinds of social practices that led to the emergence of the concept of delusion. In this genealogy, the word "delusion" is much less relevant than the broader social-conceptual practices from which the word emerged.

Given this, even if other natural languages lack a specific word for delusion, our story implies that they nevertheless engage in the same kinds of practices that are often expressed by this word today in Western, Anglophone countries.

4.1 Anthropologically Necessary and Historically Local Concepts and Practices

Drawing on recent meta-philosophical work on genealogy (Queloz, 2021; Leuenberger, 2021), we can distinguish *anthropologically necessary* practices and concepts from *historically local* ones. As the terminology suggests, anthropologically necessary practices and concepts are those that are ancient and cross-cultural, because they are required for the functioning of all recognisably human existence (Chapter 1). An example is social practices of encouraging and discouraging specific behaviours via social punishments and rewards associated with the enforcement of norms, and the closely related concepts of virtue and vice, or of right and wrong (Chapter 1, Section 3). While there is cross-cultural variation in the things deemed right and wrong (virtuous or vicious, encouraged or discouraged), it is precisely because the concepts of right and wrong themselves (and the related practices of encouragement and discouragement) are the same that differences in what they are applied to amount to substantive ethical differences (see Section 6.3 below).

In contrast, historically local concepts emerge as a function of contingent practices or institutional structures. Other cultures may lack the practice or concept, and had history turned out differently, the concept would be different or even lacking altogether. Examples of this might include concepts such as the Judeo-Christian notion of "sin" or the Western, modernist concept of "authenticity" (see Leuenberger, 2021).

It is also important to clarify the relationship between *practices* and *concepts*, since the distinction between the anthropologically necessary and the historically local applies to both. Practices are more primitive than concepts, but concepts can emerge as tools for certain practices. For example, on a Craigian analysis (Craig, 1990), the concept of knowledge emerges as a tool for the more fundamental and broader practice of flagging good sources of information, a subset of which involves knowledge attribution. Similarly, the concept of delusion emerges as a narrower tool for flagging poor sources of information, but it is only a subset of such flagging.

The notions of anthropologically necessary and historically local are not binary, but admit of a spectrum. Concepts and their associated practices can be more or less local. What is more, these can be hierarchically nested within one another as more fine-grained concepts and practices emerge. Thus, one might say that the broad genus of social-epistemic cooperation and associated practices of epistemic norm enforcement, flagging, and gatekeeping are on the anthropologically necessary side of the spectrum (and are cross-culturally universal), whereas the more fine-grained species of delusion attribution, as we know it today, is historically local (and is culturally specific and recent).

4.2 The (Relatively) Anthropologically Necessary Practice of Social Epistemic Flagging

As we explained in Chapter 1, human evolutionary success is the result of cooperation of various kinds. This ability to cooperate is primarily underpinned by the ability to regulate, as a group, the behaviour of group members. One way in which we do this is via incentives: we incentivise prosocial behaviour and disincentivise antisocial behaviour, both through *community enforcement* of norms and through partner choice and exclusion (e.g., withdrawing cooperation and social support from uncooperative individuals). These incentives are not always explicit or material: they become implicit and psychological.[6] This is one way of thinking about moral discourse and its emergence. On such a view, saying "That is wrong!" is not (at least not entirely) to describe the world, but to regulate behaviour by discouraging certain types of action. Obvious examples are behaviours that are explicitly antisocial and harmful to the group, such as killing, stealing, free riding, and so on. But as we argued in Chapter 1, our status as cultural animals means that we do not only try to discourage practical harms. There are also informational harms associated with misinformation and deception. Although we exploit psychological capacities of epistemic vigilance to protect ourselves from such harms (i.e., psychological flagging and gatekeeping), we also rely on social-epistemic norms and complex practices of encouragement and punishment (i.e., social practices of flagging and gatekeeping). For example, the deliberate telling of untruth, i.e., lying, almost always constitutes a norm violation that human communities flag and punish, either directly or indirectly via informal mechanisms of reputation, gossip, and the withdrawal of cooperation from the relevant individual.

[6] One way of understanding this is through the "internalization" of social norms (Parsons, 1951) according to which we feel pride and shame in the absence of explicit social rewards or sanctions even when we are alone.

In such cases, we see a system of norms and regulative discourse and behaviours that operate on the targeted agent (e.g., the liar or the thief) by encouraging and discouraging certain types of action. People are discouraged from the practical harm of stealing because they will be punished and, if socialised, feel guilty. They are discouraged from the informational harm of lying because they will be punished and, if socialised, will feel guilty. They will also acquire a negative reputation, undermining their access to social support. Of course, such pressures only work if the target behaviours are under the agent's control. You can only discourage theft and lies via such processes if people can refrain from stealing and telling lies. And yet, there are informational harms that are not under the agent's direct control. Some, like "carelessness", retain quite a strong moral inflection. Others, like "stupidity", are not so much moral as offensive and debasing. These discourage, but less directly. You can take steps to be less careless or less stupid, but these are not one-off acts that you refrain from doing.

However, not all forms of normative discourse serve to regulate the target agent's behaviour. Sometimes the primary function is to encourage the community surrounding the agent to take a course of action. Our proposal is that delusion attribution is like this. Castigating somebody for being a liar, or stupid, or a careless thinker, has the primary function of discouraging target agents from certain courses of action, or general practices, lest they be punished or acquire a stigmatised reputation. In contrast, to call someone delusional is not to call them a liar. The delusional person is not trying to mislead. But nor is it merely to say that they have made a mistake, based on carelessness, ignorance, or stupidity. One can take steps to correct such vices, or at least recognise what steps can be taken. In contrast, calling someone delusional acknowledges that the error is in an important sense beyond their control. Calling something a delusion is beyond calling it a mistake because it carries a certain pessimism about it being put right, even in principle. That means that, while it may indirectly motivate the target person to abandon their belief through the stigma and shame of having been negatively evaluated, the primary purpose of the discourse is to encourage others to behave in a certain way, namely, to avoid trying to correct them via ordinary processes of testimony and argument. This central idea is that the delusional individual, unlike the liar or the perpetrator of an honest mistake, is a "rational lost cause". Not only should the community not listen to them, but they will not listen to the community. The core argumentative and persuasive functions of reasoning, as reviewed in Chapter 1 (Sections 3 and 4), will hit a brick wall. The person is banished from the system of epistemic cooperation altogether, at least when it comes to the specific belief in question.

In sum, we propose that the protean, more anthropologically necessary, form of delusion attribution, which need not be expressed by the word "delusion", is not simply to flag a poor source of information. After all, liars, bullshitters, and the ignorant are poor sources of information of different kinds, and the discourse surrounding them serves to encourage them to be better (and, of course, to discourage others from following in their footsteps). In contrast, delusion attribution includes a recommendation to others within one's epistemic community of *rational disengagement*. To call someone delusional is (in part) to say: "This person's belief/assertion is a bad source of information, and you should not waste your time trying to talk them out of it". The delusional individual is a terrible source of information on the topic of their delusion, but they are neither a liar nor simply mistaken.

4.3 The (Relatively) Historically Local Practice of Delusion Attribution

Now let us move towards more historically local practices with a view to better understanding the concept of delusion as it is widely understood today, especially in Western cultures and contexts influenced by Western medicine.

Notice that, at this point, we have said nothing that requires the institutional trappings of modernity. Recommending that others do not waste conversational resources on someone who is a "rational lost cause" is a socially sophisticated practice, but it does not require institutional or technological sophistication. Alongside the development of this social-epistemic gatekeeping and flagging were institutional and technological advancements that inflected these more anthropologically necessary practices with some historically local nuance.

Consider the emergence of medicine. Although it is often beneficial to the group to be able to cure and care for those who are infirm and vulnerable, these benefits are not always obvious. Dead weights could alternatively be (and in early hominin societies plausibly often would have been) ruthlessly dispensed with for the overall good of the group (Singh, 2022). When viable forms of help and cure emerge (a technological advancement), as well as the norms that promote such actions as good (a societal development), we see the emergence of practices that help those who are cumbersome, even at high cost. This costly investment may well pay off in the long run, and it fosters *trust* in society that people will not be ruthlessly treated, which has immense value in promoting social cohesion. This marks the start of cultures of interpersonal care and healing: medical, clinical cultures.

However, with the emergence of such practices and the allowances made to the infirm (in effect, the ability of group members to adopt a primitive version of what Parsons (1951) calls "the sick role"), there emerges a new version of the free rider problem (see Chapter 1, Section 3): the problem of the malingerer. It becomes important to distinguish those who should be helped (at significant cost to the collective) from those who should not; the latter may need to be reprimanded and punished instead. In the bodily domain, it is important to distinguish fatigue or illness from laziness. At some point, humans realised that it was not just undesirable bodily states, but also undesirable mental states that could bifurcate in this way. And here the distinction between moral and medical deviance is felt all the more sharply. Does this person act and think in ways we dislike because they are morally bad or because they are sick?

What does this have to do with delusion attribution? How does this add to our genealogy? After all, we have cast delusion as a social epistemic phenomenon, not a necessarily medical one. This would help to explain why many people freely use the term "delusion" to describe non-pathological beliefs that strike them as bafflingly and incorrigibly irrational. Nevertheless, this core social-conceptual practice of delusion attribution can become medically inflected, even if the concept itself is not essentially medical.

A group member may not be able to work in the fields because they have a broken leg or a fever. Calling them sick or injured does not just describe them; it signals to society that this individual should not be castigated for laziness. To do so would not only be inaccurate but also an injustice and a waste of resources. It will do nothing to speed up their return to the fields.

By analogy, flagging someone as delusional is primarily to say that they have a bad belief and that they are a "rational lost cause". It also means that, while it may be inappropriate and futile to attempt to change their beliefs rationally, you may be able to do so via non-rational means. They are a rational lost cause, but not necessarily a lost cause *tout court*. By analogy, you cannot shame the person with a broken leg or a fever into working in the field. But if you heal the leg and cure the fever, they might return to work. Similarly, you may not be able to talk the delusional individual out of their belief, but if you fix what is wrong with them, it might go away.

Herein lies the relationship between delusion and pathology. The relationship is one of close association, but it is (i) tangential, in that it is not conceptually intrinsic, and (ii) likely relatively historically recent. The core practice of delusion attribution involves flagging that someone is a rational lost cause. Trying to argue this person out of their belief is going to be a waste of time. It is a tangential and much further step, enabled by contingent advances in both medical and clinical technologies and conceptualisations, to realise that this person's mind can be changed medically or therapeutically, rather than through the quotidian techniques of conversation and argument. In other words, problematic beliefs, moods, and experiences can be viewed as medical symptoms. But this is a contingent and relatively recent step, in both the social practices and the language used. In other historical and cultural contexts, for example, people might theorise and respond to someone's status as a "rational lost cause" through spiritual or supernatural frameworks, favouring activities such as collective rituals or demonic exorcism over medical interventions.

This is also related to one of our three central lessons as presented in Section 6. The relationship between delusion and pathology is looser than many suppose. But we can easily understand the logic behind this mistake. Just because one way of becoming a rational lost cause in the eyes of others involves pathology (e.g., schizophrenia or a brain injury), and one form of recourse you might take towards such a person is medical, it does not follow that psychological or neurobiological dysfunction is the only way to trigger this social response, nor that the concept of delusion is essentially tied to pathology or medicine.

4.4 A Brief History of the Word "Delusion"

Our genealogy expressly focused on the practices of flagging conspecifics as poor sources of information and rational lost causes, rather than on the word "delusion". After all, words can be used in different ways, by different people, for different purposes, thoughtlessly and intuitively, or by careful stipulation. However, since we make conjectures about the emergence of the concept that the word "delusion" was invented in order to express, this also makes some loose predictions about what we would see in the English historical corpus. In particular, if we are right, we would expect early uses to lack explicit medical connotations or implications of pathology.

Before looking at usage over time, let us start with etymology. The word "delusion" has roots in the Latin term *deludere* (*de-ludere*, literally to "play false", but meaning conversationally to mock, to deceive). This conveyed a sense of being misled, but these were often moral, epistemic, or spiritual failings rather than medical conditions. In ancient texts, to be deluded was to be in error, perhaps dangerously so, but not ill.

Early prominent uses of the word in English are to be found in, for example, the King James Bible (1611): "And for this cause God shall send them strong delusion, that they should believe a lie" (2 Thessalonians 2:11). There is no allusion here to medicine, illness, or pathology. Furthermore, while these people will believe a falsehood, it is not as the result of a mistake that could have been avoided, or that could be corrected; they are helpless under the power of God.

Later 17th-century examples of its use are also Christian, for example, in the work of John Bunyan (1980 [1656]), in which the word delusion appears over 120 times ("The tempter came in with his delusion", "The delusions of the Devil".) It seems that in this tradition, delusion was primarily associated with spiritual error, but of external cause. A delusional person might be someone who believed themselves to be in communion with God while actually being led astray, possibly by demonic forces. Delusion, in this context, had no connotation of illness or medical impairment, but rather of heresy or susceptibility to temptation.

This raises a question about the relationship and differences in nuance between two words that are typically used interchangeably: "delusional" and "deluded", as typically predicated of a person. First of all, "deluded" appears to be a much older term that goes at least as far back as the 16th century, and meant someone who has been misled or deceived, usually morally, intellectually, or spiritually. This fits somewhat with contemporary nuance: "deluded" retains some implication of *process*, of having been *deluded by* another agent, or oneself. "Delusional", in contrast, is a much later term that emerged in the 19th century. The adjective for somebody with a delusion was always "deluded", whereas "delusional" was likely formed as a back-formation from "delusion" plus "-al", making it an adjective that pertains specifically to a *state* of delusion. Again, the term "delusional individual" focuses on their *state* and has far less of a focus on the process, still less an agentive process, that got them into that state (contrast: "deluded individual"). It gained traction, as one might expect from the historical timing, in medical and psychiatric contexts. This is understandable given the aims of psychiatry, as an emerging branch of medicine, to extricate itself from normative and values-based frameworks that draw on morality, or, indeed, on spirituality. By the early 20th century, "delusional" became standard in psychiatry to describe clinical symptoms (e.g., "delusional belief"), and yet the word "delusion" has continued to be used in a non-clinical sense in common speech. The medicalisation of delusion as a symptom of mental disorder began with Esquirol and became codified in psychiatric texts only later in the 19th century and early 20th century by figures such as Emil Kraepelin and Karl Jaspers.

Even in such medical contexts, one can often still find reference to the core idea that delusional individuals are rational lost causes. For example, three editions of the influential textbook Clinical Psychiatry from 1954 to 1969 declared explicitly that "it is a waste of time to argue with a paranoid patient about his delusions", adding that the patient may nevertheless "still be persuaded to keep them to himself, to repress them as far as possible and to forgo the aggressive action they might suggest, in general to conduct his life as if they did not exist" (Mayer-Gross et al, 1954, p.280; see Freeman and Garety 2006, p.404). Even in the DSM's definition reviewed in Section 2.1, the claim that delusions are "firmly sustained despite what almost everyone else believes and despite what constitutes incontrovertible and obvious proof or evidence to the contrary" captures the core intuition that the delusional individual is judged to be a rational lost cause.

5. What Are We Doing When We Call Someone Delusional?

We have given a genealogy of the concept of delusion and the practice of delusion attribution. In other words, we have explained what the concept might do for us as a social, collaborative species. But what does this tell us about what we are doing when we call someone delusional? Answering a question about what we are doing when we use language has a public and a private dimension. What does the language achieve, and what mental state are we typically in when we use it sincerely? This private, or psychological, element is important because it tells us what prompts the use of language and so tells us the sorts of things that will end up as targets of delusion attribution. This also sheds light on when it is done correctly or appropriately.

5.1 Delusion Attribution as Descriptive Assertion

The definitional accounts reviewed in Sections 2 and 3 treat delusion attribution as involving *descriptive assertions*. The simplest way of thinking about "description" in the relevant sense is that a description depicts the world as being a certain way, and is accurate to the extent that the world is indeed that way. The most important part of this, for our purposes, is what we might call the "direction of fit" of the relevant utterance.[7] To say that delusion attribution

[7] The notion of direction of fit goes back to Elizabeth Anscombe (Anscombe, 1957). She illustrated this with the distinction between an inventory and a shopping list. While an inventory has a word-to-world direction of fit, a shopping list has a world-to-word direction of fit. The one is a list that responds

is a *descriptive assertion* is to say that it has a certain word-to-world direction of fit. If the words do not "fit" the world, there is inaccuracy. The "job" of the utterance is to reflect the world. In this way, to say "This man is delusional" is like saying "This man is 6 feet tall". An example of an utterance with the opposite world-to-word direction of fit is a command; it depicts a state of affairs that is not actual, and it is up to the world to satisfy it.

The public function of descriptive discourse is to *inform* audiences about the relevant state of the world. The private dimension, namely, what is typically going on in someone's mind when they sincerely assert something, is that they have the factual belief with the asserted content. To sincerely assert, in the context where you are informing an interlocutor about the world, "This man is 6 feet tall", is to express the belief that this man is 6 feet tall. On this model, then, delusion attribution—sincerely saying "This man is delusional"—expresses the factual belief that the relevant man is delusional and is accurate if this man is indeed delusional. And so, just as making correct assertions about people's height means being accurate about their height, making correct delusion attributions is about accurately detecting delusions, or delusionality, in the world.

5.2 Beyond Description: Signalling Disengagement by Expressing Bafflement

Our view, as inspired by our genealogy, denies that delusion attribution is descriptive like this. The public element, as we have seen, is to flag poor sources of information as rational lost causes, and so to recommend to others in one's epistemic community not to listen to them, and not to waste time trying to correct them.

What is the private, psychological element? Let us start with an observation about direction-of-fit and the notion of flagging. If delusion attribution is a form of flagging, what is flagging in the relevant sense? It is not merely describing the world. When you flag something, you also bring something into being for the benefit of others. For an analogy, suppose that you have a pot of red paint, and you are dabbing it on the parts of the environment that might be dangerous to a toddler. You are responsive to things in the environment, no doubt (the sharp corners of a table, for example), but you have also left the environment changed in the service of recommending a specific course of action to others.

to things as they are, that tells you the state of play (e.g., what is in your fridge), while the other tries to bring about a certain state of affairs (e.g., what you need in your fridge).

Given this, if delusion attribution is a form of flagging, descriptive assertion is surely too simplistic to capture it. To see this more clearly, reflect on what it is to disagree about flagging. When flagging something, you do not merely have factual beliefs about the world. You want to alert others. Furthermore, as with the red paint analogy, there is not simply the belief that the thing flagged has certain objective properties: there is also a judgment call about the level of threat, about what is to be *done*.

This does not mean that anything goes. But good or bad delusion attributions, like good or bad instances of flagging, are good and bad in a way that is more akin to emotional reactions, rather than factual descriptions: they can be appropriate or inappropriate, but not really accurate or inaccurate. If you dab red paint over something that is not really a threat to a toddler, your dabbing is not inaccurate: it is inappropriate. You are alerting others to something that they do not need to be alerted to. Similarly, our account suggests that wrongly calling someone delusional is not a factual inaccuracy akin to misrepresenting somebody's height. In flagging someone as delusional, you are denigrating a belief, or way of believing, that ought not to be so denigrated, and recommending a course of action (i.e., rational disengagement) to others in a way that constitutes an *injustice*, not an inaccuracy.

If you are not expressing a factual belief when you attribute delusional status to others, what state of mind are you expressing? We propose that a plausible candidate for the psychological accompaniment of delusion attribution, of this kind of flagging, is the state of *bafflement*. In treating someone as delusional, we express our inability to understand how a rational person could hold the relevant belief, given the available evidence, and thereby encourage others to treat the person as having exited the shared space of rational communication and argument, at least on the topic in question.

So understood, bafflement is a cognitive-affective response to encountering something inexplicable or that resists assimilation into your existing models of understanding. A sincere and canonical assertion of "You are delusional!" expresses an emotionally inflected state of bafflement. Just like some non-cognitivist positions in meta-ethics take sincere and canonical expressions of moral claims like "That action is wrong" to be "That action, yuk!" (e.g., Ayer 1936), this account suggests that "You are delusional" is akin to saying "That belief? Baffling!", or "I cannot wrap my head around how you could believe that". The normal processes of epistemic vigilance with which we evaluate communicated information and tailor our communication to other people do not apply to the belief in question. It does not merely strike us as implausible; it strikes us as existing outside the space of rational communication, argumentation, and the exchange of reasons altogether. (This is the grain of truth in Karl Jaspers' (1963 [1913]) famous claim that many delusions are "un-understandable". However, we suggest that this un-understandability is not a property of delusions themselves—it is the state of mind paradigmatically expressed when we evaluate people as delusional—and that "un-understandability" is better understood in terms of bafflement as we have characterised it, which arises in response to all beliefs deemed delusional, not just a subset of them.)

Importantly, such bafflement is not simply puzzlement or confusion. You can be confused about or puzzled by an inanimate phenomenon in the world. But bafflement is about other people. You might be puzzled by climate change, but baffled by your interlocutor's opinions about climate change. However, not all bafflement is about epistemic phenomena; sometimes, we are baffled by how people behave and the choices that they make. And so we need to distinguish practical bafflement (a profound failure to understand why someone is behaving in a certain way, or making a particular choice) from epistemic bafflement (a profound failure to understand why someone believes what they do). Moreover, since this epistemic bafflement in delusion attribution targets something intuitive and surface-level, rather than something theoretically sophisticated, it involves *folk*-epistemic bafflement. The attributor of delusional status is baffled by how the target's beliefs relate to evidence and commonsense epistemic norms that they, the attributor, have available to them.

Our view, therefore, looks like a development of the suggestion that Murphy (2013) makes, "that alongside folk psychology we should acknowledge a folk epistemology" and that [...] "delusions are beliefs that folk epistemology treats as inexplicable" (p.113).[8]

5.3 Correctly Calling Someone Delusional

This proposal points us towards norms of delusion attribution. We can distinguish norms of sincerity from norms of correctness or appropriateness. To say "That is delusional!" in response to something that does not actually baffle you is insincere. However, even when sincere, bafflement is not always appropriate. And when it is not, your delusion attribution inherits that inappropriateness.

[8] While there are similarities between our view and Murphy's, our engagement with genealogy and with the non-descriptive elements of delusion attribution, make the views, while compatible, different. There are also signs that Murphy takes the connection between delusion and pathology to be closer than we do. For example, he writes: "I suggest that we think less about a philosophical project of justification and turn our attention instead to commonsense judgements of the circumstances in which we see a belief as evidence of underlying pathology" (p.113).

Compare the emotion of fear. You *can* be afraid of anything, but that is not to say that you *should* be: fear is not always appropriate. For example, someone with a phobia has an inappropriate fear of something that is not dangerous. Similarly, in the case of delusion attribution, expressing sincere bafflement at a person's beliefs when they are not in any relevant sense a rational lost cause—for example, because you have simply overestimated their incorrigibility, perhaps due to a lack of empathy or thoughtfulness—is inappropriate. You are implicitly recommending inappropriate and unjust reactions to the target individual.

Just as delusion attribution can be sincere but inappropriate in this way, there can also arise cases in which an individual holds beliefs that it would be highly challenging to talk them out of, but in a way that is not baffling. Of course, this could happen because others agree with them and share the relevant beliefs, but it could also be because it is easy to understand what has led them to hold their beliefs. Beliefs arising from familiar forms of wishful thinking or self-deception are plausible examples. To return to the case of a mother in denial about her son's crimes (see Section 2.3), for example, it might be extremely challenging to convince her that the son is guilty, but this is unlikely to baffle most people. If our account is correct, it is only if such self-deception reaches a baffling extreme–suppose that the mother maintains a belief in innocence even when confronted with apparently unambiguous evidence of the crime, for example—that inclinations to treat her as delusional are likely to be felt most strongly. One way of understanding this is that when somebody's incorrigibility is wholly unsurprising and, hence, unbaffling, there is no need to flag their incorrigibility to others—and hence no need to call them delusional.

6. Three Important Lessons

Before concluding, it will be helpful to outline three implications of this account, both to clarify its assumptions and to identify lessons that will be important for understanding the rest of the book.

6.1 Lesson One: Heterogeneity

If this account is correct, the core social-epistemic practice associated with delusion attribution involves expressing folk-epistemic bafflement and flagging that the target is a rational lost cause with respect to the belief in question. Importantly, this account is silent on the causes of beliefs that trigger this social response, and so is consistent with immense heterogeneity among delusional phenomena.

First, there are many causal pathways through which individuals or groups of individuals can appear highly resistant to rational correction. For example, it could be because the person isolates themselves from such correction, because they distrust all testimony on the belief in question, or because, however much they listen to others, trust them, and respect counter-arguments, the evidence of their private experiences is so strong that it trumps all contrary testimony (see Chapter 9). As we explore in Part 2 (Chapters 3–5), it could also be because they belong to a cohesive community organised to ensure that attempts at rational correction from outsiders are either avoided or neutralised. In general, there are many pathways through which people can acquire the status of a rational lost cause, with none of them earning a claim to qualify as "true" examples of delusions.

This clarifies how our account diverges from epistemic definitional views. The irrationality that epistemic approaches take to be definitive of delusions is not the surface, folk-detectable failure of falling beyond the reach of testimonial correction and rational correction: it is a theoretically sophisticated notion of aligning your beliefs with your evidence. As we saw in Section 2, such views therefore imply that if someone endorses an apparently delusional belief because the evidence from their experience is "strong enough to support it" (Maher 1974, p.99), the belief is not really delusional (Radden, 2010). Our position has no such consequences. Being delusional is not about your private relationship to evidence. It is about how difficult it is for others to talk you out of your belief. Undergoing powerful anomalous experiences that others cannot share is simply one potential cause of being like this.

A similar lesson applies to bafflement. There are many different ways in which a belief, a way of believing, or related phenomena, such as assertion, inquiry, or reasoning, can be baffling. To see this, consider two contrasting examples. Consider the belief that one's wife is faithful. The content of the belief can be perfectly plausible in isolation, and is indeed true when believed by millions of husbands worldwide. Nevertheless, it can qualify as delusional if it is coupled with a specific husband's baffling resistance to counter-evidence (as in the case of "Reverse Othello" delusion (Butler, 2000)). At the other end of the spectrum, it matters little what evidence a delusional individual might cite for the claim, "I am the left foot of God". We just do not see how that could possibly be true. (And we would not know where to begin in talking someone out of it.) In general, there are many epistemic norms that we detect (e.g., cognitive flexibility, relevance detection, etc.), and they may all be involved in contributing to greater and lesser extents to a sense of bafflement.

6.2 Lesson Two: Against Pathocentrism

As we saw earlier, some definitional approaches have tended to tie the concept of delusion to pathology. This entails that non-pathological delusion is a contradiction in terms. Our genealogical approach rejects this view and allows us to see the relationship between delusion and pathology for what it is.

Sometimes people believe baffling things and are resistant to conversational correction because they have a medical condition. Pathology can easily set you apart from others in striking ways—for example, by producing experiences that others do not and cannot share, or by causing you to reason in abnormal ways. This makes psychiatric illness fertile territory for delusional phenomena. Moreover, this association is strengthened not merely at the level of delusions themselves but in terms of the strategies people might adopt in response. As we have seen, a delusional person is a rational lost cause, but they may not be a lost cause *tout court*. Medical intervention may help.

These observations explain why canonical cases of delusions are psychiatric, and why many are tempted to think of delusions as essentially pathological or clinical phenomena. Nevertheless, our account also illuminates why that temptation should be resisted. Just because pathology can give rise to beliefs that reliably trigger the attribution of delusional status, it does not follow that this status is essentially tied to pathology. And just because many cultures adopt medical interventions in such cases, it does not follow that the concept is essentially connected to such clinical practices. For this reason, our account can explain many people's readiness to use the language of delusion outside of clinical contexts.

6.3 Lesson Three: Delusion Attribution as Perspectival

Strictly speaking, there is no such thing as being delusional per se on our account. One is delusional according to (i.e., from the perspective of) others. The closest thing to being delusional simpliciter is being in a state that is so baffling and so resistant to rational correction that it would be deemed delusional by everyone. But that is still perspectival, even if the perspective is obscured by universal consensus.

This perspectival dimension suggests that looking for delusion as a monadic—as opposed to a relational—phenomenon in the world rests on a mistake. It also suggests that there will be cross-cultural variation in what counts as delusion, because it will be, to some extent, in the eye of the beholder. The extent of this variation needs to be clarified. To see this, consider possible variation in something being baffling, and someone being a "rational lost cause".

First, it is obvious that different people and cultures will find different things baffling. People have different worldviews and therefore find different beliefs and ways of believing variously hard to integrate. The issue of whether people being deemed a "rational lost cause" is subject to similar variation is more complicated. It can seem plausible that either one can be talked out of something, or one cannot. However, if different cultures or communities endorse very different kinds of epistemic norms, the ability to be "talked out of a belief" is not absolute. The acceptability of a certain degree of stubbornness or dogmatism will vary across people and cultures. So the question arises: "talked out of it" by whom and how; namely, based on what epistemic norms?

Second, while the application of the concept of delusion is variable, this does not prevent the concept itself from being stable. This is because it plays the same role of flagging and disengagement across different societies. Indeed, it is because the same concept is applied to different things that this constitutes a substantive disagreement, rather than merely talking past each other. The same point is made by R. M. Hare (1952) in his "Cannibals and Missionaries" examples in defence of his prescriptivist view in meta-ethics, which shares some features (especially the non-descriptivism) with our account of delusion attribution. When the missionaries see that the cannibals call "good" and encourage, and call "bad" and discourage, very different things to what they themselves do, the right way to think about this is not that the cannibals just have a different meaning of the word "good", which is what you might conclude if you thought that "good" referred to a property in the world. On the contrary, it is precisely because they mean the same thing by "good" and "bad" (i.e., that such terms express encouragements and discouragements) that this amounts to a genuine ethical conflict and reflects radically different aims for the world that they want to live in. And that is also why the missionaries are appalled by what they see. Something similar can be said about the concept of delusion. It is precisely because of its stability that disagreement about what counts as delusional feels so substantive.

Consider how religious beliefs are sometimes treated as delusions by those with strong atheistic convictions and commitments to scientific epistemic norms (Dawkins, 2007). Now consider those who disagree, either because they are religious themselves or are for various reasons sympathetic to religious belief. What is the right way to think about the nature of this disagreement? Most views of delusion would take this to be a factual disagreement. Either religious believers exemplify the property of delusion, or they do not. Our view casts things differently. Someone like Dawkins is not merely describing religious belief as having certain properties: he is denigrating it. And that is also reflected in the responses to him. They do not find his views inaccurate—they find them offensive. This is not merely factual disagreement. It is a clash of epistemic values and worldviews.

7. Summary of Chapter 2 and Part 1

In Chapter 1, we set out an account of human ultra-sociality and its three core ingredients of cooperation, culture, and competition. A central feature of this account is our epistemic interdependence: as with almost every other goal, we depend on others to acquire knowledge and regulate our beliefs. However, this dependence makes us vulnerable. We must be vigilant against misinformation and manipulation, both as individuals and as collectives policing the epistemic commons, enforcing epistemic norms, and flagging those who violate them. This chapter has drawn on this general picture to illuminate the concept of delusion. Against dominant approaches that seek to define delusions in terms of objective epistemic or psychiatric defects, we explored why human beings, understood as cooperative-cultural animals, need to attribute delusional status to one another. The core of our account is that calling someone delusional expresses folk-epistemic bafflement and flags to others that the person is a rational lost cause with respect to the relevant belief. This account, we have suggested, sheds light on the sorts of beliefs that we are disposed to call delusions, as well as when those dispositions are appropriate.

Of course, there are many further questions to be asked about this account, and many remaining details to be filled out, some of which we highlight in our concluding chapter. Nevertheless, we hope that we have done enough to illustrate some of its theoretical virtues and to identify several lessons that will be relevant throughout the rest of the book, as we now turn away from questions of delusion attribution to an exploration of why and how specific beliefs come to trigger such attributions.

Most importantly, this account's consistency with considerable heterogeneity in the characteristics and causes of delusional phenomena shapes how we approach our explanatory tasks in Parts 2 and 3. Against the influential assumption that all delusions are formed in the same or at least similar ways, our explanatory approach acknowledges that many different aetiological trajectories might be implicated in delusion formation. In the explanatory frameworks that we advance for understanding both popular and clinical delusions, for example, we embrace multifactorial, pluralistic, and dynamic explanatory models that recognise the complexity and heterogeneity of delusional phenomena and the causal pathways by which they emerge and persist.

In addition, our focus on popular delusions in Part 2 reflects our rejection of the widespread view that the concept of delusion is essentially tied to pathology. As we will see in Chapter 3, the fact that human communities sometimes embrace belief systems that seem bafflingly and incorrigibly irrational to outsiders can be described in terms of mass or collective delusions, which are just as theoretically puzzling as the strange beliefs that arise in conditions such as schizophrenia or delusional disorder. Indeed, in some ways, the absence of any apparent pathology in such cases makes them even more puzzling.

As with our treatment of delusion attribution in this chapter, the explanatory frameworks that we will advocate throughout the rest of the book are equally grounded in our status as ultra-social animals and the distinctive challenges, opportunities, and psychological processes this ultra-sociality implicates. Just as careful reflection on our social nature is necessary to understand why we call people delusional, it is equally essential for understanding the beliefs that reliably trigger this social response.

PART 2

3

The Puzzle of Popular Delusions

1. Introduction

Chapter 2 explored why we treat certain beliefs and people as delusional. Against the orthodox view that classifying beliefs as delusions is merely about detecting objective properties of beliefs or believers, we argued that such classifications are better understood in the context of social-evaluative practices of epistemic flagging and gatekeeping. Within such practices, delusion attributions arise as members of epistemic communities express their folk-epistemic bafflement at certain beliefs and signal that those who hold them fall beyond the reach of rational engagement.

In the remainder of the book, we will turn away from issues concerning delusion attribution to focus on beliefs that routinely attract such attributions. In Part 3, we will explore the characteristics and causes of beliefs that constitute what are widely thought of as paradigm cases of delusions, at least within medical psychiatry: strange beliefs labelled "clinical delusions" associated with conditions such as schizophrenia, bipolar disorder, delusional disorder, dementia, and more. In contrast, Part 2 (Chapters 3–5) will focus on what we call "popular delusions", strange beliefs characteristic of outbreaks of collective irrationality that frequently arise in non-clinical contexts.

The term "popular delusions" comes from Charles Mackay's (1841) nineteenth-century bestseller "Extraordinary Popular Delusions and the Madness of Crowds", which explored striking examples of widespread human irrationality in economic bubbles, societal panics about witchcraft, religious crusades, and many other contexts. According to modern orthodoxy within psychiatry and delusions research, such beliefs do not qualify as *real* delusions. For example, as we saw in Chapter 2, Section 2.1, the DSM-5 stipulates that irrational beliefs only qualify as delusions if they are "firmly sustained *despite what almost everyone else believes*" and are not "*ordinarily accepted by other members of the person's culture or subculture*" (American Psychiatric Association, 2013, emphasis added). According to this and similar definitions, delusions are defined not just by their epistemic defects but by the fact that

The Social Roots of Delusions. Daniel Williams, Sam Wilkinson, and Kengo Miyazono, Oxford University Press.
 DOI: 10.1093/9780191976360.003.0004

others do not share them. A belief cannot be delusional if it is popular (Bentall, 2018).

As we noted in our introductory chapter and Chapter 2, many theorists have worried that stipulations like this are arbitrary (see Coltheart, 2007; Murphy, 2013; Radden, 2010). Why could there not be mass delusions? Are those who start irrational cults or religions delusional, but the followers that they recruit are not? Does a belief cease to be delusional when it is widely embraced? Given these and other puzzles, there is a significant body of research attempting to explain in a more principled way what distinguishes delusions of the sort that arise in clinical contexts (i.e., the "real" delusions) from widespread forms of collective irrationality that arise among seemingly healthy individuals (Bentall, 2018).

We view things differently. Given Western medical psychiatry's institutional preoccupation with pathology, its decision to exclude collective irrationalities is understandable. The DSM-5's definition helps identify those in need of medical attention precisely because those cases in which the appearance of highly irrational beliefs does not indicate pathology invariably arise in communities of co-believers. Nevertheless, this need not imply that only those beliefs classified as "clinical delusions" are *real* delusions. If, as we argued in Chapter 2, the attribution of delusions expresses folk-epistemic bafflement and functions to flag that the target is a rational lost cause, there is no a priori reason why delusions should be restricted to cases involving pathology. Moreover, such a restriction does not reflect the word's everyday use. As Mackay's title illustrates, people routinely apply "delusion" (and functionally similar terms such as "mad", "insane", "crazy", and so on) in non-clinical contexts, especially to strange collective beliefs. Although some such applications might express different meanings or be viewed as merely humorous (e.g., calling a football commentator "delusional" for their pre-game predictions), they often seem to express the same sincere sense of folk-epistemic bafflement and motivation to flag that believers are a rational lost cause as one finds in clinical contexts (Kiran & Chaudhury, 2009).

More generally, our analysis suggests that the project of deciding what makes beliefs *real* delusions itself involves a kind of mistake. Once we see that delusion attribution performs expressive and signalling functions, we can see that, in some sense, delusions exist in the eye of the beholder—or, more accurately, in the social-epistemic evaluative practices of the beholders. When it comes to beliefs deemed clinical delusions in modern medical psychiatry, they are likely to be treated as delusions across diverse contexts precisely because they appear to violate social-epistemic norms that are culturally universal, for reasons that we will detail throughout Part 3. Indeed, even individuals with clinical delusions typically treat *other people's* clinical delusions as delusional (Luhrmann, 2007).

When it comes to popular delusions, things are different. Not only will a community that endorses beliefs viewed as delusional by outsiders not think of its own beliefs as delusions, but in some cases, it might be equally disposed to treat outsiders' beliefs as delusional. For example, during the Covid-19 pandemic, certain conspiracy theorists treated mainstream scientific opinion as a manifestation of "mass formation psychosis" (Fichera and Kelety, 2022). And even beyond such symmetrical attributions, which have parallels in the attitudes individuals with clinical delusions can feel towards those who do not share their beliefs, there will likely be some variation in the assessments people are disposed to make about whether a given community's beliefs qualify as delusional. To the extent that such assessments reflect people's evaluations of whether beliefs are baffling and lie beyond the reach of rational persuasion, they will depend on the evaluators' own beliefs and the kinds of social-epistemic norms they adhere to. For example, most people are reluctant to call widespread religious beliefs in their society "delusions", either because they do not view them as unusually irrational or because they view them as understandable and so expected forms of irrationality. However, religious beliefs are sometimes treated as delusions by those with strong atheistic convictions and commitments to scientific norms for regulating belief (Dawkins, 2007; Pinker, 2003).

For these reasons, our focus in Part 2 is not on any collective beliefs that happen to be viewed as delusional by some outside community. This would be a highly heterogeneous set, many of which might be perfectly rational. Instead, we will focus on cases in which groups embrace beliefs that do not just seem unusually irrational to some outsiders but are so. In such cases, the disposition to evaluate beliefs as delusional is not explained by inaccurate beliefs or irrationality in the evaluators, but rather as an understandable response to objective and genuinely puzzling epistemic defects in the target beliefs. Given this, the beliefs are likely to strike all reasonable outsiders as delusional. Indeed, as we will see (Section 3.2), such beliefs violate epistemic norms that even the believers themselves successfully apply in other domains of their lives.

Importantly, these collective irrationalities exhibit different properties and pose different explanatory challenges to the clinical delusions we will explore in Part 3. Whereas clinical delusions are typically idiosyncratic, connected to social isolation and estrangement, and socially maladaptive, the beliefs we explore in Part 2 are shared, supported by complex forms of social scaffolding and coordination, and rooted in socially adaptive motivations. Nevertheless, although the processes by which such beliefs are formed and maintained are very different, the outcome of these processes is similar: beliefs that seem bafflingly and incorrigibly irrational to most outsiders. This is why we are inclined to follow many others in using the language of "delusions" to characterise such beliefs.

As we noted in our introductory chapter, one need not endorse this terminological decision to accept the ideas and arguments we advance throughout Part 2. We aim to outline a framework for understanding the nature and causes of a particular kind of shared, irrational belief system. One can accept this framework even if one insists that such belief systems are not correctly labelled "delusions".

We will structure the chapter as follows. Section 2 provides some examples of popular delusions and introduces the "functional delusions puzzle", which asks why healthy individuals with functional psychological mechanisms sometimes embrace highly epistemically irrational beliefs. Section 3 unpacks this puzzle and identifies several features of popular delusions in need of explanation: their unusual epistemic irrationality (Section 3.1), the selectivity of this irrationality (Section 3.2), the frequent mental compartmentalisation of the relevant beliefs (Section 3.3), people's attachment to such beliefs (Section 3.4), and the social practices that generate and sustain them (Section 3.5). Section 4 then considers and criticises influential individualistic explanations of popular delusions that trace them to cognitive biases and motivated irrationality. This sets the stage for Chapters 4 and 5, in which we develop an alternative social framework for understanding such beliefs, focusing on the role of strategic social rationality and social-epistemic practices that promote and protect collective ignorance and misperceptions.

2. The Functional Delusions Puzzle

Throughout the 1980s and early 1990s, beginning in the United States and then spreading throughout other parts of the world (including Australia, Canada, the United Kingdom, New Zealand, and more), many people became convinced of a strange conspiracy theory: that their societies contained secret networks of powerful Satanic paedophiles who routinely engaged in ritual abuse involving extreme depravities such as sacrificing babies, eating foetuses, and drinking blood (Beck, 2015; La Fontaine, 1998; Nathan & Snedeker, 2001; Romano, 2016; Storr, 2021, pp.168–183). According to the theory, the networks were embedded in all mainstream institutions in society and often used daycare centres as a means to snatch and torture children. Belief in the conspiracy was popular not just among the general public but among police officers, detectives, clinicians, journalists, and other professionals, who invested considerable funding and resources into corroborating and combating the alleged Satanic ritual abuse. Hundreds of suspected individuals were formally charged, and dozens were convicted and sent to prison. Despite the extraordinary accusations, no physical evidence was ever discovered for any of the allegations concerning Satanic ritual abuse networks, which were instead supported by highly unreliable methods such as hypnosis and coercive interviews of alleged child victims (Storr, 2021). Later investigations revealed that the panic was baseless. In 1994, the National Center on Child Abuse and Neglect in the USA reported that it could not substantiate a single one of the approximately 12,000 formal accusations of Satanic ritual abuse (Goleman, 1994), a conclusion supported by numerous other investigations throughout the world (La Fontaine, 1998; Nathan & Snedeker, 2001).

The fantastical and bizarre nature of the beliefs that characterised what is now called the "Satanic panic" was hardly unique in human history (see Boyer, 2018; Brotherton, 2015; Mercier, 2020). Outlandish rumours and absurd conspiracy theories frequently grip the collective imagination of human beings. For example, across many independent societies, ethnographers and historians have documented rumours accusing individuals and groups of horrific acts involving magical or supernatural powers, a phenomenon most clearly exemplified by the cross-cultural pattern of witchcraft accusations (Boyer, 2022; Singh, 2021). During the European witch hunts of the sixteenth and seventeenth centuries, people treated as witches were alleged to engage in outrageous moral violations such as cannibalism and to conspire against the community in secret orgiastic gatherings under the cover of night. As Singh (2021) points out, surprisingly similar behaviours were also "suspected of witches among the Yamba of Cameroon (Gufler, 1999), the Santal of South Asia (Archer, 1984), and the Navajo of the American Southwest (Kluckhohn, 1944), among many other societies" (Hutton, 2017; Mair, 1969). Even the central ideas of the Satanic panic find numerous echoes throughout history, such as in common allegations that Jewish populations ritually sacrifice Christian babies (Mercier, 2020) and, more recently, in QAnon. As we saw in our introductory chapter, this American conspiracy theory alleges that powerful Satanic paedophile rings are embedded within the government, Hollywood, and elsewhere (Marwick & Partin, 2022).

Moreover, strange beliefs and narratives that seem wholly unmoored from reality are not the unique preserve of rumours and conspiracy theories. Billions of individuals today profess to hold religious beliefs that often strike those outside of the relevant community as bizarre: for example, that they have a personal relationship with a long-dead man who was the creator of the Universe, who rose from the dead, and whose mother was a virgin; that human beings are reincarnated as other life forms after they die in ways that are influenced by how they act when alive; and that the secrets of the Universe are found within an ancient book whose contents were revealed by the Universe's creator through an angel (Boyer, 2001; Iannaccone, 1992; Storr, 2021; Van Leeuwen, 2023). Smaller-scale religions and cults also embrace beliefs that strike outsiders as similarly strange, if not more so. For example, Scientologists, a modern cult composed of tens of thousands of people, profess to believe that human beings lived past lives in extra-terrestrial cultures on different planets and that an alien called "Xenu" brought billions of fellow aliens to Earth 70 million years ago before killing them with thermonuclear weapons (Wright, 2013).

Popular but strange beliefs often have considerable consequences, inspiring deep identification with their contents and significant sacrifices from those who hold them. They also play a significant role in shaping the structure and organisation of the societies within which they are endorsed. For example, numerous cultures have been organised around false and often bizarre beliefs about group differences. In India, a complex caste system has long divided the population into different groups whose membership is organised primarily by descent. Up until recently, it was widely believed that high-caste Indians would be defiled if they came into contact with the shadows of people who belonged to the so-called "untouchable" caste (Kuran, 1997). Similarly, in early modern Germany, lower social classes engaged in trades such as execution, grave digging, and latrine cleaning were believed to possess an inherited "dishonourable" status that would infect honourable citizens if they touched them (Stuart, 1999). Before the Enlightenment, many people in Europe professed to believe that the creator of the Universe granted hereditary monarchs the right to rule. More generally, many people throughout human history have believed that power relations between different groups (races, ethnicities, castes, genders, etc.) are likewise endorsed by this supernatural creator (Alexander, 1987; Sidanius & Pratto, 2001).

These and many more examples illustrate a simple lesson: even in the absence of any mental illness, human beings frequently appear to lapse into remarkable forms of irrationality, embracing beliefs that seem not just false but bafflingly irrational. Articulating this experience of bafflement, the anthropologist and cognitive scientist, Dan Sperber, writes,

> Apparently irrational cultural beliefs are quite remarkable: they do not appear irrational by slightly departing from common sense, or timidly going beyond what the evidence allows. They appear, rather, like down-right provocations against common sense rationality. (Sperber, 1985, p.85)

Whether one wants to characterise such provocations against commonsense rationality as delusions, there is still the question of why they so commonly arise. As Sperber's quote illustrates, the beliefs do not only frequently violate our folk-psychological models of human beings—that is, it is *intuitively* baffling to many people how so many could have adopted the bizarre beliefs associated with something like the Satanic panic—but they also generate a profound and enduring explanatory challenge for the psychological and social sciences (Boyer, 2018; Pinker, 2021; Van Leeuwen, 2023; Williams, 2021b). Indeed, in some ways, they pose an even more significant challenge than clinical delusions because theorists can at least appeal to psychological dysfunction or dysfunctions in explaining the latter beliefs. When it comes to popular delusions, in contrast, the challenge is to explain why seemingly healthy and otherwise broadly rational individuals could embrace beliefs that appear to many outsiders as highly irrational.

This challenge is exacerbated by the common and plausible assumption that the function of beliefs is to represent the world accurately (Fodor, 1975; Millikan, 1984; Papineau, 1984; Van Leeuwen, 2014). According to this view, beliefs are the "maps by which we steer" (see Ramsey, 1990). They guide our attempts to navigate reality in thought and action, and, like actual maps, they are well-suited to this function only if they accurately represent that reality. Given this, one would expect the psychological mechanisms underlying belief formation to be well-designed for producing accurate beliefs (Fodor, 1975; Millikan, 1984). A large body of evidence supports this expectation. Although people are not optimally rational (see Section 4 below), on most topics they seem to process information in broadly reliable and rational ways, just as one would expect on evolutionary grounds (Dorst, 2023; Lieder & Griffiths, 2020; Mercier, 2020).

Popular delusions are puzzling because they appear to violate these expectations. It is difficult to understand how even minimally rational individuals could endorse such beliefs. Specifically, they give rise to what we will call the *functional delusions puzzle*: Why do healthy individuals with normally functioning psychological mechanisms sometimes embrace popular delusions?

3. Unpacking the Functional Delusions Puzzle

Before exploring attempts to solve the functional delusions puzzle, it is important to be more precise about what we mean by "popular delusions". In Section 1, we noted that our interest is not just in collective beliefs that happen to appear puzzlingly irrational to some outsiders, but that *are* puzzlingly irrational. In this section, we outline these puzzling characteristics in more detail, identifying five co-occurring characteristics of canonical popular delusions that demand explanation: their unusual epistemic irrationality (Section 3.1), the selectivity of this irrationality (Section 3.2), the compartmentalisation of the relevant beliefs (Section 3.3), people's attachment to such beliefs (Section 3.4), and the epistemically dysfunctional social practices associated with them (Section 3.5).

3.1 Epistemic Irrationality

People who endorse popular delusions appear to exhibit epistemic irrationality to an unusual degree. As we noted in Chapter 2 (Section 2.3), epistemic rationality concerns norms conducive to forming accurate beliefs based on available evidence. Although there is controversy over precisely what this entails, an epistemically rational agent forms, evaluates, and revises their beliefs in ways that are consistent, sensitive to the quality and quantity of relevant evidence, and broadly conform to formal norms of logic, statistics, and probability theory. Of course, most people lack the technical term "epistemic rationality", but canonical popular delusions seem to violate such norms to an extreme and unexpected degree. That is, they seem bizarrely misaligned with the goal or aim of forming accurate beliefs. To quote Sperber (1985) again, they seem like "down-right provocations against common sense rationality". For example, those who endorse such belief systems seem to jump to conclusions based on little evidence, entertain implausible and often bizarre explanations of events, evaluate information in biased ways, and engage in dogmatic reasoning.

Nevertheless, in recent years, several philosophers and psychologists have argued that this appearance is misleading. They contend that beliefs that strike observers as epistemically irrational are, in fact, rational responses to partial or misleading evidence (Begby, 2021; Dorst, 2023; Levy, 2021; Tappin et al., 2020). Although this argument takes different forms and is applied to different beliefs, it typically rests on two core ideas.

The first is that the mere presence of even radically false beliefs does not demonstrate epistemic irrationality. Epistemic rationality involves forms of thinking, reasoning, and belief updating that are conducive to forming accurate beliefs *given the evidence available*. However, in many contexts, the evidence available to people is limited, misleading, or deceptive. In such cases, even ideal reasoners will form false beliefs.

The second is a central theme of this book: we are deeply cultural animals, almost always dependent on acquiring information from others when forming beliefs about aspects of reality with which we are not directly acquainted (see Chapter 1, Section 4). Given this, the primary evidence available to us in many domains consists of what other people believe and testify to. As Levy (2021) argues, this social evidence can be considered *higher-order evidence*. For example, if someone I trust claims that human activity is causing climate change, their testimony provides evidence *of* the existence of first-order evidence of human-driven climate change. This suggests that if beliefs are widespread within one's community and endorsed by authoritative and seemingly credible figures, as they often are in popular delusions, it might be rational to engage in "social referencing": to accept them even if they seem to constitute gross distortions of reality to outside observers who rely on different evidence and sources.

This is an important objection. Our beliefs about the world are often mediated by vast chains of trust and testimony that stretch back far in time. Given this, false beliefs need not result from any epistemic irrationality. For example, the broadly secular and scientific worldview common among many educated individuals within "WEIRD" (Western, Educated, Industrialised, Rich, and Democratic) societies today does not result merely from the application of individual-level rationality. It is the product of education and enculturation within a specific context shaped by centuries of local political, social, and institutional developments (Henrich, 2020). Therefore, it would be mistaken to assume that beliefs at odds with this worldview must result from individual-level irrationality. It is plausibly a recognition of this fact that explains why even most atheists are reluctant to characterise popular religious belief systems as delusions.

Moreover, the objection correctly highlights the importance of social factors and dynamics in explaining popular delusions. As we return to below (Section 4), when it comes to putatively irrational beliefs, there is a strong tendency among psychologists and philosophers to focus exclusively or primarily on individualistic factors such as cognitive biases or motivated reasoning (Bortolotti, 2015; Kahneman, 2003; Kunda, 1990; Tavris & Aronson,

2008). Although individual-level psychology is relevant to understanding human beliefs, including misbeliefs, our epistemic interdependence means that neglecting the social context within which belief formation occurs is almost always a mistake.

For these reasons, the appearance of epistemic irrationality is often misleading. Nevertheless, it is not always misleading. Even if some beliefs deemed popular delusions can be understood as rational responses to partial or misleading social evidence, it is implausible that they all can be (see Van Leeuwen, 2023; Williams, 2023a, 2023b). Although the truth is rarely self-evident, even to ideal reasoners, and people depend on social learning and so higher-order evidence to acquire most beliefs, it is difficult to deny that many canonical examples of popular delusions involve extraordinary forms of epistemic irrationality. For example, during the Satanic panic, many people appeared to believe that extreme acts of Satanic ritual abuse could routinely occur without leaving any physical evidence, and, in some cases, the very fact that children vehemently denied that they were victims of such abuse was interpreted as evidence that they *had* been abused (Storr, 2021). Similarly striking forms of irrationality occur among conspiracy theorists who interpret the lack of evidence for a conspiracy as evidence of its power (Lewandowsky et al., 2013). More generally, in cases as diverse as strange religious beliefs, ideological convictions, conspiracy theories, and rumours, people often seem highly willing to endorse such beliefs on minimal evidence and to show little interest in testing them or considering what kinds of evidence might disconfirm them (Tetlock, 2017).

This is not to deny that social learning or "referencing" plays a central role in popular delusions. Nevertheless, as with any other form of learning, social learning can exhibit epistemic irrationality (Williams, 2023a). As we reviewed in Chapter 1 (Section 4.2), even from a very young age, human beings exercise sophisticated forms of "epistemic vigilance", evaluating testimony from others through attention to factors like the message's plausibility *(plausibility checking)*, the testifier's reliability and incentives to be honest (*source evaluation*), and the quality of the testifier's arguments *(reasoning)*. In many popular delusions, such sophistication seems to vanish. For example, plausibility checking embodies the rational principle that "extraordinary claims require extraordinary evidence". However, in many cases of popular delusions, people accept claims that seem extraordinary relative to their pre-existing beliefs (e.g., claims about supernatural powers or forces that violate their intuitive models of the world) with very little first-order *or* higher-order social evidence, and they seem willing to accept testimony on flimsy grounds. For example, proponents of the conspiracy theory QAnon place significant trust in the outlandish claims issued by an anonymous user on an online message board (Marwick & Partin, 2022); during witchcraft accusations, people will often accept fantastical claims purely based on hearsay from manifestly interested parties (Boyer, 2022); and during the Satanic panic people accepted bizarre beliefs solely based on manipulated and inconsistent testimony from very young children (Storr, 2021). These look like extraordinary lapses of epistemic vigilance.

Moreover, in all the examples of popular delusions reviewed in Section 2, the relevant believers seem irrationally dismissive of all testimony from those who challenge the beliefs, including from sources they often trust on other subjects. That is, it is not just that people often seem strangely uninterested in seeking out contrary evidence, arguments, or viewpoints that might challenge the relevant beliefs. They are also frequently dismissive of such information when they encounter it. Indeed, when it comes to bizarre rumours, conspiracy theories, supernatural convictions, and so on, those who endorse them are typically aware not just that others do not share their beliefs but that many regard the beliefs *as highly irrational*, including competent, honest sources they trust on other subjects. Ordinarily—that is, by broadly rational social learners—this would be treated as powerful higher-order evidence against one's beliefs, and yet it is not.

For these reasons, there is a strong *prima facie* case that many popular delusions do not just appear to be highly epistemically irrational but are so. Of course, these remarks are schematic. In principle, one could concoct stories in which all the popular delusions we explore are epistemically rational. Indeed, if one is sufficiently creative in the beliefs one attributes to people, including about which sources are trustworthy and untrustworthy on specific subjects, almost *any* pattern of belief formation can be described as epistemically rational (Williams, 2023b). Nevertheless, we believe such interpretations are implausible. In part, our defence of this assessment will have to wait until we have outlined our positive social framework for understanding popular delusions. One important virtue of this framework, we will argue, is that it explains and reconciles the roles of epistemic rationality *and* certain forms of evidence-responsiveness in popular delusions (see Chapters 4 and 5). More specifically, it explains in what ways these belief systems are unusually epistemically irrational, whilst accounting for the fact that they seem more epistemically irrational to outsiders than to those immersed in the relevant community of believers.

3.2 Selectivity

If we are right, the unusual epistemic irrationality of popular delusions demands explanation. If one left it at that, one might think that a satisfactory explanation of such beliefs is simply that their proponents are irrational. However, this explanation confronts an obvious problem: the epistemic irrationality manifest in popular delusions is highly selective. Although those who endorse such beliefs appear highly epistemically irrational in their thought and reasoning *concerning the beliefs*, they retain their capacity to think and reason in broadly epistemically rational ways on unrelated topics.

Consider the Satanic panic again. In addition to the outlandish beliefs that characterised this episode, one must also acknowledge that such beliefs emerged atop broadly rational and reliable belief formation concerning mundane, everyday states of affairs. To navigate the world effectively, most of what people believe must be broadly accurate. Given this, even extraordinary forms of epistemic irrationality exist against a background of accurate beliefs and broadly reliable processes of belief formation (Pinker, 2021; Van Leeuwen, 2023). For example, describing groups embracing bizarre conspiracy theories who attended Donald Trump's rallies before the 2016 US presidential election, the journalist Amanda Marcotte (2016) observes,

> These folks clearly are competent enough to dress themselves, read the address of the rally and show up on time, and somehow they continue to believe stuff that's so crazy and so false that it's impossible to believe anyone that isn't barking mad could believe it. What's going on?

Sterelny makes a similar observation concerning many religious beliefs and narratives. Religion, he writes, typically involves

> a narrative, or set of connected and overlapping narratives, about the origin of the community, its neighbors, and their environment, often mixed with various recipes for causal intervention with respect to illness, fertility, and the like .... Yet the narratives that ground these costly activities seem, to the ordinary light of empirical reason, to be utterly unwarranted. Some are barely intelligible, still less credible .... *The puzzle is deepened because there is no general descent into credulity: religious communities rarely find the narratives of other groups persuasive.* (Sterelny, 2020, pp.303–304, emphasis added)

As Sterelny implies, this selectivity generates an important constraint on explanations of popular delusions. It is not enough to note that people can think and reason in epistemically irrational ways or to attribute their beliefs to across-the-board epistemic "vices" such as dogmatism or gullibility (e.g., Cassam, 2016). One must also explain why the epistemic irrationality involved is highly concentrated on these specific beliefs and occurs against the backdrop of broadly reliable, reality-tracking belief formation. To the extent that popular delusions involve losing contact with reality, this loss of contact is highly—and strangely—circumscribed. And this selectivity enhances the puzzle of popular delusions' unusual epistemic irrationality. The assessment of epistemic irrationality in such cases does not only draw on epistemic norms endorsed by those outside the community. The believers themselves successfully employ such norms on topics unrelated to the delusions.

3.3 Compartmentalisation

A related feature of popular delusions is that they often seem strangely compartmentalised within believers' mental lives (Mercier, 2020; Sperber, 1997; Van Leeuwen, 2023). In general, when we believe something, the belief is reasonably well integrated with the rest of what we think, and it guides our behaviour in all contexts where the belief's content is relevant (Fodor, 1975; Papineau, 1984). That is, our beliefs generally constitute the background mental model of reality that we draw upon to navigate the world, in thought and action. Numerous theorists have observed that popular delusions often violate this expectation. Although those who endorse such beliefs appear to be sincere and indeed frequently passionate, their endorsements rarely seem to shape their thoughts and behaviours consistently.

Mercier (2020) illustrates this with the example of Pizzagate, a precursor to the QAnon conspiracy theory, which alleged that influential Democratic Party operatives in the USA were running a child sex ring out of the basement of a Washington pizzeria. According to survey data, millions of American citizens endorsed the conspiracy theory, and even if one thinks (as seems likely) that such data overestimates the number of believers, many thousands of people still seem to have endorsed it and engaged with it. Nevertheless, only one person, a man named Edgar Welch, actually bothered to go to the pizzeria to release the children allegedly being held captive there. As Mercier (2020) points out, *if* one genuinely believed the conspiracy theory, Welch's behaviour was understandable. It is much more challenging to understand the many people who professed to believe it but did not act in ways congruent with that conviction. Similar points apply to many outlandish conspiracy theories. For example, it is a puzzling feature of many conspiratorial communities that they hold open, public meetings to discuss and criticise alleged conspiracies despite professing to believe that the conspirators who populate their stories are powerful, malevolent, and highly motivated to remain secret (Kay, 2011). In general, when people live in countries where powerful elites possess those characteristics (e.g., North Korea or the Soviet Union under Stalin), they are too afraid to acknowledge their existence openly. As we will return to in Part 3, the same is typically true of people suffering from clinical paranoia, in which beliefs and worries about hidden conspirators cause fear, anxiety, and social withdrawal. This differs greatly from the attention-seeking behaviours found among most who passionately profess bizarre conspiracy theories, such as QAnon, in countries like the USA.

Such compartmentalisation generalises to many other contexts. As with strange conspiracy theories, Mercier (2020) points out that witchcraft accusations often couple accusations of shocking and outlandish crimes—making people sick, killing them with magical powers, conspiring with the devil, planning to eat children, and so on—with strangely lenient punishments if witches confess, such as demanding certain rituals or small fines. In such cases, the professed beliefs seem bizarrely misaligned with the associated behaviours. Famously, one often sees similarly striking misalignments between beliefs and behaviours in the professed beliefs characteristic of members of many religions, cults, and ideological communities (Van Leeuwen, 2014). For example, religious believers frequently appear sincerely committed to religious doctrines such as that sins will be punished with eternal damnation and that God is always watching, and yet then proceed to act repeatedly in sinful ways. As Dennett (2006, p.227) observes, devout religious believers would not masturbate if they knew their *mother* was watching, yet many do so "in private" despite professing to believe that God (i.e., an all-powerful agent who sharply disapproves of the behaviour) is watching.

Moreover, in many popular delusions, people's commitment to the relevant beliefs seems to co-exist with at least a tacit awareness that the beliefs are unfounded. As Tanya Luhrmann (2020) observes, many religious believers are careful to pray for nebulous outcomes open to interpretation so as not to decisively test God's powers. Moreover, they often pray for outcomes that they think might happen anyway (Van Leeuwen, 2023). For example, people are much more likely to pray for a cancer to go into remission than for a body part to grow back (Rey, 2007) or for back pain to go away than for God to put money in their bank account (Bialecki, 2017). Likewise, during the Satanic panic, a famous slogan among true believers was "Believe all children!" However, this slogan was strategically applied in highly selective ways. Those interviewing children would often encourage outlandish accusations and accept them with little scrutiny, but then refuse to believe children who denied that they were victims of Satanic ritual abuse (Storr, 2021). It is difficult to see how people could know how to selectively apply epistemic standards in this way without at least an implicit awareness that the accusations were unfounded. This must be explained.

3.4 Attachment

A fourth important feature of popular delusions that demands explanation concerns people's attachment to them. When it comes to strange supernatural beliefs, ideological convictions, conspiracy theories, outlandish rumours, and so on, those who endorse the relevant beliefs rarely seem to treat them as dispassionate assessments of the nature of reality. Instead, they seem to be attached to, or invested in, the beliefs (Abelson, 1986; Festinger et al., 1956; Funkhouser, 2019; Van Leeuwen, 2023).

Such attachments manifest in different ways. When it comes to strange beliefs that unite co-believers into a community, such as religious beliefs, cultish beliefs, ideological convictions, and certain conspiracy theories, the proponents of such beliefs often seem to *identify* with their commitments in an important sense (Bortolotti, 2023). They view their beliefs as an important part of who they are, are emotionally invested in them, and react defensively to contrary evidence and criticisms of the commitments (Kahan, 2017; Lewandowsky et al., 2012). When it comes to rumours and conspiracy theories that underlie phenomena such as the Satanic panic and witchcraft accusations, attachments to the relevant beliefs often manifest differently: believers frequently seem highly motivated to embrace and propagate the beliefs and, as Boyer (2018, Ch.2) and Storr (2021) note, they will often react with frustration, anger, or outrage if their convictions are met with scepticism or dissent (Sunstein & Vermeule, 2009).

Importantly, not all cases where beliefs are associated with emotions involve attachments to the beliefs in this sense. In many cases, people's emotions are simply responses to the *contents* of their beliefs—that is, to the state of affairs they represent. Believing a poisonous spider is on one's shoulder will produce a state of terror. Believing one has won the lottery will produce an experience of joy. And so on. Similarly, if one believes that one is in a relationship with the creator of the Universe or that Satanic paedophile rings are snatching children through day-care centres, then the contents of these beliefs will elicit strong emotions. However, popular delusions often seem to involve an emotional signature that arises not just from the contents of the beliefs but from attachments to the beliefs themselves. For example, although this topic needs more empirical research, people often appear proud to endorse popular delusions and react defensively and angrily when confronted with counter-evidence or disagreement (Funkhouser, 2022; Storr, 2021; Williams, 2021a).

A theory of popular delusions should explain this signature. Because most beliefs simply comprise the mental maps we use to navigate the world, it is generally maladaptive to become attached to them. Such emotional investments interfere with the rational updating required to map the world accurately. Popular delusions do not fit this pattern. Despite their outlandish character and lack of evidential support, people often seem highly reluctant to revise or abandon such beliefs in favour of a more accurate understanding of reality. Moreover, this puzzle is deepened by the compartmentalised nature of such beliefs. There is something paradoxical about being deeply attached to, or invested in, beliefs that one fails to integrate into one's broader world model and behaviour.

3.5 Social Practices

The preceding four characteristics of popular delusions focus on individual believers: their selective epistemic irrationality and attachment to beliefs often strangely compartmentalised in their minds. As important as such characteristics are, the discussion, therefore, neglects one of the most striking features of popular delusions and the thing that seems to distinguish them most sharply from the clinical delusions that we will be exploring in Part 3 of this book: they are shared among communities of co-believers.

Of course, not all cases of epistemic irrationality involve this social dimension. As we will see below (Section 4), individuals can violate norms of epistemic rationality for multiple reasons. For example, in Chapter 2, Section 2.3, we noted a case of strong epistemic irrationality that is idiosyncratic: a mother incapable of acknowledging her son's guilt despite overwhelming evidence. Nevertheless, setting clinical delusions aside, there are generally strong limits on such cases of individual-level epistemic irrationality (see Section 4.2 below), and it is invariably only in communities of co-believers that one finds extraordinary forms of epistemic irrationality likely to elicit genuine delusion attributions. This is why most definitions of clinical delusions restrict their focus to *individual* forms of epistemic irrationality. It is typically only in such individual cases that striking forms of epistemic irrationality are truly anomalous and, hence, indicative of pathology (Bentall, 2018). The fact that the functional delusions puzzle arises in thoroughly *social* cases is a pattern that demands explanation.

One possible explanation we considered above (Section 3.1) is that popular delusions are shared because they arise through ordinary, rational social learning processes. However, the fifth and final characteristic of such delusions that requires explanation is that the social practices and dynamics sustaining the relevant beliefs seem radically different from those involved in ordinary forms of truth-seeking communication and social learning. Instead, they seem *epistemically dysfunctional*: they actively obstruct the transmission of accurate information and the formation of correct beliefs.

One important manifestation of this concerns the way popular delusions are often treated either explicitly or implicitly as *orthodoxies* within the communities that hold them (Boyer, 2018; Marie et al., 2023; Marie & Petersen, 2023; Sunstein, 2019). In line with the apparent attachment to such beliefs, dissent from or disagreement with the relevant beliefs is often socially punished in various ways, ranging from verbal attacks and coordinated reputational punishment to ostracism and violence (Kuran, 1997; Storr, 2021; Williams, 2022a). This is most obvious in extremist religious, ideological, political, and cultish sects and communities, but it also arises in numerous cases of rumours and conspiracy theories as well (Festinger et al., 1956; Iannaccone, 1992; Sunstein, 2019). In such cases, those within the relevant community of co-believers are strongly discouraged, through social penalties, from disagreeing with the relevant beliefs. For example, observing the social dynamics involved in an outbreak of the "Satanic panic" among workers in social services departments in the UK, the anthropologist J.S. La Fontaine documented the "fervent and unshakeable commitment" (La Fontaine, 1998, p.21) to the accusations and the suppression of dissent:

> In several cases, I heard an account of the extreme social pressure, up to and including complete ostracism, that had been exerted on those who doubted the diagnosis of satanic abuse in a case where their colleagues had accepted it. (La Fontaine, 1998, p.169)

Another related feature of the social dynamics surrounding popular delusions concerns what Storr (2021) calls "active belief". When it comes to such beliefs, individuals do not simply endorse them privately. Instead, the communities often engage in evangelism in which "true believers" invest considerable energy in transmitting and enforcing their beliefs through persuasion, proselytising, and other means (Hoffer, 1951). Moreover, substantial energy is often invested in producing and disseminating information and arguments that justify the relevant beliefs. This includes everything from intellectual elites who function to interpret the world and produce justifications in ways that support the supernatural convictions that unite religions and cults (Boyer, 2001), those who do the same for ideologies and belief systems that denigrate and demonise subordinate groups (Mills, 2017), and even micro-celebrities within online, conspiratorial communities who devote their time and energy to generating content designed to justify the community's conspiracy theories (Marwick & Partin, 2022).

3.6 Interim Summary

A solution to the functional delusions puzzle should not just explain why healthy individuals sometimes exhibit extraordinary epistemic irrationality. It should also explain why this irrationality is highly selective, why the beliefs involved are often compartmentalised, why people are frequently attached to such beliefs, and why they are usually associated with, maintained, and enforced by distinctive social practices. These features may be present to different degrees in different cases. Nevertheless, their co-occurrence across otherwise diverse contexts is compelling and demands explanation.

When we talk of popular delusions throughout the rest of Part 2, we mean belief systems that exhibit this cluster of co-occurring characteristics. So defined, it is an empirical question which belief systems qualify as popular delusions. Moreover, the content of belief systems is irrelevant to answering this question. For example, although some conspiracy theories, supernatural belief systems, and ideological convictions are highly likely to qualify as popular delusions in this sense, not all examples of conspiracy theories, religious beliefs, or ideologies will. Nevertheless, this heterogeneity in the contents of popular delusions does not undermine the utility of the category. Not only do we think it is clear that otherwise diverse belief systems exhibit this cluster of co-occurring properties, but by the end of Part 2, we hope to have successfully explained why the belief systems that exhibit this cluster of characteristics are most likely to appear bafflingly and incorrigibly irrational to reasonable outsiders, and hence are most likely to be viewed as mass delusions.

4. Individualistic Explanations

In the remainder of this chapter, we will explore influential individualistic explanations of popular delusions. Although we cannot be exhaustive, we will identify the most influential explanatory approaches, describing their features and limitations in enough detail to motivate the social framework we will defend and develop in the next two chapters.

4.1 Cognitive Biases

Popular delusions involve striking forms of epistemic irrationality. Decades of research in psychology and behavioural economics have revealed that human cognition is subject to numerous cognitive biases that lead people to systematically violate norms of epistemic rationality (Bortolotti, 2015; Kahneman, 2003). Perhaps, then, popular delusions result, either entirely or in part, from such biases.

The term "cognitive bias" is used in many ways in psychology and philosophy. As we will use the term here, it refers to tendencies in human cognition that involve a systematic departure from ideal norms of epistemic rationality, typically understood in terms of formal rules such as logic, statistics, and probability theory (Chapter 2, Section 2.3). Moreover, we will distinguish such tendencies that arise from structural, "cold" features of human cognition, which we will characterise as "cognitive biases", from those that occur when "hot" motivations, interests, or emotions bias belief formation, which we will characterise as "motivated irrationality" (Section 4.2). Cognitive biases have multiple sources, but two are especially important.

4.1.1 Bounded Rationality

First, in forming beliefs, accuracy must be weighed against other values such as speed, efficiency, and computational tractability. Given this, even if epistemically rational mechanisms of belief formation are adaptive and individuals are strongly motivated to think and reason in epistemically rational ways, epistemic rationality must often be sacrificed to achieve other goals. At best, we should, therefore, expect human beings to be *boundedly* rational (Kahneman, 2003). This bounded nature of human rationality shapes how we form beliefs and ensures that human cognition often involves "satisficing", not optimising, through the use of "fast-and-frugal" heuristics. Although such heuristics achieve broad reliability at a low practical cost, they also produce systematic errors under certain conditions.

For example, people often use a mental shortcut called the "availability heuristic" to estimate the likelihood of events (e.g., car accidents, terrorism, shark attacks, etc.), which exploits the ease with which instances of a phenomenon come to mind to estimate how likely they are to happen (Tversky & Kahneman, 1973). This shortcut is generally reliable because the frequency with which we encounter something affects how easily we recall it. However, it produces systematic errors when our encounters with something are unrepresentative of its prevalence or when the ease with which we recall information is biased by factors such as vividness or emotional salience.

More generally, much of human cognition is shaped by what psychologists call "type-1" processing, which produces quick and automatic judgements without the reliance on sequential, working memory-based thought or reasoning (Frankish, 2010). Although this processing is highly efficient and indispensable for navigating the world under practical constraints of time, energy, and computational tractability, it involves forming rapid judgments instead of engaging in slower, more deliberative, and more careful forms of reasoning that integrate a larger body of information (i.e., "type-2 processing") (Kahneman, 2003).

Fast-and-frugal heuristics and cognitive processing are relevant to many popular delusions. For example, the availability heuristic disposes people to overestimate the likelihood of threatening and emotionally salient events, which is plausibly implicated in many rumours and conspiracy theories (Brotherton, 2015). Moreover, hasty judgements and imperfect forms of reasoning play a role in many of the examples of collective epistemic irrationality reviewed above, which may, in some cases, be rooted in the prevalence of type-1 cognitive processing.

Nevertheless, cognitive biases underpinned by fast-and-frugal cognition cannot explain many features of popular delusions. First, these cognitive biases generally involve relatively subtle deviations from ideal epistemic rationality, contrasting with the striking and sometimes baffling forms of such irrationality manifest in popular delusions. Second, practical constraints on human cognition apply across all domains, whereas the functional delusions puzzle demands an explanation of highly selective forms of epistemic irrationality. Third, individual-level cognitive biases do not explain why popular delusions are often mentally compartmentalised or why people are attached to the relevant beliefs. Finally, in-the-head cognitive biases do not explain the social dynamics surrounding popular delusions, such as why co-believers frequently impose substantial penalties for dissent or disagreement.

4.1.2 Error Management

Another important source of cognitive biases comes from error management (Johnson et al., 2013). In making judgements and forming beliefs, organisms must be sensitive to the costs of different errors. For example, in detecting the presence of something—a predator, disease, social threat, causal relation, or anything else—an organism can make two kinds of errors: false positives (i.e., false alarms), which involve mistakenly judging that something is present when it is not; and false negatives, which involve judging that something is not present (or failing to judge that it is present) when it is. The relative costs of these errors differ according to the task and interests of the relevant agent, and such differences will inevitably alter how much evidence the agent requires before making a judgment. For example, if false alarms are less costly than false negatives, as they often are in threat detection, it is better to be safe than sorry (Stich, 1990). In such cases, detection systems will be biased towards detection based on little evidence, producing numerous false alarms. In contrast, if false alarms are more costly than false negatives, a system will require stronger evidence before detection.

These principles have shaped human cognition in many ways that are relevant to understanding popular delusions. For example, just as prey animals often have a low threshold for detecting predators because failing to detect them can be so costly, human beings exhibit what is sometimes called "hyperactive agency detection": we are disposed to detect the presence of agency behind events and regularities on minimal evidence because failing to detect the role of agents in influencing one's environment can be catastrophic (Barrett, 2000). According to many theorists, this tendency lays the groundwork for proto-religious intuitions involving the misattribution of agency as the cause of natural events (Boyer, 2001). Relatedly, as we saw in Chapter 1 and will return to in much greater depth later in Part 3, people are often also disposed not just to over-detect agency but to over-detect *social threats*. Once again, numerous theorists have argued that this tendency is relevant to rumours and conspiracy theories. Because we are highly attentive to social threats, we are excessively eager to consider conspiratorial explanations of events and behaviours (van Prooijen & van Vugt, 2018). As Hugo Mercier puts it,

> Conspiracy theories are a salient form of threat. Given the importance of coalitions during our evolution, it is plausible that we could have evolved to be particularly attuned to the risk raised by an alliance forming against us. (Mercier, 2020, p.158)

Finally, error management offers a plausible explanation for tendencies to detect spurious patterns and causal relationships manifest in superstitions and beliefs in supernatural powers (Singh, 2021). According to this view, tendencies to hallucinate patterns and causal relationships are the price we pay for detection systems that are unlikely to miss actual and often non-obvious patterns and causes.

Once again, such cognitive biases likely play significant causal roles in popular delusions. They set the background for why humans are strongly disposed to entertain specific hypotheses and are heavily oriented towards certain threats. Further, they can explain tendencies to entertain causal possibilities ruled out by a modern scientific worldview (e.g., supernatural events and magical powers). Finally, cognitive biases rooted in error management are also localised to specific domains (e.g., agency, conspiracy, and superstition). (In Part 3, we will explore why these biases are also highly relevant for understanding clinical delusions.)

Nevertheless, such biases are inadequate for explaining the core properties of popular delusions. First, although hyperactive agency detection or excessive vigilance for social threats might explain tendencies to detect agents and conspiracies where none exist, they cannot explain the broader patterns of irrational thought and reasoning involved when people endorse specific and often outlandish religious, supernatural, or conspiratorial convictions, or why people hold onto such convictions in the face of considerable contrary evidence. Second, although such biases are localised to specific domains, they struggle to explain the selectivity of this irrationality in the case of popular delusions. For example, even if people are overly ready to consider conspiracies in general, this does not explain the specific outlandish conspiratorial hypotheses associated with something like the Satanic panic or QAnon. Most importantly, cognitive biases rooted in error management fail to explain the distinctive psychological and social signature of popular delusions, including why such delusions often seem strangely compartmentalised, why people seem attached to the relevant beliefs and highly resistant to abandoning them, and why distinctive kinds of social practices and dynamics sustain them.

4.2 Motivated Irrationality

The second category of explanation we will consider appeals to motivated irrationality, which arises when non-epistemic motivations and emotions (i.e., those independent of a concern with acquiring knowledge) bias how individuals form beliefs. Historically, this phenomenon has typically been referred to as "self-deception", but in modern psychology, it is more often referred to as "motivated reasoning" or "motivated cognition" (Funkhouser, 2019; Kahan, 2015; Kunda, 1990). Whatever it is called, it involves processes in which individuals conform how they seek out, interpret, recall, and process information to goals distinct from accuracy. Such goals are typically called "directional goals" because they direct cognition towards a favoured conclusion rather than letting the available evidence speak for itself (Kunda, 1990). Beyond this, they can, in principle, take many forms, including self-esteem maintenance, emotion regulation, self-justification, and more.

There are multiple mechanisms of motivated cognition (see Bortolotti, 2015; Kunda, 1990; Williams, 2023b). *Selective exposure* occurs when individuals seek information that confirms what they are motivated to believe and avoid information that contradicts it. For example, one might actively seek out evidence and arguments that support one's preferred political views and avoid seeking out information that might challenge them. This process also has an internal analogue in which people bias their memory search to justify preferred conclusions. *Biased evaluation* occurs when individuals apply more lenient evidential standards to information that confirms their preferred beliefs than to information that challenges them. Finally, *selective forgetting* occurs when individuals selectively forget information inconsistent with their preferred beliefs.

Motivated cognition seems highly relevant to many popular delusions and addresses many of their features that need explanation. Most obviously, it can explain the epistemic irrationality manifest in such beliefs. Because motivated cognition drives individuals to embrace and maintain beliefs for reasons independent of their truth, it gives rise to systematic departures from epistemic rationality. Moreover, it illuminates why this irrationality is highly selective. Motivated cognition is not a domain-general source of epistemic irrationality. It arises only when specific directional goals distort how people sample, interpret, and recall information on particular topics. By its very nature, it also illuminates people's attachment to popular delusions. Indeed, saying that people are attached to specific beliefs or conclusions is just another way of saying they are motivated to hold or maintain those beliefs or conclusions.

Most impressively, motivated cognition offers a potential explanation for the strange compartmentalisation of many popular delusions. It has long been noted that motivated irrationality involves compartmentalisation (Funkhouser, 2019). The reason for this is simple: Because motivated cognition involves conforming how one seeks out and processes information to goals distinct from accuracy, it requires at least an implicit awareness of the unwarrantedness of the relevant beliefs. Without this awareness, it is difficult to see how people could know which information to seek out and avoid, which selective epistemic standards to deploy, and so on. For example, somebody in denial about their spouse's infidelity could not know to selectively avoid certain forms and sources of evidence without at least an implicit understanding that their beliefs must be protected from disconfirmation. More speculatively, when beliefs serve practical functions rather than epistemic ones, it would be highly adaptive for cognitive systems to quarantine such beliefs to prevent false information from automatically influencing the believer's general world model and behaviour (Williams, 2021b). We will return to this suggestion in Chapter 5 (Section 5).

For these reasons, motivated cognition provides an attractive explanation of certain features of popular delusions. Nevertheless, at least as it is typically understood, it is inadequate for three reasons. First, although motivated cognition drives epistemic irrationality, the epistemic irrationality involved tends to be relatively subtle. This is because motivated cognition is subject to a sharp "rationalisation" constraint: although it involves holding beliefs that reflect the individual's motivations, this process can only succeed if individuals can muster sufficient evidential support for their preferred beliefs (Sommer et al., 2024; Williams, 2022b). As Kunda puts it, "There is considerable evidence that people are more likely to arrive at conclusions that they want to arrive at, but their ability to do so is constrained by their ability to construct seemingly reasonable justifications for these conclusions" (Kunda, 1990, p.480). Indeed, this is why biases such as selective exposure, biased evaluation, and selective forgetting are necessary: they rationalise desired beliefs and protect them from disconfirmation. At least from an outside perspective, it is difficult to understand how many popular delusions satisfy this rationalisation constraint. Indeed, the fact that such beliefs seem radically unmoored from reality and from available evidence baffles many observers and helps explain the inclination to classify them as delusional in the first place. As we will return to in the next chapter, this consideration is not fatal to the relevance of motivated cognition to popular delusions. However, it suggests that more must be said about its consistency with the striking forms of epistemic irrationality they seem to exhibit.

Second, most research on the mechanisms underlying motivated cognition is individualistic, focusing on psychological biases in how individuals seek out, process, and recall information. Although such processes are plausibly implicated in many popular delusions, they do not explain the *social* dynamics associated with such beliefs. As we have seen, these delusions involve collective irrationalities that often seem to be sustained by social practices that obstruct the generation and transmission of accurate information. Appealing to in-the-head motivational biases does not explain such phenomena.

Finally, if motivated cognition is implicated in popular delusions, what are the relevant motivations that drive such beliefs? Like research on the mechanisms of motivated cognition, most research on its driving motivations is individualistic, focusing on the alleged psychological benefits of specific beliefs. In most cases, these benefits are alleged to be emotional. For example, many theorise that individuals are driven to embrace beliefs that provide comfort, reassurance, or positive feelings of control and certainty (Bortolotti, 2023; Kunda, 1990; Tavris & Aronson, 2008). In other cases, theorists argue that the benefits are motivational (Taylor & Brown, 1988). For example, individuals might embrace overly optimistic beliefs about their powers and future prospects to motivate themselves to pursue challenging goals. In some cases, beliefs are thought to provide motivational and emotional benefits. For example, by helping us manage our emotions, reassuring or overly optimistic beliefs might sustain our motivation and ability to persevere in the face of challenges (Bortolotti, 2020).

One problem with these individualistic theories of motivated cognition is that they are evolutionarily implausible (Kurzban, 2011; Mercier & Sperber, 2017). Not only would it be highly maladaptive for animals to let their emotions distort their world model, but purely intrapsychic benefits are irrelevant to fitness, which depends on achieving concrete material and social goals. Although some argue that the emotional or motivational benefits of motivated cognition provide indirect fitness benefits (McKay & Dennett, 2009), this argument rests on an implausible view of human evolution and psychology. For example, rather than sustaining positive emotions or motivation by convincing ourselves of potentially costly false beliefs, it would be far more adaptive to evolve emotional and motivational mechanisms that do not depend on motivated irrationality. Although these abstract evolutionary considerations are not dispositive, we will argue in Chapter 4 that a virtue of our alternative social framework is that it avoids evolutionary implausibility by drawing a more transparent explanatory connection between popular delusions and the kinds of strategic, social goals we would expect human beings to have on evolutionary grounds.

More generally, it is a puzzling feature of much research on motivated cognition that it fails to engage with our species' deepest and most consequential motivations. As we documented in Chapter 1, humans are ultra-social animals whose motivational architecture has been profoundly shaped by the challenges and opportunities of navigating an ecology organised around cooperation, culture, and competition. And yet, most attempts to explain popular delusions in terms of motivated cognition do not consider how beliefs might be shaped by our powerful motivations to win approval, trust, and esteem—our deep needs for belonging and prestige—and by the necessity of influencing others in advantageous ways. Instead, they focus overwhelmingly on inward-looking, individualistic motivations. Given the much greater evolutionary and psychological significance of outward-looking, social goals and motivations, this is a surprising oversight.

Moreover, this oversight is even more surprising given that the emotional or motivational benefits posited in traditional theories of motivated cognition are difficult to connect to most popular delusions. What psychological benefits do individuals enjoy from embracing the beliefs associated with the Satanic panic, promoting witchcraft accusations, or endorsing the kinds of beliefs related to many religions and cults? In many such cases, the contents of the beliefs are distressing. It is not reassuring to believe that children are being abused within Satanic paedophile rings, that horrifying witches are plotting against the community, or that one will be punished for eternity in hell if one acts in specific ways or refuses to accept certain kinds of doctrines. In other cases, people are likely to feel neutral about the contents of the relevant beliefs: for example, that the creator of the Universe is three persons in one, or that an alien called Xenu brought fellow aliens to Earth over seventy million years ago. Given this, although people often seem emotionally attached to such beliefs, it is difficult to explain these attachments as a direct response to the beliefs' *contents*, as we have already noted. This sharply contrasts with more everyday forms of motivated irrationality, such as refusing to believe one's son is guilty of a crime (Chapter 2, Section 2.3), where the beliefs (e.g., that one's child is innocent) seem to straightforwardly reflect what the believer wants to be true.

Proponents of motivational theories of popular delusions often postulate motivations and emotions that might seem to address this issue. For example, one of the most influential frameworks for explaining rumours and conspiracy theories derives from ideas proposed in Gordon Allport and Leo Postman's classic *The Psychology of Rumor* (Allport & Postman, 1947). They argue that rumours emerge under conditions of uncertainty and unpredictability, during which people feel significant anxiety and a lack of control. The motivation to accept rumours is then explained in terms of a "search after meaning", in which individuals reduce this anxiety and regain a sense of control by accepting beliefs that help them make sense of what is happening.

Although this and similar explanations are highly influential (see Bortolotti, 2023; van Prooijen & Acker, 2015), they confront numerous objections. First, the evolutionary objection remains. Not only is there no connection between the posited motivations and evolutionarily plausible goals, but it would seem highly maladaptive for organisms to sacrifice accurate beliefs to achieve only internal feelings of reassurance and control (Boyer, 2018; Mercier, 2020). Moreover, by focusing entirely on the state of mind of those who accept rumours, they miss the rich social dynamics that often surround them. For example, in explaining the Satanic panic, we do not just want to know why people endorsed certain propositions. We want to understand various complex social behaviours associated with the beliefs (Boyer, 2018; Storr, 2021). Finally, it is opaque why or how acceptance of most rumours and conspiracies is supposed to reduce anxiety or increase feelings of control. As we have already noted, the belief in secret networks of Satanic paedophiles does not seem reassuring, and it is difficult to see how it would reduce feelings of unpredictability or produce a psychologically desirable emotional state. In fact, although conspiracy theories are posited to have these psychological effects, evidence suggests they do not (Liekefett et al., 2023). Some theorists conclude that, although rumours emerge as *attempts* to produce feelings of certainty and control, they are unsuccessful. However, a more parsimonious explanation is that such beliefs simply do not function to produce these effects in the first place.

For these reasons, although motivated cognition seems well-suited to explaining key features of popular delusions, traditional theories of motivated cognition fail to account for several of their psychological, epistemic, and social features.

5. Chapter Summary

Let us take stock. Section 2 introduced the functional delusions puzzle, which asks why healthy, seemingly rational individuals embrace popular delusions. Section 3 identified five features of such delusions that need explanation: unusual epistemic irrationality, selectivity, compartmentalisation, attachment, and epistemically dysfunctional social practices. We then reviewed individualistic explanations of such delusions that posit cognitive biases and motivated irrationality (Section 4). Although these factors seem highly relevant to understanding popular delusions, they also seem inadequate. This inadequacy motivates the social framework for understanding such beliefs that we will develop in the next two chapters. In this framework, the cooperative, cultural, and competitive character of our species will be placed centre stage. Popular delusions, we will argue, are not merely individual cognitive failures or isolated manifestations of motivated reasoning. They are collective achievements that emerge from complex interactions between people's deepest social motivations and the norms, reputation systems, and prestige economies through which communities of co-believers scaffold, reward, and protect collective irrationalities.

4

The Social Roots of Popular Delusions

1. Introduction

In the previous chapter, we introduced the phenomenon of popular delusions. These collective belief systems are profoundly but selectively irrational, strangely compartmentalised in the minds of those who hold them, held with strong emotional attachment, and sustained by epistemically dysfunctional social practices (Chapter 3, Section 3). So understood, such delusions are diverse. They include absurd rumours and conspiracy theories, witchcraft accusations, outlandish supernatural and ideological convictions, and more. We argued that these beliefs give rise to the functional delusions puzzle, which asks why healthy and otherwise rational individuals embrace highly irrational beliefs with this strange cluster of characteristics.

We also explored individualistic explanations of popular delusions, focusing on cognitive biases and motivated irrationality (Chapter 3, Section 4). We argued that these explanations provide important insights into the causes and characteristics of popular delusions, but are nevertheless inadequate, leaving numerous features unexplained. In this chapter, we aim to address this explanatory gap.

Our central thesis is that popular delusions can only be understood by focusing on the intensely social nature of human minds and worlds. These belief systems, we will argue, are not mere cognitive mistakes. They arise from powerful social motivations adapted to social environments organised around cooperation, competition, and cultural practices regulating communication and the division of cognitive labour. More specifically, we will argue that an explanatory framework capable of illuminating such delusions must attend to two features of human social psychology and social behaviour: (i) psychological processes in which social goals of "propaganda" and signalling bias belief formation, and (ii) social processes in which shared motivations to propagate or embrace beliefs drive communities to coordinate in ways conducive to promoting, protecting, and rationalising them. This chapter focuses on (i). Chapter 5 focuses on (ii) and explains how the overall framework illuminates the five properties of delusions identified in Chapter 3.

The Social Roots of Delusions. Daniel Williams, Sam Wilkinson, and Kengo Miyazono, Oxford University Press.
 DOI: 10.1093/9780191976360.003.0005

We will structure this chapter as follows. Section 2 introduces the phenomenon of socially adaptive belief and its underpinnings in socially motivated cognition. The central idea here is that beliefs are shaped not just by epistemic and psychological goals but by social ones that can conflict with the pursuit of accuracy and psychological well-being. We then identify two different examples of this phenomenon and explore their applications to popular delusions: propagandistic cognition, which occurs when people internalise beliefs they are motivated to propagate to others (Section 3), and belief signalling, which occurs when people are motivated to adopt beliefs that signal their characteristics and allegiances (Section 4).

2. Socially Adaptive Beliefs

As noted in Chapter 3, many psychologists and philosophers understand beliefs as the mental "maps by which we steer", internal representations that help us to navigate the world in thought and action (Ramsey, 1990). Given this navigational role, it is widely held that the function of beliefs is to represent the world accurately (Fodor, 1975; Millikan, 1984). This idea invites a famous metaphor in which people forming and revising beliefs are understood as intuitive truth-seeking scientists, generating hypotheses and testing them against observations (Gopnik & Meltzoff, 1997; Sloman, 2005). Of course, it is widely acknowledged that cognitive biases and psychological factors can derail this process. As we saw in Chapter 3, Section 4, people rely on fast and frugal heuristics, they are prone to hallucinating false positives when the costs of false negatives are too high, and they sometimes subordinate the pursuit of truth to psychological goals such as emotion regulation, self-esteem protection, and the enhancement of feelings of control and certainty (Bortolotti, 2023; Taylor & Brown, 1988). In this sense, the relevant metaphor is perhaps that of a bounded and emotional scientist. Nevertheless, the primary image is one in which belief formation aims at truth, albeit in a constrained way that is sometimes derailed by intrapsychic goals.

This popular perspective on belief formation is highly plausible for most everyday beliefs. To catch the train on time, we need to know when it leaves. To avoid getting burned, we need to know whether the stove is hot. To form valuable relationships, we need to know whether people are trustworthy and kind. In such cases, our beliefs are indeed the "maps by which we steer", and their function is to help us navigate the world in ways that help us achieve our goals. Without a vast bedrock of such reality-tracking states, navigating reality would be impossible. Nevertheless, it is precisely these commonsense observations that make popular delusions so puzzling. Almost all of their characteristics, including their irrationality, compartmentalisation, and emotional intensity, seem extremely maladapted to the task of world-mapping. To make sense of such beliefs, we will argue, we must return to the intensely social character of human minds and worlds. In this world, many of their apparent bugs come to look like features, properties specialised for helping people achieve strategic social objectives rather than track reality accurately.

As reviewed in Chapter 1, much human behaviour is oriented towards influencing other people and achieving social goals, such as winning status, outcompeting rivals, cultivating a good reputation, attracting cooperation partners, displaying socially attractive traits, enforcing and following norms, and more. To understand human thought, one must, therefore, focus not just on its epistemic and psychological functions but on its social functions, and the metaphor of an isolated scientist or map maker must often give way to alternative metaphors of lawyers, press secretaries, propagandists, politicians, theologians, and apparatchiks (Haidt, 2013; Pinsof et al., 2023; Simler & Hanson, 2016; Williams, 2023b). As Tetlock puts it, this "social-functionalist" approach

> represents a sharp departure from psychological theories that have traditionally stressed the intrapsychic functions of judgment and choice and that have placed the isolated Cartesian thinker at the center of inquiry ... The focus shifts to the social functions of thought and to the embeddedness of human beings in relations with other people, institutions, and the broader political and cultural environment. (Tetlock, 2002, p.452)

Importantly, we conjecture that this social-functionalist perspective applies to human belief formation (Funkhouser, 2017; Simler & Hanson, 2016; Trivers, 2011; Williams, 2021a, 2021b). In our species, beliefs are not just the private mental maps we use to guide our thoughts and actions. They are maps that have a rich social life, shaping our interactions with others and their evaluations of us as potential partners and community members. This social life of beliefs generates a fundamentally novel set of incentives in which beliefs can be advantageous not because they represent the world accurately or serve intrapsychic functions like emotion regulation, but because they are *socially adaptive* (Williams, 2021b). Indeed, it opens the possibility that individuals can achieve social goals by forming and maintaining beliefs that conflict with goals such as accuracy or feeling good.

Our aim in the following two sections is to argue that this possibility is frequently realised in human cognition: many striking examples of epistemic irrationality are best understood not as cognitive errors or coping mechanisms but as strategic responses to the incentives of human social life. Of course, it is obvious that people can sometimes promote their interests by *communicating* in ways driven by non-epistemic goals. People lie, self-censor, bullshit, and so on. Our proposal is more radical: social goals do not just shape our outward behaviour. They shape our inner mental lives, including what we sincerely and passionately believe. Once seen in this way, we will argue, many of the puzzling properties of popular delusions become less puzzling. Their selective epistemic irrationality emerges when social incentives override epistemic norms on specific topics. Their compartmentalisation reflects the adaptive quarantining of irrational beliefs from action-guiding cognition. And the attachment to such beliefs stems not from their contents but from the social ends they serve. (In Chapter 5, we will explain how epistemically dysfunctional social practices then arise whenever entire communities are motivated to promote and protect the same socially adaptive beliefs.)

Importantly, the psychological processes involved in acquiring socially adaptive beliefs need not and do not involve *sui generis* psychological mechanisms. They are simply a manifestation of motivated cognition, as described in Chapter 3, in which non-epistemic motivations bias how individuals form and revise beliefs (Williams, 2021b). However, whereas most research on motivated cognition focuses on individualistic motivations such as emotion regulation, socially adaptive beliefs result from the interaction between social motivations—that is, *socially* motivated cognition—and the social environment. Two such motivations are significant for understanding popular delusions: propaganda (Section 3) and signalling (Section 4).

3. Propagandistic Cognition

People are often motivated to transmit—to *propagate*—false or misleading information that shapes other people's thoughts. In such cases, they behave not like intuitive scientists but like intuitive propagandists, press secretaries, and lawyers (Hoffman & Yoeli, 2021; Kurzban, 2011; Mercier & Sperber, 2017; Pinsof et al., 2023; Trivers, 2011). Their goal is not to discover and communicate the truth but to influence other people's opinions in self-serving ways.

When human beings behave as propagandists, attempting to spread ideas or narratives for self-serving reasons, it is tempting to think that this must always involve conscious and deliberate deception. According to this intuition, there is a sharp distinction between what people privately believe, which is oriented towards accuracy, and what they say, which can be deceptive and lawyerly. However, an idea that goes back at least as far as Nietzsche (1996 [1878]) (and possibly Socrates; see Melnikoff & Strohminger, 2020) is that this simple picture is often mistaken and that, in many cases, people internalise the beliefs they are motivated to transmit to others.

Several considerations lend support to this view. First, it can explain correlations between people's beliefs and their persuasive goals. We will return to numerous subtle examples of this below. However, most obviously, this phenomenon explains strong and well-documented tendencies towards self-serving, self-justifying, and self-aggrandising beliefs: people often maintain flattering self-conceptions; they portray their actions and attitudes as norm conforming; they take responsibility for good outcomes but not bad ones; they minimise the harms that they inflict on others; they denigrate rivals and diminish their qualities and achievements; and more (Alexander, 1987; Bortolotti, 2015; Kurzban, 2011; Mercier & Sperber, 2017; Pinsof et al., 2023; Taylor & Brown, 1988; von Hippel & Trivers, 2011). Such belief contents serve transparent propagandistic functions.

The standard psychological explanation of these tendencies links them to intrapsychic goals such as emotion regulation and the enhancement of one's self-image (Alicke & Sedikides, 2009; Bortolotti, 2020; Taylor & Brown, 1988). As we saw in the previous chapter (Chapter 3, Section 4.2), one problem with these explanations is their lack of evolutionary plausibility. However, a more direct problem is that they struggle to explain why such tendencies adjust in accordance with people's persuasive goals (Hoffman & Yoeli, 2021; Williams, 2023b). For example, in collectivist cultures and subcultures where self-aggrandisement is strongly discouraged, some evidence suggests that it disappears and is replaced by a tendency to hold overly flattering beliefs about relationships (Endo et al., 2000; Henrich, 2020). More importantly, people believe things they do not want to be true and find distressing when those beliefs align with their persuasion goals. For example, if it helps people win social support and sympathy, they exaggerate their victim status and pitiful qualities (Pinsof et al., 2023). We will see many more examples of this phenomenon when we turn to popular delusions.

Second, various theoretical arguments exist for why we should expect people to internalise their propaganda. First, just as the best salespeople are plausibly those who sincerely believe in the value of their product, sincere belief likely enhances the persuasive power of propaganda, a hypothesis for which there is some experimental evidence (Butterworth et al., 2022; Schwardmann & van der Weele, 2019; Smith et al., 2017). More speculatively, honest endorsement of propagandistic claims might reduce the risk that audiences will detect deception (von Hippel & Trivers, 2011), and it means that agents need not maintain the constant vigilance required when there is a gulf between private convictions and public behaviour (Funkhouser, 2017). When people believe something (as contrasted with cases where they merely pretend to believe it), there is also a strong psychological tendency to automatically generate reasons that confirm the relevant beliefs (Mercier & Sperber, 2017; see Chapter 1, Section 3.3). This obviously has many advantages when it comes to arguing for a conclusion and persuading others of its truth.

If these arguments are correct, internalising one's propaganda has positive adaptive value. However, it is also important to note that once one is motivated to transmit a belief, sincere belief would also often follow simply as a by-product of the cognitive processes involved in persuasion. When attempting to persuade others, people recall, generate, seek out, and evaluate evidence in ways conducive to this end. As a result of this process, they end up with a highly biased sample of evidence and arguments, which will likely influence their own beliefs about the issue (Williams, 2023b). Therefore, in addition to the possible adaptive benefits of self-persuasion, it is likely difficult to avoid even if one tries.

These arguments are plausible but remain largely speculative. Nevertheless, in recent years, a large body of experimental results has emerged that strongly supports the hypothesis that people internalise the beliefs they are motivated to transmit or advocate for (see Butterworth et al., 2022; Williams, 2023b). For example, Babcock and colleagues (1995) demonstrate that participants randomly assigned to represent either the plaintiff or the defendant in a legal case come to internalise beliefs that align with their side (see also Melnikoff & Strohminger, 2020). Schwardmann and van der Weele (2019) demonstrate that providing participants with incentives to persuade other agents of beliefs increases the degree to which they hold such beliefs, and Schwardmann and colleagues (2022) show that even high school debaters often increase their confidence in views that they have been randomly assigned to argue for. As with almost all psychological experiments, the effect sizes tend not to be very large. Nevertheless, it is noteworthy that the phenomenon is observed at all in low-stakes experimental conditions where persuasion or advocacy goals are randomly assigned. Moreover, it is striking that the effect seems to persist even when participants are financially incentivised to give accurate responses and explicitly warned about the biasing effect of advocacy, and even among professional lawyers trained to prevent advocacy from biasing their personal judgements (Melnikoff & Strohminger, 2020). This supports the idea that self-persuasion is difficult to avoid even if one tries.

For these reasons, there seem to be persuasive theoretical considerations and compelling empirical evidence supporting the existence of what we will call "propagandistic cognition", which arises when individuals internalise messages they are motivated to transmit for self-serving reasons (see Kurzban, 2011; Pinsof et al., 2023). As noted in Section 2, this phenomenon can be understood as a form of motivated—specifically *socially* motivated—cognition in which cognitive processes are directed towards the social goal of propaganda rather than accuracy. As with other forms of motivated cognition, then, we should expect propagandistic cognition to be subject to a rationalisation constraint (see Chapter 3, Section 4.2; see Kunda, 1990; Williams, 2022b). And this should be obvious: people do not internalise all claims they are motivated to transmit. Intentional and self-conscious deception does occur. For someone to internalise propaganda, they must be able to rationalise the relevant belief and insulate it from disconfirmation. That is, they must be convinced that the belief in question is true. This fact will be important when we turn to social mechanisms of motivated cognition in Chapter 5.

As we argued in Chapter 3, Section 4.2, a significant limitation of standard individualistic theories of motivated cognition, when it comes to popular delusions, is that it is difficult to see how such delusions could arise from the psychological goals explored in this literature (e.g., emotion regulation, self-esteem maintenance, etc.). Specifically, even though individuals often seem attached to such delusions, the delusions rarely seem to reflect what they *want* to be true. Indeed, in many cases, people seem psychologically distressed by holding the relevant beliefs. Propagandistic cognition does not confront this problem: not only can it benefit individuals to spread beliefs that depict states of affairs they feel indifferent towards, but people can be motivated to spread claims they want to be false and even find distressing to entertain. For this reason, it offers a more promising explanation of the motives driving many popular delusions, as we will now demonstrate.

3.1 Rumours and Conspiracy Theories

As we saw in Chapter 3, one important category of popular delusions is outlandish rumours, conspiracy theories, and accusations—for example, that the government and Hollywood feature networks of Satan-worshipping cannibalistic paedophiles, that the local Jewish population murders Christian children to use their blood in religious rituals, that people are being victimised by the magical spells of cannibalistic witches, and so on. As we also saw, the highly influential theory that such strange rumours and conspiracy theories arise from psychological drives to reduce uncertainty, regain feelings of control, and assign "meaning" to the world (Allport & Postman, 1947) is implausible in such cases and not supported by evidence. A superior explanation appeals to propagandistic cognition and motivations to transmit what the anthropologist Manvir Singh (2021) calls "demonizing narratives".

The recurrent appeal of demonising narratives emerges from two fundamental features of our species. First, people are often motivated to attack, victimise, exploit, or eliminate others (see Chapter 1, Section 5). Such motivations can have many different causes. For example, the targets might be perceived as rivals competing for power, status, or resources, as a burden on others, or as a threat. Second, naked acts of aggression, exploitation, manipulation, and so on tend to violate social norms. As we saw in Chapter 1, the ultra-cooperative nature of human social life means that individuals must typically cultivate a reputation as prosocial, trustworthy, norm-following, altruistic, and non-aggressive. Given this, hatred and aggression towards others must be justified in ways consistent with maintaining such a reputation. Demonising narratives emerge in response to this need: if the narratives are accurate, even reasonable and altruistic individuals would fear, hate, and attack the targets. Moreover, such narratives also unambiguously communicate hostility and hostile intentions towards targets, facilitating social coordination. Specifically, expressing beliefs that demonise targets in an extreme way sends a clear signal to anybody similarly motivated to attack the target that they can expect support and cooperation.

One can see demonising narratives of this kind in many outlandish rumours and accusations. First, anthropologists have long noted a strategic rationale underlying beliefs and rumours about witches (Boyer, 2022; Singh, 2021). In many cases, constructing and propagating accusations of witchcraft serves to target vulnerable individuals and allow communities to gang up on them whilst preserving their moral reputations among each other (La Fontaine, 1998; Gluckman, 1973). In others, the accusations provide a means for communities to coordinate attacks on individuals perceived to possess too much status and success, taking their possessions and levelling the social playing field (Kluckhohn, 1944). Whatever the motivation, the demonising narrative plays the same role: in painting the target as powerful, morally (and often aesthetically) repugnant, and threatening, it justifies their mistreatment and signals the communicator's intentions towards them. As anthropologist Pascal Boyer puts it,

> It helps to see witchcraft accusations as a form of stigmatization, providing a coordination point for coalitional alignment against a particular individual ... People who have some interest in inflicting harm on a particular individual may use witchcraft accusations rather than a direct attack because the accusation makes it possible to recruit allies against the target, whilst maintaining one's own reputation. (Boyer, 2022, p.1350)

The same underlying logic plays out in the extreme accusations levelled against minorities or rival groups that often precede pogroms, genocides, ethnic riots, and more. As Donald Horowitz (2001) has observed, deadly ethnic riots and massacres are invariably rationalised by narratives that accuse the targets of committing outrageous and often sacrilegious transgressions. For example, in the early 1900s in Kishinev (now the capital of Moldova), acts of extreme brutality against the local Jewish population were precipitated by widespread rumours that the population was draining the blood of murdered children in religious rituals (Mercier, 2020, pp.200–208). Of course, similarly baseless demonising narratives were instrumental in the much larger-scale Jewish genocide perpetrated by the Nazis and collaborators across Europe several decades later.

One can also see demonising narratives in bizarre conspiracy theories such as QAnon. The belief that shadowy "elites" within society secretly participate in Satanic paedophile networks attracts American citizens with strong anti-establishment attitudes and anti-social personality traits (e.g., narcissism, grandiosity, and psychopathy) that produce extreme antipathy towards those in positions of power and influence (Enders et al., 2022). Just as conspiracy theories, in general, often serve propagandistic functions (Cassam, 2019), bizarre and extremist conspiracy theories such as QAnon function to rationalise intense hatred of the establishment and to justify anti-democratic actions and the violation of ordinary political conventions.

Summarising the rationale behind demonising narratives, Mercier notes that the quote frequently misattributed to Voltaire, that "those who can make you believe absurdities can make you commit atrocities", gets things backwards: "As a rule, it is wanting to commit atrocities that makes you believe absurdities" (Mercier, 2020, p.202). Specifically, highly *epistemically irrational* beliefs can serve *social* functions if they enable individuals to justify and coordinate actions that would otherwise constitute strong norm violations and damage their reputations.

Importantly, our claim is not that demonising narratives and propagandistic cognition are the only explanatory factors in these cases. For example, witchcraft accusations are only likely to gain traction in cultural contexts where pre-existing beliefs allow for some possibility of magic and supernatural powers; the extreme accusations advanced before ethnic riots and acts of extreme violence are only possible against the backdrop of widespread hatred and prejudice towards the target population; and the extreme forms of demonisation found in bizarre conspiracy theories, such as QAnon, are only likely to be embraced by people with strong conspiratorial mindsets and a degree of factual ignorance that insulates them from clear counter-evidence. Moreover, many of the individualistic factors described in Chapter 3, Section 4, are likely important in such cases, including hyperactive agency-detection and threat-detection, which independently bias people's thoughts in specific directions, and fast and frugal forms of cognitive processing that lead people to jump to conclusions too readily based on little evidence.

Nevertheless, as we argued in Chapter 3, such factors fail to explain many of the properties of such popular delusions. Moreover, propagandistic cognition also seems indispensable for explaining the *extremity* of the rumours and accusations, which appear well-designed to rationalise comparably extreme hatred and mistreatment. To depict people as witches or as devil-worshipping cannibalistic paedophiles is to represent them in the worst way imaginable. The narratives paint the targets in ways that seem specialised to maximise moral outrage, disgust, and fear.

Of course, demonising narratives are often not so extreme. For example, beliefs denigrating targets are a familiar feature of intergroup competition and rivalry, ranging from ordinary partisan conflict in modern democracies to long-standing religious, ethnic, and national conflicts. In such cases, one tends to find a strong tendency among group members to exaggerate the failures, flaws, and threats posed by rival groups (Pinsof et al., 2023; Williams, 2023b). However, these demonising narratives are well suited to specific propagandistic goals and to the messages likely to be accepted in particular contexts. For example, in modern, liberal democracies, the goal of partisans is to argue that competing political parties should not be in power, not that they should be eliminated, and most citizens are unlikely to accept supernatural accusations. Given this, demonising narratives take milder forms (Williams, 2023b). It is only under conditions where extreme actions and attitudes must be justified, and such justifications have some chance of winning acceptance (even if only among those motivated to accept them), that the most outlandish demonising narratives—those most likely to be classified as popular delusions—emerge.

3.2 System-Justifying Ideologies

Demonising narratives function to justify the harsh treatment of targets and communicate clear hostility towards them. However, not all narratives that justify self-serving, exploitative behaviours take this form. In many contexts, people are motivated to propagate beliefs that justify systems and forms of social organisation from which they benefit (Eagleton, 1991; Marx & Engels, 1970 [1845–1846]; Sidanius & Pratto, 2001). Propagandistic cognition and reputation management also provide an illuminating explanation of such system-justifying beliefs.

As we saw in Chapter 1, Section 5.1, one kind of social status that human beings share with many other social animals is dominance. In dominance hierarchies, status is rooted in the ability of high-status individuals to inflict costs on subordinates. Dominance, therefore, involves coercion, whereby people higher up the hierarchy force submission from those lower down through various forms of aggression and intimidation. As a result of this coercion and the power it grants, dominants receive greater access to resources. These basic features are common to dominance hierarchies in many social species. However, in several respects, relations of domination and subordination play out uniquely in human societies (see Chapter 1, Section 5).

First, people can use sophisticated cognitive and social tools to achieve and maintain dominance. For example, dominance relationships are often maintained by complex norms, systems of social enforcement, and institutions. Second, dominance relationships occur not just between individuals and small-scale alliances but between relatively stable groups of various kinds. This includes patriarchy (in which women as a group are subordinate to men) but also dominance hierarchies relating to social classes, castes, races, ethnicities, and religious groups that have emerged in numerous forms throughout history. Finally, dominance hierarchies are firmly in tension with other features of human social life. Humans depend on cooperation and navigate environments structured around partner choice, social norms, reputations, gossip, and prestige economies. For these reasons, people benefit from cultivating a reputation as prosocial and altruistic, which motivates them to deny or obfuscate any role they might play in dominating others.

These facts provide the background for understanding system-justifying ideologies. People are motivated to propagate such ideologies to justify systems of domination from which they benefit in ways that maintain their moral reputation. As we observed in Chapter 3, Section 2, there are many examples of belief systems that perform this function, including the divine right of kings (i.e., the belief that the omnibenevolent creator of the Universe endorses a monarch's social position); supernatural belief systems in which high-status or high-caste individuals will be defiled or contaminated merely by coming into contact with subordinate individuals; the imagination of moral, cognitive, and spiritual differences between men and women that justify the former's power over the latter; unfounded belief systems that justify relationships of domination and subordination between different parts of an Empire; and belief systems of many different kinds (supernatural, religious, pseudo-scientific, etc.) that justify power relations between races and ethnicities, such as what Charles Mills calls the "white delusion of racial superiority" (Mills, 2017, p.49) that in different forms has functioned to support long-standing white supremacist forms of social organisation.

The standard Marxist and critical-theoretic analysis of such system-justifying beliefs is that they function to persuade subordinate groups to accept their oppression (Eagleton, 1991; Marx & Engels, 1970 [1845–1846]). This is one reason why dominant groups are motivated to push such belief systems, although evidence strongly suggests that they are often unsuccessful at achieving this purpose (Mercier, 2020; Turner et al., 1980). Nevertheless, just as the goal of witchcraft accusations is not to persuade the targets of such accusations, members of dominant coalitions are likely motivated to propagate system-justifying ideologies in order to maintain their reputation for pro-sociality and generosity *among each other*. If their social positions are not rooted in brutal systems of domination but in the will of God, then their privileges can co-exist with reputations for pro-sociality, generosity, and trustworthiness *among other individuals who similarly benefit from the dominance hierarchy*. As we saw in Chapter 1, this maintenance of prosocial reputation is a precondition for cooperation in social environments shaped by intense partner choice.

3.3 Supernatural Beliefs

An important category of popular delusions concerns strange supernatural beliefs often characteristic of religions, proto-religions, and cults. Although such beliefs and belief systems have complex causes, including factors related to identity formation and ingroup signalling that we return to below (Section 4.1), it has long been observed that they seem to perform social functions connected to cooperation (Durkheim, 2001 [1912]).

As we reviewed extensively in Chapter 1, Section 3, cooperation is a central challenge of human social life. Individuals are completely dependent on others' cooperation, yet cooperation is inherently challenging. People can often benefit by free-riding on other people's efforts, defecting when it is their turn to invest, or extracting a disproportionate share of the fruits of cooperation. Given this, people are strongly motivated to encourage others to cooperate, including by monitoring and punishing their selfishness and deviance, strategies usually referred to as "partner control" (Sterelny, 2012). One such strategy works via *informational* means. For example, people often invent and propagate moral principles that encourage cooperative behaviour and preach moral tales and narratives that detail what constitutes bad behaviour and its negative consequences (Boehm, 2012). According to recent research, many supernatural belief systems emerge, at least in part, from the same motivations: people are driven to propagate beliefs in the existence of supernatural agents and forces to persuade others to cooperate (Fitouchi et al., 2023; Fitouchi & Singh, 2022).

This hypothesis helps to explain a central feature of many supernatural belief systems: the postulation of supernatural agents and forces that monitor, enforce, and incentivise cooperation. This feature is obvious in Abrahamic religions, which link specific behaviours to heaven and hell, and in "karmic" religions, in which people's actions determine what karma they experience and how they will be reborn. However, it is also central to the belief systems of many smaller-scale societies, which often involve belief in deities and forces that punish transgressions such as murder, theft, and lying (Fitouchi & Singh, 2022). For example, a majority of members of the hunter-gatherer Ik people in Uganda believe in the existence of Earth spirits that harm those who do not share with others (Townsend et al., 2020), and a widespread belief among the Mentawai horticulturalists in Indonesia is that a water spirit called "Sikameinan" inflicts illness and misfortune on those who do not share their meat with fellow clan members (Singh et al., 2021). As Fitouchi and Singh summarise this idea, "People strategically endorse supernatural punishment beliefs as intuitive tools of social control to manipulate others into cooperating" (Fitouchi & Singh, 2022, p.252). Full-fledged prosocial religious belief systems then

> emerge as the macro-level cultural products of micro-level strategic interactions, iterated over cultural evolution. As people cumulatively refine religious culture to control each other's behaviour, they shape religious technologies that become intuitively better at promoting cooperation. (Fitouchi et al., 2023, p.6)

There is considerable evidence for this hypothesis (for a complete summary, see Fitouchi & Singh, 2022; Fitouchi et al., 2023). For example, people invest more in moralistic religious beliefs when their motivations to police each other increase (Jackson et al., 2021); when they perceive the beliefs to be effective in eliciting cooperation (Abrams et al., 2020); and when they judge that supernatural policing has added value over merely secular means of incentivising cooperation (Norris & Inglehart, 2011). Moreover, moralistic religious beliefs tend to preferentially target those behaviours that people have incentives to encourage in others, such that the contents of supernatural belief systems covary significantly with the specific policing problems communities confront in different cultures (Bendixen et al., 2023). Finally, the idea that people propagate prosocial religious beliefs as a way of incentivising cooperation helps to explain the common *moralisation* of such beliefs: if people believe that holding beliefs in supernatural punishment is necessary for cooperation, as most people in most societies do—indeed, atheists are one of the least trusted groups across diverse cultures (Gervais et al., 2011)—then maintaining such beliefs becomes a public good to which people should contribute (Fitouchi et al., 2023). As a result, beliefs in supernatural punishment are often associated with social norms and duties to endorse and protect such beliefs publicly, as well as social penalties for things such as public disbelief, blasphemy, and apostasy.

Further, the hypothesis is superior to alternative explanations. First, one influential explanation of supernatural belief systems treats them as a recurrent mistake arising from cognitive biases of the sort outlined in Chapter 3, especially hyperactive agency detection, combined with misguided attempts to understand the world (e.g., Boyer, 2001). However, this does not explain why supernatural belief systems often exhibit clear evidence of functional design for incentivising cooperation. For example, moralising deities, spirits, and forces inflict costs on uncooperative behaviour that outweigh its benefits; they conveniently detect uncooperative behaviour where mere humans cannot (e.g., "God is always watching"); and supernatural belief systems are often conveniently difficult to falsify, either by framing supernatural punishment in sufficiently vague ways or by postponing it to an unobservable afterlife (Fitouchi et al., 2023). Further, the idea that supernatural belief systems are just cognitive mistakes also fails to explain why people are motivated to propagate them and why their acceptance tends to be so moralised within communities.

Second, another influential explanation of supernatural belief systems is that they serve emotional and palliative purposes, providing feelings of reassurance and comfort (Freud, 1989 [1927]). Once again, this fails to account for the features of such belief systems that seem specialised for promoting cooperation. Moreover, even if it might explain why people are attached to such beliefs, it does not explain why they are motivated to propagate them or moralise their endorsement. Finally, and most problematically, many supernatural belief systems are not reassuring at all. Believing that a crocodile-like spirit hunts down uncooperative people or that one might burn in hell for eternity for acting in certain ways does not seem conducive to promoting positive emotions.

3.4 Self-Interest and Public Acceptance

In the preceding three cases, people are motivated to transmit (i.e., propagate) beliefs because an audience's acceptance of the *contents* of those beliefs bears a clear relationship to the communicator's motivations. If audiences accept demonising narratives, they will tolerate mistreatment of, or hatred towards, the targets of such narratives; if audiences accept system-justifying ideologies, they will believe that the system and its power hierarchy are just; and if audiences accept beliefs in supernatural punishment, they will (or at least it is thought that they will) be more likely to cooperate. However, there are also cases in which people's interests are more directly tied to an audience's acceptance of certain beliefs.

Consider the Catholic Church in medieval and pre-modern Europe. Although it was a powerful institution featuring individuals and coalitions of high status and influence, this exalted position depended on the public acceptance of Catholic dogmas, such as that the Church was the only legitimate interpreter of Christian scripture and that the bread and wine used in the Eucharist become Christ's body and blood. Given this, leaders within the Church had powerful incentives to propagandise on behalf of its teachings; if the public dissented from such teachings, their status and authority would crumble. Indeed, the term "propaganda" derives from the name of a committee established by the Church in early 17th-century Europe, which was responsible for propagating and enforcing the Catholic faith (DiResta, 2024).

A similar dynamic plays out in many contexts, including in popular delusions. For example, in the Satanic panic described in Chapter 3, large numbers of people (at first, Americans) in the 1980s came to believe that their society featured vast, secret networks of devil-worshipping paedophiles engaged in the ritual abuse of children, primarily through day-care centres. It is plausible that the emergence of this conspiracy theory first arose mainly through epistemic factors (that is, in response to perceived evidence and testimony; see Chapter 3, Section 3.1), albeit likely combined with some of the cognitive biases detailed in Chapter 3, Section 4, such as oversensitivity to social threats. As sociologists and historians have documented, the 1980s in the USA featured several trends and events that gave initial plausibility to the accusations among specific communities: first, there had been a resurgence of evangelical Christian groups who had pre-existing beliefs in Satan and were most likely to embrace the accusations; second, the early 1980s saw an important society-wide recognition of the existence of child abuse, which had previously been dismissed and ignored; third, apparently credible experts testified to the reliability of therapeutic practices using hypnosis and the recovery of repressed memories, which were only later debunked; and finally, in 1980 the bestseller "Michelle Remembers" was published, which was co-written by somebody who gave extensive first-hand testimony reporting her recovered "memories" of Satanic ritual abuse as a child (see La Fontaine, 1998; Nathan & Snedeker, 2001; Romano, 2016; Storr, 2021).

These and other factors conspired to make initial allegations of Satanic ritual abuse plausible to many people. Nevertheless, they cannot explain the continued commitment to the conspiracy theory even as the evidence against it accumulated, the therapeutic techniques upon which it was based were debunked, and no physical evidence emerged to corroborate any of the outlandish accusations, which, if true, should have left an enormous amount of it. Moreover, purely epistemic explanations cannot account for the extreme attachment to the conspiracy theory among many of its proponents, nor for their motivations to propagate and enforce commitment to it. For example, as we noted in the previous chapter (Chapter 3, Section 3.5), many who came to endorse the core ideas of the panic exerted intense social pressure on dissenters or anyone who so much as raised sceptical questions (La Fontaine, 1998). Those who aired such doubts were often "censured by their colleagues and discouraged from publicizing their concerns" (Nathan & Snedeker, 2001, p.11). Some were even accused of being part of the conspiracy themselves (Beck, 2015).

To understand such phenomena, one must appreciate how many people's interests became dependent on the public's continued acceptance of the conspiracy theory. First, if people came to think that the accusations were baseless and even absurd, those who had passionately advanced the allegations and used them as a basis to charge and imprison people would be guilty of shocking negligence and irrationality. Second, and just as importantly, the Satanic panic had been extraordinarily reputationally and financially lucrative for many people. As Storr argues, the "Satan hunters" during this period—that is, the journalists, therapists, police officers, social workers, and so on who fuelled accusations and claimed to fight back against Satanic ritual abuse—experienced incredible "status in the form of influence, acclaim, cash, fame, proximity to the prestigious games of law, media and government and the reputation of an avenging angel, defending the lives of America's children" (Storr, 2021, pp.180–181). Given this, such people had powerful motivations to keep the narrative alive even as its absurdity became increasingly clear to onlookers. As the Satanic panic raged on, its "explosive energy" therefore derived not primarily "from panic but from desire for acclaim" (Storr, 2021, p.181).

The Satanic panic provides a clear illustration of this dynamic, which generalises to many popular delusions and explains their auto-catalytic nature: in many cases, the more that people accept such delusions, the more that their interests—for example, their status, power, or membership in a valued community—depend on the continued acceptance of the delusion among others, which in turn produces even greater motivations to propagate the beliefs. As we will return to in Chapter 5, such motivations not only increase their confidence in their beliefs via propagandistic cognition but also drive much of the social behaviour—the evangelising, enforcing, and punishing of dissent—that surrounds them.

3.5 Interim Summary

The concept of propagandistic cognition rests on a simple but explanatorily powerful idea: people internalise their propaganda. In addition to explaining why people become attached to beliefs whose contents they find distressing, there is a transparent link between many popular delusions and the messages people are motivated to spread.

Importantly, the applications of propagandistic cognition to strange beliefs here are not exhaustive. For example, Sijilmassi and colleagues (2024) conjecture that widespread historical myths, which inaccurately depict groups such as nations and ethnicities as having a shared, distinct, and ancestral past, are rooted in propagandistic motivations. By spreading narratives that showcase a deep history of cooperation, shared experiences, and interdependence, such myths function to increase social support for the relevant group and encourage people to make sacrifices for it. Similarly, Mercier (2020, pp.119–121) argues that millenarian movements united by the belief that the end of the world is coming are often motivated to spread such beliefs to justify radical challenges to an existing social order. If the end of the world is coming, the usual "rules of the game" need not apply, a situation many millenarian movements are motivated to capitalise on. Pinsof and colleagues (2023) also propose that many otherwise strange, hypocritical features of political ideologies are rooted in motivations to spread propagandistic narratives that mobilise support for and against specific interest groups (Williams & Miyazono, 2023). Such hypotheses illustrate the explanatory fecundity of propagandistic cognition.

In addition, our application of propagandistic cognition to popular delusions has necessarily been relatively schematic, and we have not considered every possible alternative explanation for the beliefs explored here. Nevertheless, in line with our overarching aim in this book, we hope we have provided sufficient detail to demonstrate how promising and powerful this social framework is for approaching these topics. Most fundamentally, traditional, individualistic theories of motivated cognition fail to explain the popular delusions we have reviewed in this section because they do not seem to serve any apparent intrapsychic function. Such beliefs do not seem to reduce uncertainty, enhance feelings of control, or produce psychological well-being. Instead, those who believe them often seem fearful, distressed, and even horrified. Propagandistic cognition can illuminate this otherwise strange situation: people will be strongly motivated to transmit epistemically irrational beliefs that undermine their own psychological well-being if such beliefs serve strategic social functions of persuasion, social coordination, and reputation management. As we will return to in Chapter 5, this aspect of our social framework, in conjunction with the other aspects, also explains the five features of popular delusions we identified in Chapter 3.

4. Signalling

Although propagandistic cognition is an important driver of popular delusions, it is insufficient to explain many cases in which communities embrace shared beliefs that strike reasonable outsiders as highly epistemically irrational, as well as many characteristics of such beliefs. For example, when it comes to strange beliefs that unite communities of co-believers, such as one often finds in religions, cults, extremist groups, conspiratorial communities, and so on, group members frequently seem highly attached to the beliefs even when they do not serve any obvious propagandistic function. It is not clear why it would benefit the modern Flat Earth Society to propagate its belief that the Earth is a flat disc surrounded by a 150-foot wall of ice guarded by NASA (Williams, 2021a) or what members of the Heaven's Gate cult would have gained from propagating their belief that evil space aliens conspired to keep humans from developing (Davis, 2000). To understand such cases, we must turn to another form of socially motivated cognition driven not by propaganda but by social signalling.

As detailed in Chapter 1, human beings are obligate and constant reputation managers. To navigate social worlds organised around norms, gossip, prestige hierarchies, and intense social scrutiny, individuals must cultivate and display traits that make them attractive cooperation partners and win them respect from others. Much of cognition, therefore, involves social self-monitoring in which we regulate our thoughts and behaviour in response to their likely reputational consequences, and traits and dispositions are shaped in response to social rewards and punishments (Origgi, 2017; Storr, 2021; Tetlock, 2002; Tomasello, 2016).

For these reasons, people invest considerably in signalling their socially attractive qualities (Hoffman & Yoeli, 2021; Simler & Hanson, 2016). They wear expensive watches to signal their wealth; they organise lavish community feasts to signal their generosity; they volunteer for charities to signal their altruism; they go to the opera to signal their social class; they use complex, multi-syllabic words to signal their intelligence; they wear tight-fitting clothes to signal their physical fitness; and so on. Further, people also invest considerably in signalling their commitments and allegiances to others (Barclay et al., 2021; Kurzban & Christner, 2011; Raihani, 2021; Sterelny, 2012). For example, people give expensive gifts to signal their devotion to their partner and engage in elaborate rituals to signal their allegiance to their religious or cultural group (Xygalatas, 2022).

It is tempting to think that social signalling is restricted to outward behaviours: which rituals people participate in, which watches and clothes they wear, which tattoos they get, how they communicate and behave, and so on. Nevertheless, as one of us has argued elsewhere, there are good reasons to believe that it also shapes the nature and contents of people's mental lives in powerful ways, including what they believe (Funkhouser, 2017; Simler &

Hanson, 2016; Williams, 2021a). People's beliefs are not just private maps by which they steer; they are often objects of intense social scrutiny and evaluation. Given this, another driver of socially motivated cognition comes from social motivations rooted in reputation management and social signalling. In such cases, motivations to display certain qualities and allegiances influence and bias how people seek out and process information.

We will identify two examples of this phenomenon relevant to understanding popular delusions: beliefs that signal group identities and allegiances (Section 4.1) and beliefs that signal cooperative tendencies (Section 4.2).

4.1 Beliefs as Signals of Group Identity and Allegiance

As we saw in Chapter 1, humans are groupish. Much of human social life is organised around complex relationships of cooperation and competition between coalitions of various kinds. Coalitions are bounded groups that coordinate to promote shared interests and achieve common goals. They come in many forms, ranging from small-scale fleeting alliances to broader, more stable units of social organisation such as bands, tribes, gangs, ethnic groups, cults, religions, unions, political parties, and nation-states. In some cases, coalitions form to achieve narrow, predetermined goals and dissolve once those goals are achieved. In others, they function as what Tooby and Cosmides (2010) call general-purpose "amplification coalitions", amplifying the abilities of members to promote their interests in open-ended ways through networks of social support, mutual aid, heightened trust, and so on. Examples include cohesive religious groups, cults, subcultures, gangs, and ethnic groups, whose members view themselves as participants in a community organised around shared norms and interests.

Importantly, coalitions generally involve both entitlements and responsibilities. Coalition members are entitled to group benefits, such as heightened sympathy, support, protection, and mutual aid from ingroup members and, in some cases, the social status enjoyed by the group in broader society. These entitlements come with responsibilities, however. Group members must typically invest in the community, conform to group norms, aid other group members, and remain loyal and committed to the coalition.

These simple remarks provide the background for understanding many strange beliefs. First, much human behaviour involves signals of coalitional identity. Football fans wear t-shirts and paint their faces to signal their support for specific teams; religious individuals wear specific jewellery and clothes to display their religious affiliation; gang members get gang tattoos; and so on. It is plausible that motivations to signal coalitional identity also shape people's beliefs (Funkhouser, 2022; Simler & Hanson, 2016; Van Leeuwen, 2023; Williams, 2021a). Of course, many beliefs are *identity-defining* insofar as commitment to such beliefs constitutes part of the membership criteria for specific communities (Rauch, 2021; Williams, 2022a). For example, religious groups, cults, ideological groups, and so on are defined at least in part by what their members believe. Nevertheless, this observation is consistent with the possibility that people form and maintain identity-defining beliefs for purely epistemic reasons (see Levy, 2021). Our suggestion here is different: in many cases, identity-defining beliefs are formed and maintained, at least in part, for social signalling reasons, such that individuals are motivated to embrace and hold onto such beliefs to display their coalitional identity.

Several considerations lend support to this view. First, it helps to explain why groups often organise themselves around identity-defining beliefs and shared narratives that strike outsiders as strange and highly epistemically irrational. From the perspective of signalling group identity, everyday rational beliefs are useless (Tooby, 2017; Van Leeuwen, 2023; Williams, 2018). Whatever group they belong to, everybody believes that objects fall to the ground when you drop them. For beliefs to function as valuable badges of group identity, outsiders must refrain from arriving at such beliefs through ordinary processes of rational belief formation. Strange, arbitrary, and highly epistemically irrational beliefs can satisfy this need. Of course, many factors will determine which beliefs and narratives become identity-defining for specific coalitions, including beliefs that flatter and aggrandise the community (e.g., believing that one's group includes the "chosen people") and that align with the sympathies and biases of their members (e.g., people with conspiratorial mentalities organising around specific conspiracy theories); epistemic irrationality is, therefore, insufficient, but it is often plausibly necessary.

Second, considerable research shows that people's embrace of identity-defining beliefs tracks the incentives associated with holding and affirming them. For example, evidence suggests that most conversions to religious groups and sects are done for practical reasons, such that individuals weigh the relative social cost and benefits of belonging to specific communities and only convert to the relevant beliefs when they judge that the latter outweighs the former (Iannaccone, 1992; Simler & Hanson, 2016; Stark & Finke, 2000; Van Leeuwen, 2023). Likewise, defections from social groups organised around identity-defining beliefs are also largely driven by practical considerations, not evidential ones, such as whether people come to judge that their life prospects, freedom, status, or relationships will improve outside of the relevant community (Bialecki, 2017; Van Leeuwen, 2023, p.95).

Third, this explanation illuminates why people are often so attached to identity-defining beliefs, even when the beliefs do not serve any obvious emotional or propagandistic function. Bizarre beliefs about the shape of the planet, the presence of supernatural aliens, or the sacred value of holy texts do not provide obvious propagandistic or emotional benefits. Nevertheless, those who hold such beliefs often appear highly attached to them. In our analysis, people are ultimately attached to their community, not to the beliefs themselves; the specific content of their beliefs matters much less than the signalling function they perform (Williams, 2021a). Relatedly, this hypothesis helps explain the common association between social emotions and the endorsement of identity-defining beliefs. Successful group affiliation and cooperation are typically associated with feelings of security, belonging, and pride (Del Giudice, 2018, pp. 36–45). Although this topic needs more research, such feelings often seem implicated when people adopt and affirm identity-defining beliefs (Williams, 2021a).

Nevertheless, according to this view, the signalling function of identity-defining beliefs is purely assortative—that is, to signal and detect signals of coalitional identity (Van Leeuwen, 2023). Although this is likely one important factor in identity-defining beliefs, it confronts several objections as a complete explanation. First, if the aim is merely to identify and be identified by fellow group members, there are presumably easier ways to achieve this than by embracing strange and outlandish beliefs. Second, in many communities, people seem to invest substantially in displaying their commitment to identity-defining beliefs even when there is no uncertainty about their group membership. Finally, many identity-defining beliefs are not just distinctive; they are sufficiently strange and outlandish that they actively damage the reputation of ingroup members in the eyes of outsiders.

To make sense of these phenomena, we conjecture that many identity-defining beliefs are better understood not just as signals of group identity but as signals of group commitment. As noted, cooperative communities come with benefits but also with responsibilities: to be entitled to the fruits of shared cooperation, group members must be committed and cooperative group members themselves. For this reason, coalitions are inherently fragile: their dependence on collaboration makes them vulnerable to individuals who free-ride on others' cooperation or defect when it is their turn to help others (Boyer, 2018; Tooby & Cosmides, 2010). Given this, coalitions often devote significant energy to sending and monitoring signals of coalitional commitment and loyalty. Unlike merely assortative signals, these signals confront the problem of dishonesty. It typically benefits group members to be viewed as more committed and loyal than they are.

When individuals benefit from sending dishonest signals, signalling systems need mechanisms to ensure honesty. Evolutionary theorists and social scientists have identified many such mechanisms, but most boil down to the following simple insight: signals will be honest if it is either impossible or prohibitively expensive for dishonest signallers to send them (Hoffman & Yoeli, 2021; Smith & Harper, 2003). For example, as Veblen (1912 [1899]) pointed out, the conspicuous consumption of luxury goods and services is an honest signal of wealth and status because poor, lower-status people cannot afford to pay for them.

This logic of costly signalling also arises in coalitions that send and detect signals of coalitional commitment (Boyer, 2018; Sterelny, 2012). For example, groups of diverse kinds—religions, cults, gangs, subcultures, and so on—often demand initiation rites, behavioural restrictions, and rituals that involve sacrifices that would be prohibitively expensive for individuals lacking in group commitment (Iannaccone, 1992; Sosis & Alcorta, 2003; Xygalatas, 2022). Similarly, coalitions often require acts that signal ingroup loyalty by "amplifying defection costs", as Sterelny (2020) puts it. That is, members signal coalitional loyalty by acting in ways that increase the costs of defection to other groups, typically by damaging their reputation in the eyes of outsiders. There are many such examples: body modifications, including gang tattoos and tribal scarification, permanently identify group members in ways that make it impossible to join rival coalitions (Boyer, 2018); groups embrace socially stigmatised clothes, rituals, and restrictions that invite ridicule from outsiders (Iannaccone, 1992); and criminal gangs, mafias, and cults often involve "high-price defection from the norms of larger society" (Sterelny 2012, pp.295–296), such as mafias that require prospective members to commit a murder to demonstrate loyalty and gain membership. In these cases, coalition members "burn their bridges" to outside groups in ways that not only *reveal* inner commitment but also materially change their options (Mercier, 2020). By making it more difficult to join other groups, such behaviours make sticking with the relevant coalition the rational course of action—and advertise this fact to others.

We conjecture that costly signalling strategies also shape people's beliefs (see Funkhouser, 2022; Simler & Hanson, 2016; Williams, 2021a). Specifically, the stigma and perceived absurdity associated with many identity-defining beliefs are features, not bugs. By embracing shared beliefs and narratives that damage their reputations in the eyes of outsiders, individuals demonstrate to insiders that their social world is now tied to the group. For example, applying this logic to the specific case of religious beliefs, Kurzban and Christner argue that "beliefs that preclude membership in other groups are valuable because of commitment", and endorsement of strange religious beliefs has this effect because they "make one appear, to those who do not share such beliefs, mentally ill" (Kurzban & Christner, 2011, p.5). Likewise, Simler and Hanson suggest that "the craziness of religious beliefs can function as a barometer of how strong the community is" (Simler & Hanson, 2016, p.279).

These claims are too strong. Few people think of ordinary religious believers as mentally ill for endorsing mainstream religious ideas. This is likely partly because mainstream religious beliefs are sufficiently embedded in most societies that they are not considered strange. Nevertheless, the insight that certain identity-defining beliefs are specialised for eliciting a reputation for "craziness" among outsiders is plausible, especially when it comes to tight-knit cults, sects, conspiratorial groups, and extremist groups who embrace outlandish beliefs with high conviction that are sharply at odds with conventional attitudes in their society. If so, the fact that commitment to such beliefs appears delusional to outsiders is not accidental: by embracing shared narratives that cause outsiders to classify them as mass delusions (or as "crazy", "mad", "insane", etc.), believers signal a high degree of commitment to insiders.

Once again, several considerations and lines of evidence support this hypothesis. Many of these are shared with the idea that beliefs perform merely *assortative* signalling functions. For example, it can illuminate why groups are often organised around identity-defining beliefs and narratives that strike outsiders as strange and irrational, why the adoption and abandonment of such beliefs often seem to track social incentives, not epistemic considerations, and why people often appear highly attached to such beliefs and proud to endorse and affirm them.

However, unlike the merely assortative hypothesis, it helps explain the extreme strangeness and irrationality of certain identity-defining beliefs. It can also illuminate why people are often highly committed to advertising their commitment to such beliefs through various means (e.g., rituals, symbols, clothing), even when little uncertainty exists about their group identity. As Atran and Ginges observe, "Studies suggest that costly and seemingly arbitrary ritual commitment to apparently absurd beliefs deepens trust, galvanizing group solidarity for common defense and blinding members to exit strategies" (Atran & Ginges, 2012, p.855). Finally, it can explain why one often finds the most outlandish beliefs and the most extreme levels of commitment to them among close-knit sects, cults, and subcultures that constitute the only source of community for their members. For ordinary individuals who belong to numerous cross-cutting communities, embracing strategic absurdities associated with only one community will typically be impossible or highly undesirable. In contrast, the strategy will have much greater benefits and fewer costs for extremely tight-knit groups that function as people's sole source of social support (Iannaccone, 1992; Williams, 2021a).

4.2 Beliefs as Signals of Cooperativeness

In the preceding cases, the specific content of group beliefs does not matter for their signalling value. What matters is that the beliefs of group members are distinctive or that their endorsement elicits selective reputational damage among outsiders. However, other cases of belief signalling plausibly arise in which beliefs perform important social signalling functions because of a much closer relationship between their specific contents and the traits being signalled.

Most obviously, individuals can often signal their group commitment by embracing strong pro-ingroup beliefs and anti-outgroup beliefs. According to this view, one important reason why individuals embrace beliefs that glorify their favoured coalition and denigrate rival groups is precisely that endorsing such beliefs communicates their sympathy and loyalty towards fellow group members (Funkhouser, 2022; Williams, 2021a). That is, *if* one sincerely believes that one's own group is superior to others and uniquely virtuous, fellow group members will be more inclined to trust and sympathise with one. The same is true of beliefs that one's community has some special status, such as being composed of the "chosen people" or a special elect group. In such cases, there is a natural connection between the content of the relevant beliefs and positive dispositions towards the relevant group.

Nevertheless, beliefs associated with ordinary ingroup biases are rarely considered delusional, except when they take extreme forms. However, content-based social signalling can also explain a more unusual belief held in many communities: the widespread belief in supernatural forces and agents that reward cooperation and punish selfishness and cheating. As argued above (Section 3.3), such beliefs likely arise in part from propagandistic cognition. Because people intuit that others will be more likely to cooperate if they believe in supernatural punishment, they have strong incentives to propagate such beliefs to others. Yet another plausible reason beliefs in supernatural punishment are so widespread is that people also have signalling motivations to form such beliefs (Funkhouser, 2022; Williams, 2021a). Because it is widely believed that belief in supernatural punishment promotes cooperation, people's strong interest in being seen as cooperative will often motivate them to embrace and endorse such beliefs. For example, because religious people are perceived as more trustworthy than atheists (Gervais et al., 2011), individuals can enhance their reputation for trustworthiness by embracing religious beliefs. For this reason, beliefs in supernaturally-enforced cooperation are likely rooted in both propagandistic and signalling motivations.

For this strategy to be effective, sincere conviction is typically necessary. Anybody can *say* that they believe God is always watching or that a crocodile-like spirit harms those who do not share with others. To gain trust, one must convince others that this belief is sincere. This hypothesis, therefore, explains why people are often eager to display their commitment to beliefs associated with supernatural punishment (Fitouchi & Singh, 2022). Indeed, many ritual practices associated with religious and proto-religious belief systems can be understood in part as social technologies that enable individuals to signal their commitment to beliefs widely regarded as cooperation-inducing (Bulbulia & Sosis, 2011; Sosis & Alcorta, 2003). It also illuminates evidence supported by a meta-analysis revealing that those individuals who care more about reputation management are more likely to exhibit so-called "intrinsic religiosity", which roughly measures sincere belief and consistent participation in the rituals and obligations associated with such belief (Sedikides & Gebauer, 2010).

4.3 Interim Summary

As with propagandistic cognition, the idea that we have developed in this section rests on a simple hypothesis: people are motivated to embrace beliefs that send social signals about the kinds of people they are. This hypothesis is implied by two uncontroversial features of human psychology: reputation management and social signalling are deep human motivations (see Chapter 1), and motivations bias how people form and revise beliefs (see Chapter 3). In addition to explaining why people appear to become attached to beliefs even when the contents of those beliefs do not express their desires or serve any obvious propagandistic function, we have argued that this simple hypothesis illuminates many candidates for popular delusions and many of the characteristics they and their endorsers exhibit.

Like our overview of propagandistic cognition, our treatment of beliefs' signalling functions has not been exhaustive, and our exploration has necessarily been schematic. There is much more to say about how social signalling biases beliefs, and numerous examples of this phenomenon we have not explored here (Funkhouser, 2022; Simler & Hanson, 2016; Williams, 2021a). Nevertheless, we hope that we have provided sufficient detail to showcase the explanatory power of this approach, which, together with our overall social framework, constitutes a well-grounded, evolutionarily informed, parsimonious solution to the functional delusions puzzle.

Before concluding, it is worth briefly noting how propagandistic cognition and social signalling interact. As we have seen in connection with beliefs in supernaturally enforced cooperation, in some cases of popular delusions, both tendencies likely play a role in biasing people towards specific conclusions. In addition, propagandistic cognition and belief signalling likely interact more deeply in many cases. First, once people support and identify with a coalition motivated to spread specific propaganda, endorsing such propagandistic conclusions will likely signal coalitional membership and allegiance (Williams & Miyazono, 2023). For example, people who belong to highly conspiratorial communities that spread narratives designed to demonise specific elites might gain additional motivation to endorse such narratives to signal their allegiance to the community. Similarly, members of elite groups motivated to spread system-justifying ideologies that rationalise their elite status might acquire a separate motivation to endorse such ideologies to signal their membership of and allegiance to the elite group. In these cases, motivations to propagandise and signal co-occur and reinforce each other. Second, in some cases, motivations to propagandise—to evangelise, proselytise, and so on—can themselves be rooted in or supported by motivations to signal coalitional membership and allegiance. For example, if a coalition benefits from spreading coalition-serving propaganda, then making sacrifices to do so can be a costly and credible signal of coalitional allegiance (Storr, 2021). This phenomenon will be important when we turn to the social practices that underlie and sustain popular delusions in the next chapter.

5. Chapter Summary

The functional delusions puzzle asks why healthy, otherwise rational individuals embrace popular delusions, belief systems characterised by unusual and selective epistemic irrationality, compartmentalisation, emotional attachment, and epistemically dysfunctional social practices. One thing that makes this puzzle puzzling is that standard accounts of motivated irrationality seem inapplicable in most such cases. Although individuals and groups often seem highly attached to popular delusions, the delusions rarely seem to express what they want to be true, and it is usually difficult to see what emotional benefits they have for those who endorse them, except for those benefits that arise indirectly as a consequence of winning trust and approval from co-believers. We have argued that a solution to this puzzle highlights the hidden *social* rationality underlying many such delusions: what *appears* highly irrational from a narrowly epistemic point of view often serves the interests of ultra-social animals concerned with persuasion, reputation management, and social signalling.

In Chapter 5, Section 5, we will consider in more depth how this framework addresses the five properties of popular delusions identified in Chapter 3. But for at least the first four of these, the connections should already be clear. The epistemic irrationality of popular delusions reflects their origins in social goals that conflict with accuracy. The selectivity of this irrationality reflects the topic-specific nature of such goals. The beliefs' compartmentalisation emerges from the necessity of implicitly tracking their social functions and quarantining them from action-guiding cognition, where falsity can be costly. And the attachment to such beliefs ultimately derives from attachment to the social goals (e.g., justifying hostility, signalling group allegiance) that they serve.

Chapter 5 will address the fifth and final property: the dysfunctional social-epistemic practices associated with such beliefs. As we will see, this exploration will not merely supplement the ideas reviewed in this chapter. This chapter has connected popular delusions to socially motivated cognition, but this alone cannot explain how most such beliefs emerge and survive contact with reality. Even highly motivated individuals are sharply constrained by their ability to rationalise their preferred conclusions. To understand how entire communities can sustain not just mild cognitive errors but "down-right provocations against commonsense rationality" (Sperber, 1985, p.85), then, we must move beyond psychological mechanisms of motivated cognition to explore its collective machinery and the unique forms of irrationality it makes possible.

5
The Social Scaffolding of Popular Delusions

1. Introduction

Chapter 4 detailed how social goals of propaganda and signalling give rise to popular delusions, strange collective beliefs characterised by selective epistemic irrationality, compartmentalisation, emotional attachment, and epistemically dysfunctional social practices. At the psychological level, we argued that this process should be understood in terms of well-established processes of motivated cognition in which goals distinct from accuracy ("directional goals") direct how individuals acquire and revise beliefs (Kunda, 1990; Williams, 2021b). This involves motivational biases in how people seek out, ignore, interpret, process, and recall evidence (Epley & Gilovich, 2016). Such biases play important roles in popular delusions. When individuals are motivated to propagate biased beliefs or embrace them for social signalling reasons, they will inevitably seek out evidence that justifies such beliefs (*selective exposure*), lower their standards for evidence supporting them (*biased evaluation*), and selectively recall information that aligns with their preferred conclusions (*selective forgetting*).

Nevertheless, these psychological biases also seem inadequate for explaining many features of popular delusions. As detailed in Chapter 3, Section 3.5, such beliefs often involve and depend on distinctive social factors, practices, and dynamics. For example, popular delusions are often treated as orthodoxies among communities that endorse them, and "active believers" (Storr, 2021) frequently impose social pressures on dissenters and heretics (Hoffer, 1951; Kuran, 1997; Loury, 1994; Mill, 1869 [1859]). Although we have alluded to some of these characteristics in Chapter 4, we have not yet explained this important aspect of popular delusions.

Moreover, tracing popular delusions to individual biases involved in motivated cognition confronts a puzzle. As noted in Chapter 3, Section 4.2, motivated cognition is subject to a rationalisation constraint: people will only acquire beliefs they are motivated to propagate or endorse when they are genuinely persuaded by the beliefs (Epley & Gilovich, 2016; Kunda, 1990; Williams, 2022b). This is why the psychological biases implicated in motivated

The Social Roots of Delusions. Daniel Williams, Sam Wilkinson, and Kengo Miyazono, Oxford University Press.
© Oxford University Press (2026). DOI: 10.1093/9780191976360.003.0006

cognition are necessary (Kunda, 1990). People cannot just choose to believe something. Instead, they must acquire information that supports their preferred conclusions and insulate such conclusions from contrary evidence and persuasive counterarguments. This rationalisation constraint typically keeps motivated cognition on a tight leash. As Kunda observes, "People believe what they want to believe *only to the extent that reason permits*" (Kunda, 1990, p.483, emphasis added).

It is difficult to understand how people could satisfy this constraint in the case of popular delusions. Such beliefs seem bafflingly and incorrigibly irrational because those who endorse them do *not* seem responsive to reason (see Chapter 2). To quote Sperber's characterisation again (see Chapter 3, Section 2), popular delusions "do not appear irrational by slightly departing from common sense, or timidly going beyond what the evidence allows. They appear, rather, *like down-right provocations against common sense rationality*" (Sperber, 1985, p.85, emphasis added). It is difficult to see how subtle psychological biases in how individuals handle and evaluate information could produce such provocations.

In this final chapter of Part 2, we will propose a solution to this puzzle that rests on the group dynamics and social incentives implicated in popular delusions. We will argue that such social forces generate and sustain forms of collective epistemic irrationality that cannot be understood simply as an aggregation of individual psychological biases and that would be impossible for even highly motivated individuals to achieve on their own.

The idea that motivated irrationality is often a collective project is not original. For example, in their classic study of how a UFO religion reacted when their prediction of imminent apocalypse was falsified, Leon Festinger, Henry Riecken, and Stanley Schachter document the necessity of social scaffolding for strong forms of motivated irrationality:

> The individual believer must have social support. It is unlikely that one isolated believer could withstand the kind of disconfirming evidence we have specified. If, however, the believer is a member of a group of convinced persons who can support one another, we would expect the belief to be maintained... (Festinger et al., 1956, p.21)

More generally, much research in social psychology and the social sciences has documented how group dynamics can foster and sustain powerful forms of ignorance and misbelief (Janis, 1982; Kuran, 1997; Noelle-Neumann, 1974; Sunstein, 2019). This chapter builds on these and other bodies of work to outline a general framework for understanding the social scaffolding of popular delusions. Just as human epistemic success is overwhelmingly a collective achievement rooted in incentive structures of norms, reputations, and status competition (see Chapter 1, Section 4), the motivated forms of epistemic failure found in popular delusions cannot be understood without situating motivated cognition in distinctive social practices governing communication and the division of cognitive labour. These social forces, we will argue, emerge whenever communities of co-believers are motivated to propagate beliefs or adopt them for social signalling reasons. For this reason, our framework illuminates a general pattern in how collective irrationalities are socially scaffolded that recurs across otherwise very different contexts.

We will structure the chapter as follows. Section 2 revisits our discussion of epistemic cooperation from Chapter 1 and identifies conditions necessary for such cooperation to produce and transmit reliable information. Section 3 details several reasons why these conditions break down in the case of popular delusions, which are rooted in epistemic reward systems that function to promote and protect inaccurate beliefs. Section 4 describes and illustrates the consequences of this process on the suppression, amplification, and creation of specific forms of evidence. Section 5 then summarises the overall social framework we have developed in this part of the book and explains how it illuminates the five puzzling features of popular delusions introduced in Chapter 3.

2. Epistemic Cooperation

As detailed extensively in Chapters 1 and 2, human beings are epistemically interdependent. We rely on a division of cognitive labour and extensive information sharing. As with all sharing, information sharing is a form of cooperation. Like most cooperation, it is scaffolded by an incentive structure—a system of social rewards and punishments—that encourages the transmission of useful information and discourages the transmission of useless or harmful information (Boyer, 2018; Dessalles, 2007; Karabegovic et al., 2024; Mercier, 2020; Williams, 2022a). These rewards and punishments can be direct. For example, people are grateful towards those who share useful information with them and angry at liars. However, as with almost all forms of cooperation, epistemic collaboration also depends on social-epistemic norms, social monitoring, reputations, and gossip networks that relay information about people's adherence to these norms (see Chapter 1, Section 4.3). For example, in most epistemic communities, there are social norms against lying, bullshitting, and spreading unfounded gossip or rumours, with the harshness of punishments (which are often merely reputational) proportional to the perceived harms caused by the transgression. Similarly, people who are believed to share honest, accurate, and helpful information are rewarded with deference, respect, and a good reputation.

Importantly, this epistemic cooperation regulates more than just communication. Just as people often compete for prestige-based social status through acts of self-sacrificial altruism (see Chapter 1, Section 5), epistemic communities often incentivise cognitive labour—that is, processes in which people sacrifice time, energy, and resources to generate or acquire novel information, ideas, and so on—by bestowing status on those who produce and share socially valued information (Storr, 2021; Williams, 2022b).

This process is institutionalised in modern science, where scientists are driven to engage in extensive and costly cognitive labour through a "credit economy" in which novel discoveries are rewarded with social recognition (Merton, 1957). However, the more general practice of conferring status on those who sacrifice their time and energy to produce novel, socially valued information is a widespread feature of human social practices. One finds it within online software communities, in which developers who contribute useful code or solve bugs gain community status; among journalists, writers, and public intellectuals who win attention and prestige by writing articles and books that audiences value; among social media influencers on platforms like YouTube, TikTok, or Instagram, who build followers and achieve social recognition by generating videos or posts that attract audiences; and even within small-scale, foraging communities, within which individuals can achieve status by sharing novel ecological, medicinal, social, or ritual knowledge (Acerbi, 2019; Mercier, 2022). Interestingly, some theorists even speculate that one of the reasons prestige hierarchies evolved in our lineage (see Chapter 1, Section 5.1.2) was to provide a form of "payment" that individuals could offer to access other people's knowledge (Henrich & Gil-White, 2001).

These incentive structures governing human communication and the division of cognitive labour can be considered *epistemic reward systems*, systems of social rewards and punishments that coordinate and incentivise the production and transmission of socially valued information (Williams, 2022a, 2023a). In line with the primary world-mapping function of most beliefs, such reward systems usually support the production and transmission of reliable information that individuals can use to acquire accurate beliefs. Nevertheless, this outcome is not inevitable. It depends on the specific behaviours an epistemic reward system incentivises. If a given reward system encourages community members to share unreliable information or punishes them for sharing reliable information, it will facilitate the creation and spread of false or misleading ideas, evidence, and arguments.

Given this, we can ask: Under what conditions do epistemic reward systems promote the production and sharing of accurate information—or, more precisely, reliable information conducive to forming accurate beliefs? (As we will return to below in Section 4.1, accurate information can sometimes function to rationalise inaccurate beliefs when it is cherry-picked or unrepresentative of reality.) There is no single answer to this question. For example, modern science's ability to generate intellectual discoveries depends on a wide range of complex institutions, norms, and social practices (Longino, 1990). Nevertheless, two minimal conditions are plausibly necessary irrespective of context.

First, participants in the epistemic community must seek out accurate information. Because epistemic reward systems coordinate the production and transmission of socially valued information, they will produce reliable information only if people value it.[1] This is not trivial. People can have many reasons for valuing information independent of its likely truth or evidential support. For example, audiences might reward those who share information not (or not only) because it helps them form accurate beliefs, but because it is entertaining, titillating, agreeable, or because it promotes their interests in some way.

Relatedly, social-epistemic norms or other mechanisms must prevent people from poisoning the epistemic commons either by communicating or encouraging the communication of unreliable information or by discouraging the communication of reliable information. For example, they must impose social costs on liars, propagandists, and disinformation campaigns strong enough to disincentivise such behaviours. They must also discourage people from pressuring others to suppress reliable information. That is, they must prevent people from imposing social pressures that discourage the transmission of reliable information.

We will now explain why both conditions break down in the case of popular delusions. When communities are motivated to propagate beliefs or endorse them for social signalling reasons, they value information not for its *epistemic*

[1] Not everybody, or even most people, in the community must seek reliable information. In science, for example, individual scientists have many goals independent of (and sometimes in conflict with) truth, such as status (Longino, 1990; Merton, 1957). However, the system is designed in such a way to channel such motives into the generation of knowledge, a fact that is ultimately rooted in the desire for science to produce reliable information.

value but for its rationalising function. As a result, they tend to coordinate in ways that generate and sustain motivated forms of ignorance and misbelief.

3. Coordinating Epistemic Failure

As described in Chapter 3, popular delusions are often sustained by intense social pressures on communication. For example, they are frequently treated, either implicitly or explicitly, as orthodoxies within the communities that endorse them, such that those who disagree with or dissent from the beliefs are socially punished in various ways, ranging from coordinated reputational punishment to ostracism or even violence (Kuran, 1997; Marie & Petersen, 2023; Sunstein, 2019). Relatedly, those who endorse popular delusions often seem to exhibit "active belief", sacrificing time, energy, and other things in the service of evangelising, enforcing commitment to the beliefs, and uncovering and sharing novel justifications for them (Storr, 2021; Williams, 2022a).

To understand such social dynamics, one must attend to two features of popular delusions: the widely distributed motivations driving motivated cognition (Section 3.1) and the distinctive role of propagandistic and signalling motivations (Section 3.2). We will first describe how such motives give rise to delusion-promoting epistemic reward systems before describing and illustrating the consequences of such reward systems in Section 4.

3.1 Distributed Motivated Cognition

When motives to embrace specific conclusions are widespread within a community, this produces an incentive structure that discourages communication that challenges such conclusions and encourages communication that supports them.

The first step in understanding this process is to note that motivated cognition is rooted in emotional (and, more broadly, affective) reactions to information (Williams, 2023a). If an individual is motivated to propagate or endorse a belief, encountering evidence that confirms the belief or arguments that justify it will be rewarding—it will elicit positive emotional reactions—whereas encountering disconfirming evidence or persuasive contrary arguments will elicit aversive emotions such as anxiety, frustration, or anger. In this way, motivated cognition involves what Westen and colleagues call "a form of implicit emotion regulation in which the brain converges on solutions that minimize negative and maximize positive affect states associated with threat to or attainment of motives" (Westen et al., 2006, p.1947).

This emotional profile is not unique to motivated cognition. It arises whenever people encounter circumstances that promote or hinder their motivations (Del Giudice, 2018). The distinctive feature of motivated cognition is simply that the "circumstances" are evidential: motives to spread or adopt a belief shape how people seek out, avoid, and respond to evidence in ways that confirm desired conclusions and insulate them from challenges. Importantly, this process is complicated when people are motivated to spread or adopt distressing conclusions, as with many popular delusions (see Chapter 4, Sections 3 and 4). In such cases, people will respond negatively to evidence in tension with beliefs that produce negative emotions. For example, somebody strongly motivated to embrace a distressing conspiracy theory that posits powerful, malevolent, and conspiring elites will likely respond with distress (e.g., anger or frustration) to evidence that challenges the theory. However, this two-tier emotional profile is not unique to such cases. It occurs whenever people are motivated to achieve something that will produce negative emotional consequences. If someone is motivated to engage in high-risk sports or watch a terrifying horror film that will generate negative feelings of fear and stress, they will also react negatively to circumstances that prevent them from achieving their goal.

The next step toward understanding how motivated cognition becomes socially scaffolded is to note that other people are a source of evidence—in many contexts, our most important source (see Chapter 1). Not only can people inform us directly about the state of the world, but we also engage in "social referencing", treating what other people believe as a source of higher-order evidence concerning what is true (Levy, 2021; see Chapter 3, Section 3.1). Given this, when people are motivated to embrace specific conclusions, others become a source of positive or negative emotions depending on whether their communication supports or challenges such conclusions. For example, if I am motivated to endorse an identity-defining religious or ideological belief, I will react negatively to people who share evidence or arguments that contradict or disconfirm the belief (Rauch, 2021). In this way, motivated cognition shapes how we respond to and interact with others. It can even influence which individuals we want to spend time with and avoid (Ruddick, 1988).

Of course, because people are strongly motivated to win social approval, they will sometimes adjust their behaviour in response to a motivated believer's reactions to information. For example, one might be careful not to upset or distress someone by challenging a belief they are emotionally attached to, or try to win favour with someone by encouraging their self-deception. (Think of a sycophant who tries to win a boss's favour by indulging their self-aggrandisement.) Nevertheless, in cases where motivated cognition is a purely individual project, and the individual involved is not especially influential, these social pressures are unlikely to be very strong. Moreover, we often have good reasons to correct other people's motivated irrationality, such as when we are motivated to adopt alternative conclusions, when their inaccurate beliefs might negatively affect us, or when we think they would benefit from holding more accurate beliefs. As Rorty (1994) observes, friends, family members, and spouses often constrain one another's motivated irrationality for these and more reasons.

Popular delusions are different. In cases of such collective irrationalities, powerful motives to propagate or endorse beliefs are not specific to any single individual. Such delusions are *popular* because the relevant motives are widespread. For example, as we documented in Chapter 4, it is not just individuals but communities of co-believers who are motivated to spread demonising narratives, self-serving ideologies, and beliefs about supernatural punishment. The same is true of beliefs that communities are motivated to adopt to signal group allegiances and tendencies to cooperate.

This has an important consequence. When motives to adopt specific conclusions are widespread—when motivated cognition is distributed among community members—emotional reactions to confirming and disconfirming evidence also become widespread. Given this, people's communicative behaviour will affect how they are viewed and treated by entire communities, not just individuals. For this reason, the motivated cognition that underlies popular delusions generates a system of *social* rewards and punishments (i.e., *de facto* social norms), encouraging the communication of information that confirms preferred conclusions and discouraging the communication of information that challenges them (Williams, 2022a, 2023a). Of course, for complete outsiders, this need not influence their behaviour. However, for anybody inside or affected by the community who depends on being viewed favourably and cultivating a good reputation within it, this system of social rewards and punishments will inevitably influence what and how they communicate. As we will return to in Section 4, such communicative adjustment, in turn, has profound consequences for the forms of motivated irrationality that individuals can sustain.

This process constitutes our first explanation of how motivated cognition becomes socially scaffolded in popular delusions. Importantly, this scaffolding will emerge whenever communities are motivated to reach specific conclusions. Therefore, the fact that motivated cognition in popular delusions is driven—as we argued in Chapter 4—by propagandistic cognition or social signalling is incidental. One would also expect to see these dynamics if the motives involved were purely individualistic and inward-looking, as many philosophers and psychologists assume they are (see Chapter 3, Section 4.2).

3.2 The Role of Propaganda and Signalling

Although any distributed motives underlying motivated cognition will generate the social forces we have described, the role of propagandistic and social-signalling motivations in popular delusions typically motivates additional behaviours. In fact, merely appealing to the social pressures and communicative adjustment just described struggles to explain the explosive energy that often characterises popular delusions, including intense evangelising, fanaticism, and the purposeful enforcement of shared beliefs through the punishment of dissenters, heretics, and apostates, ranging from verbal, reputational attacks to ostracism and even murder (Loury, 1994; Noelle-Neumann, 1974; Storr, 2021). Such "active belief" is puzzling (see Chapter 3, Section 3.5). Even if people are strongly motivated to believe something and are disposed to react negatively to challenges against it, what motivates such additional behaviours?

The propagandistic motivations that underlie many popular delusions provide one part of the answer. If people are motivated to spread a specific belief, such as a demonising narrative, system-justifying ideology, or belief in supernatural punishment (see Chapter 4, Section 3), they will also be motivated to enforce commitment to the belief and impose costs on those who challenge it if they have the power to do so. However, in most cases of merely individual-level propagandistic cognition, such as when people are motivated to spread self-serving or self-justifying beliefs, they lack such power. Popular delusions rooted in propagandistic motives are very different. When whole communities share propagandistic motives, their power to spread and enforce preferred conclusions is much greater. Moreover, they can incentivise group members to engage in behaviours characteristic of active belief through the same reward systems that incentivise other forms of group-based cooperation (see Chapter 1, Sections 3 and 5). That is, just as individuals who make sacrifices to enforce group norms and promote group interests are often rewarded with greater trust and better reputations within the group, fanatics who devote themselves to propagating and enforcing popular delusions are often rewarded with—and hence motivated by—reputational and status rewards among those motivated to spread the same beliefs (Atran & Ginges, 2012; Boyd, 2017; Ridgeway, 2019; Storr, 2021).

This is a common pattern within tight-knit religious, conspiratorial, and ideological groups (Storr, 2021). In such cases, fanatics—active believers—can be thought of as epistemic enforcers and warriors: just as groups reward members who enforce group norms and make sacrifices to promote group goals, those who make sacrifices to spread and enforce propagandistic beliefs win social rewards among those who share the same propagandistic motives (Williams, 2022a)

A similar dynamic emerges from social signalling motives. As we documented in Chapter 4, many popular delusions are plausibly rooted in motives to signal group identity, allegiance, and conformity to moral norms. In such cases, active belief is likely motivated by a desire to demonstrate sincere commitment to those beliefs. That is, through costly sacrifices involved in evangelism, the punishment of dissenters, and general fanaticism, active believers credibly signal their sincere endorsement of the relevant beliefs and, hence, their possession of the traits that sincere belief reveals, such as ingroup commitment and cooperative tendencies.

For example, if someone wants to win social trust and inclusion within a sect or cult organised around identity-defining convictions, then making visible sacrifices to express, spread, and enforce those convictions sends an unambiguous signal of their commitment to the group. This appears to be a common pattern underlying the collective punishment of heretics (Pinker, 2011; Storr, 2021). Once endorsement of beliefs or norms signals commitment to a coalition, it becomes important for individuals who depend on the coalition's acceptance and approval to prove that their public endorsement is sincere. Given this, even those who do not privately endorse the relevant beliefs can become motivated to punish dissenters and heretics (Willer et al., 2009). Similarly, in religious contexts, active belief can play the same role as costly religious rituals (see Chapter 4, Section 4). Just as participation in such group rituals can signal sincere commitment to underlying religious beliefs, which are often believed to be cooperation-inducing, so can the costly behaviours associated with active belief.

In these ways, propagandistic and signalling motivations create additional pathways for belief-supporting social incentives to emerge. Moreover, as we noted in Chapter 4, Section 4.3, many popular delusions are likely fuelled by both propagandistic and social signalling motives. For example, when it comes to widespread, cross-cultural beliefs in supernatural punishment, people are motivated both to propagate such beliefs to encourage others to cooperate and to endorse them to signal their own cooperative motivations (Fitouchi & Singh, 2022). This combination plausibly explains why such belief systems are so frequently associated with intense fanaticism, collective punishment of dissenters and heretics, and evangelism.

3.3 Interim Summary

For epistemic reward systems to facilitate the production and transmission of reliable information, audiences must value reliable information, and people must be prevented from poisoning the epistemic commons. Both conditions break down in the case of popular delusions. Widespread motives to embrace specific conclusions encourage communication that supports them and discourage communication that challenges them. Propagandistic and social-signalling motivations then often strengthen such incentives and drive additional behaviours characteristic of active belief. The consequence is epistemic reward systems that function not to promote shared knowledge but to generate and protect shared delusions.

Before identifying and illustrating the consequences of such reward systems, it is important to clarify people's awareness of them. In many cases, people deliberately encourage and discourage communication in ways designed to protect certain beliefs or narratives, and they understand the function of their behaviour. For example, in totalitarian and authoritarian regimes, leaders are likely aware of both the consequences and aims of censorship and other pressures on speech. Nevertheless, individuals will lack such awareness in many communities that embrace popular delusions (Williams, 2023a).

First, as Stanley Cohen (2001, p.45) observes, the social pressures underlying collective forms of denial and self-deception are frequently reflexive, discouraging their acknowledgement. Given this, even when social pressures discourage people from challenging preferred conclusions, people are also discouraged from acknowledging such pressures.

Second, even when social pressures on communication are acknowledged, their origin in motives to propagate beliefs or embrace them for signalling reasons will not be acknowledged. Much psychological research documents that people are often ignorant of the causes of their behaviours and emotional reactions, leading to *post hoc* rationalisations designed for reputation management rather than accuracy (Carruthers, 2011; Mercier & Sperber, 2017; see Chapter 1, Section 3.3). For this reason, communities endorsing shared delusions typically converge on inaccurate understandings of the social pressures that support them. For example, they might rationalise such social pressures as serving social harmony, justice, God's wishes, or truth (Cohen, 2001; Kuran, 1997; Mill, 1869 [1859]).

4. Consequences and Illustrations

The epistemic reward systems associated with popular delusions incentivise forms of communication and cognitive labour that promote, protect, and justify them. This occurs through three primary pathways: by influencing which features of the world people attend to and ignore, by affecting the distribution of social, higher-order evidence people are exposed to, and by encouraging forms of cognitive labour intended to rationalise specific beliefs. We will first describe these consequences (Section 4.1) before offering two brief illustrations of them (Section 4.2).

4.1 Consequences

First, the most obvious effect of the epistemic reward systems described in Section 3 concerns the skewed information people are exposed to about the world. As psychologists, social scientists, and philosophers have long documented, social pressures on communication and the self-censorship they create systematically "distort, corrupt, and impoverish the knowledge in the public domain" (Kuran, 1997, p.155; see also Mill, 1869 [1859]; Noelle-Neumann, 1974; Janis, 1982; Sunstein, 2019). Given this, communities motivated to spread specific beliefs or embrace them for social-signalling reasons are typically shielded from aspects of the world that are in tension with them. Similarly, because people are socially rewarded for drawing attention to evidence that confirms such beliefs, the communities are also disproportionately exposed to features of the world that support their preferred conclusions. In consequence, whereas the task of confirming desired beliefs and shielding them from disconfirmation falls on the individual in individual cases of motivated cognition, this task is effectively outsourced to broader social pressures and incentives in the case of popular delusions. Describing this dynamic, Timur Kuran writes:

> The holder of a publicly unquestioned belief faces no reminder of its weaknesses. He finds public discourse to be loaded with facts and arguments

> consistent with his belief. By contrast, the holder of a belief at odds with public discourse is routinely reminded of the flaws in his thinking. He feels pressured, therefore, to revise his beliefs. If nothing else, he finds himself gripped by doubt and confusion. (Kuran, 1997, p.179)

Second, other people do not just draw our attention to features of the world. We also engage in "social referencing", treating other people's beliefs as evidence—specifically, higher-order evidence—about what is true, especially when such people are trusted fellow group members (Levy, 2021). Given this, the epistemic reward systems associated with popular delusions also shape the distribution of higher-order *social* evidence, which becomes systematically skewed towards confirming such delusions. For example, when motivated rumours build momentum, information and arguments that support them are eagerly shared, while those that challenge them are discouraged (Boyer, 2018). In addition to influencing which features of the world people attend to and ignore, the appearance of widespread community endorsement provides additional evidence—often called "social proof"—for the rumours, lending them much greater subjective plausibility. A similar dynamic plays out in many other popular delusions, ranging from the extreme social pressures on group members to avoid any public doubts or criticism of identity-defining beliefs to how beliefs that rationalise systems of domination are often associated with rewards for those who affirm the beliefs and punishments for those who challenge or dissent from them (see Marx & Engels, 1970 [1845–1846]; Mills, 2017; Sidanius & Pratto, 2001).

The kinds of behaviours associated with active belief greatly exacerbate this dynamic. Active believers—for example, those who eagerly enforce commitment to specific beliefs, evangelise, and exhibit other behaviours associated with fanaticism—do not just exert further pressures on other people's communication. Social referencing is modulated by confidence (see Mercier, 2020). All else being equal, we are more influenced by more confident people. By revealing extreme confidence (and in some cases certainty) in their convictions, active believers therefore provide robust higher-order evidence for those convictions among community members. As Henrich (2009) observes, this is a general pattern in many religious communities, where the costly sacrifices made by fanatics lend credibility to their beliefs among people who might otherwise be sceptical.

Finally, the epistemic reward systems associated with popular delusions do not just influence how people communicate (or avoid communicating) their pre-existing thoughts, ideas, or beliefs. As with epistemic cooperation more broadly (see Section 2), they also incentivise forms of cognitive labour in which individuals invest time, energy, and ingenuity into producing novel ideas and information. Specifically, popular delusions tend to be associated with a *marketplace of rationalisations* (Williams, 2022b), a kind of informational economy in which individuals can win social rewards by devoting themselves to producing novel information—ideas, evidence, arguments, and so on—designed for rationalising the beliefs a community is motivated to propagate or enforce.

The logic underlying rationalisation markets is simple. First, when individuals are motivated to propagate or embrace a specific conclusion, they are motivated to rationalise it. In standard theories of motivated cognition, it is assumed that this task of producing rationalisations falls on individuals motivated to reach the relevant conclusions. However, with popular delusions, motives to propagate or embrace a predetermined belief are widespread. The result is a widespread "demand" for rationalisations. Given this, individuals can win attention and status by devoting their ingenuity, time, and energy to satisfying this demand. As with all markets, the resultant marketplace of rationalisations should be viewed through the lens of competition: communities motivated to spread beliefs or embrace them for social signalling reasons will search for the highest-quality rationalisations, which incentivises competition among "rationalisation producers" to win attention and status by producing and sharing the highest-quality rationalisations possible.

Rationalisations can take many forms, including novel evidence, structured arguments, connections between preferred conclusions and existing bodies of knowledge, and theories that support such conclusions. The only constraint is that the relevant information can be used to justify the belief in question. That is, to qualify as a rationalisation, communicated content must provide a genuine epistemic justification of a given belief or system of beliefs, at least among those motivated to embrace them. Importantly, outright fabrications or misinformation can rarely satisfy this constraint.

An analogy with lawyers or public relations teams helps to illuminate this situation. Such professionals rarely just invent outright falsehoods or present bald-faced lies. Instead, they are skilled at uncovering, selecting, framing, and interpreting information—typically accurate information—in ways that rationalise the predetermined conclusion they are paid to justify (e.g., "my client is innocent") (Haidt, 2013). The same is typically true of those who succeed in rationalisation markets. For example, highly partisan pundits and media outlets almost never fabricate content. Instead, they select, omit, frame, interpret, and comment on accurate information in ways designed to support partisan narratives (Williams, 2022b). Moreover, because the goal of rationalisation producers is to justify preferred beliefs, they often devote themselves not just to rationalising such beliefs directly but to addressing counter-evidence and challenges—"epistemic threats"—to the relevant beliefs and to finding ways to discredit those who disseminate such evidence and challenges (Williams, 2022a).

4.2 Illustrations

So far, the discussion has been highly abstract. This is purposeful. In describing how popular delusions are socially scaffolded, we have aimed to describe an abstract pattern in how collective forms of motivated irrationality become socially scaffolded. If our analysis is correct, this pattern is not unique to specific examples of collective irrationality; instead, it will recur across otherwise extremely diverse contexts. To illustrate this, we will briefly focus on how the epistemic reward system we have characterised manifests in the case of two very different popular delusions: what Charles Mills (2017) calls "the white delusion of racial superiority" and what an article in *The New York Times* has recently called "the QAnon delusion" (Edsall, 2021).

4.2.1 The White Delusion of Racial Superiority

First, Mills (2017) has famously analysed the social forces underlying what he calls "white ignorance", which can roughly be understood as systems of false beliefs and ignorance that have historically functioned to support and legitimise white supremacist forms of social organisation (see also Gould, 1996; Kendi, 2016). In our social framework, the motives driving such belief systems are primarily propagandistic, rooted in the interests of a coalition (groups who have historically identified as "white") to spread claims and narratives that promote their interests and support an exploitative, hierarchical social system from which they benefit (see Chapter 4, Section 3.3). However, social signalling also plausibly plays a role, with a commitment to racist beliefs and narratives functioning as signals of identity and allegiance to dominant racial groups.

In line with our arguments in this chapter, Mills suggests that white ignorance manifests a form of "structural group-based miscognition" (Mills, 2007, p.49), a form of motivated collective-epistemic dysfunction that cannot be understood merely as an aggregation of individual-level epistemic failures. In this social system, "evasion and self-deception become the epistemic norm" (Mills 1997, p.97), involving ignorance that "resists... that fights back [...], [that] is militant, aggressive, not to be intimidated [...] presenting itself unblushingly as knowledge" (Mills 2007, p.49). Whereas research on motivated irrationality and self-deception has traditionally been "located within an individualistic framework", Mills' work seeks to "extrapolate some of this literature to a social context", identifying how "interests may shape cognition" in ways that go far beyond in-the-head psychological biases, influencing "what we and society choose to remember, whose testimony is solicited and whose is not, and which facts and frameworks are sought out and accepted" (Mills, 2007, pp.69–72).

There are many nuances and insights in Mills' (1997, 2007) work that go beyond our analysis in this chapter, not least because there are many features of white ignorance that are specific to the extremely deep-rooted, long-lasting system of white supremacy he analyses. Nevertheless, several aspects of his analysis can also be understood in terms of the social framework we have outlined (see Williams 2023a). For example, characterising social pressures on communication, Mills observes how "testimony about white atrocities—lynchings, police killings, race riots—would often have to be passed down through segregated information channels, black to black, *too explosive to be allowed exposure to white cognition*" (Mills, 2007, p.68, emphasis added). Similarly, he also quotes a woman describing her experience of racial apartheid: "My problems started when I began to comment on what I saw... I insisted on being accurate. *But the world I was born into didn't want that*" (Mills, 2007, p.68, emphasis added; quote from Litwack, 1998, p.34). Here, one clearly sees a dysfunctional epistemic reward system in play, one that discourages and punishes any threats to preferred beliefs.

As others have done (e.g., Gould, 1996; Kendi, 2016), Mills (1997, 2007) also documents how much intellectual labour has historically been invested in rationalising white superiority. Focusing on attempts to justify the cognitive superiority of white people, for example, he documents the evolution and elaboration of sophisticated religious, pseudo-scientific, and historical theories, "the feature putatively correlated with intelligence varying, but *the desired outcome of confirming nonwhite intellectual inferiority always achieved*" (Mills, 1997, p.60, emphasis added). According to Mills, it is through social forces that "the white delusion of racial superiority inoculates itself against refutation" (Mills, 2007, p.55).

4.2.2 The QAnon Delusion

For a radically different example of how epistemic reward systems emerge from distributed motivated cognition, consider the American conspiracy theory, "QAnon", which we introduced in our introductory chapter (Marwick

& Partin, 2022; Wendling, 2020). Centred on claims made by an anonymous individual named "Q" on an online message board, QAnon emerged during Donald Trump's first presidency. Although the content of the conspiracy theory has evolved (and continues to evolve) over time, its defining conviction is that the world contains an elite cabal of Satan-worshipping, cannibalistic paedophiles operating a global child sex trafficking ring. Claiming to be a high-level government official, Q publishes cryptic evidence for this conspiracy on fringe online message boards, as well as suggestions that Trump will eventually expose it.

There is continuing controversy both over how many people endorse QAnon and what characteristics such supporters have (see Enders et al., 2022). Nevertheless, numerous scholars and observers have documented its "cult-like" character, including the degree to which the theory's core convictions are treated as orthodoxies among a relatively cohesive (primarily online) community that endorses it, and the energy invested into signalling commitment to the conspiracy theory, evangelising on its behalf, and engaging in coordinated punishment of dissenters and heretics (Conner & MacMurray, 2022; DiResta, 2024; Edsall, 2021; Marwick & Partin, 2022). As we argued in Chapter 4, support for the theory is likely rooted in propagandistic motives to spread a demonising narrative (targeting left-wing elites and establishment institutions despised by its proponents), as well as motivations to signal a commitment to the community of like-minded individuals motivated to spread it (see Chapter 4, Section 3.1). Indeed, the strong community dimension underlying support for the conspiracy theory is reflected in one of its most popular slogans: "WWG1WGA!" ("Where we go one, we go all") (Wendling, 2020; Williams, 2022a).

Interestingly, the QAnon community also supports a highly active, competitive marketplace of rationalisations. Drawing on qualitative fieldwork documenting the online dynamics within a community of believers, Marwick and Partin document how such believers participate in a "collective, knowledge-making activity... designed to construct specific facts and theories that maintain QAnon's cohesion over time" (Marwick & Partin, 2022, p.2535). Specifically, the community rewards and encourages cognitive labour designed to rationalise the conspiracy theory and insulate it from contrary evidence and objections. Its members "work together to construct 'proofs'":

> A "proof" is a document that decodes Q's obscure and vague posts, known as "drops", and links them to real-world events that happen days, months,

> or even years before or after. To Q devotees, these linkages prove that Q is who they claim to be… They are used to refute claims that the Q conspiracy is counter-evidentiary and to demonstrate the accuracy of Q's predictions to both insiders and outsiders. (Marwick & Partin, 2022, p.2542)

Against a popular and journalistic consensus depicting the QAnon community as passive, "gullible dupes", Marwick and Partin (2022) document how much intense energy is invested by members into actively participating in the community and sustaining its defining convictions. Specifically, influential QAnon participants called "Bakers" or "Anons", who can be viewed as rationalisation producers within our framework, draw "upon the participatory affordances of the social web to collectively construct knowledge that maintains the social and political cohesion of the conspiracy across time" (Marwick & Partin, 2022, p.2536). Such practices, they write, "produce, legitimize and make rational what might otherwise seem counterfactual" (ibid, p.2551).

5. Summary of Part 2

Chapter 3 introduced the functional delusions puzzle, which asks why groups of otherwise healthy, rational individuals embrace beliefs that strike outsiders as highly epistemically irrational. More specifically, we argued that any solution to this puzzle must explain five characteristics that tend to co-occur in popular delusions: the unusual epistemic irrationality of group beliefs, the selectivity of this irrationality, the mental compartmentalisation of the beliefs, the believers' attachment to them, and the epistemically dysfunctional social practices and dynamics that sustain them. We argued that although individualistic explanatory paradigms for understanding popular delusions offer various insights, they cannot solve the functional delusions puzzle.

To overcome these limitations, Chapters 4 and 5 have outlined a social framework for understanding popular delusions. This framework is rooted in the general picture of human beings that we introduced and defended in Chapter 1, in which human minds are fundamentally social minds adapted to complex social environments characterised by cooperation, culture, and competition. In the framework we have developed, popular delusions arise from fundamental motivations to influence others through propaganda or signalling, and from complex forms of social coordination and scaffolding that promote, protect, and rationalise such delusions.

This framework is necessarily schematic. It aims to identify very general social factors and the interactions among them that recur across various contexts. This breadth of coverage inevitably means a sacrifice of explanatory depth (see our Introductory chapter). To understand specific popular delusions, a wealth of idiosyncratic social, cultural, historical, and institutional factors will no doubt be relevant. For example, as we noted in Chapter 4, Section 3.4, something like the Satanic panic cannot be understood outside of the context of specific cultural and historical circumstances that characterised America (and, more broadly, the Western world) in the 1980s. Moreover, much more could and should be said about propagandistic cognition, the role of social signalling in beliefs, and the social scaffolding of popular delusions, both in clarification and defence. Nevertheless, we have aimed to introduce and defend an integrative, empirically well-informed, high-level social framework for understanding popular delusions and the recurrent patterns they exhibit, and we hope that this framework will spur future developments, elaborations, and critiques.

We will conclude this part of the book by returning more systematically to the five characteristics of popular delusions detailed in Chapter 3.

5.1 Epistemic Irrationality

Any explanation of popular delusions must address the high degree of epistemic irrationality they seem to exhibit. One part of our explanation points to the roots of popular delusions in non-epistemic, social goals of propaganda and signalling. Because such beliefs are driven by socially motivated cognition, it is unsurprising that they involve systematic departures from ideals of epistemic rationality. However, an equally important part of our explanation concerns how popular delusions are socially scaffolded and incentivised by epistemic reward systems that function to promote, protect, and rationalise them. It is due to this social support that those who endorse popular delusions can sustain forms of ignorance and misbelief that would fall beyond the reach of merely individual forms of motivated irrationality. For this reason, our framework explains not just the epistemic irrationality of popular delusions but the unusual and frequently baffling degree of irrationality they appear to exhibit to outsiders.

In Chapter 3, we noted that some psychologists and philosophers have argued that popular delusions that *appear* epistemically irrational to outsiders are rational responses to misleading, higher-order evidence (e.g., Levy, 2021).

If the framework that we have outlined is correct, this analysis is mistaken. Nevertheless, the role of social scaffolding in popular delusions suggests it contains an important insight. The epistemic reward systems detailed in this chapter ensure that communities motivated to spread beliefs or embrace them for social-signalling reasons are exposed to very different forms of evidence from those outside the relevant communities. As a result, even though motivated irrationality still plays a vital role in driving individual-level cognitive biases and generating the relevant reward systems, there is an important sense in which delusions are less epistemically irrational for those who endorse them than they appear to outsiders (see Williams 2023a). That is, although such beliefs might appear extremely irrational to outsiders, and those who endorse them might seem like rational lost causes, they will seem epistemically rational to believers. In this way, our framework accommodates both the intuition that popular delusions are bafflingly and incorrigibly irrational—that they constitute collective outbreaks of madness—and the insight that those who endorse them are exposed to skewed, misleading evidence. We will return to this nuance of our framework in our concluding chapter.

5.2 Selectivity

Because the framework we have detailed posits motivated cognition, it can also address the selective epistemic irrationality exhibited in popular delusions. As we noted in Chapter 3, a virtue of motivational explanations is that they can explain why epistemic irrationality is often highly targeted toward specific conclusions. If our framework is correct that popular delusions have roots in specific propagandistic or signalling motivations, nothing is puzzling about why communities that embrace popular delusions can keep track of reality on topics distinct from their delusions. Their goal is to form accurate beliefs on such topics, not propagate or embrace predetermined conclusions.

5.3 Compartmentalisation

The connection to compartmentalisation requires more explanation. As we argued in Chapter 3, popular delusions often seem to involve strange forms of mental compartmentalisation: although people frequently seem sincere in embracing such delusions—indeed, they sometimes seem fanatical—they often do not seem to integrate such delusions into their thoughts and actions in ways that one would expect if they fully internalised them. For example, people often seem to maintain an implicit awareness of the unfoundedness of the relevant beliefs, and they act in ways that would seem strange if the beliefs were true. Conspiracy theorists who believe in an all-powerful deep state hold open, well-advertised meetings in public halls; devout religious believers profess a belief in hell but then act in ways that by their own lights would bring eternal damnation; those levelling accusations of extreme witchcraft often accept strangely lenient punishments if the target confesses and accepts their subordinate role; and so on. For these reasons, some theorists have argued that popular delusions do not really involve beliefs or perhaps involve a distinct kind of belief (Mercier, 2020; Sperber, 1997; Van Leeuwen, 2014).

Our primary explanation of this feature of popular delusions once again draws on their motivational character. As has long been noted, motivated irrationality is often strangely compartmentalised and plausibly *must be* at least partly compartmentalised. Without at least an implicit awareness of the truth and ability to track reality, motivated believers would be unable to shape how they seek out, interpret, and process information in ways conducive to justifying and protecting favoured conclusions (Funkhouser, 2019). In this way, the beliefs that people sincerely profess in cases of popular delusions sit atop cognitive mechanisms that are—and plausibly must be—fundamentally reality-oriented.

More generally, it would be highly maladaptive for cognitive systems to treat beliefs rooted in social goals similarly to ordinary world-modelling beliefs. Because most beliefs function to help us navigate reality by tracking it accurately, their functional properties are specialised for this function. For example, sensitivity to evidence helps them track how things are, and automatic integration with the rest of our beliefs helps them guide our thoughts and actions whenever their contents are relevant (Van Leeuwen, 2023). The situation is very different with socially adaptive beliefs: because they emerge from social goals rather than attempts to model the world accurately, properties such as evidence-responsiveness and non-compartmentalisation would be maladaptive (Williams, 2021b). Given this, it is unsurprising that such beliefs do not just exhibit epistemic irrationality—they are less evidence-responsive than ordinary world-modelling beliefs—but are also more compartmentalised (Trivers, 2011; Williams, 2021a).

Nevertheless, more research is needed to understand this picture and the underlying psychology involved. For example, some philosophers and psychologists have sought to draw distinctions among different kinds of cognitive attitudes that are often lumped together under the general term "belief" (Bratman, 1992; Van Leeuwen, 2023; Mercier, 2020; Sperber, 1997). Moreover, some have applied such distinctions to argue that what we have called "socially adaptive beliefs" constitute a distinct kind of cognitive attitude (Van Leeuwen, 2023). Although we are sceptical of such proposals (Williams, 2021a, 2021b; for a parallel issue about clinical delusions, see Bortolotti, 2009; Bortolotti & Miyazono, 2015; Miyazono, 2018), working out the precise psychological details involved if the framework that we have developed is correct is an important task for future work.

5.4 Attachment

Because the framework that we have developed is rooted in a kind of motivated cognition, in which beliefs emerge from deeper motivations to spread claims or signal the believer's traits, it can explain people's puzzling attachment to popular delusions. In our framework, this attachment is ultimately to the desired outcomes such beliefs help bring about (e.g., encouraging cooperation or winning social approval), not the beliefs themselves. For this reason, it can explain people's attachment to beliefs they do not want to be true and might even feel distressed to believe, as is often the case with popular delusions (see Chapter 4, Section 2). Moreover, it can illuminate forms of attachment that go beyond motivated cognition, such as people's frequent identification with popular delusions in the case of beliefs that signal group identity, as well as the kinds of practices (e.g., fanaticism, evangelism, and orthodoxy enforcement) associated with "active belief".

5.5 Social Practices

As detailed in this chapter, our framework can also explain the social practices and dynamics implicated in popular delusions. As we have argued, the popularity of popular delusions turns motivated irrationality into a team project. Widespread motives to spread beliefs or embrace them for social signalling reasons create epistemic reward systems that transform shared misrepresentations into orthodoxies, orient communication towards the affirmation and confirmation of such orthodoxies, and reward individuals for rationalising, enforcing, and signalling commitment to them. The result is an incentive structure regulating communication and the division of cognitive labour in ways geared to generating and protecting what DiResta (2024) calls "bespoke realities".

Our overarching project in this book is to draw on the nature of human sociality to address various questions about delusions. In Part 1, we introduced a basic picture of human sociality (Chapter 1) and drew upon it to analyse social practices of delusion attribution (Chapter 2). Our account claims that delusion attribution typically functions to express folk-epistemic bafflement and flag that the believer in question is a rational lost cause. Given this, such attributional practices are not restricted to clinical cases, either in principle or in practice. In Part 2 (Chapters 3, 4, and 5), we have developed a high-level social framework for understanding the collective irrationalities that often trigger such attributions in non-clinical contexts. We have argued that such "popular delusions" are not mere cognitive mistakes. They are a kind of collective "achievement" that channels shared motivations into a self-reinforcing social reality, one cut off from reality and corrective testimony from outsiders.

In Part 3, we will turn to the third explanatory challenge we have set ourselves: understanding the clinical delusions that arise in contexts of mental illness and psychopathology. Unlike the popular delusions we have explored in Part 2, such beliefs are usually idiosyncratic, associated with significant social isolation and distress, and socially maladaptive. And they arise not from the functional operation of our psychology but in the context of dysfunction and distress. Nevertheless, we will argue that human sociality is still highly relevant for understanding the characteristics and causes of these beliefs, including their connection to social experiences like abuse and marginalisation, their predominant focus on social themes like persecution, status, and surveillance, and their strange resistance to social correction.

PART 3

6
Individualistic Accounts of Clinical Delusions

1. Introduction

In Part 3 (Chapters 6–9), we turn from popular delusions to clinical delusions, strange beliefs that occur in the context of a wide range of psychiatric and neurological conditions, including schizophrenia, delusional disorders, bipolar disorder, amnesia, dementia, drug abuse, and various forms of brain damage (American Psychiatric Association, 2013). Canonical examples of clinical delusions include the conviction that one's thoughts are being broadcast on television (thought broadcasting), that one is the target of organised persecution (persecutory delusions), that one's spouse has been replaced by an identical-looking impostor (Capgras delusion), or that one is dead or does not exist any longer (Cotard delusion) (Bortolotti, 2009).

As with popular delusions, clinical delusions strike most observers as bizarrely and incorrigibly irrational. That is, they trigger the same folk-epistemic bafflement and motivation to flag that the believer in question is a rational lost cause that underlie our account of delusion attribution in Chapter 2. Nevertheless, in line with our emphasis on the profound heterogeneity in the phenomena that reliably trigger such responses, popular and clinical delusions exhibit several fundamental differences that necessitate separate explanatory treatments.

First, with extremely rare exceptions (see Chapter 9, Section 5), clinical delusions are idiosyncratic. Unlike bizarre conspiracy theories or supernatural convictions that unite communities of co-believers, individuals with clinical delusions endorse beliefs that sharply diverge from those that prevail in their broader culture or subculture. (Clinical definitions of delusions often highlight this divergence to distinguish them from beliefs that look similar in their falsity and resistance to evidence; see Chapter 2, Section 2.)

Second, because clinical delusions arise in the context of disorders, injuries, and other forms of psychological dysfunction, they do not give rise to

The Social Roots of Delusions. Daniel Williams, Sam Wilkinson, and Kengo Miyazono, Oxford University Press.
 DOI: 10.1093/9780191976360.003.0007

the functional delusions puzzle, which asks why healthy people endorse seemingly absurd beliefs (see Chapter 3, Section 2). That is, although it is puzzling why individuals with well-functioning psychological mechanisms would embrace strange and seemingly highly irrational beliefs, it is much less puzzling why somebody suffering from a psychiatric disorder or brain injury would do so. Of course, this does not mean that clinical delusions are easy to understand or explain. As we will review in this chapter and the rest of Part 3, it is highly challenging to explain why individuals with clinical delusions embrace strange beliefs that appear highly resistant to evidence and rational correction. The point is simply that the nature of this challenge is different when explanations can invoke dysfunctions or aberrations in the psychological processes underlying belief formation.

Finally, we identified five recurring characteristics of popular delusions: epistemic irrationality, selectivity, compartmentalisation, attachment, and epistemically dysfunctional social practices. In contrast, clinical delusions are too heterogeneous to allow for such a uniform treatment, including not just in their aetiology but in their contents, the manner in which they are held, and their mental compartmentalisation. For example, some clinical delusions have extremely implausible ("bizarre") content (e.g., the belief that one is dead or has ceased to exist), whereas others have a more everyday ("mundane") focus (e.g., that one's spouse is having an affair) (Cermolacce et al., 2010). Some delusions are monothematic (i.e., focused on just one theme), whereas delusions in psychotic disorders such as schizophrenia are often polythematic and highly elaborated into complex belief systems (Bortolotti, 2016; Coltheart, 2013). Some delusions are accompanied by a wide range of psychotic symptoms, including hallucinations and disorganised thought and speech, whereas others appear amidst a "sea of apparent normality" (Davies & Egan, 2013, p.690). And some delusions are remarkably compartmentalised (e.g., a person fails to show concern for the loved one they believe has been replaced by an impostor), whereas others lead to tragic behavioural consequences (e.g., a person who attacks a loved one they believe to be an impostor) (de Pauw & Szulecka, 1988).

This profound heterogeneity makes it much more challenging to identify a set of co-occurring explanatory targets for clinical delusions, as we did with popular delusions. Moreover, there is a principled reason why we should expect this asymmetry, grounded in what is sometimes called the "Anna Karenina principle" after Tolstoy's famous observation that "All happy families are alike; each unhappy family is unhappy in its own way" (see Diamond, 1997).

As we saw in Part 2, popular delusions involve fragile "achievements". They depend on the successful coordination of complex psychological processes and social practices designed to promote, protect, and rationalise highly irrational beliefs that would ordinarily be extinguished by contact with reality. To succeed, they must satisfy multiple constraints, including incentive alignment, dissent suppression, and insulation from disconfirmation. As with most other complex achievements, there are very few ways to get this "right". Hence, despite significant variation in the contents of popular delusions, their roots in socially adaptive motivations and sophisticated forms of social coordination ensure that they exhibit a set of recurring characteristics. In contrast, because clinical delusions result from breakdowns in or disturbances to normal psychological functioning, there are many more ways in which such failures can occur, which lies behind the profound heterogeneity we observe in clinical delusions themselves.

For these reasons, our explanatory aims when it comes to clinical delusions are different from our aims concerning popular delusions in Part 2. Nevertheless, as with popular delusions, we will argue that most existing theoretical approaches to these beliefs also neglect their important connections to human sociality, and that, despite their heterogeneity, it is possible to identify three social patterns that cut across most clinical delusions: their predominant social focus, their connection to social experiences, and their strange resistance to social correction. Ultimately, we will also argue that whereas popular delusions involve a collective, motivated distortion of the complex web of norms, trust, and testimony that constitutes the human social-epistemic system (see Part 1), clinical delusions involve complex causal pathways through which individuals lose access to this system.

The first half of this chapter (Section 2) reviews four of the most influential explanatory frameworks in research into clinical delusions, each of which can be understood as providing an answer to the question of why the delusional person believes what they do (i.e., something deeply implausible) in a way that appears highly resistant to evidence and rational correction (Coltheart et al., 2011). (Henceforth, when we refer to "delusions", we refer to beliefs classified as delusions in clinical contexts unless stated otherwise.)

- **Cognition-Based Accounts**: Delusions arise from aberrations in how individuals think or reason about the world (Section 2.1).
- **Experience-Based Accounts**: Delusions arise from anomalous experiences (Section 2.2).
- **Two-Factor Accounts**: Delusions arise from two dissociable factors; e.g., anomalous experiences and cognitive difficulties (Section 2.3).

- **Predictive Processing Accounts**: Delusions arise from disturbances in the brain's hierarchical prediction error-minimisation systems (Section 2.4).

Our overview of this literature is necessarily selective. First, we omit consideration of several theoretical frameworks, including causal approaches that trace clinical delusions directly to neurological problems (Campbell, 2001; Wilkinson 2016), psychoanalytic approaches that emphasise unconscious conflicts (Freud, 1958), and phenomenological approaches that focus on alterations in basic existential orientations (Sass & Pienkos, 2013). (Although we will not discuss these approaches explicitly in this section, we will refer to some of them in later chapters. For example, in Chapter 9, Section 4.2, we refer to a phenomenological analysis of anomalous self-experiences in schizophrenia and its impact on group identification.) We also follow psychiatric orthodoxy in assuming that delusions are a kind of belief. Although some interesting psychological and philosophical research contests this assumption and offers "non-doxastic" models of delusions, space constraints prohibit us from engaging with such work here (see Bortolotti & Miyazono, 2015). Second, our treatment of the theoretical approaches we review is brief and schematic. Our aim is not to be exhaustive but to identify features of such approaches relevant to the arguments and ideas we advance in later chapters in Part 3.

In Section 3, we extract two such features. First, many influential explanations of clinical delusions restrict themselves to one or two explanatory factors. We argue that this restriction is implausible in many cases and often rests on a spurious argument according to which delusions research should focus exclusively on clinically abnormal factors. Second, most research on clinical delusions is individualistic, positing psychological factors like experiential abnormalities or domain-general cognitive difficulties in which human sociality plays no distinctive role.

The second half of the chapter (Sections 4–6) identifies three challenges for such individualistic explanatory approaches:

- **The Challenge of Social Determinants**: Without supplementation, individualistic approaches do not seem to explain the causal relevance of social factors like abuse and marginalisation to delusions (Section 4).
- **The Challenge of Social Focus**: Without supplementation, individualistic approaches do not seem to explain why delusions overwhelmingly focus on social themes (Section 5).

- **The Challenge of Social Evidence**: Without supplementation, individualistic approaches do not seem to explain why social and non-social evidence are treated differently in delusion formation (Section 6).

These challenges set the stage for the rest of Part 3, which critically evaluates existing social accounts of delusions (Chapter 7) before developing our preferred theoretical approach to these challenges in Chapters 8 and 9. Specifically, Chapter 8 will address the challenges of social determinants and social focus, while Chapter 9 will address the challenge of social evidence.

2. Individualist Accounts

2.1 Cognition-Based Accounts

Because delusions strike others as highly irrational, it is natural to try to explain them by appealing to problems or defects with how individuals think or reason about the world (von Domarus 1944; Garety 1991; Garety & Hemsley, 1997). This might take the form of a cognitive bias distinctive of those with delusions, or a cognitive impairment caused by dysfunctions or disturbances to the psychological mechanisms underlying reasoning.

Before proceeding, we note two terminological decisions. First, we use "cognition" to refer to psychological processes underlying (non-perceptual) judgement, belief formation, and decision making. Although there are ongoing psychological and philosophical debates about the perception-cognition boundary (Firestone & Scholl, 2016), the distinction is helpful in distinguishing approaches to delusions that posit perceptual versus post-perceptual aberrations, and it is assumed in much delusions research (although not all; see Section 2.4). Second, cognition is broader than reasoning, a distinctive form of cognition characterised by conscious, slow, sequential, working-memory-based processes (Kahneman, 2003). This is important because some accounts positing cognitive biases or abnormalities in delusion formation do not focus on reasoning in this sense.

There are different ways in which accounts of delusions might appeal to problematic or aberrant cognition. One view is that a severe and generalised reasoning impairment is the only causal factor underlying clinical delusions (von Domarus, 1944). This view has very few proponents today. It conflicts with the striking fact that people with clinical delusions often seem capable of largely typical forms of reasoning on topics unrelated to their delusions. As Bell and colleagues observe,

> [T]his is clearly apparent during conversation with someone with delusions. All things being equal, they can generate normative conclusions about matters not relating to their delusional beliefs and come to seemingly atypical conclusions only when reasoning relates to the specific focus of the delusions. Therefore, most people with delusions appear not to have a generalized problem with rationality but a circumscribed irrationality by which conclusions are irrational solely in relation to the delusional content. (Bell et al. 2021, p.25)

Moreover, there is little scientific support for the idea that reasoning impairments are the main cause of clinical delusions. For example, assumptions early in psychiatry that delusions might result from problems with syllogistic logical reasoning (von Domarus, 1944) have long been discredited by the failure to identify any specific difficulties delusional individuals have with such tasks once general cognitive ability (i.e., IQ) is controlled for, which is known to be reduced in conditions such as schizophrenia (Watson & Wold, 1981).

More recent research has explored subtler kinds of cognitive bias. For example, there is a large body of research on the Jumping To Conclusions bias ("JTC bias"), a tendency whereby individuals reach conclusions based on less evidence than others. A seminal experimental study of the JTC bias (Huq, Garety, & Hemsley, 1988) focuses on the "beads task". In a typical set-up, subjects must determine which of two jars with different proportions of red and black beads a sequence of beads is drawn from. Studies suggest that delusional people with schizophrenia tend to require less evidence than experimental controls before reaching a conclusion (Dudley et al., 2016).

There is also a growing body of research on the Bias Against Disconfirmatory Evidence ("BADE"), a tendency whereby individuals stick to their prior hypotheses in the face of conflicting evidence (Eisenacher & Zink, 2017). For example, experimental studies of BADE (e.g., Moritz & Woodward, 2006; Woodward et al., 2006) reveal that delusional people with schizophrenia have a greater tendency than experimental controls to stick to their original interpretation of an abstract drawing (e.g., that it is a lemon) even when more details are added to the drawing suggesting their original interpretation is mistaken (e.g., showing that it is a frog rather than a lemon).

These biases appear well-supported by empirical research, although their role in delusion formation remains unclear. Moreover, they seem relatively subtle and insufficient on their own to explain delusions without additional factors. For example, meta-analyses (Dudley et al., 2016; So et al., 2016) report that patients with delusions drew on average 0.6 fewer beads than non-delusional individuals in the beads task and that between 40% and 50% of delusional individuals showed no evidence of the bias at all. McLean and colleagues (2017) explore a wide range of putative cognitive biases, including BADE, and find some average differences between the performance of delusional individuals and non-delusional individuals on tasks designed to measure them. Once again, however, the effect sizes are relatively small, and the causal relationship between the putative bias and delusions is often opaque. Further, McLean and colleagues do not control for general cognitive ability, which, as noted, is known to be reduced in many individuals with clinical delusions.

2.2 Experience-Based Accounts

Another influential paradigm appeals to anomalous experiences to explain clinical delusions. Maher (1974) developed this idea into a general explanatory approach. He argued that clinical delusions result from attempts to make sense of anomalous and highly misleading experiences produced by some underlying dysfunction or damage, such that "the locus of the pathology is in the neuropsychology of experience, not in the neuropsychology of deductive or inferential reasoning" (Maher, 1999, p.551). Indeed, Maher argued that the thinking and reasoning of individuals with clinical delusions is normal and even scientific:

> Strange events, felt to be significant, demand explanation. It is the core of the present hypothesis that the explanations (i.e. the delusions) of the patient are derived by cognitive activity that is essentially indistinguishable from that employed by non-patients, by scientists, and by people generally. [...] In brief, then, a delusion is a hypothesis designed to explain unusual perceptual phenomena and developed through the operation of normal cognitive processes. (Maher, 1974, p.103)

This conjecture has several attractions (see Noordhof & Sullivan-Bissett, 2021). Most obviously, it neatly explains the so-called "loss of contact" with reality that delusions appear to manifest to others. If people are exposed to strange and misleading experiences, it is unsurprising that they draw inaccurate inferences about the world. Insofar as these experiences are private, it is also unsurprising that others will regard the resulting beliefs as highly irrational and unresponsive to publicly available evidence. Moreover, if the experiences are sufficiently strange and misleading, attempts to interpret or explain them might require sharp revisions to one's understanding of the world. This could help to explain the bizarreness of some delusional contents.

Researchers have linked various delusions to specific anomalous experiences (Ellis & Young, 1990; Davies et al., 2001). For example, one early hypothesis claimed that Capgras delusion, in which the individual comes to believe that somebody (typically a loved one) has been replaced by an impostor, can be thought of as "inverse prosopagnosia" (Ellis & Young, 1990). Whereas in prosopagnosia ("face-blindness") (Bauer, 1984), people cannot consciously recognise familiar faces but show preserved covert recognition via autonomic arousal (measured by skin conductance response), individuals with Capgras delusion exhibit the opposite pattern: intact conscious recognition but impaired autonomic responses. This creates a surprising and disturbing "looks right, feels wrong" experience when viewing loved ones' faces, which the delusional belief ("this is an impostor") resolves. Empirical research lends some support to this hypothesis, including confirmations of reduced autonomic responses to familiar faces in individuals with Capgras delusions (Ellis et al., 1997; Hirstein & Ramachandran, 1997), as well as neuroimaging evidence of specific lesion patterns affecting connections between face recognition areas and emotional processing regions (Thiel et al., 2014).

Similar experience-based accounts have been developed for other monothematic delusions. For example, theorists have proposed that Cotard delusion (the delusional belief one is dead, dying, etc.) is linked to global affective disturbances causing derealisation and depersonalisation (Davies & Coltheart, 2022), and that Fregoli delusion (the belief that strangers are familiar people in disguise) reflects inappropriate autonomic responses to unfamiliar faces (Langdon et al., 2014).

For polythematic delusions that arise in conditions like schizophrenia, two prominent experience-based accounts are Frith's (1992) self-monitoring deficit account and Kapur's (2003) aberrant salience account.

Frith's (1992) hypothesis is that some delusions in schizophrenia can be explained by an underlying problem with the brain's self-monitoring mechanisms. To differentiate self-generated from externally generated stimuli, brains must predict and attenuate the sensory consequences of the organism's actions. If this process breaks down, self-generated actions and thoughts may seem surprising and be misattributed to external sources. Frith conjectures that this happens in schizophrenia. When self-produced movements lack the accompanying sense of agency, they feel externally controlled; when inner speech lacks the "self" tag, it is experienced as alien voices. Evidence supporting this account includes experimental demonstrations that individuals with schizophrenia show impaired ability to discriminate self-generated from externally generated sensations (Blakemore et al., 2000), reduced sensory attenuation for self-produced tactile stimuli (Shergill et al., 2005), and deficits in predicting the sensory consequences of their actions (Ford & Mathalon, 2004). Perhaps most famously, individuals with passivity experiences can tickle themselves, a sensation normally suppressed by intact self-monitoring prediction models (Blakemore et al., 2000).

According to Kapur (2003), dopamine typically assigns motivational and reinforcing value to rewarding stimuli. Given this, pathological increases in dopamine transmission can lead to a dysfunctional attribution of motivational significance (i.e., aberrant salience) to otherwise neutral events, including external occurrences and experiences within the individual's mind. Phenomenologically, this might lead individuals to imbue neutral or irrelevant events with great but inexplicable importance. According to Kapur (2003), this matches the subjective reports often given in the early stages ("prodromal phase") of psychosis in schizophrenia, during which the individual's experience of the world comes to be infused with a kind of significance they cannot fully understand. After continued repetition of such aberrant salience over an extended period, delusions arise as "a 'top-down' cognitive explanation that the individual imposes on these experiences of aberrant salience in an effort to make sense of them" (Kapur, 2003, p.15).

Although more empirical research is required to probe how specific experiential abnormalities connect to specific delusions, these experience-based accounts have numerous explanatory virtues. Nevertheless, as we will see in Section 2.3, among those who recognise the importance of anomalous experiences in delusion formation, some theorists, "two-factor theorists" in particular, argue that they are insufficient.

2.3 Two-Factor Accounts

According to two-factor accounts (Coltheart, 2007; Coltheart et al., 2011; Davies et al., 2001; Davies & Coltheart, 2024), delusions involve two dissociable causal factors ("first factor" and "second factor") that play different explanatory roles. The first factor, which is typically connected to anomalous experience, explains the theme of the delusional hypothesis. The second factor explains why the relevant delusional belief is adopted or maintained. Although most applications of the two-factor framework have been to monothematic delusions (Davies et al., 2001), some have suggested extensions of the framework to polythematic delusions in conditions such as schizophrenia as well (Coltheart et al., 2007). However, it is widely recognised that this extension is much more challenging and under-researched (Coltheart, 2013).

According to this framework, different monothematic delusions have different first factors, which can give rise to distinct anomalous experiences. For example, reduced autonomic responses to familiar faces might be the first factor in Capgras delusion, whereas self-monitoring problems might be the first factor in delusions of control. In contrast, many two-factor theorists assume that all monothematic delusions share the same second factor, which is often related to right-prefrontal damage (Coltheart et al., 2011).

Different theorists propose different accounts of the nature of this second factor. Roughly, they locate it either in the process by which a delusional hypothesis is adopted or in the process by which it is maintained despite conflicting evidence. Coltheart and colleagues' (2010) account belongs to the latter kind. They argue, echoing Maher, that adopting a delusional hypothesis based on the first factor can be reasonable. Given this, the second factor lies not in the initial adoption process but in the maintenance process, causing delusional individuals to ignore or discount evidence that conflicts with prior (delusional) beliefs. McKay and colleagues' (McKay, 2012; Miyazono & McKay, 2019) two-factor account belongs to the former kind. They argue that adopting a delusional hypothesis based on the first factor is unreasonable. Hence, the second factor targets the adoption process. It involves a "bias towards observational adequacy", prioritising new observations over prior beliefs. (In Bayesian terminology, this amounts to over-weighting the likelihood ratio relative to the prior probability ratio.)

Two-factor theorists have advanced various arguments for why the first factor alone cannot explain delusions (for an overview, see Miyazono, 2018). First, they point to cases where the first factor allegedly exists without fully fledged delusions. For example, people with ventromedial prefrontal damage exhibit an anomalous autonomic response to familiar faces analogous to the one observed in cases of Capgras delusion, but do not typically develop a full-fledged delusion.

Second, the first factor cannot explain everything about the process of delusion formation. For example, an anomalous autonomic response to a familiar face alone might not explain why a person adopts the preposterous hypothesis that their loved one has been replaced by an impostor rather than other, more reasonable hypotheses, such as the hypothesis that there is something wrong with their brain (which is much more likely, especially in the context of

Capgras delusion after an obvious brain injury). Similarly, anomalous experiences alone might not explain the persistence of delusions in the face of mounting contradictory evidence.

Third, people with delusions exhibit not only experiential abnormalities but also some cognitive biases or abnormalities, and they are not epiphenomenal. As reviewed above (Section 2.1), there is relatively strong evidence that people with delusions exhibit cognitive biases, including the JTC bias or the BADE. Although the role of such biases in delusion formation is not fully understood, it is plausible that they at least play some causal role in the process.

Fourth, in cases of delusions due to neurophysiological deficits, it is highly unlikely that the relevant brain damage is restricted to perceptual or experiential processes, while other processes (including cognitive ones) remain intact. For example, Capgras delusion due to brain damage is not only associated with autonomic abnormalities but also other neurophysiological abnormalities, including right-prefrontal abnormalities (Coltheart et al., 2011).

Collectively, these arguments present a persuasive case that experiential abnormalities are rarely sufficient to produce or sustain clinical delusions (Miyazono, 2018). Nevertheless, they are all controversial (e.g., Corlett, 2019; Sullivan-Bissett, 2022). One important source of controversy concerns the meaning of "factor" in these discussions. For example, Sullivan-Bissett (2020; see also Noordhof & Sullivan-Bissett, 2021) defends a one-factor account by arguing that the cognitive biases relevant to delusional beliefs fall "within the normal range" (i.e., are not "clinically abnormal"), and, hence, do not count as an additional "factor" in delusion formation. This touches on broader issues concerning delusional explanation, which we will return to in Section 3.

2.4 Predictive Processing Accounts

The predictive processing framework is often presented as a paradigm shift in theorising about delusions. It proposes reconceptualising the relationship between perception and cognition (and, hence, hallucinations and delusions) through the lens of hierarchical Bayesian inference (Hohwy, 2004; Corlett et al., 2010; Fletcher & Frith, 2009; Adams et al., 2013). To simplify significantly, its core principles as a general framework for understanding brain function are as follows (see Clark, 2013, 2015; Friston, 2005; Hohwy, 2013):

1. **Hierarchical Prediction**: The brain contains hierarchically organised generative models that predict incoming sensory data based on

hypotheses about their causes. Lower levels of the hierarchy are closer to sensory surfaces and more "perceptual". Higher levels are further away from sensory surfaces and more abstract, "cognitive", and multimodal. For example, an auditory input (e.g., impacts on the eardrum) might be disambiguated as having a particular pitch and timbre at low levels, a squeaking door at higher levels, and an old friend entering the room at even higher levels.

2. **Prediction Error Minimisation**: The brain's primary computational function is to minimise prediction errors—discrepancies between predictions and actual sensory input—either by updating predictions (perceptual inference) or by generating actions that bring sensory input in line with predictions (active inference).
3. **Precision-Weighted Prediction Errors**: The influence of prediction errors on belief updating is modulated by their estimated precision (i.e., reliability), which determines how strongly prediction errors drive revisions of the brain's hypotheses.
4. **Bidirectional Processing**: Information flows both "top-down" (predictions from higher to lower levels) and "bottom-up" (prediction errors from lower to higher levels).
5. **Bayesian Inference**: Hierarchical, precision-weighted prediction error minimisation implements a form of approximate Bayesian inference, which is widely understood as the optimally rational method for updating hypotheses in light of new evidence.

As a general computational framework for understanding brain function, predictive processing has been highly influential within the burgeoning field of computational psychiatry (Griffin & Fletcher, 2017). An early predictive processing account of delusions (Fletcher & Frith, 2009) targets schizophrenia and aims to explain not just delusions but also hallucinations. Roughly, it proposes that excessive dopamine in the brain (as per Kapur, 2003) leads to the assignment of inappropriately high *precision* to sensory prediction errors, thereby imbuing them with a kind of "newsworthiness" or attention-grabbing salience. These precise prediction errors then drive deep revisions in the brain's model of the world. At lower, more sensory levels, these revisions correspond to hallucinations. At higher, more cognitive levels, they correspond to delusions.

This proposal and its later developments correspond to what is sometimes called the "canonical predictive coding account of psychosis" (Sterzer et al., 2018). ("Predictive coding" is often used synonymously with "predictive processing"; see Clark, 2015.) However, because predictive processing is a highly flexible modelling framework, the scientific and philosophical literature contains many different predictive processing accounts that link delusions to distinct aberrations in processes of hierarchical precision-weighted prediction error minimisation (Harding et al., 2024; Hohwy, 2013; Miyazono & McKay, 2019; Rappe & Wilkinson, 2023; Williams & Montagnese, 2023).

The predictive processing approach has many theoretical and empirical virtues. For example, neuroimaging studies document aberrant prediction error signals in individuals with psychosis (Murray et al., 2008; Corlett et al., 2007), computational simulations demonstrate that alterations in precision-weighting can produce psychotic phenomenology (Adams et al., 2013; Sterzer et al., 2018), and pharmacological studies reveal that psychosis-inducing drugs (such as ketamine and amphetamines) disrupt prediction error signalling (Corlett et al., 2007; Honey et al., 2008). Moreover, by rejecting a sharp boundary between perception and cognition, predictive processing offers a rich framework for understanding anomalous experience and thought in delusions. Within the context of hierarchical prediction error minimisation, there are lower-level hypotheses that are clearly perceptual and higher-level hypotheses that are clearly cognitive, but there are also in-between states, and information flows up and down the hierarchy. This gradualistic, bi-directional framework seems well-suited to explaining the complex, dynamic interactions and blurry boundaries between strange experiences and delusional thought often characteristic of psychosis in conditions like schizophrenia (Fletcher & Frith, 2009).

We are sympathetic to the predictive processing approach. Nevertheless, it is important to reiterate that the predictive processing framework is highly flexible and consistent with many distinct hypotheses about how aberrations in prediction error minimisation drive delusions. Moreover, although predictive processing offers a sophisticated, lower-level neurocomputational framework for understanding perception, cognition, and the porous boundary between them, most existing applications of predictive processing in delusions research share the dominant assumption that delusions result from experiential and/or domain-general cognitive difficulties (regardless of whether the experiential/cognitive boundary is sharp or not). For example, the canonical predictive coding account of psychosis strongly resembles the aberrant salience account, even if it recasts salience in terms of precision-weighting of prediction errors. Similarly, two-factor accounts of delusions can be re-framed in the language of hierarchical prediction error minimisation (Miyazono & McKay, 2019). For this reason, our treatment of predictive processing will largely assimilate it to these other experiential/cognitive explanatory approaches in what follows.

3. Factors, Abnormality, and Individualism

As we have seen, the four explanatory approaches we have reviewed trace delusions to cognitive difficulties, experiential abnormalities, combinations of the two, or aberrations in prediction error minimisation that underlie experiential and cognitive difficulties. Although these proposals have significant theoretical and empirical virtues, the second half of this chapter will identify three challenges for them. First, however, we will flag two important features all approaches share: their restriction to a small number of explanatory factors (Section 3.1) and their individualism (Section 3.2).

3.1 Explaining Delusions

As the debate between experience-based and two-factor accounts illustrates, much research into delusions restricts itself to positing only one or two explanatory factors. This is surprising. Psychiatric phenomena typically have many causes that interact in complex ways (Borsboom & Cramer, 2013). Why would multifaceted, heterogeneous phenomena like clinical delusions be different? As Daniel Freeman argues,

> Debates about delusions being caused by either one or two factors are outdated. The complexity of causation in delusions is apparent in discussions with patients but also when the results of empirical studies are considered. Many contributory factors are implicated in persecutory delusions. It is most certainly not a matter of one or two causes. (Freeman, 2016, p.686)

We share this perspective. Although some delusions, especially monothematic delusions linked to discrete brain injuries, might have only one or two explanatory factors, we will argue in Chapters 8 and 9 that many delusions are likely caused by complex, dynamic interactions among multiple cognitive, experiential, affective, behavioural, and other factors. In this respect, our approach to clinical delusions will mirror our multifactorial approach to popular delusions, which posits many causes (cognitive biases, motivated reasoning, social-epistemic norms, status competition, etc.) and subtle, often self-reinforcing interactions between them (see Chapters 4 and 5).

One possible reason theorists resist this multifactorial approach is a restrictive, pathocentric understanding of what counts as an explanatory factor in delusion formation. For example, according to Ema Sullivan-Bissett,

> Factors ... are not merely causal contributions. The task is not to create an inventory of everything to which we need to appeal in order to explain delusional belief. Even in everyday cases, if that were the task, the inventory would be substantial. We would need to appeal to the subject having oxygen in her environment, having suitably developed cognitive capacities to form beliefs, being in such-a-such a place p at such-and-such a time t to receive evidence e, and so on. Background conditions are not factors. (Sullivan-Bissett, 2024b, p.415)

According to this argument, factors are intended to explain why some people form delusions, and others do not. Given this, any contributing causes to delusions shared between people with and without delusions are irrelevant. Researchers must identify factors unique to delusional people: "In addition to causally contributing to the formation or maintenance of a delusional belief, the term *factor* picks out a contribution which is *abnormal*" (Sullivan-Bissett 2024b, p.415).

There are at least two reasons to resist this line of argument:

First, the boundary between "normal" and "abnormal" functioning is often ambiguous and theoretically contested. In some cases, such as delusions connected to localised forms of brain injury or damage, the term "clinically abnormal" is relatively uncontroversial. However, most traits, including many relevant to understanding experiences and behaviours of clinical interest, exist on a continuum, and there is rarely a clear line distinguishing extreme values and outright pathology (Kotov et al., 2017). Moreover, it is often difficult to distinguish between dysfunction and the behaviour of well-functioning mechanisms when exposed to extreme conditions such as heightened distress, sleep problems, worry, and so on (e.g., Wilkinson et al., 2017).

These remarks barely scratch the surface of this complex issue, which is the topic of a vast philosophical and scientific literature. Nevertheless, given the significant controversy over what it means for factors to be clinically abnormal and how to apply this concept in many cases, we should not insist on clinical abnormality as a necessary condition for something to qualify as an explanatory factor.

Second, and more importantly, contrasting mere background conditions with clinical abnormalities presents a false dichotomy. Although there are countless uninteresting contributory causes of delusions, such as oxygen in the subject's environment, they are not uninteresting because they are "normal". They are uninteresting because they do not explain what distinguishes delusional people from non-delusional people. They are not "difference makers"

(Strevens, 2008). However, whether something is a difference maker is orthogonal to whether it is clinically abnormal. For example, suppose that a distinctive reasoning style is necessary to explain why some people with anomalous experiences embrace delusions, and others do not. In that case, it is a difference maker and, hence, a relevant explanatory factor even if it exists within "the normal range". It is worth noting that this understanding of factor (namely, as an explanatorily relevant difference maker rather than a clinically abnormal difference maker) is in line with how it is generally used in the natural and social sciences, including the medical sciences.

Understanding factors this way opens up several important possibilities. First, many factors might be relevant to understanding delusions. For example, in a recent factor analysis of paranoia, extreme forms of which manifest as persecutory delusions, Freeman and Loe (2023) find that 66.7% of the variance in paranoia was explained by thirteen factors, many of which do not seem "clinically abnormal" in any interesting sense, such as negative images, anxiety sensitivity, worrying, and distinctive behaviours. Although a factor analysis cannot identify causes, this multifactorial approach aligns with empirical research into persecutory delusions (Freeman, 2016), as we will return to in Chapters 8 and 9.

Second, the causation involved in delusions can be highly complex, including interactions between multiple factors and dynamic processes involving subtle, self-reinforcing feedback loops. That is, rather than delusions emerging in a simple linear way from underlying dysfunctions, some might emerge gradually over time through interactions between many different emotional, cognitive, experiential, and behavioural factors, which might in turn involve bidirectional relationships between delusions and their causes (e.g., paranoia might be partly caused by anxiety, strange experiences, social withdrawal, and insomnia, all of which are exacerbated by paranoia; see Freeman, 2016).

The possibility of these subtle and complex interactions demonstrates why something can be highly relevant to explaining delusions even if it is not individually unique to delusional people. Just as many causes cut across psychiatric disorders, factors such as anxiety or distinctive reasoning styles need not be unique to people with delusions for them to form part of a complex, dynamic pattern of interacting factors relevant to explaining why some people become delusional, and others do not.

Finally, some beliefs treated as delusional in clinical contexts might not involve any clinically abnormal factors. For example, Sullivan-Bissett (2024b) argues that cognitive biases within the "normal range" do not count as explanatory factors. However, just as there is "normal-range" variation in cognition, there is also significant "normal-range" variation in people's propensities to have anomalous experiences (see Van Os et al., 2000), which are central to her preferred "one-factor" account. Given this, strange experiences that exist within the "normal range" might interact with many other complex factors (cognitive biases, strong emotions, coping problems) to produce clinical delusions, even if no such factors are individually clinically abnormal. Of course, it is an empirical question whether this situation ever obtains. Nevertheless, once one rejects the view that delusions are essentially pathological (see Chapter 2) and understands delusional explanation in the way we have described, the role of clinically abnormal factors is something to be discovered in delusions research, not simply assumed.

3.2 Individualism

The second noteworthy feature shared by the explanatory frameworks reviewed in Section 2 is their individualism. More specifically, there are at least two respects in which human sociality is irrelevant to these approaches. First, they focus on psychological factors internal to individuals. Cognitive difficulties, strange experiences, and dysregulated prediction error minimisation all reside inside the minds of delusional individuals.

Second, the psychological factors posited by such approaches are typically not essentially tied to our social psychology. For example, the fact that we are intensely social animals highly preoccupied with social motivations, goals, interests, fears, and so on is typically absent from such accounts. And although some experience-based accounts posit anomalous social experiences (e.g., hearing voices) or anomalous experiences interpreted or explained in social terms (e.g., as an impostor or a hidden plot), the cognitive difficulties posited by the frameworks we have reviewed are *domain-general*. For example, the JTC bias concerns conclusions about any topic, social and non-social, and the aberrations in prediction error minimisation posited in predictive processing accounts typically affect the brain's capacity to revise hypotheses about all subject matters (see Williams & Montagnese, 2023).

In the remainder of this chapter (Sections 4–6), we will identify three underappreciated social dimensions of delusions that generate challenges for these individualistic approaches. These challenges share the same structure: individualistic approaches that restrict themselves to anomalous experiences, domain-general cognitive difficulties, or global disruptions in prediction error minimisation do not seem to explain a striking fact about delusions. First, they do not seem to explain the causal relevance of social factors like abuse and marginalisation to delusions (Section 4). Second, they do not seem to explain why delusions overwhelmingly focus on social themes (Section 5). Finally, they do not seem to explain why social and non-social evidence are treated differently in delusion formation (Section 6).

Importantly, we will not argue that individualistic approaches *cannot* explain these social dimensions of delusions. Instead, we will argue that they *do not* explain them without theoretical supplementation. That is, experiential abnormalities, domain-general cognitive difficulties, or global disturbances to hierarchical prediction error minimisation alone do not seem to explain them.

As with our review of the individualistic approaches to delusions in Section 2, our treatment of these challenges is necessarily selective. Instead of reviewing all attempts to address these challenges, we aim to introduce them in enough detail to highlight why they create challenges that must be addressed.

4. The Challenge of Social Determinants

One important respect in which the theoretical frameworks for understanding clinical delusions reviewed above are individualistic is that they focus on psychological factors that are within the individual's mind. Anomalous experiences, domain-general cognitive difficulties, and predictive processing aberrations all reside within the relevant person. However, as has long been documented in research on delusions and psychosis more broadly, there also appear to be powerful *social risk factors* for delusions. These are social experiences or features of the social environment that increase the likelihood that individuals will develop delusions, in some cases substantially (Arseneault et al., 2011; Luhrmann, 2007; Selten et al., 2013; Van Os et al., 2010; Varese et al., 2012).

Before reviewing some of these factors, it is important to clarify how to interpret them. As we have noted (Section 1), the beliefs labelled "clinical delusions" in modern medical psychiatry are highly heterogeneous, arising from a vast range of different psychiatric and neurological illnesses and as unwanted side effects from various drugs. Given this heterogeneity, it is unclear what it would mean to study risk factors for clinical delusions as such. Therefore, most research in this area focuses on risk factors for conditions or symptoms strongly associated with clinical delusions, especially psychosis (typically understood to include delusions and hallucinations) in conditions like schizophrenia. In this context, well-confirmed social risk factors often supported by meta-analyses include physical and sexual abuse, bullying, poverty, low socio-economic status, urban environments, and membership of minority (e.g., racial, ethnic, or religious) groups. Several of these are worth expanding on.

First, there is strong evidence that childhood adversity, including physical, sexual, and emotional abuse and bullying, substantially increases the likelihood of psychosis (Arseneault et al., 2011; Morgan & Gayer-Anderson, 2016; Read et al., 2005; Varese et al., 2012). For example, one meta-analysis reviewing over thirty studies reveals that patients with a psychotic disorder were 2.72 times more likely to have suffered childhood adversity than controls (Varese et al., 2012). Similarly, a large Australian study discovered an approximately 2- to 2.5-fold increase in psychosis risk among victims of childhood sexual abuse (Cutajar et al., 2010). Finally, Arseneault and colleagues (2011), using data from a longitudinal UK cohort, found that children who were maltreated by adults were more than three times as likely to develop psychotic symptoms later on, and those who were bullied by peers were about two and a half times as likely. In contrast, accidental injuries showed only a weak association, underscoring the particular impact of intentional interpersonal trauma.

Second, one of the most replicated findings in the epidemiology of psychosis is that minority ethnic and religious groups seem to be susceptible to substantially higher rates of it (Leaune et al., 2019). However, this finding is nuanced by what is known as the "ethnic density effect", which is that this enhanced psychosis risk is partly ameliorated when those minorities form a greater proportion of the local population (Baker et al., 2021). Given that this effect applies to settled minority groups, it is misleading to describe the relevant risk factor as applying specifically to migration, although some research suggests that the incidence of psychotic disorders may be higher among refugees specifically (Hollander et al., 2016). In addition, there is also a considerable body of research showing elevated risks of psychosis and psychotic disorders in urban areas, and more specifically in densely populated areas (Vassos et al., 2012), as well as among people of lower socio-economic status (Castillejos et al., 2018).

These risk factors are correlational and do not themselves establish causation. For example, it could be that the correlations arise because having or being susceptible to psychosis causes people to act in ways that make them more likely to have the relevant social experiences or inhabit the relevant social environments. Nevertheless, although causality is challenging to establish, there is a broad consensus that social factors play a genuinely causal role. This assessment partly rests on common sense. For example, it is difficult to see how a susceptibility to psychosis later in life would make one substantially more likely to be abused as a child. However, it is also supported by findings of dose-response relationships in which the strength of association increases with the intensity and duration of social adversity (Shevlin et al., 2008; Pedersen & Mortensen, 2001), as well as longitudinal studies demonstrating that social adversity typically precedes psychosis onset (Morgan et al., 2014; Bebbington et al., 2004). Finally, a causal interpretation is consistent with a large body of evidence on the significant impact of adverse social experiences and conditions on mental health more generally (see Hughes et al., 2017; Kirkbride et al., 2024). Given this, we will discuss social "determinants" in what follows, not just social risk factors.

In summary, there is strong evidence that social experiences and features of an individual's social environment increase the likelihood of forming delusions. This poses an explanatory challenge to the individualistic approaches reviewed in Section 2. As noted already, we are not claiming that such approaches cannot be supplemented to explain the relevance and importance of social factors in delusion formation. For example, theorists might explore how adverse social interactions or environments affect anomalous experiences, domain-general cognitive difficulties, or disturbances to processes of probabilistic prediction and inference (e.g., Sloan et al. 2025). Nevertheless, this would involve going beyond the core explanatory posits of individualistic approaches.

5. The Challenge of Social Focus

The second challenge for individualistic approaches concerns a striking fact: delusions overwhelmingly focus on the delusional individual's "place in the social universe" (Bentall et al., 1991, p.14), a pattern that appears consistent across cultures and historical periods (see Bell et al, 2021; Gold & Gold, 2015).

Although there are some disagreements over which precise categories to include and their cultural variability, standard psychiatric taxonomies typically identify a surprisingly constrained set of delusional themes such as the following (American Psychiatric Association, 2013):

1. **Persecutory Delusions**: Beliefs that others are intentionally causing harm or planning to harm the individual.
2. **Referential Delusions**: Beliefs that environmental events, objects, or people have special significance specifically related to the individual.

3. **Grandiose Delusions**: Beliefs about having exceptional abilities, wealth, or special identity.
4. **Erotomanic Delusions**: Beliefs that another person, typically of higher status, is in love with the individual.
5. **Nihilistic Delusions**: Beliefs that the individual, others, or the world is nonexistent, destroyed, or dying.
6. **Somatic Delusions**: Beliefs about abnormalities in bodily functioning or anatomy.
7. **Thought-Related Delusions**: Beliefs about thought insertion, withdrawal, broadcasting, or control by external forces.
8. **Control Delusions**: Beliefs that one's actions, emotions, or volition are controlled by external forces.
9. **Jealous Delusions**: Beliefs that a romantic partner is unfaithful.
10. **Religious Delusions**: Beliefs involving religious themes, divine communication, or special religious identity.
11. **Guilt Delusions**: Beliefs that one has committed unforgivable sins or crimes.
12. **Misidentification Delusions**: Beliefs involving misattribution of identity to people, places, or objects.

The fact that the themes of delusions can be listed in this way is noteworthy, given that technical definitions of delusions place no constraints on their content. Given this, individualist approaches are consistent with the prediction that delusions will range freely over all possible contents of thought (Gold & Gold, 2015). Although there is some disagreement over the size and variability of delusional themes, this prediction appears to be false.

The concept of "theme" here should be distinguished from the specific contents of delusional beliefs. For example, the delusional belief that one is the reincarnation of Elvis Presley and the delusional belief that one is the reincarnation of Napoleon differ in content. However, they both share the theme of grandiosity. Any given delusional theme is consistent with an indefinite range of possible delusional contents, and one should expect specific delusional contents to be shaped in powerful ways by idiosyncratic individual and cultural factors. Nevertheless, it is noteworthy that the profound variation in the individual contents of delusions seems to occur within a surprisingly circumscribed set of delusional themes across otherwise diverse cultural contexts (Bell et al., 2021).

Once one focuses on delusional themes rather than specific delusional contents, it is plausible that standard delusional taxonomies can be divided into an even smaller number of overarching themes (see Gold, 2017). For example, although persecutory delusions (#1) are often distinguished from delusions of thought (#7), control (#8), and jealousy (#9), all these delusions are preoccupied with how other agents are intentionally harming or controlling the delusional individual. This theme also applies to many misidentification delusions (#12), such as the Capgras delusion, in which the delusional individual believes that an impostor has replaced a loved one. Similarly, although grandiose delusions (#3) are often distinguished from erotomanic delusions (#4), both delusions express an elevated social position, either directly in the case of grandiose delusions or indirectly in the case of erotomanic delusions through being the object of romantic attention from a high-status person. Finally, although religious delusions (#10) are often separated from other themes by their focus on religious content, most religious delusions simply introduce supernatural elements into more basic themes of persecution, reference, or grandiosity (Gold, 2017).

More importantly, delusions do not just cluster around specific themes. They are also overwhelmingly focused on social themes (see Bell et al., 2021; Bentall et al., 1991; Gold & Gold, 2015; Williams & Montagnese, 2023). This is true if one simply counts the number of delusional themes that focus in some way on the relationship between the delusional individual and other agents, either real or imagined, natural or supernatural. By this definition, 9–10 of the themes directly involve social themes: persecutory, referential, grandiose, erotomanic, thought-related, control, jealous, religious, guilt, and most misidentification delusions all centre on the individual's relationship to other agents. Only nihilistic and somatic delusions lack an explicit social theme.

However, this mode of analysis is misleading because individual themes also differ radically in prevalence. For example, persecutory delusions are by far the most common delusional theme worldwide. In a recent meta-analysis surveying the prevalence of different delusional themes, Collin and colleagues (2023) demonstrate that 65% of people with delusions have persecutory delusions, 40% have referential delusions, 28% have grandiose delusions, 22% have control delusions, and 18% have religious delusions. They also find that although the prevalence of different themes varies according to disorder, such themes and their prevalence appear to be approximately constant across different countries.

In other words, most delusions across time and cultures appear to have social themes. As Gold and Gold put it, "There is a clear pattern in the phenomena of delusion, and any theory worth its salt is going to have to be able to explain why it is there" (Gold & Gold, 2015, p.166). The challenge of social focus arises because it is unclear how the individualistic approaches reviewed in Section 2 explain it. Consider their limitations:

1. **Cognition-Based Accounts**: Cognitive biases like JTC or BADE do not predict the social focus of delusions. Such domain-general biases should affect how individuals think about all topics equally. They do not explain why social content would predominate.
2. **Experience-Based Accounts**: While anomalous experiences plausibly constrain possible delusional content, the space of possible anomalous experiences is vast, as is the number of ways of interpreting and explaining them. Given this, such accounts do not explain why experiences that generate social interpretations occur more frequently than those that suggest non-social content.
3. **Two-Factor Accounts**: These accounts explain specific delusional content through the first factor (or anomalous experiences that it gives rise to) but offer no principled reason why these experiences should be overwhelmingly concerned with or understood in social rather than non-social ways.
4. **Predictive Processing Accounts**: While these frameworks elegantly explain the process of delusion formation, they do not inherently predict the social focus of delusional content (see Williams & Montagnese, 2023). Aberrant prediction errors could occur in any perceptual or cognitive domain.

As before, we are not arguing that these accounts are inconsistent with the predominant social focus of delusions, nor that they cannot be supplemented in ways that address this challenge. The point is simply that they would require some form of supplementation to address it.

6. The Challenge of Social Evidence

The third and final challenge is that individualistic approaches do not explain why delusional beliefs resist social correction by other epistemic agents, or in other words, why they are uniquely insensitive to social forms of evidence, particularly testimonial evidence. Instead, such approaches tend to assume a coarse-grained conception of evidence where experiential and social evidence are not distinguished.

Descriptions of delusions often emphasise their "imperviousness to counterevidence" as a defining feature (Jaspers, 1913/1963; American Psychiatric Association, 2013). For example, Bortolotti writes,

> What seems a potentially central and distinctive feature of delusions is that delusions are unshakeable. They are not typically given up under the weight of counterevidence and counterargument. The most common outcome of a delusion being challenged is that either the challenge is dismissed, or the delusional belief is elaborated to neutralize the challenge. (Bortolotti, 2023, p.69)

Nevertheless, in Section 2, we reviewed compelling reasons for thinking that delusions are often connected to experiential forms of evidence. As Bortolotti writes,

> In a broad sense of "evidence", we do have some evidence for our delusional beliefs and thus delusions are not entirely groundless. Even in the case of delusions with bizarre contents [...] there is usually a puzzling experience that demands an explanation, and the delusion is an explanation that fits that experience. (Bortolotti, 2023, p.56)

Importantly, this acknowledgement that delusions are *sensitive* to experiential evidence does not mean they are *rationally responsive* to such evidence. Maher (1974) is often interpreted as saying that delusional people respond to the evidence of anomalous experiences in a broadly "rational" manner, in that their response to such experiences is not less rational than scientists' response to scientific evidence. Stone and Young (2007) disagree with Maher and argue that delusional individuals exhibit a bias towards observational adequacy, which is oversensitivity to new observations relative to prior beliefs in the belief revision processes (see also McKay, 2012 and Miyazono & McKay, 2019). Note, however, that Stone and Young do not deny that delusional individuals are sensitive to experiential evidence. Indeed, Stone and Young claim that, in effect, delusional individuals are *too sensitive* to experiential evidence. In short, while the claim that delusional individuals are rationally responsive to experiential evidence is contested, there is much broader agreement that they are sensitive to experiential evidence.

How, then, can we make sense of the fact that delusional individuals appear simultaneously sensitive (and perhaps overly sensitive) to some forms of evidence yet profoundly unresponsive to others? This puzzle is analogous to what

Furl and colleagues (2024) call "a fundamental puzzle concerning the manner in which deluded individuals integrate new experiences with their prior beliefs", which they express as follows:

> How can deluded individuals have beliefs that cannot be changed by counterevidence but yet are adopted on the basis of too little evidence? We observe that many of the scientific studies in this field have historically adopted a position on one side or the other of this contrast. As per the dominant psychiatric conception, some studies indicate that individuals with delusions possess some trait that disposes them to rely inflexibly on their existing beliefs and to be less influenced by new experience than healthy people. But other evidence and theoretical work suggest that deluded individuals are disposed to neglect their prior convictions and to be unduly swayed by weak evidence. (Furl et al., 2024, p.241)

We take this puzzle to show that delusions are not insensitive to all forms of evidence, and that there is a particular kind of evidence to which they are not sensitive. We hypothesise that it is social forms of evidence, and testimonial evidence in particular, to which delusions are particularly insensitive. (As we saw in Chapter 3, Section 3.1, this social evidence can be understood as a distinctive kind of higher-order evidence (Levy, 2021).) This hypothesis is coherent with the fact that, when people describe delusions as being insensitive to evidence, what they typically have in mind are cases in which delusional people resist social correction by others, or testimonial counterevidence from others. They are cases in which others challenge a delusional person in a testimonial exchange, but the delusion persists. For example, a person with Capgras delusion about his wife is told by the clinician that the woman in front of him is his real wife, but his delusion persists. Indeed, the delusion persists not just in the face of contradictory testimonial evidence, but also under-cutting testimonial evidence, such as being told, "The only reason that you believe this is because of your brain injury".

Strictly speaking, delusional individuals are not only insensitive to "testimonial evidence" in a narrow sense. For example, a person with Capgras delusion about his wife may be insensitive not only when the clinician tells him that the woman in front of him is his wife, but also when the clinician presents a DNA identification of the woman, which is not "testimonial evidence" narrowly construed, in the sense that the clinician is not telling the person anything but rather *showing* them. However, such cases count as testimony in the broader sense that they involve a deliberate informational transfer that relies on basic trust. In Craig's (1990) terminology, the clinician is here an informant, not merely a source of information. Social worries about the trustworthiness of other agents can therefore undermine such evidence. We will come back to this issue in Chapter 9.

The discussions above suggest that, in accounting for delusion, we must adopt a fine-grained conception of evidence in which different forms of evidence, including experiential and testimonial, are distinguished. In contrast, existing individualist approaches tend to (implicitly or explicitly) adopt a coarse-grained conception of evidence, in which different forms of evidence are not distinguished from one another, except perhaps by the relative strength of different kinds of evidence.

This is most clearly seen in cognition-based accounts, including accounts that trace delusions to JTC bias or BADE. Simonsen and colleagues make a similar point in discussing existing reasoning-based accounts:

> [Previous research of reasoning in schizophrenia] neglects that we usually make inferences based on a multitude of information sources that vary both in type and reliability. This is the case for low-level perception, but perhaps even more so for our social lives, where we constantly have to deal with different people that say or do different things with different degrees of certainty. This information has to be combined with our own experiences and beliefs, which may be more or less certain. In short, the classical beads task [for testing the JTC bias] fails to address how we simultaneously balance and integrate heterogeneous information sources. (Simonsen et al., 2021, p.1604)

According to the JTC account, delusional individuals tend to jump to conclusions *in facing all forms of evidence*. But this is implausible. Delusional individuals do not seem to jump to conclusions when facing testimonial evidence. After adopting a delusional belief, an individual with Capgras delusion does not jump to the conclusion that the woman in front of him is his real wife when his clinician tells him that she is his real wife. Indeed, this is related to one of the most serious worries about the JTC bias account, i.e., that it fails to explain the maintenance of delusion where delusional beliefs persist in the face of clear counterevidence (e.g., Davies et al., 2001). According to the BADE account, delusional people tend to stick to prior beliefs in the face of counterevidence *in facing all forms of (counter)evidence*. However, this is also implausible. Delusional individuals do not stick to prior beliefs in the face of experiential evidence. For example, when an individual with Capgras delusion initially adopts his delusional belief in response to some anomalous experience, he revises his prior non-delusional belief (i.e., that this woman, who looks exactly like his wife, is his wife).

Similar problems arise for the other explanatory approaches. For example, the second factor in two-factor accounts is also typically characterised in domain-general terms rather than as a specific deficit in responding to social evidence, and predictive processing accounts rarely accommodate differences between social and non-social evidence in their models of prediction error minimisation.

The situation with experience-based accounts is somewhat different. The problem with such accounts is that they do not explain why testimonial evidence fails to counterbalance or override the experiential evidence they posit. This is puzzling given our general reliance on testimony (see Chapter 1, Section 4) and the fact that the testimonial counterevidence could not be stronger in most cases of delusion (see Chapter 9). Of course, as we will argue in Chapter 9, it is possible to supplement experience-based accounts with a recognition of the distinction between different kinds of evidence and an explanation of the asymmetry in question, but that is just what it would be—a supplementation. Without supplementation, the asymmetry in question is puzzling. The resistance of delusional beliefs to social evidence is left unexplained.

7. Chapter Summary

This chapter has critically reviewed dominant individualistic frameworks for understanding clinical delusions: cognition-based (Section 2.1), experience-based (Section 2.2), two-factor (Section 2.3), and predictive processing accounts (Section 2.4). Each approach provides valuable insights into the psychological processes that may contribute to delusion formation, from cognitive biases and anomalous experiences to hierarchical prediction processes. Nevertheless, each also encounters limitations in accounting for the social dimensions of delusions.

We have identified three social challenges for these accounts: explaining the robust epidemiological evidence linking social adversity to delusions (the challenge of social determinants; Section 4), explaining the predominantly social themes of delusional content across cultures (the challenge of social focus; Section 5), and explaining why social evidence appears to be treated differently from experiential evidence in the delusion-forming process (the challenge of social evidence; Section 6).

As we have stressed throughout, these challenges are not intended as decisive objections to individualist accounts. Nevertheless, they suggest that research on delusions must engage more with human sociality. In the remainder of Part 3, we will explore two ways this engagement might unfold. In Chapter 7, we will examine and scrutinise social accounts of delusions that posit abnormal social cognition instead of the factors identified in individualistic approaches. We will argue that although this approach offers important insights, it also encounters significant limitations. This will pave the way for our positive framework in Chapters 8 and 9, which aims to address the three social challenges we have identified by integrating individual and social approaches. This integration will involve situating experiential and cognitive difficulties in intensely social minds inhabiting uniquely complex and challenging social environments.

7
Existing Social Accounts of Clinical Delusions

1. Introduction

Chapter 6 reviewed individualistic frameworks for understanding clinical delusions, including cognition-based, experience-based, two-factor, and predictive processing accounts. We argued that these individualistic approaches confront three challenges related to social dimensions of delusions: first, they do not have a clear explanation of the social determinants of delusions (the challenge of social determinants); second, they do not directly explain why the contents of delusions overwhelmingly focus on the individual's place within the social world (the challenge of social focus); third, they do not explain the fact that non-social and social evidence appear to be treated in different ways in the delusion formation process (the challenge of social evidence).

Chapters 8 and 9 will develop our preferred way of addressing these social challenges, which situates delusions in a multifactorial framework in which perceptual, cognitive, and other factors interact with distinctive features of human sociality and the social environment in complex causal processes. In this chapter, we will first explore a very different, more direct social approach, which seeks to explain delusions through selective disorders of social cognition (Bell et al., 2021; Frith, 2004; Gold & Gold, 2015).

As with previous chapters, our review and discussion are not exhaustive. Instead, we will focus primarily on Ian and Joel Gold's (Gold, 2017; Gold & Gold, 2015) hypothesis that delusions are symptoms of disorders of a special-purpose "suspicion system" designed to detect and manage social threats. We focus on this account because we regard it as the most promising and well-developed of its kind and because several of our criticisms will generalise to similar accounts that trace delusions to targeted disorders in specialised sociocognitive processes.[1]

[1] Chris Frith (2004, 2014) has famously proposed that delusions in schizophrenia result from mentalising deficits. Although we agree that abnormal mentalising is likely implicated in many delusions, it

The Social Roots of Delusions. Daniel Williams, Sam Wilkinson, and Kengo Miyazono, Oxford University Press.
 DOI: 10.1093/9780191976360.003.0008

We structure the chapter as follows. Section 2 makes the preliminary case that social threat management is relevant to delusions. Section 3 details the central claims of Gold and Gold's account. Section 4 outlines several reasons for being sceptical of these claims. Section 5 summarises this chapter and extracts a general lesson: that although heightened vigilance for social threats seems highly relevant to many delusions, it is a mistake to assume that this relevance must take the form of localised disorders in a highly modular social threat detection system.

2. Social Vigilance and Delusions

The greatest danger humans must navigate is typically other humans (see Chapter 1, Section 5.2.2). Whether such dangers take the form of everyday selfishness and free riding or brutal forms of domination and violence, the competitive nature of human social life means that other people constitute and have always constituted a universal, persistent, and highly consequential threat (Green & Phillips, 2004; Wrangham, 2019). Moreover, unlike other threats, such as diseases or physical accidents, social threats involve rational agents with sophisticated capacities for reasoning, planning, and social coordination, including the ability to conceal or deliberately misrepresent their actions and intentions (Williams & Montagnese, 2023).

Given these persistent dangers and unique complexities of social threats, it is highly plausible that humans have evolved sophisticated motivations and capacities specialised for detecting, anticipating, and responding to them. We have already introduced epistemic vigilance, which involves cognitive processes targeted at informational threats posed by others (Mercier, 2020; Sperber et al., 2010; see Chapter 1, Section 4.2). However, such capacities are just one part of more general capacities adapted to the dangers posed by other people, which we will refer to as "social vigilance".[2]

Social vigilance seems to involve at least the following four characteristics. First, individuals' feelings of social suspicion and threshold for social threat detection are calibrated to their degree of risk, which depends on the level of social danger in their environment and their vulnerability to such dangers

does not follow that delusions emerge from a selective disorder to mentalising, and mentalising deficits are most strongly associated with the negative symptoms of schizophrenia, not psychosis (Freeman, 2016; Garety & Freeman, 2013; Korver-Nieberg et al., 2013).

[2] The term "social vigilance" is sometimes used more narrowly to refer to the active monitoring of social threats (White et al., 2024; Wright et al., 2020), which is one manifestation of more general motivations and capacities specialised for detecting and responding to them.

(Raihani & Bell, 2019). Both factors vary significantly between contexts and individuals. For example, one's vulnerability to exploitation depends both on one's capabilities (i.e., one's ability to manage or rebuff social threats) and the degree of social support one can expect from others. Evidence suggests that individuals track these individual and environmental features and adjust their suspicious tendencies accordingly (Kraus et al., 2011; Raihani & Bell, 2019; Singh, 2021). Moreover, as with many features of human cognition, such tendencies seem to be especially impacted during sensitive periods such as childhood and adolescence, when deep-rooted expectations about the world are acquired and become challenging to unlearn (Fuhrmann et al., 2015; Giudice, 2018).

Second, except for those who can be very confident of high social support and safety, one would expect social vigilance to be somewhat biased towards producing false alarms to avoid the risk of failing to detect real threats (Haselton & Nettle, 2006; Singh, 2021). As documented in Chapter 3, this is an adaptive ("error management") feature of detection systems whenever false positives (e.g., detecting a non-existent threat) are less costly than false negatives (e.g., failing to detect a real threat). This likely explains why mild forms of paranoia are widespread within the non-clinical population (Freeman et al., 2005; Raihani & Bell, 2019).

Third, in addition to tracking social threats in one's immediate environment, social vigilance includes motivations and abilities specialised for anticipating and exploring more distant, threat-related scenarios arising from complex plans and conspiracies deliberately concealed by their perpetrators (Williams & Montagnese, 2023). Once again, this task is challenging because exploitative scenarios can take many forms, and exploiters can misrepresent their intentions and take into consideration their victim's beliefs and expectations. (Recall the example we mentioned in Chapter 1, Section 5.2.2, in which a group of Yanomamö men conspired to trick someone into laying down his weapons so they could execute him.) For these reasons, once suspicions of exploitation or victimisation occur, people are often driven to explore complex possibilities and scenarios and "expect the unexpected". Moreover, given the possibilities of deception and concealment, such suspicions about social threats are often uniquely difficult to falsify. For example, it is difficult to disconfirm the suspicion that one is the victim of a deliberately and carefully concealed plot.

Finally, detecting social threats is only worthwhile if one responds appropriately. Given this, social vigilance involves motivations, emotions, and capacities specialised for responding to such threats. Because the dangers posed by others can take multiple forms and an individual's available reactions depend on many factors (e.g., their capabilities and level of social support), these responses must be highly flexible and context-sensitive. For example, sometimes one should try to respond to attempted exploitation with aggression, sometimes one should try to recruit support from others, sometimes one should accept one's situation because no responses are available, and sometimes one should hide or isolate oneself.

Several theorists have speculated that social vigilance is relevant to delusions (e.g., Abed & Abbas, 2014; Freeman, 2007; Green & Phillips, 2004; Raihani & Bell, 2019). Although such proposals take different forms, the focus is usually on the connection between delusions and an excessive vigilance for social threats, producing false positives (i.e., detecting non-existent social threats) that either constitute or give rise to paranoid delusions. For example, Abed and Abbas allege that "the core psychopathology of schizophrenia involves hypervigilance and overattribution of malicious intentions to others" (Abed & Abbas, 2014, p.3), and Green and Phillips conjecture that "clinical levels of paranoia [including persecutory delusions] may represent the inevitable cost of efficient threat perception" (Green & Phillips, 2004, p.336).

Even when stated in this highly schematic way, one can see the attractions of such proposals by returning to the three social challenges to traditional accounts of delusions identified in Chapter 6. First, if excessive vigilance for social threats is relevant to some delusions, this would illuminate their leading social risk factors (e.g., childhood abuse, bullying, marginalisation), which all plausibly increase an individual's suspicion of other people's intentions. Second, it would help to explain why the most common delusional theme cross-culturally is persecution, which, by definition, involves unfounded suspicions of social threats. Finally, it would illuminate why people with delusions are strongly resistant to testimonial evidence in some cases. If individuals are suspicious of other people's intentions, they will be less likely to accept testimony that contradicts their beliefs. In other words, excessive social vigilance will naturally drive excessive epistemic vigilance.

Nevertheless, there are multiple ways to elaborate on such ideas. For example, one might view social threat management as an explanatory factor that can supplement the focus on perceptual and domain-general cognitive abnormalities in traditional explanatory frameworks (e.g., Freeman, 2016). We will favour this approach in Chapters 8 and 9. Alternatively, one might treat disorders of social vigilance as an alternative to traditional explanatory frameworks. This is the explanatory strategy developed by Gold and Gold, at least on the most ambitious interpretation of their account.

3. Delusions and a Disordered Suspicion System

Gold and Gold's account of delusions is complex and has evolved (Gold, 2017; Gold & Gold, 2015). Here, we will isolate just those features of the account relevant to understanding its core ideas. We will first identify what the account seeks to explain (Section 3.1) and what it assumes (Section 3.2) before turning to the explanation itself (Section 3.3).

3.1 The Target of the Explanation

Gold and Gold assume clinical delusions form a unified class of beliefs amenable to a shared causal explanation. That is, despite the profound heterogeneity in the characteristics and causes of beliefs classified as delusions within medical psychiatry (see Chapter 6, Section 1), they assume such beliefs share a common aetiology that cuts across the diverse psychiatric and neurological disorders and conditions associated with delusions. Moreover, their account seeks to explain several alleged characteristics of such beliefs that much traditional research ignores or fails to appreciate sufficiently.

We have already identified two of these social characteristics in Chapter 6, Sections 4 and 5. First, Gold and Gold note that delusions have important social determinants in factors like abuse, discrimination, and marginalisation. Second, they observe that delusions mainly focus on a relatively small number of overwhelmingly social themes, a "clear pattern in the phenomena of delusion, and any theory worth its salt is going to have to be able to explain why it is there" (Gold & Gold, 2015, p.166). Specifically, Gold (2017) argues that most clinical delusions fall into three broad categories. In delusions of social threat, individuals believe other agents (real or imaginary) intentionally seek to harm, control, or interfere with them. This includes persecutory delusions, delusions of reference, delusions of jealousy, delusions of control, delusions of thought, and religious delusions in which the social threat is a supernatural agent. In delusions of social power, individuals believe they possess high social status due to special abilities, identity, or connections to other high-status people. This includes grandiose delusions, erotomanic delusions, and religious delusions in which grandiosity is understood through a supernatural lens. Finally, delusions of social inferiority involve beliefs depicting the relevant individual as weak, damaged, or vulnerable. This includes somatic delusions, nihilistic delusions, and delusions of guilt or sin.

Third, Gold and Gold argue that delusions involve a highly circumscribed form of irrationality. That is, although people with delusions seem to think and reason in disordered ways, this aberrant cognition is highly concentrated around the delusions themselves. As Vaughan Bell and colleagues note, "[M]ost people with delusions appear not to have a generalized problem with rationality but a circumscribed irrationality by which conclusions are irrational solely in relation to the delusional content" (Bell et al., 2021, p.25). Given this, Gold and Gold argue against accounts of delusions that posit domain-general reasoning abnormalities, which would predict more global disturbances in delusional cognition. This observation differs from their claim that delusions tend to have social themes. The latter focuses on the contents of delusions, the former on delusional cognition. For example, even if delusions focus overwhelmingly on social themes, people with delusions could still exhibit global disturbances to cognition.

3.2 The Explanation's Assumptions

Gold and Gold's (2015) account of delusions assumes that social vigilance is underpinned by interactions between a "suspicion system", a special-purpose evolved module "designed to act as a quick-and-dirty 'early warning system' for social threats" (Gold, 2017, p.108), and a "reflective system", a part of the mind capable of sophisticated reasoning and of drawing on a much broader range of information to evaluate whether suspicions of social threat are warranted.

This account assumes a "dual systems" model of cognitive processes (Frankish, 2010; Kahneman, 2003; see Chapter 3, Section 4). According to this model, the mind involves two distinct kinds of systems or forms of cognitive processing. "System 1" cognitive processes are typically unconscious, automatic, fast, and effortless. They generate rapid and automatic judgements or decisions through processes that individuals have no conscious access to. In contrast, System 2 processing is typically conscious, effortful, slow, subject to executive control, and capable of drawing on a much more comprehensive range of relevant information.

The suspicion system is a form of System 1 cognition, "the purpose of which is early detection of the threat of exploitation" (Gold & Gold, 2015, p.232). The central target of the system is malign intentions, which it detects and anticipates by responding to potentially subtle and ambiguous cues. Because the costs of false positives are typically much lower than those of false negatives, it is biased towards producing false positives. Moreover, the suspicion system is modular in certain important respects (Fodor, 1983). First, it is *domain-specific*: "It is only interested in input of a certain kind—evidence of social threat" (Gold & Gold, 2015, p.261). Second, it is *informationally encapsulated* "to a high degree" (Gold, 2017, p. 110), meaning it processes evidence of social threat in ways that are highly compartmentalised from (and hence uninformed by) most of the information people possess. Thus, whereas domain specificity concerns "the range of questions for which a device provides answers (the range of inputs for which it [i.e., the relevant module] computes analyses)" (Fodor, 1983, p.103), informational encapsulation concerns the degree to which its operations can access information elsewhere within the mind. This modularity is supposed to explain how the system's operations can be so fast and automatic—that is, how it can "act as a quick-and-dirty 'early warning system' for social threats" (Gold, 2017, p.108).

In typical forms of social vigilance, this modular processing of the suspicion system interacts with System 2's "reflective system", which is neither domain-specific nor informationally encapsulated. Instead, it integrates a much broader range of evidence and deploys slow, conscious reasoning to determine whether the suspicious thoughts generated by the suspicion system are warranted. If it deems them unwarranted, the suspicion system's activity is inhibited, and the suspicion subsides. If it deems them well-founded, the individual integrates the threat into their broader web of beliefs and deploys defensive strategies.

3.3 The Explanation

This provides the background for understanding Gold and Gold's account. "Delusions", Gold writes, "are disordered versions of thoughts that function as warning signals about dangerous others as well as disordered thoughts that function as strategies to combat these social threats" (Gold, 2017, p.102). Specifically, Gold and Gold speculate (i) that delusions of social threat result from a disordered suspicion system that generates false alarms of social threats; (ii) that delusions of social power are a disordered manifestation of a strategy allegedly used to rebuff social threats by inflating one's social status, an approach analogous to how other animals often make themselves look bigger in response to threats and dangers; and (iii) that delusions of social inferiority are a disordered version of a strategy aimed at appeasing threatening individuals through the manifestation of submission.

Gold and Gold argue that such speculations provide a framework for addressing the two fundamental questions of delusion research: why specific delusional ideas occur to people and why individuals retain such ideas in the face of apparent counter-evidence. Their answer to the first question is that delusional ideas either occur to people as part of the natural operation of the suspicion system—fleeting paranoid thoughts occur to most of us, after all—or through a malfunction that renders the system hypervigilant for social threats.

Their answer to the second question is that delusional thoughts are retained as beliefs when the reflective system cannot inhibit the alarms of the suspicion system. They identify multiple reasons why this might be the case. For example, it might be that a disordered suspicion system produces warning signals even in the presence of the reflective system's inhibitions or because of a functional disconnection between the suspicion system and the reflective system, which means the former's warning signals cannot be inhibited. (Note that in the latter case, the disorder targets the inhibition of warning signals from the suspicion system rather than the system itself. Nevertheless, because the disorder is specific to the system's output, we will follow Gold and Gold in referring to this as a disorder of the suspicion system.)

Whatever the cause, Gold and Gold argue that one would expect a period of conflict between the outputs of the two systems during which the individual recognises the implausibility of their suspicious thoughts. They suggest this corresponds to the prodromal phase of psychosis in schizophrenia, when individuals often retain insight into the falsity of their delusional ideas. After this, they suggest that the delusional thoughts will eventually "win out," and the role of the reflective system will shift from scrutinising the suspicion system's alarm signals to integrating the social threat into the individual's broader worldview.

As Gold and Gold acknowledge, these conjectures are highly schematic. Nevertheless, one can see in broad outline how they could begin to address the targets of their explanation. First, they argue that "the social determinants of psychosis [...] may be stressors that increase our need for vigilance and in the long run 'overload' the suspicion system" (Gold & Gold, 2015, p.292). That is, experiences of victimisation and marginalisation increase the risk of delusions by increasing people's vigilance for such threats.

Second, they argue that the social focus of delusions across cultural contexts reflects their origins in a cognitive module dedicated to the narrow domain of social threats: "The dozen or so forms of delusion are stable across time and culture because they reflect the function (or malfunction) of the suspicion system which, as an old, hardwired, and modular form of cognition, is not plastic" (Gold, 2017, p.115).

Finally, this modular character of the suspicion system can also illuminate the allegedly circumscribed nature of irrationality as manifested in delusional cognition. Because delusions result only from disorders of the suspicion system, one would not expect delusional individuals to exhibit domain-general disturbances to how they think and reason about the world. Except for its inability to inhibit the warning signals generated by the suspicion system, the reflective system—the individual's domain-general ability to think and reason about the world—is intact on their account.

4. Evaluating the Account

In this section, we will identify several reasons why we do not think this account and the approach it exemplifies are promising. We will not explore all potential objections. We will focus only on those that most clearly motivate our alternative approach to addressing the three social challenges identified in Chapter 6. First, we will argue that social vigilance is unlikely to involve a highly modular "suspicion system" (Section 4.1). Second, we will argue that the account conflicts with the heterogeneity manifest in delusional contents, cognition, and causes (Section 4.2). Finally, we will argue that excessive vigilance for social threats alone is unlikely to produce persecutory delusions, let alone all delusions (Section 4.3).

4.1 Does a Modular Suspicion System Underpin Social Vigilance?

The central hypothesis of Gold and Gold's account of delusions is that delusions arise from disorders of a highly modular cognitive system tasked with detecting social threats. Although we share their view that humans have evolved psychological processes specialised for managing social threats (Chapter 1, Section 5) and that such processes are relevant to understanding delusions in many cases, their assumption that such processes involve a highly domain-specific, informationally encapsulated detection module is implausible.

Some theorists have identified general objections to modular accounts of human cognitive architecture (Anderson, 2010; Prinz, 2014; see Chapter 1, Section 2). Whatever the merits of such general criticisms, there are specific reasons for being sceptical that social threat detection and anticipation involve a highly compartmentalised, special-purpose module.

The fundamental problem concerns the uniqueness and complexity of social threats. As noted above (Section 2), unlike other threats, social threats involve rational agents with sophisticated abilities in reasoning, planning, coordination, and deception. This means they can involve complex scenarios spanning different time scales, cooperation between multiple agents, and deliberate misrepresentation and concealment. Moreover, such agents can strategically adapt in response to attempts to identify their hostile or exploitative intentions. Given this, detecting and, more importantly, *anticipating* social threats are uniquely challenging and cannot simply be modelled on much simpler detection tasks where modular processing is most plausible.

First, consider the claim that the suspicion system is domain-specific. By this, Gold and Gold mean that the system "is only interested in input of a certain kind—evidence of social threat" (Gold & Gold, 2015, p.261). The problem with this assumption is that anything could conceivably qualify as evidence of social threat. Unlike with tasks like face recognition or language parsing, where inputs are relatively clearly defined and predetermined, there is no natural, predetermined class of inputs for social threat detection.

Consider coming home after being away to discover a cigarette butt in your garden. Is that evidence of a potential social threat? If the only person you live with is your spouse, and they do not smoke, and they tell you that nobody has been in the house whilst you have been away, it might provide evidence for, say, infidelity or any number of other possibilities. Whether it does would depend on a wide range of factors: the likelihood that the cigarette arrived there accidentally, your trust in your partner, the plausibility of alternative explanations, and so on. Or consider noticing that what somebody says contradicts something else they said in a different context. Whether that contradiction should qualify as evidence of social threat will, once again, depend on countless other factors, such as the specific content of their contradictory claims, their trustworthiness, their relationship with you, and so on.

These examples demonstrate that social threat detection cannot be restricted to a predetermined range of inputs. Whether something qualifies as evidence for a social threat depends on how it relates to specific hypotheses about other people's intentions and the relationship between them and your distinctive circumstances. Given that rational agents with exploitative or hostile intentions can deliberately and inadvertently alter the perceptible environment in countless open-ended ways, including ways intended to evade and mislead detection, anything could conceivably qualify as evidence of a social threat, and the same "input" can mean radically different things according to context.

For these reasons, it is equally implausible that social threat detection could be highly informationally encapsulated. Because something only qualifies as evidence of social threats relative to specific hypotheses about exploitative or hostile intentions, detecting and anticipating such threats must integrate a vast and open-ended body of information, including perceptual, social, contextual, and historical information. In other words, detecting or anticipating potential social threats cannot be isolated from one's broader beliefs, concerns, and interests; tracking such threats inevitably draws on hypotheses and knowledge only accessible by engaging with such information.

Some of Gold and Gold's discussions of social vigilance acknowledge the complex, unique, and global informational and cognitive demands it raises. However, they do not appreciate the problems that such demands pose for their assumptions about the modularity of the suspicion system. For example, they cite studies on how rapidly people intuit the trustworthiness of faces as evidence "that the Suspicion System is a special-purpose [modular] mechanism" (Gold & Gold, 2015, p. 257), but focusing on such rapid intuitions as representative of social threat detection is highly misleading. First, whether a facial expression qualifies as evidence of a threat depends on a wide range of additional contextual factors. What are their intentions? Whom is their expression directed at? The same facial expression can mean countless distinct things depending on the broader context (Chanes et al., 2018). More importantly, the example ignores what makes social vigilance so challenging: people often deliberately misrepresent or conceal hostile or manipulative intentions. For this reason, there is no reliable behavioural evidence of deception (Mercier, 2020), and a smile can qualify as evidence for a social threat just as much as a scowl, depending on the broader context. Finally, most evidence for social threats has nothing to do with people's facial expressions, appearance, or behaviour. And it is noteworthy that the cases where quasi-perceptual social threat detection systems are most plausible, such as detecting signs of direct physical aggression in somebody's face, are very far removed from the kinds of fears and worries central to typical persecutory delusions (Freeman, 2016).

These observations are not intended to challenge the assumption that humans possess psychological processes specialised for detecting and anticipating social threats. Instead, the point is that the highly modular cognitive system posited by Gold and Gold seems incapable of effectively performing this task. In general, it is a mistake to infer from the fact that the human mind is specialised for performing specific functions that it is divided into encapsulated, domain-specific modules dedicated to those tasks (Barrett, 2014).

Because different tasks impose very different requirements on cognition, including their necessary degree of integration with more global cognitive and informational resources, no single cookie-cutter template applies to all the psychological processes that underlie different functions. By assimilating social vigilance to much simpler perceptual or quasi-perceptual detection tasks, Gold and Gold ignore the very features of social threats that make them uniquely complex and challenging to navigate. Social threat detection and anticipation must integrate complex social signals, evaluate social and cultural context, process linguistic input, track relationships and other historical information over time, evaluate social status and context-variable roles, and much more. A highly modular, encapsulated cognitive system would be incapable of satisfying such constraints.

Why does this matter? First, the allegedly modular nature of the suspicion system is central to Gold and Gold's account. It is supposed to explain why delusions focus on a narrow range of themes, why the cognitive disturbances exhibited in delusions are highly localised, and why suspicious thoughts cannot be inhibited by an individual's broader body of beliefs about the world. It is also supposed to explain how the disorders associated with delusions could selectively target social threat detection whilst leaving other cognitive processes intact.

However, these objections are also important for a more constructive reason. Once one appreciates social vigilance's unique informational and computational demands, including its reliance on integrating a wide range of information and cognitive resources, it opens up theoretical space for alternative ways in which social vigilance might be relevant to delusions. For example, in Chapter 8, we will argue that such complexities partly explain why social vigilance is uniquely fragile and vulnerable to producing paranoia when individuals confront experiential or global cognitive disturbances.

4.2 Heterogeneity

At least on the most ambitious interpretation of Gold and Gold's account, they assume that delusions exhibit sufficient homogeneity to be treated as a unified class of beliefs amenable to a shared causal explanation. This conflicts with our analysis of delusion attribution (see Chapter 2) and emphasis on the profound heterogeneity in the character of delusions and delusional cognition (see Chapters 2 and 6). Clinical delusions vary massively in their focus, the bizarreness of their content, the degree to which they are circumscribed, their developmental trajectory throughout a disorder, their persistence, the degree of distress they cause, and the disorders and disturbances with which they are associated. In the context of Gold and Gold's account, three especially problematic forms of heterogeneity concern delusional contents (Section 4.2.1), delusional cognition (Section 4.2.2), and delusional causes (Section 4.2.3).

4.2.1 Content Heterogeneity

The main explanatory target of Gold and Gold's account is the cross-cultural clustering of delusional content around social themes (see also Bell et al., 2021). Because this is a pattern allegedly exhibited by all delusions, not just delusions associated with specific disorders or disturbances, it motivates them to treat delusions as a unified class amenable to the same underlying explanation. As argued in Chapter 6, Section 5, we agree with Gold and Gold that the cross-cultural clustering of delusions around predominantly social themes is an important and underappreciated phenomenon that warrants explanation. Nevertheless, Gold and Gold's account seems to posit too much homogeneity in the contents of delusions.

The first and most obvious problem is that some delusions do not seem to have social content. Consider delusional parasitosis, which typically involves the belief that one's body is infected with parasites, or Cotard delusion, often expressed as the belief that one has ceased to exist. Moreover, one might worry that standard taxonomies of delusional themes (e.g., Gold, 2017) undercount the prevalence of non-social delusions by arbitrarily excluding certain widespread delusion-like beliefs from the category. For example, as Stephen Gadsby argues (2024), psychiatrists typically resist the use of the term "delusion" to describe strange beliefs about the body and body weight in anorexia nervosa, even though such beliefs satisfy many conventional medical criteria for delusional status. The belief that one is overweight when on the brink of starvation would strike most people as delusional, especially if our analysis of delusion attribution is correct (see Chapter 2), and yet it is arbitrarily excluded from most analyses of delusional themes (e.g., Gold, 2017).

Insofar as Gold and Gold seek to explain the social focus of delusions by tracing them to disorders of social cognition, the fact that certain delusions do not seem to focus on social phenomena poses a clear problem for their account. In response to this worry, they argue that delusions that do not seem to have social content are indirectly connected to social themes and social threat management. For example, they claim that somatic delusions and some nihilistic delusions (e.g., the Cotard delusion) are delusions of "social inferiority" because they "represent the delusional person as particularly damaged, weak, or vulnerable" (Gold, 2017, p.102). This leads them to interpret such delusions as "distorted versions of self-deprecatory behaviors, the purpose of which is to defend against social threat by appeasing threatening individuals" (Gold, 2017, p.113).

There are several problems with this account. First, it is inapplicable to some non-social delusions. For example, reduplicative paramnesia involves the delusional belief that one's current setting (e.g., a hospital) has been duplicated or moved to another location (Coltheart & Davies, 2024a). It is difficult to see how this could be even indirectly connected to the theme of social inferiority. Second, the claim that somatic and nihilistic delusions are delusions of social inferiority that arise in response to perceived social threats is no just highly speculative but implausible. Cotard delusion often appears to be linked to depressed mood and affect, not paranoia (Berrios & Luque, 1995; Faunce & Tennant, 2024). Moreover, the connection between such fixed and strange delusions and submissive behaviours seen in other animals is tenuous.

Another problem with Gold and Gold's account is that it also seems to impose too much homogeneity among delusions with explicit social themes. First, Gold and Gold bundle multiple delusional themes together as delusions of social threat. However, this seems unwarranted in certain important cases. For example, delusions of reference are one of the most common delusional themes across cultures (Collin et al., 2023). Although they typically have a social focus (e.g., the suspicion of being observed, discussed, followed, or the focus of covert messages) and often develop into persecutory delusions, they need not involve the attribution of threatening intentions to others. Sometimes, their content is neutral or positive. It is this feature that distinguishes such delusions from persecutory delusions and explains why they can mutate into grandiose delusions as well as delusions focused on social threats (Freeman, 2016). This poses a problem for Gold and Gold's analysis of the prodromal phase of schizophrenia, according to which suspicions of social threat morph into persecutory delusions over time as individuals lose the ability to inhibit such suspicions. This phase is often characterised by delusions of reference that are not inherently connected to social threats.

Second, Gold and Gold assimilate grandiose and erotomanic delusions to a general category of delusions of social power, which they seek to explain as an attempt to rebuff perceived social threats. So understood, these delusions are supposed to be similar to cases in which other animals attempt to deter threats by making themselves look bigger (e.g., elephants sticking out their ears, puffer fish inflating themselves, and so on). Once again, this interpretation seems to be driven by the demands of their account rather than by the delusions' features. For example, although grandiose delusions sometimes arise from paranoia and persecutory delusions (if others are out to get you, this can imply that you must be very important or unique), they can also arise in mania, when individuals are experiencing highly elevated status-related emotions in which they are, if anything, excessively *un*vigilant against social threats. In such cases, grandiose delusions co-occur with abnormally high energy, inflated self-esteem, and exaggerated sensitivity to rewards, rather than hypervigilance for social threats (Del Giudice, 2018, p. 506). Moreover, as with Gold and Gold's analysis of delusions of social inferiority, the connection between grandiose delusions and cases in which animals inflate their appearance to rebuff social threats is highly tenuous. For example, this analogy fails to explain many features of grandiose delusions, including that their contents are often highly elaborated and connected to fantasy elaboration (in which people imaginatively withdraw into pleasurable grandiose fantasies). It is also opaque why people would sometimes keep their grandiose delusions private if this account is correct (see Freeman, 2018).

In summary, although Gold and Gold are correct to highlight the cross-cultural clustering of delusional themes around primarily social concerns, their account seems to impose too much homogeneity on delusional content. A framework for understanding delusions must be sensitive to both the general patterns exhibited by delusional content and its heterogeneity. By exaggerating the former, Gold and Gold's account struggles to explain the latter.

4.2.2 Cognitive Heterogeneity

Another strong assumption of homogeneity in Gold and Gold's account concerns delusional cognition. They claim that abnormal cognition in people with delusions is narrowly concentrated around the delusions themselves and does not affect broader cognitive processes. This allegedly makes it plausible that delusions result from disorders of a highly modular special-purpose suspicion system, leaving the "reflective system"—the cognitive processes that underpin domain-general capacities for thought and reasoning—intact.

The problem with this assumption is that there is profound variation in the degree to which abnormal cognition is circumscribed in delusions. The case where highly circumscribed abnormalities are most evident is in monothematic delusions following discrete brain injuries. However, in these cases, there is already a highly influential explanation of their circumscribed nature: that they are connected to comparably circumscribed perceptual abnormalities (see Chapter 6, Section 2.2). There is controversy over whether such abnormalities are sufficient to produce delusions in such cases. Nevertheless, their narrow focus is widely thought to be connected to relatively narrow anomalous experiences (Noordhof & Sullivan-Bissett, 2021). This offers an alternative explanation for the circumscribed cognitive abnormalities observed in such cases. Moreover, Gold and Gold's account seems inferior. For example, if people with delusions were suffering a disorder in their suspicion system or in their ability to inhibit suspicious thoughts, one would expect people with such delusions to feature much more expansive hypervigilance for social threats, generating suspicion and suspicious explanations of events across the board. However, we are unaware of any evidence for this prediction, and monothematic delusions frequently involve contents wholly unrelated to social threats.

Nevertheless, even if Gold and Gold's account could explain highly circumscribed cognitive abnormalities, many delusions seem to be associated with global cognitive abnormalities. For example, in the polythematic, highly elaborated delusions often associated with schizophrenia and other psychotic disorders, there seem to be very general disturbances to how individuals evaluate and process information, which correlate with global neural differences (Del Giudice, 2018, Ch.8; McCutcheon et al., 2020; Reed et al., 2020). Although Gold and Gold and other proponents of social accounts of delusions are likely correct that these relatively subtle global disturbances are insufficient to explain the frequently striking forms of abnormality manifest in delusions themselves (see Bell et al., 2021), the latter might arise from complex interactions between global cognitive disturbances and many other factors (e.g., experiential and affective) over time, as we will explore in the next chapter. That is, Gold and Gold seem to present a false dichotomy: either cognitive disturbances must be highly localised, or they must be severe enough to directly cause delusions through global impairment. This overlooks a more nuanced possibility in which delusions often emerge from dynamic interactions among multiple factors—including both local and global cognitive changes—that compound and reinforce one another over time.

In summary, one of the central assumptions of Gold and Gold's account is that the irrationality manifest in delusional cognition appears to be highly circumscribed. This motivates their attempt to link delusions to highly targeted disorders in a special-purpose, encapsulated module. However, as with their assumptions about delusional themes, their assumption about delusional cognition seems to impose too much homogeneity on delusional cognition.

4.2.3 Causal Heterogeneity

A third problematic form of homogeneity in Gold and Gold's account concerns their analysis of the causes of delusions. The most ambitious interpretation of their account assumes that all delusions result exclusively from disorders of a single, modular suspicion system. This understanding of delusional causality is, therefore, highly *localised* (it traces delusions to one specific cognitive system), *low-factorial* (it traces delusions to a small number of factors affecting the system and the inhibition of its outputs), *delusion-specific* (the factors producing delusions are unique to delusions), and *pathocentric* (the factors all involve disorders).

There are several problems with these assumptions. First, Gold and Gold's unified and simple causal model seems to lack the resources to address the heterogeneity manifest in delusions, including (but not restricted to) delusional contents and cognition. As we have seen, if delusions are downstream of hypervigilance for social threats, why do some delusions not seem to involve such hypervigilance? If delusions result from highly localised disturbances to a cognitive module, why are delusions often associated with global cognitive disturbances? A more complex, flexible explanatory framework seems necessary to accommodate these and many other forms of heterogeneity.

Second, delusions are associated with a vast range of conditions, injuries, and disturbances. They can arise from many psychiatric conditions, neurological disorders, brain injuries, and the use and abuse of various psychoactive substances. Even focusing just on clinical paranoia and persecutory delusions, the most natural explanatory target of Gold and Gold's account, they arise not just in schizophrenia but in bipolar disorder, dementia, delusional disorder, Parkinson's disease, brain injuries, epilepsy, and many other conditions. They are also linked to phenomena such as sleep deprivation, drug use (especially cannabis and amphetamines), and severe stress (Freeman, 2016; Raihani & Bell, 2019). As Raihani and Bell observe, "In terms of the causes and contexts in which it appears, paranoia is perhaps most remarkable for being associated with such a wide range of difficulties, impairments and stresses" (Raihani & Bell, 2019, p.114). Although not impossible, it seems implausible that these diverse difficulties, impairments, and stresses all produce localised disorders within the same highly specialised sociocognitive module. Instead, such heterogeneity seems to fit better with an explanatory framework in which multiple kinds of experiential, cognitive, and emotional disturbances can be channelled into persecutory delusions (see Chapter 8).

Third, Gold and Gold's account neglects the importance of many highly relevant factors to understanding delusions. For example, although we agree with Gold and Gold that factors such as perceptual abnormalities and global cognitive abnormalities are insufficient on their own to explain phenomena such as the social focus of delusions (Chapter 6), there are both persuasive theoretical reasons and some compelling evidence that they are relevant to delusions in many cases (Freeman, 2016; Noordhof & Sullivan-Bissett, 2021; Sterzer et al., 2018; see Chapter 8). Strange experiences seem to be associated with many monothematic delusions, and the polythematic delusions characteristic of psychotic conditions in schizophrenia often seem to be preceded by and related to perceptual abnormalities, such as hearing voices and seeing otherwise everyday objects as loaded with special significance (Freeman, 2016; Kapur, 2003). It seems implausible that such experiences are epiphenomenal. Moreover, because their content is not always social and is often neutral or even positive when it is social, it is also implausible to treat all of them as consequences of hypervigilance for social threats.

Fourth, Gold and Gold's account also neglects the relevance of non-pathological and "non-specific" causal factors, i.e., factors that contribute to delusions and the maintenance of delusions that are not unique to delusions (Freeman, 2016; see Chapter 8, Section 2). Much empirical research supports a transdiagnostic view of many disorders in which they arise from interactions between factors and processes that cut across traditional psychiatric categories (Freeman, 2024; Krueger & Eaton, 2015). For example, anxiety seems to play a significant causal role across many psychiatric conditions, including delusions. By biasing people's attention towards threats, driving worrying and rumination on threat-related scenarios, and motivating people to engage in safety-seeking behaviours where they seek isolation from others, anxiety can contribute to paranoid ideation and persecutory delusions (Freeman, 2016; see Chapter 8). However, such anxiety need not itself be pathological and is not unique to persecutory delusions.

The example connects to a fifth and final worry: Gold and Gold's account ignores complexity in the causal processes underlying delusions. Many psychological difficulties arise not directly from a single or a handful of underlying dysfunctions but from complex webs of interacting factors that shape one another over time, often involving feedback loops through which seemingly small changes cascade into significant effects. Although such factors can include dysfunctions, they frequently include other factors, including non-pathological ones, and subtle interactions between them (Borsboom & Cramer, 2013; Freeman, 2016; Giudice, 2018). In the context of persecutory delusions, for example, strange experiences can increase anxiety, which can affect sleep, which can limit people's cognitive abilities to cope with strange experiences, which can increase anxiety. Anxiety can lead people to avoid threatening situations, which results in social isolation, which increases feelings of vulnerability, which increases anxiety and stress. And so on. Such complex processes involve substantial path dependency, distributed causation, and probabilistic, dose-response relationships between different causes and the phenomenon of interest, rather than a simple linear relationship between dysfunctions and disorders.

Although it is an empirical question whether this more complex model of delusional causality is appropriate in a given case, it aligns with leading explanatory approaches in modern psychiatric research. It also seems to have empirical support regarding delusions (Freeman, 2016). For example, one of the best-supported interventions against persecutory delusions, the "Feeling Safe Programme", targets diverse factors like sleep, worry, self-confidence, the impact and interpretation of hallucinated voices, reasoning processes, and feelings of safety (Freeman et al., 2021). In contrast, it is unclear why such interventions would heal a disordered suspicion system.

4.3 Is a Disordered Suspicion System Sufficient for Delusions?

The final objection we will raise is that even if one sets aside worries about the cognitive architecture and homogeneity assumed in Gold and Gold's account, it is unclear why a disordered suspicion system would be sufficient to produce persecutory delusions, let alone all delusions.

The core hypothesis of Gold and Gold's account is that persecutory delusions are downstream of a hyperactive social threat detection system or an inability to inhibit the suspicious thoughts produced by the system. Although this connection between persecutory delusions and false alarms in social threat detection is superficially plausible, it is unclear why a tendency to generate false alarms should specifically produce delusions. Instead, one might expect traits such as heightened social anxiety, excessive submissiveness or aggression, social withdrawal, difficulty trusting others and forming relationships, and hypervigilance regarding social cues, driving frequent misinterpretations of their meanings in paranoid directions. Although such traits frequently accompany persecutory delusions, many people characterised as having "paranoid personality disorder" demonstrate that it is possible to exhibit such characteristics without forming delusions (Lee, 2017). This should be unsurprising: it is unclear why hypervigilance for social threats should give rise to many traits often associated with delusions, including the profound "loss of contact with reality" exhibited in strong convictions in highly outlandish ideas. That is, it seems possible to have disordered social vigilance, including systematic tendencies to produce paranoid thoughts and difficulties inhibiting such thoughts, without developing the fixed, strange beliefs often characteristic of clinical delusions.

Gold and Gold might respond to this challenge by arguing that disorders of the suspicion system are not sufficient for producing persecutory delusions but are necessary. This is similar to the explanatory strategy we will develop in the following two chapters. However, once one treats hypervigilance for social threats as just one factor among others, the motivation for assuming social threat detection must be selectively disordered in delusions becomes less apparent, as we will return to in Chapter 8.

5. Chapter Summary

We have identified three general critiques of Gold and Gold's attempt to explain delusions by appealing to disorders within a special-purpose social threat detection system.

First, unlike more straightforward detection tasks, social threats involve the hidden intentions of rational agents with sophisticated planning, coordination, and deception capabilities. It is difficult to see how a highly encapsulated detection module focused on a predetermined range of inputs could cope with such challenges. Second, Gold and Gold's account struggles to accommodate the profound heterogeneity of delusional content, cognition, and causes. The attempt to impose unity on such diversity through a single and simple explanatory framework seems driven more by theoretical demands than empirical evidence. Finally, disorders of a specialised suspicion system seem insufficient to produce persecutory delusions, let alone all delusions. Hyperactive social vigilance alone would more naturally predict the heightened but non-delusional psychological profile typically associated with paranoid personality disorder, not the dramatic departures from reality often characteristic of clinical delusions.

Although such observations focus specifically on Gold and Gold's account, they have broader implications for theorising about delusions. Most importantly, Gold and Gold's account exemplifies a more general explanatory approach that links human sociality to delusions by appealing to localised disorders in special-purpose sociocognitive modules (e.g., Bell et al., 2021). Our critiques generalise to this broader approach: the complexity and challenges of navigating the social world are in tension with special-purpose, informationally encapsulated modules; the heterogeneity manifest in delusional contents, cognition, and causes is in tension with simplistic explanatory models in which all delusions emerge directly from a small number of disorders of the same underlying module; and it is unclear why localised dysfunctions in social cognition would predict delusions specifically instead of generic challenges with dealing with people and social situations.

Of course, we do not assume that these considerations constitute knockdown arguments. Nevertheless, they are sufficiently strong that they motivate a search for alternative ways of addressing the three social challenges for theories of delusions that we identified in Chapter 6. We will now turn to such a framework.

8
The Social Determinants and Focus of Clinical Delusions

1. Introduction

In Chapter 6, we reviewed individualistic frameworks for understanding clinical delusions, which focus on experiential abnormalities, domain-general cognitive problems, and global information-processing aberrations in how the brain manages uncertainty and responds to prediction errors (Chapter 6, Section 2). We argued that although such frameworks likely identify important causal factors, they fail to address three challenges concerning the social dimensions of delusions (Chapter 6, Sections 4, 5, and 6): why social experiences such as abuse, discrimination, and marginalisation significantly increase the risk of developing delusions (the challenge of social determinants); why delusions tend to focus on social themes across different cultural contexts (the challenge of social focus); and why people with delusions seem to respond differently to social and non-social evidence (the challenge of social evidence).

Chapter 7 explored Ian and Joel Gold's (2015) attempt to integrate human sociality into our understanding of delusions by tracing them to selective disorders in a sociocognitive module (a "suspicion system") tasked with detecting and anticipating social threats (Chapter 7, Section 3). Although this account contains important insights, we identified several reasons for scepticism (Chapter 7, Section 4). First, social threat detection is likely too complex, adversarial, and informationally demanding to be handled by a highly encapsulated mental module. Second, the account struggles to accommodate the profound heterogeneity in delusional contents, cognition, and causes. Finally, it is unclear why hypervigilance for social threats alone would give rise to delusions rather than more general suspicious tendencies and difficulties in social functioning.

In this chapter and Chapter 9, we develop an alternative framework for integrating human sociality into our understanding of delusions. Instead of replacing traditional accounts focused on experiential and domain-general

The Social Roots of Delusions. Daniel Williams, Sam Wilkinson, and Kengo Miyazono, Oxford University Press.
 DOI: 10.1093/9780191976360.003.0009

cognitive problems with an appeal to selective dysfunctions in social cognition, we aim to supplement such accounts in ways that address the three social challenges. Our general approach is *multifactorial* in positing that multiple factors typically interact to produce and sustain delusions, *dynamic* in emphasising the complex ways such factors often unfold and interact over time, and *pluralistic* in allowing that different causal processes will often be relevant to different delusions (see Freeman, 2016). As we have argued in Chapters 6 (Section 3.1) and 7 (Section 4.2), this multifactorial, dynamic, and pluralistic framework appears to be well supported by the available evidence and is necessary to account for the complexity and heterogeneity of clinical delusions.

The question, then, is how to address the social determinants, focus, and resistance to social correction of delusions within this framework. The rest of Part 3 outlines our answer. Our overarching thesis is that the relevance of human sociality is far broader, deeper, and more complex than existing social accounts assume. Instead of isolating "social factors" in a malfunctioning module, we argue that human sociality and its distinctive vulnerabilities constitute the primary context within which all delusion-causing factors operate, including anomalous experiences and domain-general cognitive abnormalities.

Our framework begins with the general picture assumed throughout this book: Humans are intensely social animals. We confront uniquely complex social worlds organised around cooperation, culture, and competition. And we depend on such worlds for basic material, psychological, and epistemic functioning (Chapter 1). This ultra-sociality is the source of our ability to know and navigate our environments in highly flexible ways. However, it rests on psychological and social processes that are inherently fragile and vulnerable to distinctive failure modes under conditions of confusion and stress, which shape the formation, focus, and maintenance of delusional beliefs.

First, because we depend on social support, approval, and trust, losing access to such social goods produces wide-ranging, catastrophic psychological, physical, and behavioural effects. We become suspicious, stressed, depleted, and isolated. Although these disturbances are rarely sufficient to produce delusions on their own, they exacerbate and interact with factors like anomalous experiences and cognitive disturbances to make delusions much more likely.

Second, because human attention, rumination, and thought are disproportionately focused on social phenomena, we tend to explain anomalous experiences in terms of domains involving agency, threat, and social evaluation. And because such domains are highly complex, adversarial, and opaque, they constitute a natural magnet for delusional ideation that can be uniquely challenging to escape from.

Finally, because the processes of epistemic vigilance with which we evaluate testimony and social evidence must balance trust and scepticism under conditions of profound uncertainty, they are brittle. When operating under stressors such as unusual experiences, confusion, cognitive deficits, or mood dysregulation, this balance can easily tilt towards scepticism, driving social isolation and suspicion of other people's competence and honesty. As a result, people can lose access to the very social feedback they need to form accurate beliefs, retreating into private worlds that mark them as "rational lost causes" in their community's eyes.

In broad outline, these are our answers to the challenges of social determinants, social focus, and social evidence. In this framework, the very features of our psychology and behaviour that adapt us to the complexities and challenges of social life make us highly vulnerable to delusions under conditions of confusion, stress, and isolation. Given this, our overarching message is that human sociality is not merely another factor or set of factors in the formation of delusions. It is the fundamental and fragile context within which delusion-causing factors like experiential and domain-general cognitive abnormalities operate, making delusions more likely, socially focused, and stubborn.

This chapter begins by illustrating our preferred approach with an application to persecutory delusions, by far the most common delusional theme and therefore a useful test case (Section 2). After extracting general explanatory principles from this case study, we will then outline our analysis of the social determinants (Section 3) and social focus of delusions (Section 4). Because of the importance of the challenge of social evidence, we dedicate a separate chapter to it (Chapter 9).

2. Understanding Persecutory Delusions

Persecutory delusions (i.e., unfounded beliefs that others intend to harm, control, or interfere with oneself) are by far the most common theme of clinical delusions across different cultural contexts (Collin et al., 2023; Gold, 2017; Raihani & Bell, 2019). In the previous chapter, we identified various reasons to be sceptical about the claim that such beliefs emerge solely from localised dysfunctions in social threat detection. Instead, the evidence appears to support a multifactorial framework that encompasses factors identified in traditional approaches to delusions, as we have reviewed elsewhere (Freeman, 2016; see Chapter 6, Section 3.1; and Chapter 7, Section 4.2).

We will first briefly review several of these factors, most of which are not unique to persecutory delusions (Section 2.1). We will then outline a framework for understanding the complex roles that human sociality plays in such dynamic, multifactorial processes (Section 2.2). Finally, we will step back and extract some general principles from this case study (Section 2.3), which will inform our explanations of the social determinants, social focus, and testimonial insensitivity of delusions in this and the next chapter.

2.1 A Multifactorial Framework

Multiple lines of empirical research suggest that complex interactions among the following factors are typically implicated in persecutory delusions (Freeman, 2016; 2024; Freeman & Loe, 2023). Our review here is not intended to be exhaustive. For example, we will postpone consideration of the roles of human social psychology and the social environment until Section 2.2. Moreover, our overview will be brief as we have already touched on several of these factors in Chapter 6.

2.1.1 Experiential Abnormalities

There are compelling theoretical and empirical reasons to think that experiential abnormalities are causally implicated in delusions (see Chapters 6 and 7), including persecutory delusions (Freeman, 2016; Freeman et al., 2013; 2015a; So et al., 2018). In some cases, the relevant experiences are social, such as hearing voices or experiencing a peculiar unfamiliarity when seeing known faces. In others, they involve more general disturbances to experience. For example, in psychotic conditions such as schizophrenia, delusions often seem to emerge against the backdrop of "aberrant salience" (Kapur, 2003; So et al., 2018; Sterzer et al., 2018). Other relevant experiences likely include feelings of dissociation (Černis et al., 2021) and experiences rooted in source-monitoring failures that lead to self-generated imagery (e.g., in imagination, rumination, and fantasy) being attributed to external events (Griffin & Fletcher, 2017; Keefe et al., 1999). Although such experiences rarely directly determine how they will be interpreted, they provide the raw material that violates people's expectations and drives them to revise their understanding of reality to interpret or explain them. For this reason (and others; see Chapter 6, Section 2.2), although we think that anomalous experiences are rarely sufficient to produce delusions, we agree with "empiricist" frameworks that they are likely necessary factors in most and perhaps all cases of delusion formation. (We will return to this point in our concluding chapter.)

2.1.2 Domain-General Cognitive Factors

Research suggests that abnormalities in how individuals think and reason about the world are also often implicated in delusion formation. For example, some studies suggest that three-quarters of patients with clinical delusions do not consider alternative explanations for the events they cite as evidence (Freeman et al., 2004), and general cognitive abnormalities such as jumping-to-conclusions bias (Chapter 6; Dudley et al., 2016) and difficulties with analytic reasoning seem to be relatively well-supported by empirical evidence (Freeman et al., 2014). As we saw in Chapter 6, research in computational psychiatry has also linked various global information-processing disturbances to prediction error minimisation and probabilistic inference in persecutory delusions (Sheffield et al., 2022). Although there remains significant uncertainty over the nature and causes of such domain-general cognitive disturbances, they seem to play an important role in many persecutory delusions by impairing people's ability to evaluate evidence and critically assess implausible ideas.

2.1.3 Affective Disturbances

As Ritunnano and colleagues document, a recurring characteristic in the experience of delusions is "a radical rearrangement of the lived world dominated by intense emotions" (Ritunnano et al., 2022, p.458). Empirical research suggests that this affective dimension is not merely an effect of being delusional but often a contributory cause (Freeman et al., 2015b). Emotions modulate a wide range of psychological processes, including perception, attention, memory, inference, learning, and categorisation, and they also have a wide range of physiological consequences. Given this, strong emotions and affective disturbances can have powerful, diffuse effects on many processes that interact with and exacerbate anomalous experiences and cognitive abnormalities. When it comes to persecutory delusions, diverse findings suggest that anxiety precedes and contributes to paranoid ideation, directing attention towards threats, biasing people's interpretations and explanations in threat-oriented directions, motivating rumination on (i.e., repetitive worrying about) possible threat-related scenarios, and producing high physiological arousal that is associated with perceptual abnormalities and can itself be misinterpreted as additional evidence of danger (Freeman et al., 2010; Freeman et al., 2013; Startup et al., 2007). Individuals experiencing persecutory delusions exhibit a worry-thinking style similar to that of patients with generalised anxiety disorder (Freeman & Garety, 1999).

2.1.4 Safety-Seeking Behaviours

As with anxiety more generally, people experiencing persecutory suspicions typically engage in what are called "safety-seeking behaviours" to protect themselves from perceived threats. The most common behaviour is seeking isolation from others (i.e., social withdrawal) (Freeman et al., 2007). Although an understandable response to perceived social danger, this can strengthen persecutory beliefs and exacerbate initial paranoid worries in multiple ways. Not only does it prevent individuals from receiving testimonial evidence that might challenge their paranoid thoughts (see Chapter 9), but it is easy to misinterpret the association of safety-seeking behaviours with safety as evidence of their efficacy. Moreover, as we return to below, social withdrawal can have wide-ranging negative psychological and physiological consequences that exacerbate other delusion-causing factors (Section 3).

2.1.5 Impaired Coping

Finally, what might be called people's "coping resources" seem to play an important role in persecutory delusions. For example, chronic stress causes a wide range of deleterious mental and physical health consequences, and dealing with phenomena such as anomalous experiences, cognitive difficulties, intense emotions, and social isolation can all be extremely stressful, as can delusional ideation itself. Such stress, in turn, can heighten anomalous experiences, weaken people's cognitive resources to deal with such experiences and critically evaluate worries, and exacerbate intense emotions and emotion dysregulation (Freeman, 2016). Likewise, just as the stress engendered by paranoid suspicions and ideation can create fatigue, including by leading to insomnia, this fatigue and sleep deprivation can in turn contribute to the further development and elaboration of persecutory delusions, both by exacerbating factors like strange experiences and mood dysregulation and by making it harder to step back from immediate reactions and carefully evaluate evidence (Myers et al., 2011; Reeve et al., 2015).

2.2 The Role of Human Sociality

Except for specific perceptual abnormalities such as voices and behaviours such as social withdrawal, the factors that we have described are not distinctively social. How, then, does human sociality fit into this framework?

As we saw in Chapter 7, one possibility is that a localised malfunction in an encapsulated "suspicion" module is an additional factor (Gold & Gold, 2015). Although we share Gold and Gold's assumption that human psychology is specialised for social threat detection (what we call "social vigilance") in ways relevant to understanding persecutory delusions, we gave several reasons to be sceptical of this specific hypothesis (see Chapter 7, Section 4). For example, it is unlikely that a highly encapsulated, domain-specific module could handle the distinctively complex and adversarial character of social threat detection. And the wide range of causes and conditions associated with persecutory delusions makes it unlikely that they all involve the same highly localised point of cognitive failure.

Instead, we conjecture that social vigilance contributes to persecutory delusions through more complex, diffuse pathways.

First, independent of delusions, social threats are a uniquely salient and consequential focus of human thought and experience. As we have argued in Chapters 1 and 7, other people typically constitute the most consequential and complex danger we confront, not least because they have sophisticated capacities for reasoning, planning, social coordination, and deception that make them fundamentally unlike all other threats. Given this, when people are confronted with strange or surprising events, they typically look for agential explanations, both because of the risks of failing to detect agential causes and because other agents have unique abilities to affect our experiences and environments in subtle and hard-to-detect ways (Singh, 2021). That is, this deep-rooted tendency likely reflects both an "error management" bias (see Chapter 3, Section 4.1.2) and a rational response to the unique capacities of agents to interfere with the environment in surprising ways. This means that factors such as anomalous experiences and confusion arise in minds that are independently highly attuned to the risks of social exploitation and manipulation and biased toward considering suspicious, agency-based explanations of surprising events (Williams & Montagnese, 2023). In other words, even if social vigilance is not selectively disordered in delusions, our baseline social vigilance will often channel delusional ideation in persecutory directions, especially if we are already anxious or distressed, as people experiencing anomalous experiences or cognitive disturbances usually are.

Second, once suspicious thoughts and explanations of anomalous experiences are seriously entertained, they are uniquely challenging to disconfirm. If others intend to harm or manipulate you, they will typically take active measures to conceal this fact. As we saw in Chapter 6, this strategic, adversarial nature of social threats makes social vigilance highly complex in ways that have no parallels in simple detection tasks. However, just as importantly, it also makes paranoia an inherently "sticky" domain of attention and thought. It is challenging to disconfirm the suspicion that you are the victim of a deliberately concealed plot. The more carefully concealed the threat, the less likely it is that unambiguous evidence for that threat will exist. Given this, not only are humans independently biased to consider social threat-based explanations of unusual or anomalous experiences, but the nature of social threats makes such explanations unusually resistant to disconfirmation once they are seriously entertained.

Third, this epistemic stickiness is exacerbated by paranoid worries' tendency to trigger a cascade of self-reinforcing feedback loops (Freeman, 2016). For example, once people start entertaining suspicious thoughts, they become more anxious, which can further bias attention towards threats, which can create further anxiety. Relatedly, suspicious thoughts motivate people to explore social threat-related risks in their imagination, driving worry and rumination that lead to heightened anxiety and greater social vigilance, which leads to further rumination. Further, paranoid worries can drive people to engage in safety-seeking behaviours such as social withdrawal, which can create additional anxiety and stress, thereby weakening coping resources even more and removing people from corrective feedback, which exacerbates paranoid worries. And finally, as we will explore in Chapter 9, paranoid worries and feelings can drive not just testimonial isolation but mistrust of any testimony individuals encounter, cutting them off from the epistemic support often needed to regulate beliefs.

For these reasons, paranoid ideation can be thought of as the spider's web of psychosis. When an insect gets caught in a spider's web, its natural response is to struggle. Although understandable, this struggle typically results in the insect becoming more entangled and alerting the spider to its presence. Similarly, when individuals begin to entertain paranoid thoughts, natural and even rational responses, such as anxiety, social withdrawal, heightened vigilance, safety-seeking behaviours, and mistrust, often make the situation worse. If such cycles continue unchecked, paranoid thoughts can become increasingly difficult to escape as multiple feedback loops strengthen and reinforce each other.

Finally, such processes are all exacerbated by the complexity and fragility of social vigilance. Unlike simpler detection tasks, tracking and anticipating social threats must integrate vast perceptual, social, and contextual information and recruit the most sophisticated and complex cognitive abilities people possess (see Chapter 7, Section 4.1). Effective social vigilance is, therefore, highly fragile. Just as the performance of relatively more complex and challenging physical tasks is disproportionately affected by general impairments such as fatigue or dizziness (consider tasks like dancing or juggling), global cognitive difficulties or confusion will have outsized effects on the performance of highly complex and challenging cognitive tasks, such as social vigilance. In other words, precisely because social vigilance involves tracking the hidden intentions of adversarial, strategic agents capable of sophisticated planning, coordination, and deception, it is highly challenging to get right at the best of times. When people are impaired, disoriented, or confused, it is likely to be placed under unique stress. Contra Gold and Gold (2015), this need not be because social vigilance is a malfunctioning, special-purpose module. Instead, precisely because it requires access to a vast and open-ended range of information, as well as the full range of cognitive capacities underlying attention, reasoning, working memory, and mental time travel, it is disproportionately affected by global disturbances.

In summary, the nature, complexity, and fragility of human social vigilance contribute to the emergence and maintenance of persecutory delusions in multiple, interacting ways:

- **Natural Focus**: Social threats constitute a highly salient focus of human attention and thought.
- **Sociocognitive Bias**: We have a built-in tendency to attribute unusual, surprising events to human agents.
- **“Stickiness”**: Suspicious thoughts are uniquely challenging to disconfirm once they are entertained.
- **Feedback Loops**: Suspicion can trigger self-reinforcing cycles of anxiety, social withdrawal, and mistrust.
- **Inherent Fragility**: The complexity and uncertainty of social threat detection and anticipation make the task highly prone to error.

Before any delusions form, human minds are vigilant for social threats and biased toward seeking agential explanations of unusual experiences. Given this, paranoid explanations provide a natural focus of attention, thought, and rumination once anomalous experiences emerge, especially if individuals are anxious and distressed. And once such suspicions take root, they are uniquely challenging to dispel due to the complexity of social threats, the stickiness of social threat-based explanations, and the tendency of suspicion to trigger self-reinforcing cycles of worry, anxiety, social withdrawal, and mistrust. In this analysis, then, social vigilance is not an encapsulated module but a diffuse, fragile suite of motivations, capacities, and tendencies that make social threats salient, sticky, and hard to falsify.

Importantly, this analysis does not assume that individuals with persecutory delusions are suffering from a malfunctioning social module, or even that they have unusually high baseline levels of vigilance concerning social threats. Nevertheless, it should also be clear from these considerations why the likelihood of developing persecutory delusions would be increased among individuals with heightened social vigilance, either as a result of temperament or as a consequence of life experiences (see Section 3).

First, heightened social vigilance predictably increases people's propensity to interpret or explain anomalous experiences through the lens of social threats. Due to the "stickiness" of paranoia as a domain of thought and the tendency of paranoid suspicions to initiate self-perpetuating feedback loops, this increases the probability of developing delusions. Second, heightened social vigilance involves heightened anxiety, which, for the reasons already documented, biases people's attention and thoughts towards threats, increases tendencies to worry and ruminate on such threats, and creates heightened physiological arousal, all of which can play causal roles in the formation of persecutory delusions. Third, heightened social vigilance typically undermines people's coping abilities, increasing stress levels and sleeping difficulties, making it harder for individuals to evaluate evidence and step back from immediate cognitive reactions. Finally, as we will return to in Chapter 9, because heightened social vigilance increases epistemic vigilance—when individuals are excessively vigilant for social threats, they become less likely to seek, trust, and incorporate feedback from others—it will inevitably make it more challenging for individuals to correct initial delusional worries and ideas.

2.3 Principles of the Framework

We can extract several principles from this treatment of persecutory delusions that inform our broader theoretical framework that we will apply in addressing the social determinants, focus, and insensitivity of delusions.

First, we assume that multiple factors are typically implicated in the formation, maintenance, and elaboration of delusions (Freeman & Loe, 2023). Moreover, many of these factors (e.g., anxiety, safety-seeking behaviours, heightened social vigilance, fatigue, etc.) are not individually unique to delusions and need not (although they might) be "clinically abnormal" in the sense of emerging from underlying dysfunctions (Krueger & Eaton, 2015; see Chapter 6, Section 3.1). For all the factors we have described (e.g., strange experiences, domain-general cognitive abnormalities, mood dysregulation, social vigilance, etc.), research suggests that they exist on continua and that their relationship to delusions is typically probabilistic and dose-responsive (Freeman, 2016).

Second, this framework is dynamic, highlighting that delusion formation typically involves complex interactions among factors that unfold over time, including feedback-driven processes (Borsboom & Cramer, 2013; Hofmann, 2014). For example, initial paranoid suspicions can trigger cascading changes in emotion, attention, behaviour, and mistrust that exacerbate and protect people's paranoia, creating self-reinforcing cycles that are increasingly difficult to escape from. Similarly, anxiety does not just bias people's attention and interpretations towards threats. It also exacerbates perceptual abnormalities, drives safety-seeking behaviours, and increases stress and sleeping difficulties, all of which can, in turn, create further anxiety and impact delusions through alternative pathways.

Third, our approach is pluralistic in that we do not assume all delusions involve the same aetiology. Given the profound heterogeneity in the manifestations and correlates of delusions (see Chapter 6, Section 1), including persecutory delusions, we find it highly likely that different combinations and interactions of perceptual, cognitive, affective, and behavioural disturbances can give rise to such beliefs. For example, in some cases, strange experiences might be sufficiently overwhelming that they lead directly to delusions without any domain-general cognitive abnormalities. In others, relatively mild perceptual abnormalities may produce delusions solely through their interaction with additional affective, cognitive, and behavioural disturbances. A flexible, multifactorial modelling framework can accommodate this heterogeneity.

As Freeman argues (2016, p.686), one fruitful way of understanding this complex modelling framework is in terms of "inus" conditions (Mackie, 1974): as *i*nsufficient but *n*on-redundant parts of *u*nnecessary but *s*ufficient conditions. Consider lighting a match to start a fire (see Mackie, 1974). Although this suffices to cause a fire when certain other conditions obtain (e.g., oxygen in the environment), and in such a situation, the fire would not arise without lighting the match (i.e., it is non-redundant), it is insufficient in the absence of such conditions, and also unnecessary in the sense that fires can emerge for reasons unrelated to lighting matches. Similarly, although many combinations of factors can suffice to produce delusions, with each element in the multifactorial process playing a non-redundant role, each factor would be individually insufficient, and any specific causal process is unnecessary, in the sense that other complex combinations of factors could also give rise to delusions. The only possible exception to this is anomalous experiences, which, as noted above (Section 2.1), are likely necessary factors in delusion formation, even if they are not individually sufficient.

Finally, although human sociality plays a central role in our analysis, and we assume that human minds are specialised for navigating distinctive social challenges and opportunities, our framework does not assume that a special-purpose, encapsulated social module has malfunctioned as a part of the delusion-forming process. Instead, we demonstrate how distinctive features and vulnerabilities of human sociality provide the background context for delusion formation, exacerbating and interacting with other delusion-causing factors in ways that make delusions more likely, more likely to focus on social phenomena, and more likely to resist social correction. To the extent that social cognition is causally relevant in such processes, it is because of how it behaves under abnormal conditions and stressors (experiential abnormalities, affective disturbances, global cognitive difficulties), not because it has selectively malfunctioned. That is, to use terminology that we will clarify in greater depth in the next chapter, social cognition *misfunctions* in such cases; it does not malfunction (see Miyazono, 2018; Chapter 9, Section 3).

The principles of this framework will now serve as the theoretical background for our answers to the three challenges we identified in Chapter 6. Sections 3 and 4 discuss the challenges of social determinants and focus, respectively. And Chapter 9 presents our answer to the challenge of social evidence.

3. The Social Determinants of Delusions

As reviewed in Chapter 6, Section 4, there is strong evidence that adverse social experiences and conditions increase the likelihood of developing delusions, at least in the context of psychotic disorders such as schizophrenia (Luhrmann, 2007). For example, childhood adversity, including physical and sexual abuse and bullying, substantially increases psychosis risk (Morgan & Gayer-Anderson, 2016; Read et al., 2005; Varese et al., 2012). Similarly, occupying a minority or minoritised status within a given social context (e.g., minority ethnic and religious groups) increases the likelihood of psychosis (Jongsma et al., 2021). However, this risk is partly ameliorated when individuals live in populations with a higher proportion of members from their minority group (the "ethnic density effect") (Baker et al., 2021; Raihani & Bell, 2019).

As reviewed in Chapter 7, Section 2, one influential way to understand such risk factors is by examining their effects on social vigilance (Raihani & Bell, 2019). For example, Gold and Gold argue that "[t]he social determinants of psychosis [...] may be stressors that increase our need for vigilance and in the long run "overload" the Suspicion System" (Gold & Gold, 2015, p.292). Another influential framework draws on the concept of "social defeat" taken from animal behaviour research, which refers to situations in which one animal assumes a subordinate status after being defeated by another (e.g., in a dominance contest) (Luhrmann, 2007). There is evidence that such defeats have numerous adverse impacts on psychological and physical health in ways that are partly mediated by effects on the release and re-uptake of dopamine (Selten et al., 2013). The social defeat hypothesis of schizophrenia proposes that analogous forms of social defeat and subordination in humans also lead to dopaminergic dysregulation, which is widely thought to be causally linked to psychosis, perhaps through its effects on the attribution of salience.

We think there are insights in both analyses. Because of our intense sociality and interdependence (Chapter 1), social adversity has wide-ranging and highly damaging effects on mental and physical health. Snyder-Mackler and colleagues survey extensive evidence demonstrating that measures of social status, social integration, and early-life adversity "are among the strongest and most consistent predictors of health and survival outcomes" (Snyder-Mackler et al., 2020, p.4). For example, low social integration predicts a well-replicated ~50% increase in all-cause mortality, which either rivals or exceeds the mortality risks documented for obesity, alcoholism, or moderate smoking (Holt-Lunstad et al., 2010), and social adversity is strongly linked not just to a wide range of psychiatric disorders beyond schizophrenia but also to physical diseases as diverse as diabetes, cardiovascular disease, tuberculosis, and cancer (Snyder-Mackler et al., 2020). Even the ethnic density effect does not seem to be specific to psychosis (Bécares et al., 2012). Although such research is almost always merely correlational, the causal impact of social adversity is strongly supported by experimental research on other social mammals, including primates (Snyder-Mackler et al., 2020). It is also precisely what one would expect given our ultra-sociality and, hence, dependence on other people for basic psychological, material, and epistemic functioning.

For these reasons, it seems clear that the social determinants of psychosis are not unique to, and so are individually insufficient for, psychosis. Given this, we propose that they increase delusion risk not through highly localised impacts on sociocognitive mechanisms (e.g., by "overloading" a modular "suspicion system"; see Gold & Gold, 2015) but through wide-ranging effects that exacerbate and interact with several of the delusion-causing factors already reviewed. Specifically, we propose three general pathways:

First, there is a *heightened vigilance pathway*. We have already explained why heightened social vigilance will likely increase the risk of delusion (see Section 2), and it should be clear why experiences such as abuse and discrimination increase people's social vigilance. As reviewed in Chapter 7, Section 2, people's sensitivity to social threats is determined by two overarching factors: their estimation of (i) how dangerous the social environment is and (ii) their vulnerability to such dangers (Raihani & Bell, 2019). By increasing people's perception both that their environment is socially threatening and that they are vulnerable, experiences such as abuse and marginalisation will predictably heighten people's social vigilance, especially when such experiences occur during so-called "sensitive periods" such as childhood and adolescence, when deep-rooted expectations of the world are acquired and become difficult to unlearn (Del Giudice, 2018). As we have noted already (Chapter 7, Section 4.3), such heightened social vigilance is not sufficient on its own for delusions, and it need not involve any dysfunction in the mechanisms underlying social threat detection. Considered in isolation, it might simply be an adaptive response to the relevant individual's circumstances. However, through its exacerbation of and interaction with other factors, such as experiential abnormalities, anxiety, safety-seeking behaviours, and mistrust (see Chapter 9), heightened social vigilance can significantly increase the probability of delusion formation in at-risk individuals via the pathways we have already described.

Second, there is a *stress-dysregulation pathway*. Feelings of vulnerability engendered by subordination, isolation, humiliation, or a lack of social support inevitably have wide-ranging effects on cognition and behaviour beyond their impact on social vigilance (Snyder-Mackler et al., 2020; see Chapter 1). For example, social isolation and chronic subordination seem to cause dysregulation of multiple biological systems, including those involved in the stress response, inflammation, and neurotransmitter function, all of which are corrosive to mental and physical health (Sapolsky, 2005). This stress might directly contribute to creating or exacerbating anomalous experiences through dopaminergic dysregulation, as suggested by the social defeat theory of psychosis. However, it can also drive mood dysregulation, weaken people's cognitive resources, and undermine general coping abilities, all of which can increase delusion risk in vulnerable individuals.

Finally, there is a *behavioural-feedback pathway*. Social adversity often leads to changes in behaviour that can create problematic feedback loops. For example, discrimination and marginalisation can drive people to engage in safety-seeking behaviours such as social withdrawal. Although this can be an adaptive response to social danger, it can also exacerbate people's feelings of vulnerability, reduce their access to corrective feedback (see Chapter 9), and increase the challenges of social interaction. Such outcomes can, in turn, motivate further withdrawal, creating cycles that reinforce one another over time. Such cycles seem especially prevalent in clinical paranoia and persecutory delusions (Freeman, 2016).

As should be clear, these pathways do not operate in isolation. Instead, they interact in complex ways, and relatively minor initial difficulties can snowball into more serious problems without intervention. For example, feelings of vulnerability and powerlessness created by social exploitation or subordination can heighten stress, potentially contributing to perceptual abnormalities, but also increase social vigilance, which can increase perceptions of social danger in ways that increase stress.

This framework illuminates several patterns in how social adversity affects delusion risk. First, it illuminates why there often appears to be a dose-response relationship between social adversity and psychosis risk (Freeman, 2016). Not only do more adverse experiences increase people's estimations of social danger and personal vulnerability, but they also create more opportunities for problematic cycles to develop and strengthen over time. Second, it explains why early-life adversity appears particularly damaging (Varese et al., 2012). This is when more deep-rooted beliefs and expectations are acquired, and feedback loops that begin early have more time to become entrenched and shape future development. Finally, it illuminates why social support and associated feelings of social safety can be protective and therapeutic (Raihani & Bell, 2019). Even if delusions are initially triggered by non-social causes, such as neurological changes or recreational drug use that creates anomalous experiences (Freeman et al., 2015a), social support and feelings of social safety reduce people's perceptions of social danger and vulnerability and provide coping resources for disrupting problematic cycles.

In this framework, the social determinants of psychosis are neither specific to nor sufficient for psychosis. Instead, some individuals have pre-existing vulnerabilities to developing delusions, perhaps rooted in genetic predispositions to experiencing perceptual abnormalities or difficulties in belief updating and reality testing. However, whether and how such vulnerabilities manifest in delusions will often depend on exposure to social stressors that can initiate and strengthen the problematic cycles we have described. For this reason, the framework also illuminates why similar forms of social adversity can contribute to many different psychological difficulties and psychiatric conditions beyond psychosis. Human ultra-sociality ensures that social adversity affects biological and psychological systems in profound and diffuse ways, but its impacts on individuals will depend on their specific vulnerabilities and circumstances.

4. The Social Focus of Delusions

The second social challenge that we identified in Chapter 6 concerns the thematic content of delusions. Cross-culturally, delusions tend to cluster around a surprisingly circumscribed set of themes, most of which focus on the individual's place within the social world. This observation has motivated several existing social accounts of delusions, which seek to explain their social focus by tracing it to localised dysfunctions in social cognition (Bell et al., 2021; Gold & Gold, 2015). However, among several other problems with this conjecture, it struggles to explain why delusions are not universally social in their content (see Chapter 7, Section 4.2). Given this, we propose an alternative framework for understanding the social focus of delusions in which their predominant social focus (Section 4.1) and clustering around specific themes (Section 4.2) result from the way delusion-forming factors arise within minds that are independently preoccupied with uniquely complex, challenging, and ambiguous social phenomena.

4.1 The Generic Question of Social Focus

To understand why delusions so commonly focus on the social world, we must first return to three fundamental features of human minds and social environments identified above (Section 2).

First, human minds are deeply and pervasively social. As we have repeatedly emphasised throughout this book, the fundamental challenges we confront are connected to issues of cooperation, culture, and social competition. Given this, the disproportionate social preoccupation of human thought shows up in numerous non-delusional contexts. We are constantly thinking about the social world: what others are doing, what they are thinking, what they think about us, how we relate to them, and so on. For example, research on the default mode network—brain regions that activate when people are daydreaming or mind-wandering—suggests that people naturally drift towards social content when not engaged in specific tasks (Mars et al., 2012). Similarly, most human communication involves transmitting social information, especially gossip (Dunbar, 2004), and the overwhelming majority of art, storytelling, and news focuses on the behaviours of real or imagined agents. For these reasons, it is doubtful that the predominant social focus of delusions must be explained in terms of delusion-specific factors.

Second, humans exhibit strong biases towards detecting agents and interpreting and explaining anomalous events through the lens of agent causation. As Luhrmann observes, our species is "wildly anthropomorphic", predisposed to "see agents everywhere" (Luhrmann, 2020, p.7). For example, we readily see faces in clouds, attribute complex intentions to simple geometric shapes moving on screens, and are predisposed to explain unusual occurrences or patterns in terms of agent causation, especially when they are negative or distressing (Heider & Simmel, 1944; Singh, 2021). As noted above (Section 2.2), such tendencies likely have two sources: evolutionary pressures of error management that made it costly to miss the behaviour of genuine agents, leading to what researchers call "hyperactive agency detection" (Barrett, 2000), and the simple fact that agents are uniquely capable of altering our experiences and environment in subtle and unpredictable ways. Once again, this suggests that the tendencies that bias delusional ideation in social directions are not unique to delusions. When confronted with unusual or surprising experiences, perfectly "normal" social cognition will ensure that individuals' attention and thoughts gravitate towards agency-based explanations.

Finally, the social world poses unique challenges for understanding, prediction, and explanation. Unlike the immediate physical environment, which is relatively perceptible and highly predictable, rational agents possess sophisticated capacities for reasoning, planning, coordination, and deception. This makes the intentions and behaviours of agents far more complex and challenging to understand and predict than the behaviours of inanimate, physical objects. Moreover, whereas the physical world generally cooperates with hypothesis testing, or at least does not wilfully block our attempts to understand it, agents can actively conceal evidence and adapt to attempts at detection. Given this, not only is it unsurprising that individuals disproportionately attend to possible agential explanations of their anomalous experiences, but it is equally unsurprising that people find it most challenging to maintain accurate representations of the social world when confronted with experiential and cognitive disturbances (Sterzer et al., 2018).

In conjunction with each other, these simple observations can explain the predominant social focus of delusions without positing localised disorders in social cognition or any factors unique to delusions. When faced with inexplicable experiences and domain-general cognitive disturbances, human minds naturally gravitate towards social explanations simply because the social world is the most powerful attractor in human sense-making.

This generic answer to the challenge of social focus has several virtues. First, although our explanatory framework is consistent with the possibility that localised dysfunctions in social cognition give rise to delusions, it does not presuppose this controversial hypothesis to explain the striking pattern that such dysfunctions are posited to explain, and hence does not confront the various objections to this hypothesis that we outlined in Chapter 7.

Second, because these observations identify species-universal features of human psychology and social environments, they can explain the cross-cultural clustering of delusions around overwhelmingly social themes. That is, in contrast to theorists who seek to explain the thematic focus and content of delusions by appealing solely to individually and culturally variable factors (e.g., Kapur, 2003), our framework can illuminate why the predominant social focus of delusions is cross-culturally universal. To the extent that all humans share an ultra-social mind confronting uniquely complex, high-stakes social environments, the social focus of delusions across otherwise diverse cultural contexts is unsurprising.

Finally, this framework explains why the social world is not an inevitable focus of delusional ideation. In conjunction with and in interaction with each other, human ultra-sociality, agency-detection biases, and the unique complexity of the social world illuminate broad tendencies in our attention, experience, and thought. However, such tendencies do not guarantee that delusions will have a social focus. For example, in some cases, specific kinds of perceptual abnormalities, such as certain bodily experiences, might strongly suggest particular non-social interpretations connected to internal organs or physical health rather than the behaviour of other agents. In contrast, theories that aim to explain the social focus of delusions by tracing them to localised dysfunctions in social cognition have a much harder time with exceptions to this pattern (see Chapter 7, Section 4.2). We will return to this relative virtue of our analysis in greater depth in Section 4.3.

4.2 Specific Delusional Themes

The foregoing observations illuminate why the social world is such a common focus of delusional ideation and belief. Nevertheless, they say nothing about the specific themes of delusions. We will now address this issue for the five most common delusional themes identified in Collin and colleagues' (2023) recent meta-analysis of 123 studies featuring 20,979 subjects across thirty countries, which estimates the following frequencies of delusional themes in clinical groups:

- Persecutory delusions: 64.5%
- Delusions of reference: 39.7%
- Grandiose delusions: 28.2%
- Delusions of control: 21.6%
- Religious delusions: 18.3%

Our remarks here are necessarily schematic and speculative. However, they are not more so than similar speculations about the themes of delusions proposed by existing social accounts of such delusions (e.g., Bell et al., 2021; Collin et al., 2023; Gold & Gold, 2015), and we hope that they illustrate the fruitfulness of our preferred explanatory approach and identify important areas for future research.

4.2.1 Persecutory Delusions

Paranoia is by far the most common theme of delusions cross-culturally. Moreover, it is striking that persecutory delusions are associated with a vast range of conditions and disorders, including schizophrenia, delusional disorder, bipolar disorder, dementia, amnesia, post-traumatic stress disorder, and various forms of brain injury and drug abuse. As noted by Raihani and Bell, "In terms of the causes and contexts in which it appears, paranoia is perhaps most remarkable for being associated with such a wide range of difficulties, impairments and stresses" (Raihani & Bell, 2019, p.114). These facts cry out for explanation. Why is persecution the most common delusional theme? And why are such delusions such a recurring failure mode of human cognition across diverse conditions and disorders?

Because we have dealt with persecutory delusions already in Section 2, our remarks here will be brief. In that section, we noted multiple interacting reasons why delusions are so commonly channelled in persecutory directions, even in the absence of any localised impairment to social vigilance. However, implicit in that discussion was also an explanation of why paranoia is the most common theme of delusional ideation and belief, and why it is such a recurring failure mode across a wide range of different disorders and disturbances.

First, anomalous experiences and the broader range of disturbances and difficulties commonly associated with delusions (e.g., confusion, impairment) are likely to create feelings of distress, anxiety, and vulnerability. Paranoia predictably feeds on such experiences (Freeman, 2024). As Raihani and Bell note, this process can be understood in terms of a "cognitive failsafe" (Raihani & Bell, 2019, p.118). Because impairment makes people more vulnerable to exploitation and manipulation, increased social vigilance can have a protective effect. However, when this enhanced social vigilance interacts with anomalous experiences, cognitive deficits, and general confusion, this protective defence can trigger unfounded paranoid ideation. In other words, anomalous experiences and associated disturbances often create precisely the anxiety and vulnerability under which ordinary tendencies to seek suspicious agency-based explanations of surprising events are likely to be activated and exaggerated.

Second, once people's attention and thoughts are directed towards social threats, the vulnerabilities of social vigilance identified in Section 2 kick in, making this domain uniquely challenging to escape, especially when people's cognitive facilities and coping abilities are impaired. The "stickiness" of social vigilance makes it inherently challenging to receive disconfirming evidence for social threat-based worries. The unique complexities of social vigilance ensure that social threat detection and evaluation are likely to be disproportionately affected by global cognitive impairments and disturbances. And the tendency of suspicious worries to trigger the cascade of self-reinforcing feedback loops we have already described can easily entrench and exacerbate initial paranoid worries. As we will return to in Chapter 9, one especially toxic feature of such processes from the perspective of maintaining delusional beliefs is the role of paranoid suspicions in causing testimonial isolation (social withdrawal from other people's corrective testimony) and testimonial discount (mistrust of any corrective testimony that is encountered).

In summary, the reason persecutory delusions are such a common failure mode of human cognition is not that a wide range of conditions and disturbances involve selective dysfunctions in a special-purpose suspicion module. It is because a wide range of conditions and psychological disturbances are likely to induce feelings of anxiety and vulnerability, because social threats constitute a highly sticky, complex, and challenging domain of thought, and because unfounded suspicious worries are uniquely positioned to trigger reactions that become self-reinforcing and highly maladaptive, especially under conditions of stress and strain.

4.2.2 Delusions of Reference

Delusions of reference (sometimes called "ideas of reference") involve unfounded thoughts and beliefs that otherwise ordinary or innocuous events (e.g., news bulletins, people's gestures, the placement of objects) are being intentionally targeted at the individual. Given this, they also typically involve thoughts, worries, and beliefs of being observed, followed, spied upon, discussed, or the covert focus of messages. Delusions of reference are, therefore, almost always social in nature—they focus on phenomena such as communication and surveillance by other agents—and they also exhibit an obvious overlap with persecutory delusions. In fact, delusions of observation, a kind of delusion of reference in which the individual believes they are being spied upon or gossiped about, plausibly are a kind of persecutory delusion as standardly defined and can be understood through the same causal pathways already identified. In delusions of communication, in contrast, individuals mistakenly view themselves as the real but covert target of messages or signs (Startup & Startup, 2005). Insofar as these do not necessarily involve the attribution of exploitative or malevolent intentions, they are not persecutory.

As has long been noted, delusions of reference have a clear connection with aberrant salience theories of psychosis (Kapur, 2003). Incorrectly treating otherwise innocuous messages, signs, and behaviours as targeted at oneself appears to be a special case of mistakenly attributing salience to otherwise innocuous experiences and events, although delusions of reference also seem to be connected to other experiential abnormalities (Freeman, 2016). The question, then, is why a general disturbance in the attribution of salience and other kinds of anomalous experiences should so frequently lead to delusions focused specifically on communication and surveillance.

One can answer this question without appealing to psychological factors unique to delusions of reference. Not only is the social world the most salient domain of attention and interest independent of delusions, but it is a world in which surveillance and social attention are central, not least because extensive social monitoring and gossip are necessary for achieving the distinctive forms of social cooperation on which our species depends (see Chapter 1). When coupled with the fact that other people are the most important factor determining our well-being and survival, we are highly attuned to other people's intentions and attention. Indeed, just as we are biased towards detecting agency generally and social threats specifically, we also tend to overestimate the extent to which we are the target of other people's interests and communications, especially when under stress (Collin et al., 2023; Fenigstein, 1984). Given the interactions of this bias with the wide range of other factors we have identified, including our bias towards agency detection and explanation, the inherent complexity of social cognition, and the unique difficulty of disconfirming certain kinds of agential hypotheses once they are entertained (e.g., that others are deliberately concealing their attempts to monitor or follow you), it is not surprising that a generic disturbance to salience attribution should be channelled into ideas of reference.

Moreover, as has long been noted, delusions of reference are very often just the initial basis of delusional ideation that then gets elaborated into persecutory delusions or grandiose delusions (Kapur, 2003). Their common elaboration into persecutory delusions should be evident from our treatment of persecutory delusions. Once thoughts of being the covert object of attention from other agents interact with factors such as anxiety and heightened vigilance for social threats, it is easy for such thoughts to be channelled towards persecutory worries and hypotheses, which can then be difficult to escape from. Why would they sometimes be channelled into grandiose delusions?

4.2.3 Grandiose Delusions

Individuals with grandiose delusions believe themselves to possess special and inflated traits, identities, or missions. In some sense, grandiose delusions are the opposite of persecutory delusions. Emil Kraepelin famously remarked that "the various directions, which the delusions take in paranoia [by which he roughly meant delusional disorder rather than paranoia as we understand it today], correspond in general to the common fears and hopes of the normal human being", and therefore "appear in a certain manner as the morbidly transformed expressions of the natural emotions of the human heart" (Kraepelin, 1921, p.255). Whereas persecutory delusions and other delusions oriented around social threat reflect the most basic fears of human beings, grandiose delusions reflect the most powerful dreams and hopes—namely, for status and, specifically, prestige status (see Chapter 1, Section 5.1.2). In grandiose delusions, individuals believe they possess identities or traits associated with considerable prestige—that would win them intense respect, admiration, and social importance.

Importantly, connecting grandiose delusions to status does not imply that grandiose delusions involve an explicit belief in the individual's superiority over others. As Isham and colleagues (2021) point out, the explicit content of grandiose delusions is typically that the individual possesses exceptional abilities or an exceptional identity, not that they are better than others. For this reason, they suggest renaming grandiose delusions as "delusions of exceptionality". However, the pursuit of exceptionality is precisely rooted in the desire for, and the rewards associated with, status, and the kinds of exceptionality reflected in grandiose delusions are precisely those associated with status

(Ridgeway, 2019; Storr, 2021). For this reason, Isham and colleagues' (2021) observation that individuals with grandiose delusions typically describe the subjective importance of their delusions in terms of their "meaningfulness" rather than status is misleading. People rarely acknowledge status as one of their primary motivations. To do so is to risk losing status. This is the "reputation tightrope" we highlighted in Chapter 1, Section 5.1.2. Nevertheless, "meaning" is often just a euphemism for prestige (Storr, 2021). Our lives feel meaningful and purposeful when we believe we have traits or accomplishments that are, or would be, socially approved of, respected, and admired (Hoffman & Yoeli, 2021).

Given this, whereas persecutory delusions embody fundamental fears of social threat, grandiose delusions plausibly embody the profound motivation for prestige. Moreover, much of what we have said about why delusions are so commonly channelled into persecutory themes can be applied with modification to the topic of grandiose delusions.

First, just as social threats are independently a highly salient domain of thought and attention, so is prestige (Chapter 1, Section 5.1.2). Moreover, just as we are independently biased towards detecting social threats, we are also independently biased towards interpreting evidence in ways that are conducive to propagating a status-maximising self-image (Williams, 2021b; see Chapter 4). We tend to selectively seek out, interpret, and evaluate information in ways that facilitate the spread and justification of inflated beliefs about our traits and social status, giving rise to so-called "positive illusions" that are pervasive among the general population (Bortolotti, 2015; Taylor & Brown, 1988). This means that factors that predispose people to delusions arise in minds within which status is already a fundamental interest and within which information is already selectively acquired and interpreted in ways biased towards forming a high-status self-image.

Second, just as anxiety and negative affect bias attention and thought in a paranoid direction in persecutory delusions, grandiose delusions seem to be causally linked to positive emotions and heightened mood. In contrast with persecutory delusions, they appear to be correlated with higher explicit self-esteem and lower depression and anxiety scores (Garety et al., 2013; Moritz et al., 2010; Smith et al., 2006), and elevated mood seems to be a contributing cause of such delusions, not merely a correlate or consequence of them (Isham et al., 2021). For example, grandiose delusions are especially common during manic episodes in bipolar disorder, which are typically characterised by inflated self-esteem, increased energy, persistently elevated and expansive mood, and the activation of status- and achievement-related emotions such as pride and ambition (Del Giudice, 2018, p.506). This will predictably bias attention and interpretation towards the domain of status.

Once delusional ideation becomes preoccupied with this domain, numerous factors similar to those implicated in persecutory delusions can maintain and exacerbate this focus (Isham et al., 2021). For example, just as worry and rumination bring paranoid thoughts to mind, enrich threat-based scenarios, and increase conviction, grandiose delusions are strongly associated with fantasy elaboration in which individuals repetitively ruminate on and immerse themselves in grandiose scenarios, in part because this sustains the positive affect associated with such fantasies. Moreover, grandiose delusions can also likely be sustained by a generalised impairment to coping abilities, which undermines individuals' ability to distance themselves from their intuitive reactions and tendencies and increases their motivation to withdraw into pleasurable fantasies. As with persecutory delusions, for example, there is evidence that sleep problems are a contributory factor in grandiose delusions (Sheffield et al., 2021). Finally, as we will explore in Chapter 9, Section 4, once individuals perceive themselves as having high status, they may also discount the competence of testimony from those now perceived as having low status.

In this analysis, then, the grandiose theme of delusions involves a confluence of interacting factors: our innate, powerful drive for prestige, amplified by elevated emotions that bias attention and thought towards ideas of social importance, which then becomes amplified by fantasy elaboration, entrenched by impaired coping abilities, and protected by mistrust of corrective testimony. This differs from Gold and Gold's (2015) speculation about grandiose delusions, which posits that individuals attempt to protect themselves against social threats by projecting a high-status image. As we argued in Chapter 7, this conjecture is difficult to understand on its own terms—when individuals feel under threat, this generally creates social anxiety, negative affect, and social withdrawal, not grandiosity—and it is difficult to reconcile with many features of grandiose delusions, including their connections to elevated mood, fantasy elaboration, and a range of other factors. According to our account, grandiose delusions typically build directly on positive affect and mood rather than on heightened perceptions of social danger. They are connected to powerful prestige motivations rather than to defence against social threats.

However, our analysis must also be qualified regarding frequent situations in conditions like schizophrenia where persecutory and grandiose delusions co-occur. In some cases, this co-occurrence arises because grandiose delusions are simply a logical consequence of holding persecutory delusions. For example, if one believes oneself to be the victim of a hidden conspiracy perpetrated by powerful interests, one may reasonably come to infer that one possesses a special identity or holds a position of great importance. In these cases, grandiosity is simply a by-product of more fundamental tendencies towards persecutory delusions. In other cases, persecutory delusions might follow logically from grandiose delusions. For example, Lake (2008) suggests that grandiose delusions can lead people to worry that others will harbour negative intentions towards them or try to steal their special "gifts", thereby generating paranoia. In this case, the processes leading to grandiose delusions are primary.

4.2.4 Delusions of Control

In delusions of control, individuals believe that their actions, thoughts, feelings, and inclinations are being influenced or controlled by other agents, including imagined and supernatural agents. Despite being classified differently from persecutory delusions, they have a strong paranoid element and fall within the more general category of delusions oriented around the theme of social threat. Although there is still considerable uncertainty about their causes, a leading theory traces them to failures in source monitoring and self-prediction, which causes individuals to find their thoughts and actions surprising (Frith, 2005). In this sense, delusions of control might be different from standard persecutory delusions in having a close connection to very specific experiences. Given what we have said already, our explanation of why people reliably interpret or explain such anomalous experiences by attributing them to other agents should not be surprising: even if the specific contents of the relevant experiences (e.g., the feeling of surprise at self-generating thoughts or actions) do not logically imply that another agent lies behind them, distinctive features of human minds and the social world make this the most plausible hypothesis to consider.

4.2.5 Religious Delusions

Finally, religious delusions are standardly defined as delusions that feature a religious theme or content. Here, we agree with Gold and Gold (2015) that such delusions are unlikely to be best characterised as a distinct delusional theme. Instead, they typically express more fundamental persecutory or grandiose themes in religious language, which is unlikely to reflect a significant difference at the level of underlying psychological processes which give rise to them. Specifically, although psychiatrists and psychologists studying delusions might draw a sharp distinction between secular and religious phenomena, this distinction is plausibly not reflected in the belief systems of patients with delusions. Given this, the belief that one is the reincarnation of

Napoleon likely does not involve fundamentally different underlying mechanisms from the belief that one is Jesus. Therefore, religious delusions do not need a separate explanatory treatment here.

4.3 A Three-Level Explanation of Social Focus

The five delusional themes we have considered are not exhaustive, and our remarks are highly schematic and conjectural. Nevertheless, they illustrate a promising general approach to explaining delusional themes. In this approach, the thematic focus of delusions is explained not by directly linking specific delusional themes to delusion-specific impairments in specific psychological mechanisms. Instead, it is explained by identifying the background features of human minds and worlds within which factors such as anomalous experiences and domain-general cognitive abnormalities arise.

More specifically, our preferred framework for understanding delusional themes has three levels. At the highest level, we explain the general focus and themes of delusions by identifying general features of human minds and worlds within which delusions arise. At this level, for example, we can explain why the social world is a magnet for delusional ideation by appealing to universal features of human social psychology that we reviewed in Chapter 1 (for example, our independent preoccupation with and interest in social phenomena and biases towards detecting agency) and social environments (for example, the distinctive complexity, evidential opacity, and frequently adversarial character of agents' actions and intentions).

At an intermediate level, our framework identifies variables and complex interactions among them that can explain the themes of specific delusions. Here, several variables are especially important. First, there is variation in the kinds of anomalous experiences implicated in delusions. For example, in some cases, specific anomalous experiences might be closely linked to the focus of specific delusional themes (e.g., in delusions of control). In contrast, in others (e.g., generic disturbances in the process of salience attribution or feelings of dissociation), the experiences might be interpretable across multiple themes. Second, there are variations in individual traits. For example, some people may be highly vigilant for social threats, either due to relatively stable personality traits or heightened exposure to such threats in their current or past environments (see Section 3). Such traits will then bias the direction that delusional ideation takes. Third, there are variations in emotions and mood, which can bias people's attention and interpretations in specific directions—for example, by determining whether people are predisposed to ruminate on threats and dangers or fantasise about hopes and dreams. Finally, there are behavioural tendencies. As we have seen, behaviours such as social withdrawal can exacerbate persecutory ideation, and people are likely to vary in the degree to which they engage in specific behaviours.

At the lowest level, this framework can be supplemented to explain the specific content through which delusional themes manifest. This is where variation in individuals' pre-existing beliefs and the broader cultural context is significant. Even if two individuals within the same cultural group develop persecutory or grandiose delusions, their idiosyncratic life experiences and pre-existing interests and beliefs make it likely that the specific content of their delusions will differ. Similarly, one would expect the general contents associated with specific themes to differ substantially between cultural and sub-cultural groups. For example, one interesting study of Egyptian patients by el Sendiony (1976) shows that those with lower education tended to express delusions with religious content related to Islam. In contrast, more educated, middle-class patients tended to express delusions with more secular and science-based themes.

Significantly, this framework can explain why similar kinds of experiential abnormalities can be channelled into very different delusional themes. For example, even if individuals are confronted with a generic disturbance in the process of attributing salience to experiences and events, variations in other factors such as individual traits, mood, and psychological tendencies will inevitably bias attempts to grapple with and explain such experiences in different directions.

Just as importantly, it can also illuminate why different kinds of anomalous experiences can be channelled into the same delusional theme. As noted above, persecutory delusions arise from a surprisingly diverse set of underlying conditions and disturbances. To the extent that one sought to explain such delusions by appealing to particular experiences or impairment to a highly specialised psychological suspicion module, this would be puzzling (see Chapter 7, Section 4.2.3). In our framework, in contrast, it arises because factors that predispose people to delusions emerge in minds within which the domain of social threat is independently highly salient, and because feedback loops can easily take hold whenever paranoid suspicions are seriously entertained.

5. Chapter Summary

This chapter introduced a novel framework for understanding the roles of human sociality in delusions. In contrast to alternative social accounts that connect delusions to selective malfunctions in special-purpose social modules, we have argued that the vulnerabilities of human sociality provide the primary context and amplifier within which complex interactions among all delusion-causing factors arise.

When it comes to the social determinants of delusions, we argued that they increase delusion risk not by breaking or "overheating" compartmentalised sociocognitive modules but through complex, diffuse interactions involving three causal pathways: heightening social vigilance, dysregulating biological systems, and driving behaviours like social withdrawal and other self-reinforcing feedback loops that protect and amplify delusional tendencies and cut individuals off from corrective social feedback. These profound, wide-ranging impacts are neither specific to nor sufficient to produce delusions, but they can significantly increase delusion risk in vulnerable individuals.

When it comes to the social focus of delusions, we argued that delusions gravitate towards social themes not because they result from broken social modules but because factors like anomalous experiences and domain-general cognitive disturbances arise within minds that are obsessively social, biased to see agency behind unusual experiences and events, and navigating uniquely complex, opaque, and adversarial social environments.

In these analyses, human sociality is not a malfunctioning sub-system of the mind. It provides the background focus and preoccupation that channels strange experiences towards social interpretations. It creates forms of profound interdependence that ensure abuse, marginalisation, and the loss of social support have catastrophic effects that exacerbate all other delusion-causing factors. It involves distinctive complexities that make navigating the social world exceptionally challenging, sticky, and vulnerable to disruption under conditions of stress, confusion, and impairment. And it explains why social suspicions are likely to drive distinctive feedback loops that reinforce and amplify delusional beliefs.

Throughout this chapter, we have also repeatedly highlighted how delusional individuals can become cut off from and mistrustf,ul of the testimony, corrective feedback, and collective sense-making that people rely upon to acquirknowledge and regulate their beliefs. Of all these roles, it is this final one—the isolation of delusional individuals from other people's knowledge—that is most directly connected to their status as "rational lost causes" in their community. In the next chapter, we explore this phenomenon and the broader challenge of social evidence in full.

9

The Social Insensitivity of Clinical Delusions

1. Introduction

Chapter 6 identified three explanatory challenges for individualistic accounts of clinical delusions that posit factors like anomalous experiences and domain-general cognitive abnormalities: the challenge of social determinants (why adverse social experiences are causally relevant to delusions; Chapter 6, Section 4), the challenge of social focus (why delusions predominantly focus on social themes; Chapter 6, Section 5); and the challenge of social evidence (why delusions are uniquely insensitive to social evidence; Chapter 6, Section 6). Chapter 8 advanced our solution to the first two challenges. Instead of tracing delusions to a malfunctioning sociocognitive module (see Chapter 7), our framework posits that human sociality and the distinctive challenges of social life provide the fragile context within which all delusion-causing factors, including anomalous experiences and domain-general cognitive abnormalities, emerge and interact. Specifically, we argued that the unique complexities and vulnerabilities of human sociality explain both why delusions become more likely when at-risk individuals experience social stressors (e.g., abuse, bullying, and marginalisation) and why delusional ideation is typically channelled towards social themes (e.g., social threats, surveillance, and status).

This chapter extends this framework to the challenge of social evidence: why delusional beliefs are particularly insensitive to testimonial evidence, and social sources of evidence more broadly. Of course, given our argument in Chapter 2 that beliefs attract delusional status when they are viewed as being impervious to conversational correction—when an individual is treated as a "rational lost cause" on the topic in question—our solution to this final challenge serves not only to explain features of those things that we call delusions, but also to illuminate why they are counted as delusions in the first place. Relatedly, it explains the property that most sharply distinguishes clinical delusions from the popular delusions that we explored in Part 2: their idiosyncratic

The Social Roots of Delusions. Daniel Williams, Sam Wilkinson, and Kengo Miyazono, Oxford University Press.
© Oxford University Press (2026). DOI: 10.1093/9780191976360.003.0010

nature (see Chapter 3, Section 1). In the overwhelming majority of cases, clinical delusions are confined to the individuals who hold them. As Bentall observes, they "are believed by only one person": "they do not seem to come from anywhere—the patient does not hear them from someone else—and they do not go anywhere" (Bentall, 2024, p.567). Of course, if delusions are partly rooted in private anomalous experiences, as we have argued (see Chapter 8, Section 2), the impression that they do not "come from anywhere" is highly misleading. However, it remains deeply puzzling that they are maintained even in the face of unanimous feedback from the delusional individual's social environment that their beliefs are mistaken.

Our central thesis is that delusions' insensitivity to social evidence arises not from a broken "testimony module", but from two distinct failure modes ("testimonial failures") that occur when processes of social learning operate under anomalous conditions and stressors. In the case of "testimonial isolation", individuals fail to receive corrective social feedback on their delusional ideation and beliefs. In the case of "testimonial discount", individuals discount the corrective testimonial evidence that they do receive, both because of general properties of epistemic vigilance, and because of various processes by which this generic vigilance is amplified in delusional individuals.[1]

The chapter begins with an overview of testimonial failures and their roles in delusion formation (Section 2). We then discuss testimonial isolation and testimonial discount in detail (Section 3) before surveying possible causes of testimonial discount (Section 4). We close the chapter by extending our framework to *folie à deux* (i.e., shared delusions), where the idiosyncratic, socially insensitive character of delusions and associated testimonial failures appear to be absent (Section 5).

2. Problems in Testimonial Exchanges

Let us begin with a brief reminder of what the challenge of social evidence is. The challenge is to explain why delusional beliefs are particularly insensitive to social forms of evidence, and testimonial evidence in particular. Consider the following case of somatic delusion (the "ORGAN case", hereafter) as a concrete example.

[1] For related proposals, see the papers by Freeman and colleagues, including Freeman, Garety, Kuipers, Fowler, and Bebbington (2002). See also Cameron (1959) and Fuchs (2015). For a philosophical discussion of testimony in delusions and religious beliefs, see Radden (2010) and Murphy (2013).

> A Thirty-Three-Year-Old Man with Chronic Schizophrenia. The patient had been ill for fourteen years. At the time of the interview, he was preoccupied and distressed by the firm belief that he had no internal organs. Although his doctors had told him that this was a physiological impossibility [...] the patient said that he could not rid himself of the belief. The patient also expressed the belief that spirit doctors had come to his room one night to perform a magical operation in order to remove his internal organs. This happened, he believed, because he was being punished by God for some evil or sin that he had committed, although he was uncertain about the nature of that sin. The most distressing aspect of the delusion for this patient was the pervasive worry that, when he died, he would be rejected from heaven because he was no longer a proper human being. (Davies et al., 2001, p.136)

The delusion in this case is likely formed at least partly as a response to anomalous somatic feelings. This suggests that the delusion is sensitive, at least, to experiential forms of evidence. In contrast, it is not sensitive to the doctor's testimonial evidence ("Although his doctors had told him that this was a physiological impossibility [...], the patient said that he could not rid himself of the belief"). Of course, this specific example of explicit testimony barely scratches the surface of contrary testimonial evidence that delusional individuals typically confront and dismiss. Most obviously, they are usually made aware that both their loved ones and seemingly authoritative figures (e.g., medical professionals) consider their beliefs *to be delusional*, which would seem to constitute extremely strong social evidence against their beliefs. (For a discussion of how conflicting testimony can be understood as higher-order evidence, see Chapter 3, Section 3.1.) More generally, it is the inability of delusional individuals to respond to contrary testimony of any kind that explains why they are treated as delusional in the first place.

Given this, the challenge of social evidence is to explain why delusional individuals appear to be sensitive to experiential evidence but insensitive to social evidence. For example, in the ORGAN case, why does the individual seem to be sensitive to the evidence provided by anomalous somatic feelings but reject the social evidence received from his doctors, as well as from everyone else he encounters who tells him that his belief is mistaken and presents evidence and arguments against it?

One tempting answer to such questions is that the experiential evidence in delusions is so strong that it simply outweighs any relevant testimonial evidence. If so, delusional individuals need not be unusually insensitive to testimonial evidence. They are merely basing their beliefs on the strongest evidence available to them, which they interpret as coming from their experience.

One might find this view especially plausible if one embraces a one-factor account of delusions, according to which the only clinically abnormal factor in their formation and maintenance is anomalous experiences (see Chapter 6, Section 3).

As we return to in greater depth in Section 3.2.1, we are open to the possibility that this response to the challenge of social evidence is applicable in some cases. Nevertheless, as we noted in Chapter 6, Section 6, unless this claim is supplemented with additional details, it merely re-describes the challenge of social evidence; it does not address it. As we have stressed repeatedly throughout this book, individuals are deeply reliant on others to acquire knowledge and to regulate their beliefs. We are an epistemically interdependent species (see Chapter 1, Section 4). As Goldman observes, "What people believe and know is largely a function of their community and culture, narrowly or broadly construed. Most of what we believe is influenced, directly or indirectly, by utterances and writings of others" (Goldman, 1999b, p.3). This epistemic interdependence makes it highly surprising that delusional individuals appear to discount all social evidence against their beliefs. Such evidence could not be any stronger in many cases. Delusional individuals often encounter repeated, unanimous testimony, including from highly trustworthy, competent testifiers, that their delusional beliefs are false. Given this, even if it is true that delusional individuals simply judge their experiential evidence to be much stronger than testimonial evidence, this is a puzzling fact that demands a deeper explanation.

As with the framework that we outlined in Chapter 8, our solution to the challenge of social evidence will be multifactorial, dynamic, and pluralistic, exploring how multiple relevant factors and their complex interactions unfold against the backdrop of vulnerabilities associated with human sociality. Specifically, we will identify two distinct kinds of failure modes that arise when social learning and epistemic vigilance operate under conditions of anomalous experience and other delusion-relevant stressors, which we will refer to as "testimonial failures".[2]

The first testimonial failure, "testimonial isolation", refers to processes by which people become isolated from corrective testimony, thereby failing to receive the social evidence that might cause them to question or abandon delusional ideas and beliefs. The second, "testimonial discount", refers to processes by which delusional individuals discount testimonial evidence relative to experiential evidence, thereby prioritising the latter over the former when

[2] An earlier paper by one of us (Miyazono & Salice, 2021) calls testimonial isolation and discount "testimonial abnormalities". In this book, we call them "testimonial failures" instead. The "failure" talk is preferable because it is more neutral than the "abnormality" talk on some open empirical issues, including the issue as to whether testimonial isolation and discount are caused by underlying pathology.

they conflict. As we will see, this phenomenon of testimonial discount can involve universal tendencies to exercise epistemic vigilance towards testimony that conflicts with experientially grounded beliefs, but it can also implicate additional processes that amplify this natural vigilance.

Importantly, testimonial isolation and testimonial discount address the challenge of social evidence in different ways. The challenge is to explain why delusional beliefs are particularly insensitive to social forms of evidence. Processes of testimonial discount provide a direct answer to this challenge, while testimonial isolation offers a "deflationary" response. To the extent that delusional individuals are isolated from contrary testimony and broader social feedback, they might appear insensitive to social evidence when in fact they have simply not been exposed to it. That is, they might only appear to be insensitive to "available" testimonial evidence; as a matter of fact, the evidence is not actually "available" to them.

Before proceeding, three clarifications are necessary. First, although we think that both testimonial failures are typically relevant to delusions in schizophrenia, which will be our primary focus in what follows, our commitment to pluralism implies that different causes of testimonial failures might be relevant in different cases. Moreover, we do not assume that both kinds of testimonial failure are relevant in all cases. For example, there might be delusions in which testimonial discount is relevant but testimonial isolation is not. The possibility of testimonial isolation without testimonial discount is more complex. On our expansive understanding of the concept of testimonial discount, such cases would not seem to qualify as delusions. An individual who does not discount contrary testimony would relinquish the relevant belief, thereby ceasing to be delusional. However, there might be cases in which people are misinterpreted as delusional because they are assumed to be unpersuadable by contrary testimony, when in reality they have simply not encountered enough of it. Moreover, in Section 5, we will consider rare cases in which genuinely delusional individuals seem to discount all testimony except that of another delusional individual.

Second, the term "testimonial failure" refers to failures to receive and integrate testimonial evidence. It is neutral on the question of what causes such failures, including whether they involve irrationality or underlying pathology. In line with the framework that we outlined in Chapter 8, we are sceptical that testimonial failures are rooted in dysfunctions that selectively target social cognition, including the psychological processes of epistemic vigilance with which we evaluate communicated content. Instead, as we will return to below (Sections 3 and 4), we find it more plausible that the primary factors driving testimonial isolation and discount involve complex interactions between the unique vulnerabilities of human sociality and the abnormal conditions and stressors associated with delusions.

Finally, many researchers divide the aetiology of delusion into three stages: adoption, maintenance, and elaboration. The adoption stage is the initial stage where a delusional person adopts a delusional hypothesis (e.g., "I have no internal organs") rather than an alternative, non-delusional hypothesis (e.g., "My internal organs are not very healthy"). The maintenance stage is the next stage where, despite apparently obvious counterevidence (e.g., the doctor's telling the person that it is physiologically impossible that he has no internal organs), the delusional person maintains the delusional hypothesis. As we saw in Chapter 2, a belief is not going to be deemed a delusion without this step. However outlandish a belief may be, if it is easily corrected, then it lacks the status of "rational lost cause" characteristic of delusions. The elaboration stage is then an optional stage ("optional" in the sense that not all delusions go through this stage), where delusional hypotheses are elaborated and polythematised, forming an intricate delusional system of beliefs (e.g., the delusional person comes to believe not only that he has no internal organs, but also that spirit doctors removed his internal organs, that he was punished by God for some evil or sin, that he will be rejected from heaven, and so on).

The testimonial failures that we explore in this chapter are primarily relevant to the maintenance stage. Delusional people maintain their delusional beliefs because they do not receive sufficient testimonial feedback for correcting their delusional beliefs (testimonial isolation), and/or because they discount or neglect available testimonial feedback (testimonial discount). Nevertheless, although this neat distinction between stages can be analytically helpful, the idea of a simple temporal sequence can also obscure the complex, dynamic processes often implicated in the aetiology of delusions, which can involve highly complex causal interactions and feedback loops in which the lines between formation, maintenance, and elaboration are blurry. As we saw in the previous chapter, for example, the process through which strange experiences, anxiety, and heightened social vigilance develop into full-blown persecutory delusions is frequently extended over significant timescales, and testimonial isolation and discounting can be highly relevant in this process.

Moreover, testimonial failures can fuel the elaboration of delusional beliefs, which can in turn further entrench them and make them even more resistant to correction. As we reviewed in Chapter 1 (Section 4.2), human reasoning typically has a lawyerly character: although we are instinctively vigilant and sceptical when evaluating other people's claims and arguments, we tend to exhibit a "myside bias" when producing reasons (Mercier & Sperber, 2017). That is, the ideas and arguments that we spontaneously generate when we reflect and reason about the world tend to align with and rationalise what we already believe. In ordinary social contexts with sufficient communication and mutual trust, this myside bias is highly adaptive. It ensures that we are effective at persuasion, advocacy, and reputation management, and that others are effective at correcting our natural biases. As Mercier and Sperber argue, however, myside bias makes reasoning in the absence of such social processes and their corrective feedback highly unreliable. Precisely because "the normal conditions for the use of reasoning are social, and more specifically dialogic", the results of reasoning outside of this social context can "spell disaster for the lone reasoner":

> As she reasons, she finds more and more arguments for her views, most of them judged to be good enough. These reasons increase her confidence and lead her to extreme positions. (Mercier & Sperber, 2017, p.247)

Although Mercier and Sperber do not apply this insight specifically to clinical delusions, it provides a powerful explanation for why testimonial isolation and discounting can be so epistemically dangerous in such cases. In our introductory chapter, we quoted Keynes' observation that, "It is astonishing what foolish things one can temporarily believe if one thinks too long alone" (Keynes, 1936, p.vii). We can now see that these dangers arise not just because thinking alone isolates us from the social feedback we depend on to acquire knowledge and regulate our beliefs, but also because such isolation separates reasoning from the social, dialogic context within which it functions well.

3. Isolation and Discount

Let us now more closely at testimonial isolation (Section 3.1) and testimonial discount (Sections 3.2 and 4).

3.1 Testimonial Isolation

It has long been noted that delusional individuals often experience considerable social isolation, especially in schizophrenia. As Jaspers observes:

> It is to a certain extent characteristic for the large group of those who are *mentally ill in the narrower sense* and whom we nowadays class together as schizophrenic that they should exclude themselves from human society in

> some form or another. They erect a new world inside themselves in which they predominantly live even though to the superficial observer they may seem to be quite in touch with the real world. [...] The individuals who—in typical cases—shut themselves off from others without seeming to notice it or suffering in any way from it have always formed a group of socially dead people. (Jaspers, 1963, pp.724–725)

Moreover, it has also already been hypothesised that the testimonial isolation brought about by such isolation can causally contribute to the development of delusions, directly or indirectly. For example, Freeman and colleagues argue that, "If the person is isolated, unable to revise his or her thoughts on the basis of interactions with supportive others, then ideas of threat are more likely to flourish" (Freeman et al., 2002, pp.335–336). Similarly, Feyaerts and colleagues emphasise "the importance of social relations in counteracting the excessive hyper-reflexive self-focus that often sustains delusional experience", observing that "the phenomenology of psychotic conditions is often marked by social disconnection, isolation, or loneliness, which are therefore essential targets for treatment" (Feyaerts et al., 2021, p.245).

What causes testimonial isolation in individuals with delusions? In Chapter 8, Section 2, we presented a multifactorial approach in which causal factors of different kinds—including perceptual abnormalities, domain-general cognitive factors, affective disturbances, safety-seeking behaviours, and coping abilities—interact with the unique complexities and vulnerabilities of human sociality. Among others, it is easy to see how affective disturbances, such as heightened anxiety, as well as heightened social vigilance more broadly, might causally contribute to testimonial isolation. The same is true of safety-seeking behaviours and social withdrawal. In schizophrenia specifically, these behavioural tendencies are then likely to be exacerbated by social skill problems (the lack of appropriate skills and competence in social and communicative exchanges; see Mueser et al., 1991), which deprives people of the skills and competence necessary for testimonial interaction, or social anhedonia (the reduced ability to experience pleasure from social relationships; see Blanchard et al., 2001), which deprives them of the motivation for testimonial interaction.

Moreover, not all relevant causal factors need to be located within the relevant delusional individual's head. In addition to "internal factors" such as affective disturbances or motivations to engage in safety-seeking behaviours, there can also be "external factors" that exist or arise from outside delusional individuals, as well as complex interactions between such external factors and internal factors. That is, isolation can happen not only when a person with some internal factors avoids interaction with other people but also when the person is excluded, discriminated against, or stigmatised by other people. (This form of testimonial isolation caused by external factors can be called "testimonial quarantine".)

As we argued in Chapter 8 (Section 3), for example, the social determinants of psychosis, including factors like childhood abuse and marginalisation, are highly relevant to explaining testimonial isolation, both by increasing people's feelings of social vulnerability and vigilance (what we called the "social vigilance pathway") and by initiating safety-seeking behaviours like social withdrawal (the "behavioural feedback pathway"). External factors might also include general tendencies in modern society where individuals with delusions tend to be stigmatised and so treated in an unfriendly, even hostile manner. For example, Crichton and colleagues (2017) discuss the possibility that negative stereotypes about schizophrenia can contribute to epistemic impairment:

> Such negative stereotypes are problematic for several reasons, beyond their empirical inadequacy. They encourage unwarranted attitudes of suspicion and distrust towards people with schizophrenia, which, in turn, can contribute to their social isolation; this is in itself epistemically impairing. Many of our epistemic practices are intrinsically social, such as testifying (giving information to others) and interpreting (making sense of one's experiences)[...] Social isolation and epistemic impairment can be mutually reinforcing. (Crichton et al., 2017, p.69)

Of course, individuals with delusions can, in turn, anticipate such hostile reactions and stigma and adjust their behaviour accordingly. As we have stressed repeatedly throughout this book, human beings are obligate reputation managers, engaging in extensive social self-monitoring to elicit social approval and avoid social disapproval. Hence, in sharp contrast to the socially adaptive beliefs relevant to popular delusions that we reviewed in Part 2, the socially maladaptive character of clinical delusions—the fact that expressing such beliefs can significantly damage the relevant individual's reputation—provides them with strong incentives to conceal their beliefs from others. Although this can reduce the degree to which others disapprove of or stigmatise them, it can also ensure that their strange beliefs become isolated from corrective testimony that they might epistemically benefit from.

One intriguing possibility is that the practice of delusion attribution, which we discussed in Chapter 2, is itself an external causal factor contributing to testimonial isolation. Flagging someone as delusional is primarily to say that they are a "rational lost cause", according to our analysis of delusion attribution. When people attribute delusional status to a person and thereby regard him as a "rational lost cause", they are discouraged from having testimonial interactions with him; he is effectively testimonially isolated. Moreover, sensing that they do not regard the person as trustworthy, he in turn might lose his motivation to have testimonial interaction with others. It is challenging for an individual to be motivated to have testimonial interactions with others when it is clear that they regard him as extremely untrustworthy.

This suggests an interesting and important possibility: delusion attribution and delusion formation causally interact so that the former is part of the cause of the latter. Delusion formation is, according to this proposal, partly due to testimonial failures, including testimonial isolation, which is itself partly due to delusion attribution. That is, delusion attribution can function as a self-fulfilling prophecy; by calling someone "delusional", we effectively contribute to her actually being delusional. This is, of course, slightly overstated. In most (if not all) cases of clinical delusion, people call somebody "delusional" because the person is already delusional at least to some extent. It is not the case that delusion attribution turns a completely non-delusional person into a fully fledged delusional person. Also, the causal contribution of delusion attribution to delusion formation is only partial and indirect. It is partial because there are other causal factors as well, and it is indirect because its causal contribution to delusion formation is mediated by testimonial isolation.

Thus, delusion attribution is not a self-fulfilling prophecy in a pure sense; we cannot turn a person into being delusional purely by calling her "delusional". Still, we do think that delusion attribution can play some role, even if it is partial and indirect, in the delusion formation process by, for example, causally contributing to testimonial isolation, which makes it very difficult for delusional people to get rid of delusional beliefs on the basis of testimonial feedback.

3.2 Testimonial Discount

Let us now turn to testimonial discount, which involves neglecting or discounting testimonial evidence. We focus on two forms of testimonial discount: general testimonial discount (Section 3.2.1) and amplified testimonial discount (Section 3.2.2).

3.2.1 General Testimonial Discount

Testimonial discount can take different forms. What we call "general testimonial discount" refers to a general tendency not unique to delusional individuals. As we already noted in Chapter 1, Section 4.2, in our discussion of epistemic vigilance, there are strong independent reasons to think that people tend to be vigilant in the social exchange of information, which is useful to guard against being manipulated or misled by others, who often have strong incentives to be deceptive, biased, or lazy in their communication. The same reasoning does not apply to one's own senses, which evolve for the specific purpose of providing reliable information about the environment. Thus, McKay and Mercier write:

> There is now a large amount of evidence that people systematically discount information communicated by others. [...] The discounting of others' opinions can be overcome if we have positive reasons to trust them or if they present good arguments—in particular, if our prior opinions are weak. However, in the absence of such positive reasons, discounting is a pervasive phenomenon. There is no such systematic equivalent when it comes to perception. Although in some cases we can or should learn to doubt what we perceive (e.g., when attending to the reminder that "objects in mirror are closer than they appear" while driving), this is typically an effortful process with uncertain outcomes. (McKay & Mercier, 2023, p.126)

It is expected, then, that people in general have a tendency to put more weight on their own perceptual information over testimonial information from others, which is not peculiar to people with delusions. There are some supportive empirical findings reviewed in Morin and colleagues' (2021) on the phenomenon of "egocentric discounting", which suggests that testimonial and other social information is systematically discounted in nonclinical populations. And in contexts where people are presented with even unanimous testimony that conflicts with strong experientially-based beliefs, most people maintain their beliefs, even if they often *publicly* misrepresent them to avoid reputational damage (see Mercier, 2020, pp.74–75 for a review).

This feature of epistemic vigilance might be understood in terms of a distinction between what has been called a Cartesian as opposed to a Spinozan model of belief formation (Curley, 1975). A Cartesian belief formation process is an "opt-in" process which evaluates the plausibility of a hypothesis before accepting it in the belief system. By default, the process does not accept a hypothesis;

it is accepted only when it is evaluated as plausible. This nicely fits McKay and Mercier's description of testimonial belief formation; "the discounting of others' opinions can be overcome if we have positive reasons to trust them", but "in the absence of such positive reasons, discounting is a pervasive phenomenon". In contrast, a Spinozan belief-formation process is an "opt-out" process which accepts a hypothesis in the belief system before evaluating its plausibility. By default, the process accepts the hypothesis, and it is removed from the belief system when it is evaluated as implausible. This fits McKay and Mercier's description of perceptual belief formation; "although in some cases we can or should learn to doubt what we perceive [...], this is typically an effortful process with uncertain outcomes".

Some researchers defend a Spinozan model of belief formation for both empirical and philosophical reasons (e.g., Gilbert, 1991; Gilbert et al., 1993; Egan, 2008; Mandelbaum, 2014). And some apply a Spinozan model to delusional beliefs (e.g., Bongiorno, 2022; Davies & Egan, 2013), arguing that this model explains some features of delusional beliefs or the processes by which they are produced and maintained. However, we need not choose between the Spinozan model and the Cartesian model. Rather, we propose that some cases of belief formation are Spinozan, carrying with them in-built doxastic force, while other cases of belief formation can be Cartesian, allowing for a neutral suspension of judgement from the outset. As we already noted in Chapter 1, Section 4.2, there are good reasons to be epistemically vigilant about testimonial information from others, which is why a Cartesian, opt-in process is appropriate when it comes to handling testimonial input (Orchinik et al., 2024, 2025). On the other hand, there are no obvious reasons to be epistemically vigilant about perceptual information. Indeed, perceptual information is generally trustworthy. For these reasons, a Spinozan opt-out process is more appropriate for handling perceptual input. This is not to say that perceptual input cannot be doubted, but it is in very unusual circumstances that we doubt our senses and perform an effortful override (arguably, that's why visual illusions are so much fun).

Of course, this usually adaptive process of epistemic vigilance can become highly maladaptive when some underlying pathology or other disturbances produce systematically unreliable perceptual inputs. In such cases, the very properties of epistemic vigilance that protect people from social manipulation can instead shield highly unreliable beliefs from social correction. This is likely what happens in many cases of delusions, thereby illustrating a central theme developed in Chapter 8: the very features of our psychology and behaviour that ordinarily adapt us to the complexities and challenges of social life can simultaneously make us highly vulnerable to delusions under the abnormal conditions often associated with delusions.

In this way, the properties and vulnerabilities of epistemic vigilance provide a deeper, principled explanation of something that would otherwise be extremely puzzling: why delusional individuals often interpret their experiential evidence as trumping social evidence even when, from an outsider's perspective, this social evidence seems overwhelmingly strong (see Section 2). In such cases, general testimonial discount is not an additional difference-making factor in the delusion-formation process. It is rather a universal property of epistemic vigilance, and one which is ordinarily highly adaptive. Hence, just as our explanation of the social focus of delusions identified features of human social psychology that are not unique to delusions, part of our answer to the challenge of social evidence identifies generic features of epistemic vigilance that are also not unique to those with delusions. Nevertheless, without attending to these universal features of human social psychology, the tendency of delusional individuals to weight misleading experiential evidence more strongly than extremely powerful social evidence would be deeply mysterious. It is only by attending to the unique complexities and vulnerabilities of human sociality that this mystery can be partly solved.

3.2.2 Amplified Testimonial Discount

Importantly, the fact that general testimonial discount is likely to be involved in all delusions does not imply that it is the only relevant feature of epistemic vigilance in such cases. For example, McKay and Mercier hypothesise that delusions involve what we will call "amplified testimonial discount", which is something over and above a general form of testimonial discount that can be seen in the non-clinical population. "Whereas in healthy individuals the scales are adaptively tipped in favor of trusting the perceptual over the ostensive", they write, "this imbalance may be maladaptively exacerbated in delusions" (McKay & Mercier, 2023, p.126).

Amplified testimonial discount can manifest itself as a difference in handling testimonial evidence between delusional and non-delusional people. There are some suggestive empirical findings in line with this possibility, including a recent study by Simonsen and colleagues (2021). Their experiment involves a task where participants are supposed to infer the colour of the next marble to be drawn from a jar on the basis of sensory information (i.e., the colour of the marbles that were drawn already) and testimonial information (i.e., predictions of other people). Compared to people in the control group, people in the schizophrenic group exhibit a tendency to rely on sensory information rather than testimonial information, which appears to be correlated with poor social cognitive function rather than general cognitive deficits such as working memory deficit or executive function deficit.

How should we understand amplified testimonial discount? Of course, one possibility is that some cases of clinical delusions involve a localised dysfunction in psychological processes of epistemic vigilance. Although this possibility should not be ruled out a priori and warrants empirical research, there are reasons to be sceptical. For example, many of our objections to the idea that social vigilance involves a highly encapsulated module susceptible to localised dysfunction extend to epistemic vigilance specifically (see Chapter 7, Section 4.1). Indeed, determining the likely competence and trustworthiness of testifiers requires access to a vast and open-ended body of information, not least because all of one's beliefs are relevant to evaluating the plausibility of testimony, and because testifiers can and do take active measures to misrepresent their trustworthiness in highly complex ways designed to evade detection.

More importantly, the idea that testimonial discount is maladaptively exacerbated need not imply that some underlying mechanism is malfunctioning or damaged. When cognitive mechanisms underlying the evaluation of testimony and social evidence behave sub-optimally, there are two interpretations of the sub-optimal performance: misfunction and malfunction (Miyazono, 2018; see also Millikan, 2004; Sullivan-Bissett, 2024a). In the misfunction case, they perform sub-optimally because of abnormal inputs to relevant mechanisms or abnormal conditions under which they operate. (By way of analogy, a coffee maker misfunctions when it does not successfully perform its function, of producing coffee, when nobody has put water in it.) In the malfunction case, in contrast, the relevant social cognitive mechanisms fail to perform their functions because they are intrinsically damaged. (By way of analogy, a coffee maker malfunctions when it does not successfully perform its function, of producing coffee, due to physical damage to its electric circuit.)

In Chapter 8, we reviewed many cases in which otherwise adaptive social-psychological processes misfunction under the anomalous conditions and stressors associated with delusions. For example, general features of social vigilance can easily produce self-reinforcing cycles of paranoid ideation, worry, mistrust, and social withdrawal when anxious individuals have strange experiences, such that psychological processes usually protective against social threats end up instead facilitating the emergence and persistence of unfounded fears and thoughts about social threats. Similarly, as we saw in Section 2, reasoning's ordinarily adaptive tendency towards myside bias misfunctions when testimonial failures remove the normal social context within which reasoning functions well.

Importantly, general testimonial discount itself can involve a kind of misfunctioning: ordinarily adaptive processes of epistemic vigilance become maladaptive when normally reliable perceptual systems become dysfunctional or disturbed, producing misleading experiential evidence. As we have noted, in some cases of delusion, this is likely the only form of testimonial discount. For example, it is conceivable that general testimonial discount is relevant to Capgras delusion after brain injury in a car accident, where we do not have any reason to posit anything stronger than testimonial discount in the general sense. Nevertheless, we will now explore various ways in which this general discounting is amplified in many delusions, especially in schizophrenia. And in most of these cases, this amplification is rooted in misfunctioning, not malfunctioning.

4. Causes of Amplified Testimonial Discount

In this section, we first review how epistemic vigilance is modulated by assessments of the competence and sincerity of testifiers (Section 4.1) before speculating about how such assessments become distorted in some cases of delusions (Section 4.2).

4.1 Competence and Sincerity

There are some independent reasons to think that, at least in the cases of delusion in schizophrenia, there are some peculiar causes that can amplify testimonial discount. As we saw in Chapter 1, Section 4.2, epistemic vigilance involves a careful examination of both the testimony itself and the testifier's characteristics. The former concerns how the content of the relevant testimony is plausible, especially how coherent it is with prior beliefs. The latter, which is crucial in this context, concerns how competent the testifier is with regard to the relevant topic as well as how sincere and honest they are in the relevant context. The more competent the testifier is, other things being equal, the more trustworthy she is. And, the more sincere the testifier is, other things being equal, the more trustworthy she is. As we will see in the next section, delusions (in schizophrenia, in particular) are likely to involve some peculiar causal factors that can lead to discounting the competence and sincerity of testifiers in testimonial exchanges.

Importantly, the underestimation of competence and sincerity can undermine more than just testimony in a narrow sense, i.e., "a statement of someone's thoughts or beliefs, which they might direct to the world at large and to no one in particular" (Sosa, 1991, p.219). This is because the trustworthiness of evidence that is not testimonial in a narrow sense can be undermined by doubts about the competence and sincerity of some of the people involved in producing or transmitting it. This explains why, as we noted in Chapter 6, Section 6, delusional people are not only insensitive to testimonial evidence in the narrow sense.

For example, consider the case in which a doctor presents a delusional individual with a body of scientific data that strongly indicates the impossibility of the delusional hypothesis he adopts (e.g., "I have no internal organs"). If the individual underestimates the competence and sincerity of testifiers, he might not trust the scientific evidence, thinking, for example, that the data were fabricated by the people trying to harm or harass him or that the relevant researchers are not as competent as he, who, from his own point of view, has special and privileged insights. Moreover, as we have explored in Parts 1 and 2, the trustworthiness of testimony is upheld by complex systems of social norms and incentive structures ("epistemic reward systems"; see Chapter 5) in which testimony judged to be competent and sincere is socially rewarded, whereas testimony judged to be incompetent or dishonest is punished. To the extent that someone becomes mistrustful of this broader social-epistemic structure—for example, coming to believe that people will not be held socially accountable and punished for asserting specific falsehoods—this mistrust can then influence their assessment of all cooperative (epistemic and non-epistemic) behaviour within it.

Relatedly, in the "Truman syndrome", which can sometimes be seen in the prodromal phase of schizophrenia, a person has the impression that "the world ha[s] changed in some way that other people [a]re aware of, which he interpret[s] as indicating he [i]s the subject of a film and living in a film set (a 'fabricated world')" (Fusar-Poli et al., 2008, p.168). Here is a case reported by Fusar-Poli and colleagues:

> Mr M.A., a 26-year-old postman, presented with the feeling there was something subtle going on around him that others knew about but he didn't. He had a vague sense that people around him were 'acting', he was the focus of their interest and they knew a secret that was being kept from him.

> Furthermore he felt 'detached from the environment' and had a sense the world was slightly unreal, as if he was the eponymous hero in the film *The Truman Show*. (Fusar-Poli et al., 2008, p.168)

A person with Truman syndrome feels that he has been the victim of a massive deception in a fabricated world, just as in the film *The Truman Show*. And, because of his feelings and thoughts about the massive deception, he might discount not only testimonial evidence but also many, if not all, forms of evidence.

Thus, social worries about the trustworthiness of other agents can undermine not only testimonial evidence in the narrow sense but also a variety of evidence. After all, untrustworthy agents can deceive or mislead others by manipulating a variety of evidence. An extreme example of this can be found in the history of philosophy; i.e., Descartes' evil demon thought experiment in the First Meditation. A remarkable fact about Descartes's thought experiment is that he motivates (methodological) scepticism by a kind of social worry, i.e., a worry about an agent, the evil demon, who is an extremely untrustworthy agent who tries to deceive us all the time.

> I will suppose therefore that not God, who is supremely good and the source of truth, but rather some malicious demon of the utmost power and cunning has employed all his energies in order to deceive me. I shall think that the sky, the air, the earth, colors, shapes, sounds and all external things are merely the delusions of dreams which he has devised to ensnare my judgment. I shall consider myself as not having hands or eyes, or flesh, or blood or senses, but as falsely believing that I have all these things. (Descartes, 1984, p.15)

This thought experiment nicely illustrates (among other things) the fact that one cannot even trust basic forms of evidence such as one's sensory experiences in the presence of a highly untrustworthy and powerful agent.

Of course, there is an important difference between the evil demon case and delusional cases such as the ORGAN case. The person in the ORGAN case is not sceptical about experiential evidence (e.g., anomalous somatic feelings), while Descartes in the First Meditation is sceptical about it. But this difference is a matter of degree, not in kind. Social worry concerning a deceptive agent is the common factor between these two cases. It is relatively weak in the ORGAN case, undermining testimonial evidence but not experiential evidence. In contrast, social worry is so strong in the evil demon case that it undermines not only testimonial evidence but also experiential evidence.

4.2 Discounting Competence and Sincerity

As we noted above, delusions (especially in schizophrenia) are likely to involve some unusual causal factors that can contribute to discounting competence and sincerity of testifiers in testimonial exchanges. Let us now discuss some candidates for those causal factors. These speculations are not intended to be exhaustive, and it is likely that different instances of delusion may involve different combinations of factors.

Affective Factors: Several affective factors in schizophrenia can contribute to the discounting of competence and sincerity of testifiers in testimonial exchanges. For instance, anxiety and paranoid feelings, which can be regarded as affective factors, can easily cause delusional people to underestimate the sincerity of testifiers. If someone feels that a stranger is trying to harm or harass her, then she probably will not think of the stranger as a very sincere testifier. Perhaps the stranger has the malicious intent to deceive her as part of his strategy to harm or harass her. Another possibility is that grandiose feelings, which are also common in schizophrenia (and bipolar disorder), cause delusional people to underestimate the competence of testifiers. When someone feels that she is special and has some special capacities (special cognitive capacities, in particular) that other people do not have, then she will probably be inclined to think that testifiers, in comparison to herself, are not very competent, at least when it comes to certain topics.

Experiential Factors: There are many possible ways in which the specific contents of abnormal experiences might lead to amplified testimonial discounting. For example, the experience of unfamiliarity, especially the unfamiliarity of other people, can induce people to discount those people's trustworthiness. As we saw in Chapter 6, Section 2.2, a widely accepted account of Capgras delusion holds that a person with Capgras delusion has an abnormal experience in which familiar people are felt to be unfamiliar. More precisely, a face that is familiar in a semantic sense (i.e., the features of the face match the stored semantic memory of the person) is nonetheless felt as unfamiliar in an affective sense (i.e., the recognition of the face is not accompanied by affective or autonomic responses of the right kind). This kind of experience, where other people are experienced as unfamiliar in an affective sense, might also be exaggerated in other cases, such as Cotard delusion (Ramachandran & Blakeslee, 1999; Gerrans, 2002; but see Billon, 2016).

According to Kapur's aberrant salience hypothesis, which we have seen in Chapter 6, delusions in psychotic disorders like schizophrenia are a response to aberrant salience, which "induces a somewhat novel and perplexing state marked by exaggerated importance of certain percepts and ideas" (Kapur, 2003, p.15). Aberrant salience, on the one hand, suggests that relevant percepts and ideas have some significance, and, on the other hand, suggests a somewhat grandiose thought that one has a sharp awareness of things that other people do not have. Arguably, the aberrant salience in itself does not have any grandiose-related content, but it can lead to a grandiose thought that one is in a better epistemic position than others. In fact, many of the subjective reports that Kapur refers to as the expressions of aberrant salience suggest such a grandiose thought; e.g., "I developed a greater awareness of . . . . My senses were sharpened. I became fascinated by the little insignificant things around me"; "Sights and sounds possessed a keenness that he had never experienced before"; "It was as if parts of my brain awoke, which had been dormant"; or "My senses seemed alive . . . . Things seemed clearcut, I noticed things I had never noticed before" (quoted in Kapur 2003, p.15). This is important because, as we noted in Chapter 1 (Section 4.2), people's assessments of a testifier's competence are highly granular, estimating not just general character traits but whether testifiers are likely to have information relevant to specific topics. To the extent that delusional individuals believe themselves to possess esoteric knowledge or insights, they will, therefore, underestimate the competence of those whom they judge to lack such information.

Behavioural and Cognitive Factors: Some behavioural and cognitive factors in schizophrenia can also contribute to testimonial discount. An obvious candidate would be social cognition problems in psychosis (Penn et al., 2008), including emotion perception problems, mentalising problems, and attribution biases; for instance, problems in emotion perception or mentalising can lead to a lower evaluation of the trustworthiness of a testifier. Note that these social cognitive problems, even if they are causally relevant to testimonial discount, do not necessarily suggest a social cognitive malfunction (as opposed to misfunction). For instance, neurotypical adults without mentalising deficits can exhibit systematic errors in mentalising tasks such as the false belief task (e.g., Birch & Bloom, 2007).

Another candidate is a failure of "group identification". It is highly plausible that many delusional people, especially those with schizophrenia, have difficulty in group-identifying, which causes them to discount the trustworthiness of testifiers. We will spell out this possibility in some detail below.

An individual "group-identifies" with a group G (or acquires the "group identification" as a member of G) when she achieves a primitive form of self-conception as a member of G. It has been suggested in social psychology and philosophy that group identification plays a crucial role in collective, cooperative, and collaborative action and cognition (Turner, 1982; Brewer,

1991; Brewer & Gardner, 1996; Pacherie, 2013; Salice & Montes Sánchez, 2016; Salice & Miyazono, 2019; Miyazono & Inarimori, 2021; Pickard, 2021).

Experimental studies involving the minimal group paradigm (for an overview, see Diehl, 1990) show that group identification motivates pro-group behaviour. In a classic study by Tajfel and colleagues (1971), for example, a person with the group identity as a Kandinsky-lover (as opposed to a Klee-lover) was motivated to be helpful to other Kandinsky-lovers (as opposed to Klee-lovers). In the experiment, participants first indicated their aesthetic preferences for given pairs of paintings. Based on their preferences, they were told that they were either Kandinsky-lovers or Klee-lovers (while, unbeknownst to them, they were randomly assigned to either the Kandinsky-lover group or the Klee-lover group). In the next task, participants were asked to distribute real monetary rewards to other participants, including other Kandinsky-lovers and Klee-lovers. The result revealed an in-group favouritism: in distributing monetary rewards, Kandinsky-lovers favoured other Kandinsky-lovers over Klee-lovers, and Klee-lovers favoured other Klee-lovers over Kandinsky-lovers.

How does group identification work, exactly? One possibility is that group identification is a form of framing; people identify themselves as members of a group when they adopt a group frame to represent themselves and the agents with whom they are interacting (Bacharach, 2006). In this case, group identification's influence on cognition and behaviour involves a kind of framing effect (Bermudez, 2022). Salice and Miyazono (2020) propose a representational account of group identification, according to which group identification is understood in terms of non-doxastic representations. They reject the idea that group identification is a doxastic process in which, for example, a person X comes to believe that X is a member of a group G. Such a belief does not account for the motivational force of group identification. Rather, group identification involves a "pushmi-pullyu representation" (Millikan, 1995, 2004), a primitive kind of representation with both the world-to-mind direction of fit as well as the mind-to-world direction of fit. When X group-identifies with G, X forms a representation with both descriptive content (e.g., describing oneself as a member of G) as well as directive content (e.g., directing oneself to behave as a member of G).

Group identification is related to testimonial trust. In particular, it is relevant to testimonial exchanges such that X, with a group identity as a member of G, tends to regard a testifier, Y, who is also a member of G, as trustworthy (sincere and/or competent). Once one group identifies, one regards other group members as, other things being equal, more cooperative and sincere in group activities, including testimonial exchanges, than non-group members. For example, in Tajfel's experiment (1970; Tajfel et al., 1971), a participant, who identifies as a Kandinsky lover, might regard other Kandinsky lovers as, other things being equal, more cooperative and sincere in group activities, including testimonial exchanges, than Klee lovers. This is what Brewer calls "depersonalized trust", i.e. a form of trust (understood as an expectation of cooperation) that is "extended to any member of the ingroup whether personally related or not" (Brewer, 1999, p.433). More speculatively, it could be suggested that, once one group identifies, one regards other group members as, other things being equal, more competent in some activities, possibly including testimonial exchanges, than non-members. When one identifies oneself as a Kandinsky lover, one might regard other Kandinsky lovers as more competent in testimonial exchanges, at least on some particular topics (e.g., aesthetic topics), than Klee lovers. This can be understood as a group version of the self-enhancing positive illusion.

Salice and Henriksen (2015, 2021) argue that group identification is compromised by anomalous self-experiences in schizophrenia, where individuals feel themselves as different from others, including the feeling of ontological dissimilarity (i.e., anomalous self-experience as being very different from other people) or the loss of common sense (i.e., an inability to take for granted what other individuals consider obvious, self-evident, or even trivial). If this is correct,[3] there can be the following causal chain leading to testimonial discount; (i) because of anomalous self-experiences, the delusional individual fails to group-identify; i.e. fails to recognise any other in-group members; (ii) because of the failure to recognise any other in-group members, the delusional individual discounts either sincerity or competence of testifiers; (iii) because of discounting of testifiers' sincerity or competence, the delusional individual discounts the testimony of others. Of course, failures of group identification might also be caused by numerous other factors, including processes of social isolation and feelings of rejection and exclusion that delusional individuals can experience in relation to those around them.

5. *Folie à Deux*

Our central hypothesis in this chapter is that delusional individuals exhibit testimonial failures, including testimonial isolation and testimonial discount. We will now consider a phenomenon that seems to pose a clear challenge to

[3] The empirical evidence for this is rather mixed. For example, a recent study by Greenburgh et al. (2024) found that paranoia tendency is positively correlated with social identification.

this hypothesis: rare cases of *folie à deux* in which people seem to be delusional without exhibiting any testimonial failures.[4]

Folie à deux (FAD) involves a delusion that is shared by multiple individuals. Gralnick defines FAD as "a psychiatric entity characterized by the transference of delusional ideas and/or abnormal behavior from one person to one or more others who have been in close association with the primarily affected patient" (Gralnick, 1942, p.232). Let us call the person who initially comes up with the delusional belief the "primary" individual, and the person who receives the delusional belief from the primary individual the "secondary" individual. Often, primary and secondary individuals belong to the same nuclear family, and there is a very strong psychological relationship (of trust, dependence, etc.) between them.

Although high-quality empirical research into FAD is sparse, there are some important documented similarities between FAD and psychotic delusions. Just like in psychotic delusions, for example, persecutory themes are very common in FAD, and social isolation is a major risk factor. Interestingly, not only delusions but also hallucinations can be shared in the case of FAD. For example, a mother and her son might share not only the delusional belief that the person living in the next flat is harassing them, but also the hallucinatory auditory experience of that person's shouting and hitting the wall, which might be due to a top-down influence on sensory experience. Insofar as primary and secondary individuals often belong to the same family, it is also highly likely that the individuals involved often share genetic risk factors for psychosis as well.

In some cases of FAD, physical separation from the primary individual is sufficient for the secondary individual to abandon the delusional commitment, but not in other cases. Relatedly, FAD can come in different subtypes, where primary and secondary individuals play different roles (Gralnick, 1942; Shimizu et al., 2007). In some cases, the secondary individual passively receives the delusion from the primary individual (*folie imposée*). In other cases, the secondary individual, who is initially sceptical, is persuaded by the primary individual, and then later actively committed to the delusional idea (*folie communiquée*). There are also cases where primary and secondary individuals simultaneously come up with the same or similar delusional ideas (*folie simultanée*), where primary and secondary individuals mutually influence each other (*induction réciproque*), where primary and secondary individuals play different roles (*division du travail*), etc.

[4] Another example of this type is Koro (Yap, 1965; Bartholomew, 1994; Li, 2010; Coltheart & Davies, 2024b). Koro is seen in South and South-East Asia, and is characterised by a delusion-like belief that one's penis is shrinking into one's abdomen, accompanied by the fear that this may be lethal.<

FAD cases do not seem to involve any general problems in testimonial exchanges. As Radden notes:

> [i]n light of the ways of normal (and normative) social learning, particularly among intimates, the inducing of an idea in one person by another in *folie à deux* seems likely to conform to epistemic norms governing the acquisition of those states: their mode of transfer will be unexceptional. (Radden, 2010, p.81)

Let us now focus on the following case ("the SISTERS case" hereafter) where three sisters share delusional beliefs with some religious content, which motivate them to break into somebody else's house illegally:

> This case of shared psychotic disorder involved three biological sisters [Sister 1 (21), Sister 2 (23), Sister 3 (22)] without documented mental health histories before the incidents. [...] Approximately 18 months before the incidents [...] Sister 3 became fearful of harm coming to her children at the hands of her mother due to the mother's mental illness. Within six months, Sisters 1 and 2 moved in to assist with childcare, but later moved to the home next door at the request of the husband of Sister 3. [...] In the next several months, the three sisters became inseparable. They were increasingly preoccupied with religion and spent hours praying together. They began holding their own prayer service and Bible study group. They became isolated from everyone, including other family members. [...] For three days before their arrest, the sisters prayed continuously without sleeping. Sister 1 became convinced that God had special plans for her and her sisters and would provide for them. She also concluded that the Bible had been tampered with and was now incorrect due to the alternate spellings of Immanuel and Emmanuel. She had become convinced that God was trying to tell her something, and she convinced her sisters of the same. [...] On the day of the incident, the sisters disrobed in their home to "free themselves from the confines of clothing". Upon reading a Bible verse, Sister 1 believed that God wanted her to have the house that she and her sisters were accused of burglarizing [...] that God was going to provide for all her needs in that house [...] that her situation was similar to that of Moses when God told Moses to claim the Promised Land. The three sisters drove to the victims' house wearing only pajamas. They also brought the children of Sister 3 with them. They prayed while driving and believed "anything was possible at the time... God had intended for us to stay at that house for a while...He was guiding us. (Joshi et al., 2006, pp.512–513)

The SISTERS case seems to be a "successful" case of testimonial exchange in which Sister 1 (the primary individual) transmits information to Sisters 2 and 3 (the secondary individuals) by testimony. There is neither testimonial isolation (i.e., Sisters 2 and 3 are not testimonially isolated from Sister 1) nor testimonial discount (i.e., Sisters 2 and 3 do not discount testimony from Sister 1). Thus, people seem to be delusional, while they do not seem to exhibit any testimonial failures in FAD cases.

In response, one might deny the idea that the beliefs of secondary individuals in FAD are delusional (e.g., Munro, 1999). According to this proposal, Sister 1 is the only person in this case who is delusional; Sisters 2 and 3 are not. For example, Sister 1 has the delusional belief that God intends for them to occupy the house. Sisters 2 and 3 also believe the same thing, but their belief is not a delusion; rather, it is just a false belief that is formed in response to the testimony of an untrustworthy testifier (i.e., Sister 1).

This response is not compelling because it is difficult to see a principled reason—one that goes beyond mere stipulation—to deny the possibility that the beliefs of the secondary individuals can be genuinely delusional, given that they often seem practically indistinguishable from what we take to be genuine delusions. Such a claim seems motivated by the kind of pathocentrism we reject. The beliefs of the secondary individuals appear to be equally appropriate candidates for the status of a "rational lost cause" that is central to our analysis of delusion attribution (see Chapter 2).

Another response, which is more promising, would be to deny the claim that testimonial processes are entirely unproblematic in FAD cases. Let us think about testimonial isolation first. It is certainly true that Sisters 1, 2, and 3 are testimonially connected rather than isolated, but there is an important sense in which they are collectively isolated from others. For instance, while on the one hand "the three sisters became inseparable", and they "were increasingly preoccupied with religion and spent hours praying together", on the other hand they "became isolated from everyone, including other family members". A possible suggestion, then, is that FAD cases involve a collective form of testimonial isolation where primary and secondary individuals are collectively isolated from outsiders.

A similar suggestion about testimonial discount is possible. It is certainly true that Sisters 2 and 3 are testimonially persuaded by Sister 1, but nonetheless they are likely to be resistant to testimony from outsiders, especially when it comes to those issues that are directly or indirectly relevant to their collective delusions. For instance, it is very likely that, even if other family members had provided testimony offering some (counter)evidence relevant to their delusional beliefs, the sisters would not have been responsive. FAD cases, then, involve a collective form of testimonial discount where primary and secondary individuals collectively discount testimony from outsiders. Indeed, if they did not discount all relevant testimony from non-delusional sources, they would cease to be delusional.

Another possibility is that FAD involves testimonial failures of a different kind, e.g., an overrating (rather than discounting) of testimonial evidence from some particular individuals (e.g., Sister 1). And so, relatively speaking, there is a testimonial override of outsider testimony, and the testimony from Sister 1 plays for Sisters 2 and 3 a role that is analogous to the compelling experience in some experience-based accounts of delusion. Such an overrating might be caused by the overestimation (rather than underestimation) of the competence and sincerity of the particular individuals, which in turn might be due to excessive (rather than fragile) group identification with the individuals. The idea of excessive group identification in FAD cases is coherent with the observation that FAD is often seen in nuclear families, and that in general nuclear families are characterized by particularly intense group identification among their members (Sani, 2012). The fact that group identification tends to be strong among nuclear families is coherent with our discussion of kin selection and epistemic vigilance in Chapter 1, Section 4. For an obvious evolutionary reason, it is expected that people tend to be less vigilant towards their family members, typically exhibiting much higher baseline trust towards them.

6. Summary of Part 3

After setting out our general understanding of human ultra-sociality in Chapter 1, Chapter 2 aimed to establish that attributing delusional status to people and their beliefs involves the motivation to flag them as a "rational lost cause". This implies that "delusion" is an overarching and heterogeneous category, which can encompass non-pathological beliefs. Part 2 was then dedicated to explaining popular delusions and their features, while Part 3 aimed to explain clinical delusions and their features.

Chapter 6 clarified three explanatory challenges concerning clinical delusions: the challenge of social determinants, the challenge of social focus, and the challenge of social evidence. These challenges suggest that individualistic accounts of clinical delusions that have been dominant in the philosophical and empirical literature—including cognition-based accounts, experience-based accounts, two-factor accounts, and predictive processing accounts—are incomplete at best. Chapter 7 critically evaluated Gold and Gold's (2015) social account of clinical delusions and argued that their commitment to a selectively malfunctioning sociocognitive module (a "suspicion system") is empirically and theoretically implausible.

Chapters 8 and 9 have introduced our own explanatory framework, which offers a multifactorial, dynamic, and pluralistic approach to understanding delusions. It postulates multiple interacting factors, not all of which are unique to delusions or clinically abnormal, and models delusion formation as a complex, extended process, acknowledging the highly heterogeneous nature of delusions and their varied origins. This framework supplements rather than replaces existing individualistic accounts. While it recognises the importance of individual factors like anomalous experiences, it emphasises the crucial explanatory role of human sociality and its distinctive complexities and vulnerabilities, the relevance of which is far broader, deeper, and more complex than social accounts that restrict themselves to malfunctioning sociocognitive modules. Chapter 8 discussed the challenges of social determinants and social focus, while Chapter 9 focused on the challenge of social evidence.

We conclude Part 3 by summarising how our framework addresses the three explanatory challenges.

6.1 Social Determinants

Our framework addresses the challenge of social determinants by proposing that adverse social experiences, such as abuse and discrimination, increase the risk of delusions not through isolated impacts on specific socio-cognitive mechanisms, but through wide-ranging effects that interact with and exacerbate multiple delusion-causing factors. This framework suggests that adverse social experiences heighten social vigilance, making individuals more attuned to social threats and increasing their feelings of vulnerability, dysregulate stress systems and impair coping abilities, contributing to anomalous experiences, mood dysregulation, weakened cognitive resources, and reduced overall coping, and drive problematic behavioural patterns like social withdrawal, which, while initially protective, can create self-reinforcing cycles that strengthen paranoid thoughts, ultimately explaining the dose-response relationship between adverse social experiences and delusions, the uniquely damaging impact of early-life adversity, and the protective role of social support, all while emphasising that these social factors are neither specific to nor sufficient for psychosis.

6.2 Social Focus

Our framework addresses the challenge of social focus—why delusions tend to focus on themes that are about the delusional individual's place in the social universe—in terms of the inherently social nature of human minds navigating uniquely complex, opaque, and often adversarial social environments. Such universal features of human sociality channel delusional ideation rooted in anomalous experiences and domain-general cognitive abnormalities towards social interpretations. The framework further explains specific delusional themes (e.g., persecutory, grandiose) by integrating individual traits, mood, and cultural context, illuminating why similar experiences can lead to diverse delusional themes and why diverse experiences can converge on the same theme. This comprehensive approach highlights that the social nature of delusions stems from general cognitive and experiential disruptions manifesting in an ultra-social species. It contrasts with theories relying solely on localised social-cognitive impairments, offering a broader and more nuanced understanding of delusion content and its origins in fundamental aspects of human sociality.

6.3 Social Evidence

Our framework addresses the challenge of social evidence—why delusions are insensitive to testimonial evidence—by postulating "testimonial failures". These include testimonial isolation, where individuals lack exposure to relevant social evidence due to internal (e.g., anxiety, social withdrawal) or external (e.g., stigmatisation) factors, and testimonial discount, where experiential evidence is prioritised over conflicting testimonial evidence. This discount can be general or amplified. Amplified testimonial discount stems from various interacting factors, such as affective factors (paranoid/grandiose feelings impacting testifier sincerity/competence), experiential factors (compelling anomalous experiences or unfamiliarity leading to discounting testimony), and behavioural/cognitive factors (social cognition problems or difficulty with group identification affecting trust). The framework is pluralistic, recognising that not all delusions involve both isolation and discount, and that rare cases, like *folie à deux*, may exhibit different patterns, such as collective isolation/discount or an overrating of specific testimonies.

Conclusion

1. Introduction

The central thesis of this book is that human sociality in the broadest sense is highly relevant to a wide range of puzzles and questions related to delusions, including what it means to be delusional, why delusions arise, what forms they take, and why they persist.

We began in Chapter 1 by outlining in more detail what we mean by human sociality. Humans are not just another social species. We are intensely cooperative and cultural animals, radically reliant on others for our survival and success, including our abilities to know and navigate our environment. And this environment is itself intensely social. It involves uniquely complex systems of norms, reputations, gossip, surveillance, and partner choice, as well as high-stakes opportunities and threats associated with competition for prestige and power between individuals and shifting coalitions.

This picture of human sociality then informed our analysis of delusions. First, we argued that what it means to be delusional is best understood in the context of norm-governed, social-evaluative practices of epistemic flagging and gatekeeping (Chapter 2). In such practices, treating beliefs as delusional does not involve the application of an objective medical diagnosis or the detection of a natural kind. It is part of an ancient social practice in which members of epistemic communities express their bafflement at certain beliefs and signal that those who endorse them are "rational lost causes"—people who have exited the shared space of reasons (see Sellars, 1956) altogether on the topic in question, unreachable by ordinary processes of communication, persuasion, and rational argument.

We then advanced explanatory frameworks for understanding two pathways, or two kinds of pathways, through which people reliably trigger this social response. In Part 2 (Chapters 3–5), we argued that mass or "popular" delusions emerge from interactions between socially motivated cognition and complex forms of social scaffolding. When communities share motivations to propagate beliefs or to adopt them for social signalling reasons, they produce systems of norms, incentives, and distributed cognition that function to

The Social Roots of Delusions. Daniel Williams, Sam Wilkinson, and Kengo Miyazono, Oxford University Press.
© Oxford University Press (2026). DOI: 10.1093/9780191976360.003.0011

promote and protect those beliefs. Through such "epistemic reward systems", communities scaffold and sustain levels of motivated irrationality that their members could not achieve on their own.

In Part 3 (Chapters 6–9), we turned to clinical delusions. Because such beliefs typically separate individuals who endorse them from their community, one might think that the social nature of human minds and worlds plays no role in such cases. We argued that this is mistaken. Although the proximate causes of clinical delusions typically involve strange, private experiences and domain-general cognitive difficulties, such disturbances unfold within social minds confronting uniquely complex social challenges in ways that influence their formation, persistence, and predominant focus on social themes. One critical example of this social relevance concerns the processes through which social isolation and mistrust cause delusional individuals to lose access to the collective knowledge and corrective testimony that people rely on to regulate their beliefs. That is, whereas popular delusions emerge from a motivated, collective distortion of social knowledge-generating practices, clinical delusions involve a catastrophic withdrawal from such practices.

It should now be clearer how this explanatory framework can illuminate and reconcile the seemingly conflicting ideas expressed in the two quotes from Nietzsche and Keynes that we referenced in our introductory chapter. The first quote, from Nietzsche, holds that "[m]adness is rare in the individual—but in groups, parties, nations, and epochs it is the rule" (Nietzsche, 1996 [1886], p.70). According to this perspective, our social nature explains our most common and spectacular epistemic failures. The second quote, from Keynes, remarks that "it is astonishing what foolish things one can temporarily believe if one thinks too long alone" (Keynes, 1936, p.vii). Here, we see the idea central to much research in modern cognitive science, cultural evolution, and social epistemology that human sociality is our species' epistemic superpower, the source of our ability to remain tethered to reality and to acquire and accumulate knowledge.

In our framework, both quotes capture something important. Humans are dependent on epistemic cooperation to regulate our beliefs and acquire knowledge. When social isolation or suspicion causes individuals to lose access to such cooperation, it is easy for their beliefs to become dangerously unmoored from reality, especially when they experience unusual things or have difficulties integrating and processing information. However, such individual "madness" is relatively rare because most humans are tightly integrated into social-epistemic networks that constrain individual departures from collective belief systems. In sharp contrast, there are no such constraints on the collective irrationalities identified in Nietzsche's quote. Precisely because they emerge from widespread, adaptive motivations to co-opt the social-epistemic machinery of norms, reputations, and coordination to non-epistemic ends, they are a common outcome of perfectly "normal" psychological and social processes.

In this concluding chapter, we will briefly identify the book's main contributions and unifying themes (Section 2), connect our ideas to prominent debates and rival approaches (Section 3), and set out an agenda for future research based on some of the book's most significant limitations (Section 4).

2. Interdependence and the Fragility of Knowledge

Our main aim in this book is to establish the fruitfulness of centring human sociality in delusions research. We also hope to have broadened readers' appreciation of the rich and complex character of our social nature and its relevance to thinking about human belief formation and knowledge. In our framework, human sociality is not merely one factor among others; it provides the fundamental context in which phenomena such as experience, classification, and cognition unfold. To paraphrase William James (2000 [1907], p.68), the trail of human sociality is over everything.[1] It shapes the experiences and evidence we encounter, the threats and opportunities that dominate our attention and interests, the phenomena that pose our most complex and consequential challenges, and the processes through which we acquire knowledge and regulate our beliefs.

Throughout the book, we have advanced many claims, conjectures, and hypotheses that reflect this overarching ambition of connecting human sociality to delusions. Instead of simply repeating these ideas, it will be helpful to extract two unifying themes that recur throughout the book.

The first theme concerns the profound and wide-ranging relevance of human interdependence to questions about belief formation and delusions. As we stressed in Chapter 1, human beings are not isolated cognitive agents who happen to live in groups. We are radically interdependent, reliant on complex networks of social cooperation, coordination, and competition to achieve the overwhelming majority of our goals, including our epistemic goals. This interdependence informs every aspect of our analysis.

Most fundamentally, because we depend on epistemic cooperation and a division of cognitive labour to acquire knowledge, communities must enforce

[1] The original quote is, "The trail of the human serpent is thus over everything".

social-epistemic norms and police the epistemic commons. This sets the stage for our analysis of delusion attribution, which emerges as a way of flagging those who not only threaten to poison the epistemic commons with false ideas but who have exited the system of epistemic cooperation altogether, at least on the specific topic in question.

Interdependence is also central to the emergence and persistence of popular delusions. Because we depend on others and their assessments, our psychology often prioritises social goals of persuasion, advocacy, and reputation management over the disinterested pursuit of truth. This is where socially motivated cognition and socially adaptive beliefs come from. And because we rely on others to regulate our beliefs and acquire evidence, including "higher-order" evidence, the systematic distortion of social-epistemic practices by socially motivated cognition can easily transform such practices into powerful mechanisms of shared ignorance and misbelief.

In the case of clinical delusions, human interdependence ensures that experiences of abuse, marginalisation, and social exclusion are not just unpleasant but psychologically, physically, and behaviourally catastrophic. They increase feelings of vigilance, vulnerability, and mistrust, dysregulate mood and biological systems, and promote social withdrawal, all of which increase the likelihood of delusions in at-risk individuals. Interdependence also ensures that the social world is the most salient and high-stakes focus of human attention, thought, and imagination, channelling delusional ideation towards social phenomena that are uniquely challenging to track and anticipate. And precisely because we rely on substantial social scaffolding to regulate our beliefs, it explains why the loss of access to corrective testimony and collective knowledge in delusions is so damaging.

The second overarching theme concerns the relationship between human sociality and the fragility of knowledge. In much research into delusions, it is assumed that knowledge of reality constitutes a kind of "default" state relative to which false beliefs are a puzzling aberration. This assumption explains why there is a vast body of psychological, social-scientific, and philosophical research specifically focused on why people believe false things. In such projects, true beliefs are thought to be unmysterious, a simple consequence of naturally truth-seeking mechanisms functioning properly. One also sees this assumption in the popular idea that delusions involve a "loss of contact with reality", the presupposition being that "contact" with reality is the natural condition of human minds, as well as in the widespread assumption that if someone endorses a radically mistaken belief, there must be something "wrong" with their belief-forming processes.

The framework developed in this book challenges this perspective. Although we have explored the causal pathways through which people embrace popular and clinical delusions, we have situated these explorations in a broader picture of human sociality that involves an "explanatory inversion" of the relationship between human knowledge and error.

The term "explanatory inversion" comes from the philosopher Joseph Heath (2022, p.2), who argues that such inversions "arise as a consequence of discoveries or theoretical insights that have the effect of changing, not our specific explanations of events, but rather our fundamental sense of what needs to be explained". He gives the example of crime. For a long time, it was assumed that the primary challenge of criminology was to explain the causes of crime, in part due to the commonsense observation that most people in most places obey the law most of the time. In the 19th century, sociologists like Émile Durkheim criticised this perspective, pointing out that the motives underlying crime and social deviance more broadly are typically perfectly ordinary and largely unmysterious. Instead, the deep mystery of criminology is not crime but law-abidingness:

> Common sense is wrong on this point because we are all reasonably well-socialized adults, living in a well-ordered society, and so we take for granted the institutional arrangements that secure our compliance with the rules. But the underlying mechanisms are ones that we do not really understand, as a result of which it is difficult to explain why more people do not break the law more often (since it is so often in their interest to do so) ... There is an explanatory inversion at work, because of the change in our understanding of what needs to be explained. (Heath, 2022, p.4)

We view our book similarly. At least when it comes to forming beliefs outside the scope of immediate first-person experience, knowledge is not the "default" state of human beings. We are not automatically "in touch with reality". Rather, knowledge is a collective achievement that typically depends on a precarious system of social support and epistemic cooperation. "Common sense" misleads us about this state of affairs because we always assume that we hold accurate beliefs; this is simply what it means to believe something. However, when we step back and reflect on the social, cultural, and epistemic situation of human beings, we should appreciate that knowledge is often a complex achievement of fragile psychological and social processes.

This fragility is central to our framework for understanding popular delusions. Much of cognition does not "naturally" aim at truth. Indeed, when it comes to beliefs about socially relevant domains—for example, people's beliefs about themselves, their groups, their society, and those features (or imagined features) of reality relevant to intra-group cooperation and intergroup competition—propagandistic and signalling motives typically predominate (Chapter 4). Similarly, our treatment of epistemic reward systems (Chapter 5) reveals just how easily the social-epistemic practices through which we produce, share, and acquire information can become systems that sustain ignorance and delusion. In this framework, it is the fact that some systems of epistemic cooperation (e.g., modern science) partly escape the distorting factors identified in Part 2 that is aberrant and puzzling, not the collective madness identified in Nietzsche's aphorism (see Rauch, 2021; Williams, 2024b).

The connections between human sociality and the fragility of knowledge are also central to our analysis of clinical delusions. The most transparent source of fragility here concerns our epistemic dependence on other people's testimony. In this case, knowledge is fragile not just because we rely on such social inputs to acquire information and avoid mistakes but because the psychological and social processes through which we access and evaluate testimony are themselves fragile. In general, social learning involves a high-stakes dilemma: we must be sufficiently open to other people's testimony to acquire knowledge but sufficiently vigilant to avoid misinformation and manipulation. It is easy to get this wrong in such a way that "epistemic vigilance" works not to protect us from deception but to protect our mistaken beliefs from correction.

Moreover, precisely because the social world is uniquely complex, opaque, and potentially adversarial, involving strategic agents with sophisticated capacities for reasoning, planning, coordination, and deception, it poses unique epistemic challenges. To cope with these challenges effectively, we typically need not just sufficient social support and trust, but also cognitive resources that adverse social encounters, strange experiences, and emotional dysregulation can easily strain. Indeed, once one appreciates how easy it is for perceptual abnormalities, cognitive difficulties, and mood disturbances to trigger the mutually reinforcing cycles of suspicion, social withdrawal, and rumination relevant to paranoia and what we have called the "spider's web of psychosis" (see Chapter 8), it becomes surprising that paranoid ideation and delusions are not more common than they are.

For these reasons, our framework suggests that there is often nothing fundamentally mysterious about why people embrace even radically mistaken beliefs about reality. Of course, this does not mean that there is nothing to explain in such cases, any more than Durkheim's explanatory inversion in criminology implies that criminal behaviours need not be explained. Our book attempts to provide such explanations. The point is instead that appreciating the degree to which individual knowledge is often a fragile achievement should demystify delusional phenomena. Instead of assuming that something must have gone terribly wrong inside a delusional individual's mind, we should consider why the precarious support structures necessary to support knowledge acquisition are absent or have withered away. Psychological dysfunction might be relevant to that question in some cases, but it need not be in many others. And even when it is relevant, it is likely so only because of its role in dynamic, multifactorial processes that involve universal human vulnerabilities, highlighting the profound continuities between delusions and "normal" belief formation.

3. Core Debates and Existing Views

Before identifying limitations of our project and setting out an agenda for future research, it will be helpful to briefly comment on how our book connects to broader debates and rival positions in delusion research.

3.1 Delusions and Rationality

One central debate concerns the relationship between delusions and rationality (Bortolotti 2009, 2015, 2023). For example, many have found it plausible that part of what it means to be delusional is holding beliefs that are highly epistemically irrational, i.e., that violate norms such as evidence sensitivity and rational coherence to an unusual degree. Similarly, many have argued that irrational psychological processes are central to the formation and persistence of delusional beliefs.

Our arguments in this book have complicated implications for such debates. First, we have argued that delusion attribution is not best understood as picking out mental states demarcated by objective epistemic failures. Instead, it involves conferring a social-epistemic status on individuals or groups, treating their beliefs not just as mistaken but as falling beyond the reach of rational persuasion and argument. In this sense, the *appearance* of epistemic irrationality central to delusion attribution, the thing that triggers folk-epistemic bafflement and the motivation to flag rational disengagement, could be misleading. For example, if somebody's beliefs are partly responses to private (e.g., experiential) evidence, or to evidence not available to another epistemic community, they might be treated as a "rational lost cause" even though their beliefs are rationally responsive to the evidence they have encountered.

Of course, this possibility might never be realised in practice. That is, the causal processes that give rise to beliefs that trigger this response might always involve objective epistemic irrationality. Our frameworks for understanding the aetiology of popular and clinical delusions suggest that this is partly correct, but that epistemic irrationality is only part of a much broader and more complex causal story.

First, the socially motivated cognition central to our analysis of popular delusions involves seeking out and processing information in ways that are biased away from truth-seeking and, hence, epistemically irrational. In this way, our account differs from a recent body of research across philosophy and cognitive science that models seemingly irrational beliefs in the non-clinical population (e.g., conspiracy theories, science denial, political misperceptions, etc.) as rational responses to inadequate, ambiguous, or misleading evidence, including higher-order social evidence (e.g., Begby, 2021; Levy, 2021; see Chapter 3, Section 3.1). Nevertheless, this observation must be nuanced in several ways.

To begin with, although popular delusions involve unusual forms of epistemic irrationality, such irrationality is not a "mistake". Socially adaptive beliefs emerge from adaptive social processes that prioritise strategic social objectives over epistemic ones. In this sense, the appearance of extreme irrationality in many popular delusions *is* often misleading. Such beliefs are not irrational *tout court*. They involve forms of *epistemic irrationality* that are *instrumentally rational*, at least in the sense that they function to promote an individual's short-term practical interests of persuasion and reputation management. Of course, as with all behaviours that arise from individually adaptive motivations, socially adaptive beliefs can produce terrible and highly unjust collective outcomes, but they nevertheless emerge from well-functioning psychological mechanisms.

In addition, our framework locates the epistemic irrationality of popular delusions not only in individual psychology but in distributed social processes. Specifically, although individual-level motivational biases play a significant role in our explanation of popular delusions, the task of rationalising unfounded beliefs and insulating them from disconfirmation is primarily outsourced to the social environment (see Chapter 5). When communities share motives to propagate or adopt beliefs, they produce systems of social rewards and punishments (e.g., the enforcement of orthodoxy, the suppression of dissent, the encouragement of fanaticism, and a marketplace of rationalisations) that amplify and hide evidence in ways geared to providing epistemic support for those beliefs. This is the sense in which our framework treats motivated irrationality as an irreducibly collective achievement, and it explains why popular delusions are less *individually* epistemically irrational than they seem to those outside the relevant system of epistemic cooperation.

The role of epistemic irrationality within our framework for understanding clinical delusions is also complicated. Although there is significant uncertainty regarding the nature and impact of domain-general cognitive biases or global information-processing abnormalities on such beliefs (see Chapter 6), we acknowledge that they likely play an important role in many cases. Nevertheless, the emergence and persistence of clinical delusions involve far more than brute epistemic irrationality.

First, as we will return to shortly (Section 3.2), we share the core "empiricist" assumption that clinical delusions are sensitive to private but misleading experiential evidence. For this reason, it is a mistake to treat such delusions as wholly insensitive to or divorced from evidence, even if they appear unresponsive to publicly available evidence. Moreover, we have argued that talk of "evidence sensitivity" *tout court* is highly misleading (Chapter 9, Section 2). There are principled reasons why human beings should and do treat experiential evidence differently from testimonial evidence. Insofar as clinical delusions are distinguished by their insensitivity to the latter, this is less about extreme epistemic failures on the part of delusional individuals than about the vulnerabilities of epistemic vigilance and the ease with which mistrust, strange experiences and expectations, and various stressors can erode our openness to corrective testimony.

More generally, our framework suggests that the processes through which clinical delusions emerge and persist often involve locally rational, reasonable, or adaptive responses to perceived conditions. For example, if you are abused or marginalised, it is perfectly rational to become more mistrustful of testimony and more vigilant for social exploitation or manipulation. If you feel threatened by others, it is typically highly adaptive to become anxious and more disposed to ruminate on possible threat-related scenarios. If you begin to worry that you are the victim of a deliberately concealed plot, it is reasonable to search for evidence of this plot and to refuse to treat the absence of clear evidence as clear evidence of the plot's absence. Nevertheless, when people are confronted with anomalous experiences and other stressors, it is easy for these and other processes, all individually understandable, to interact in ways that produce and sustain delusions.

Ultimately, then, our framework's emphasis on the fragility of knowledge and the weaknesses of unaided individual cognition should reframe our understanding of the connection between clinical delusions and irrationality. Once we appreciate how unreliable unaided individual cognition is, we should also recognise how even relatively mild experiential, affective, and cognitive disturbances can snowball into seemingly bizarre beliefs when individuals lose access to the social support and epistemic scaffolding that humans rely on for knowledge.

3.2 Delusions and Experience

One central debate about the aetiology of delusions concerns the role of anomalous experience. In this context, philosophers often distinguish "empiricist" from "rationalist" accounts (see Bayne & Pacherie, 2004). In a nod to the empiricism of early modern philosophers such as Locke, Berkeley, and Hume, the former claim that delusions are at least partly the result of erroneous evidence presented in perceptual experiences. In a nod to rationalist philosophers like Descartes, Spinoza, and Leibniz, the latter accounts allege that delusions are the result of disruptions to how individuals think or reason about the world, which are distinct from experience but may in turn influence how the world is experienced.

Anomalous experiences do not play a central role in our explanations of popular delusions, which are driven instead by widespread motivations to propagate ideas or adopt them for social signalling reasons. In such cases, community members might be encouraged or discouraged from providing testimony about their personal experiences. For example, cults or sects might socially reward members who report experiences of miracles or divine revelation that provide evidence for shared belief systems. Nevertheless, the ultimate drivers of these belief systems are social motivations. In contrast, our framework for understanding clinical delusions embraces the core empiricist idea that anomalous experiences are typically and perhaps always relevant in the delusion-forming process (see Chapter 8, Section 2). How, then, does our empiricist framework connect to existing debates in this literature?

First, we have argued that strange experiences alone do not explain the social determinants of delusions, the predominant social focus of delusions, or why those who embrace delusions are so resistant to corrective testimony. To account for these social dimensions, one must understand how the character of human ultra-sociality ensures, first, that phenomena such as abuse, marginalisation, and social isolation exacerbate strange experiences and undermine people's abilities to cope with them (Chapter 8, Section 3); second, that delusional ideation is disproportionately focused on uniquely complex and challenging social threats and opportunities (Chapter 8, Section 4); and third, that people with delusions are often separated from and suspicious of testimonial evidence (Chapter 9).

Relatedly, our framework also stresses that anomalous experiences are rarely sufficient to produce or sustain delusions on their own. Instead, delusion formation typically involves complex, dynamic processes that unfold over time, featuring interactions between strange experiences and emotional disturbances, psychological tendencies (e.g., rumination or fantasising), domain-general cognitive biases, behavioural tendencies, and changes to how individuals evaluate testimony, all of which unfold within ultra-social minds confronting uniquely complex and ambiguous social threats and opportunities. On the surface, this multifactorial framework sharply diverges from both one-factor and two-factor models of delusion formation. Nevertheless, this claim is complicated by disagreements over how to understand and individuate "factors" (see Chapter 6, Section 3). For example, at least when it comes to monothematic delusions, Ema Sullivan-Bissett (2024b) argues for a "one-factor" empiricist model, not because she thinks anomalous experiences alone produce delusions, but because she believes they are the only "clinically abnormal" factor involved.

As we noted in Chapter 6, our disagreement with this perspective is partly methodological and partly substantive. First, questions of clinical abnormality are orthogonal to questions of explanatory relevance. To understand the causes and characteristics of delusions, one must often focus on many factors that are individually perfectly "normal" or within the "normal" range. Second, if one insists that the term "factor" should be reserved for clinically abnormal or pathological factors, there is an important sense in which we are *zero*-factor theorists. That is, although we acknowledge that clinically abnormal experiences (i.e., experiences rooted in underlying psychological or neurobiological dysfunction) are relevant in many and perhaps most cases of delusion formation, we do not assume they are always necessary. As with most human psychological traits, propensities to have strange experiences are distributed throughout the population and modulated by numerous factors (Van Os et al., 2000). It is easy to imagine how anomalous experiences and a wide range of other factors, none of them individually pathological or connected to dysfunction, might nevertheless interact in complex, dynamic processes to produce beliefs that become dangerously unmoored from shared reality and unreachable by rational persuasion.

Another debate among empiricists concerns how to understand experience itself. For example, although empiricist models of delusions are often conflated with "bottom-up" models in which delusions emerge from erroneous "inputs" to belief formation, empiricists can reject bottom-up models of experience. To maintain the analogies with early modern philosophers, they might embrace a "Kantian" view in which experience emerges through a combination of bottom-up influences with top-down categories and expectations. Relatedly, there is a prominent debate over whether clinical delusions involve attempts to explain anomalous experiences or whether they simply endorse the contents of such experiences. To take Capgras delusion as an example, the alternatives are: "Something is not right. This person feels unfamiliar. How do I explain this? Must not be Dad", as opposed to the experience directly presenting: "Not Dad".

When it comes to the latter debate, our framework has focused primarily on explanation. For example, our account of the social focus of delusions assumes that the raw material of strange experiences is often logically consistent with multiple possible hypotheses, and that it is features of our social psychology and the social environment that explain why individuals frequently embrace delusional hypotheses that focus on recurrent social themes of persecution, surveillance, control, or status. Nevertheless, our pluralistic framework is consistent with the possibility that, in some cases, the content of anomalous experiences might be sufficiently specific and rich that delusions simply endorse their content. This is especially likely if one accepts a model of the mind in which top-down influences on perception can contribute to the creation of experiences with complex content (see Wilkinson, 2021). For example, specific social threat-based expectations triggered by heightened social vigilance might shape attention and perceptual processing, producing experiences or outright hallucinations congruent with those expectations, which might then be treated as further confirmation of them. In line with this, there is some evidence from studies using virtual reality headsets suggesting that individuals with strong social threat expectations experience identical visual stimuli differently from others (Freeman et al., 2008).

This possibility of dynamic, bidirectional influences between bottom-up and top-down processes in perception and cognition naturally leads us to a discussion of predictive processing.

3.3 Delusions and Predictive Processing

One of the most influential frameworks for understanding delusions and psychosis more broadly is predictive processing (see Corlett et al., 2010; Fletcher & Frith, 2009; Adams et al., 2013). As described in Chapter 6, Section 2.4, predictive processing models the brain as a hierarchical prediction machine. Perception and cognition emerge through processes in which brains exploit hierarchically organised generative models to predict sensory information, register prediction errors, and then use them to update the model. Moreover, these prediction errors are weighted by their estimated "precision" (roughly, their reliability), which determines the relative influence of bottom-up information and top-down expectations in driving inference and learning.

We are sympathetic to the main ideas of predictive processing (Wilkinson 2014, Williams 2018, Miyazono and McKay 2019), including its emphasis on the porous boundaries between paradigmatically perceptual and cognitive processing, and on the dynamic, bidirectional interactions between the two. How, then, do the ideas in this book relate to this influential framework?

When it comes to popular delusions, it is unclear how to integrate phenomena like socially adaptive beliefs and socially motivated cognition into the language of predictive processing. One reason for this is that such cognitive processes are not geared towards epistemic goals, such as minimising prediction error or resolving uncertainty, but to outward-facing, strategic ones. Another is that the "beliefs" in question behave differently from ordinary world-modelling beliefs (see Chapter 5). Precisely because they arise through processes aimed at social transmission and signalling rather than modelling the world, they are typically compartmentalised in people's mental lives and cordoned off from broader cognition and behaviour. It is a task for future research to explore how such phenomena could be made consistent with, or illuminated by, the core ideas of predictive processing.

Our framework for understanding clinical delusions can be more straightforwardly translated into the language of predictive processing. For example, heightened social vigilance could be recast as strong social threat-related "priors" and increased precision on related prediction errors, testimonial discounting could be recast in terms of various processes through which brains lower the precision of prediction errors coming from testimony, and the predominant social focus of delusions could be understood in terms of how generative models assign disproportionate weight to certain social predictions and struggle to resolve uncertainty in the uniquely complex domains associated with social dynamics (see Sterzer et al., 2018). In this sense, we view our hypotheses as consistent with predictive processing, and it is an important task for future work to explore possible connections (see Section 4 below).

Nevertheless, these examples also illustrate what our framework adds that a narrow focus on the formal properties of the brain's information-processing mechanisms will miss. Although the human brain might be accurately described as a hierarchical, generative model-based prediction machine at one level of abstraction, this description says nothing about what kinds of animals we are, what goals most powerfully motivate us, which features of our environment are most salient to us, which opportunities and threats pose the most complex computational challenges we confront, and why we would be disposed to treat prediction errors differently depending on whether they originate in experience or from testimony. It also says nothing about the degree to which we rely on complex, fragile social practices of epistemic cooperation to regulate our beliefs and acquire knowledge, and how this dependence drives us to police the social flow of information and regulate our interactions with one another, placing some people within the shared space of reasons and some people outside of it. Importantly, none of these observations is *inconsistent* with predictive processing, or with other lower-level theories about the brain's information-processing mechanisms. However, they go beyond such theories to reveal features of the human condition highly relevant to understanding the properties and formation of delusions.

Recently, proponents of predictive processing have criticised the "social turn" in delusions research, arguing that paranoia and persecutory delusions are best explained not by selective dysfunctions in specialised socio-cognitive processes but by aberrations in domain-general learning mechanisms (see Corlett et al. 2025). We hope that the framework we have developed in Part 3 of this book demonstrates why this line of reasoning is mistaken. As we argued in Chapter 7, we share their scepticism about the relevance of malfunctioning sociocognitive modules in delusion formation. Nevertheless, this scepticism does not imply that human sociality is irrelevant to understanding the causes or characteristics of delusions. In our framework, delusions emerge from complex interactions between perceptual, cognitive, affective, and behavioural factors that unfold within obsessively social animals navigating uniquely complex, high-stakes social environments. Unless you engage with this specific character of our social nature and social ecology, you will not understand clinical delusions, including why social adversity substantially increases their likelihood of arising, why delusions predominantly focus on social themes, and why people with delusions are so resistant to testimonial evidence. And yet this engagement does not require the postulation of broken sociocognitive modules.

4. An Agenda for Future Work

As we acknowledged in our introductory chapter, our project has been highly ambitious, synthetic, and speculative. Although we have tried to ground our claims and conjectures in empirical evidence and persuasive arguments, we are aware that the ideas we have advanced and defended have been limited and incomplete in various ways. We will conclude by highlighting some of these limitations to outline an agenda for future research.

First, one central task for future research is to test the empirical conjectures that we have advanced. For example, the framework for understanding delusion attribution that we advanced in Chapter 2 rests on a speculative genealogy about the emergence of delusion-attribution practices in human social life and their contingent connection to medical practices. Although we provided some general theoretical arguments and historical evidence supporting this picture, future research should explore the extent to which it is consistent with detailed historical and anthropological studies of the nature of social-epistemic practices across time and cultures. Similarly, we argued that the attribution of delusional status is rooted in feelings of folk-epistemic bafflement and the motivation to flag targets as rational lost causes. Future research could draw on methods from experimental philosophy to test this account (e.g., Rose et al., 2014; for related experimental work on conspiracy theories, see Napolitano & Reuter, 2023), perhaps presenting participants with carefully crafted, contrasting case-studies and asking them to report their disposition to characterise them as delusional, or asking participants whether they deem certain statements (e.g., "This is a delusion but they could be talked out of it".) contradictory or infelicitous.

Importantly, such studies and their results must be designed carefully because our account does not imply that all uses of the term "delusion" will align with our account. For example, although many people are happy to use the term "delusion" in non-clinical contexts (e.g., Edsall, 2021), its widespread use in modern medical psychiatry today might encourage some people to think that the specific term is essentially tied to pathology or mental illness. Nevertheless, if we are correct, there is a core conceptual practice that involves expressing folk-epistemic bafflement and recommending rational disengagement that is cross-cultural, precedes the use of "delusion" in modern medical psychiatry, and is often articulated with expressions like "delusional", "mad", "crazy", or "insane", and this conjecture could in principle be tested.

Future research should also seek ways to test the conjectures central to our explanatory accounts of popular and clinical delusions. For example, experimental psychologists could test the degree to which activating social goals of propaganda (e.g., persuasion or advocacy) and reputation management biases cognitive processes (see, e.g., Babcock et al., 1995; Melnikoff & Strohminger, 2020; Schwardmann et al., 2022). Careful sociological and ethnographic research could also explore the degree to which the characteristics of epistemic reward systems (e.g., "active belief", self-censorship, and rationalisation markets) that we have posited are present in specific belief-based communities (see, e.g., Marwick & Partin, 2022; Storr, 2021). Similarly, future research could test our explanation of the social focus of delusions by evaluating the degree to which human thought naturally gravitates towards social explanations of anomalous or surprising events under specific conditions. There are also many opportunities to test our conjectures about how asymmetries in the treatment of experiential and social evidence are relevant to the maintenance of clinical delusions, and how phenomena such as failures of group identification result in testimonial discount.

Future work should also seek to connect our conjectures to lower-level research about cognitive and neurobiological mechanisms. Although we hope to have established that there are important insights and explanatory contributions one can make without in-depth engagement with such issues, these mechanistic questions are nevertheless essential for a complete understanding of delusional phenomena. As we have already noted, one crucial part of this project involves connecting our ideas to existing neurocomputational frameworks such as predictive processing. However, our explanatory accounts also leave many other issues open. For example, there are important questions about how phenomena such as socially motivated cognition operate in terms of cognitive processes and neurobiological mechanisms, and how to understand socially adaptive beliefs. Although we provided a functional explanation of why such beliefs are often strangely compartmentalised in the minds of those who hold them, the mechanisms underlying such compartmentalisation remain unclear. Countless questions also remain concerning the mechanisms underlying clinical delusions if our explanatory approach is correct. For example, it is unclear why at least some examples of such beliefs are also compartmentalised. And although we have criticised highly modular accounts of complex sociocognitive processes such as social vigilance, these questions about cognitive architecture and how the mind is organised to perform specialised functions must ultimately be adjudicated by detailed mechanistic research.

Another limitation of our explanatory frameworks is their qualitative, verbal character. That is, although complex, dynamical causal processes are central to our account of both popular and clinical delusions, models of these processes should ideally use quantitative, formal frameworks better suited to representing them. For example, this might include sophisticated agent-based modelling in the case of our analysis of epistemic reward systems in popular delusions (see O'Connor & Weatherall, 2019), or complex network analyses of the multivariate causal processes and feedback loops central to our account of many clinical delusions (see Borsboom & Cramer, 2013).

Finally, our project has been primarily descriptive and explanatory. We have aimed at understanding the functions and practices underlying delusion attribution, and the general psychological and social processes by which individuals and collectives develop beliefs that attract such attributions. Nevertheless, if our arguments and conjectures are even broadly correct, they carry many important ethical, social, and political implications. Exploring these implications is a central task for future research.

For example, our aetiological accounts of popular and clinical delusions carry significant lessons for how we should respond to such belief systems and the individual and collective harms that they often produce. In the case of popular delusions, our account implies that such belief systems are not best understood as simple cognitive errors. Instead, they reflect powerful social motivations. Given this, although our account does not imply that fact-checking initiatives or attempts at rational persuasion will be futile in such cases—recall that motivated cognition is subject to a rationalisation constraint (see Chapter 3)—it does imply that they are likely to be of limited effectiveness, and that interventions that more directly target the social motivations and pressures that produce and sustain such belief systems might be more effective. Similarly, although our account of clinical delusions is not inconsistent with the importance of traditional pharmaceutical and other medical interventions, it highlights the need to consider a much broader range of causal processes and intervention points, including adverse social experiences such as isolation and marginalisation. It also suggests that people's ability to "unlearn" delusional beliefs will often depend on increasing their exposure to and trust in testimony, and that facilitating and scaffolding *experiential* learning will often be far more effective than social learning. In line with this, a central feature of Daniel Freeman and colleagues' highly successful "Feeling Safe Programme" for people with persecutory delusions is that it helps people learn (or relearn) safety through guided behavioural experiments in feared situations (see Freeman et al., 2021).

Our framework for understanding delusion attribution also raises numerous important ethical and political questions. If delusion attribution expresses folk-epistemic bafflement and involves a motivation to recommend rational disengagement, there are important questions about how we should evaluate this practice and its connection to phenomena such as epistemic injustice and stigma, which warrant more in-depth treatment in future work. Moreover, as we have already stressed in Sections 2 and 3, if our accounts of why people embrace and hold onto popular and clinical delusions are correct, they demystify such beliefs and reveal that those who endorse them are much less irrational than they initially appear. For this reason, our book on delusions might have the strange consequence of convincing readers that there is much less delusion in the world than people think.

Of course, these highly schematic remarks barely scratch the surface of the complex issues that we have raised in this concluding section. Nevertheless, we hope that they offer at least a glimpse of what a research agenda based on the ideas in this book might look like, and that they encourage some readers to address these complex issues in future work.

References

Abed, R. T., & Abbas, M. J. (2014). Can the new epidemiology of schizophrenia help elucidate its causation? *Irish Journal of Psychological Medicine*, 31(1), 1–5.
Abelson, R. (1986). Beliefs are like possessions. *Journal for the Theory of Social Behaviour*, 16, 223–250.
Abrams, S., Jackson, J. C., Vonasch, A., & Gray, K. (2020). Moralization of Religiosity Explains Worldwide Trends in Religious Belief. OSF. https://doi.org/10.31234/osf.io/5a2db
Acerbi, A. (2019). *Cultural Evolution in the Digital Age*. Oxford University Press.
Adams, R. A., Stephan, K. E., Brown, H. R., Frith, C. D., & Friston, K. J. (2013). The computational anatomy of psychosis. *Frontiers in Psychiatry*, 4, 47.
Aktipis, A., Cronk, L., Alcock, J., Ayers, J. D., Baciu, C., Balliet, D., ... Winfrey, P. (2018). Understanding cooperation through fitness interdependence. *Nature Human Behaviour*, 2(7), 429–431.
Alexander, R. D. (1987). *The Biology of Moral Systems*. Aldine de Gruyter.
Alicke, M. D., & Sedikides, C. (2009). Self-enhancement and self-protection: What they are and what they do. *European Review of Social Psychology*, 20(1), 1–48.
Allport, G. W., & Postman, L. (1947). *The Psychology of Rumor*. Henry Holt.
American Psychiatric Association. (2013). *Diagnostic and Statistical Manual of Mental Disorders* (5th ed.). American Psychiatric Publishing.
Anderson, C., Hildreth, J. A. D., & Howland, L. (2015). Is the desire for status a fundamental human motive? A review of the empirical literature. *Psychological Bulletin*, 141(3), 574–601.
Anderson, M. L. (2010). Neural reuse: A fundamental organizational principle of the brain. *Behavioral and Brain Sciences*, 33(4), 245–266.
Anderson, M. L., & Finlay, B. L. (2014). Allocating structure to function: The strong links between neuroplasticity and natural selection. *Frontiers in Human Neuroscience*, 7, 918.
André, J. -B., Baumard, N., & Boyer, P. (2023). Cultural evolution from the producers' standpoint. *Evolutionary Human Sciences*, 5, e25.
Anscombe, G. E. M. (1957). *Intention*. Harvard University Press.
Archer, W. G. (1984). *Tribal Law and Justice: A Report on the Santal*. Concept.
Arseneault, L., Cannon, M., Fisher, H. L., Polanczyk, G., Moffitt, T. E., & Caspi, A. (2011). Childhood trauma and children's emerging psychotic symptoms: A genetically sensitive longitudinal cohort study. *American Journal of Psychiatry*, 168(1), 65–72.
Atran, S., & Ginges, J. (2012). Religious and sacred imperatives in human conflict. *Science*, 336(6083), 855–857.
Ayer, A. J. (1936). *Language, Truth and Logic*. Gollancz.
Babcock, L., Loewenstein, G., Issacharoff, S., & Camerer, C. (1995). Biased judgments of fairness in bargaining. *The American Economic Review*, 85(5), 1337–1343.
Bacharach, M. (2006). *Beyond Individual Choice: Teams and Frames in Game Theory*. Princeton University Press.
Baker, S. J., Jackson, M., Jongsma, H., & Saville, C. W. (2021). The ethnic density effect in psychosis: A systematic review and multilevel meta-analysis. *The British Journal of Psychiatry*, 219(6), 632–643.
Baker, S. J., Jackson, M., Jongsma, H., & Saville, C. W. N. (2021). The ethnic density effect in psychosis: A systematic review and multilevel meta-analysis. *The British Journal of Psychiatry*, 219(6), 632–643.
Barclay, P. (2013). Strategies for cooperation in biological markets, especially for humans. *Evolution and Human Behavior*, 34(3), 164–175.

Barclay, P. (2020). Reciprocity creates a stake in one's partner, or why you should cooperate even when anonymous. *Proceedings of the Royal Society B: Biological Sciences*, 287(1929), 20200819.

Barclay, P., Bliege Bird, R., Roberts, G., & Számadó, S. (2021). Cooperating to show that you care: Costly helping as an honest signal of fitness interdependence. *Philosophical Transactions of the Royal Society B: Biological Sciences*, 376(1838), 20200292.

Barrett, H. C. (2014). *The Shape of Thought: How Mental Adaptations Evolve*. Oxford University Press.

Barrett, J. L. (2000). Exploring the natural foundations of religion. *Trends in Cognitive Sciences*, 4(1), 29–34.

Bartholomew, R. E. (1994). The social psychology of 'epidemic' koro. *International Journal of Social Psychiatry*, 40(1), 46–60.

Bauer, R. M. (1984). Autonomic recognition of names and faces in prosopagnosia: A neuropsychological application of the guilty knowledge test. *Neuropsychologia*, 22(4), 457–469.

Baumard, N., André, J.-B., & Sperber, D. (2013). A mutualistic approach to morality: The evolution of fairness by partner choice. *Behavioral and Brain Sciences*, 36(1), 59–78.

Baumeister, R. F., & Leary, M. R. (1995). The need to belong: Desire for interpersonal attachments as a fundamental human motivation. *Psychological Bulletin*, 117(3), 497–529.

Bayne, T., & Pacherie, E. (2004). Bottom-up or top-down: Campbell's rationalist account of monothematic delusions. *Philosophy, Psychiatry, & Psychology*, 11(1), 1–11.

Bebbington, P., Bhugra, D., Brugha, T., Singleton, N., Farrell, M., Jenkins, R., ... Meltzer, H. (2004). Psychosis, victimisation and childhood disadvantage: Evidence from the second British National Survey of Psychiatric Morbidity. *The British Journal of Psychiatry*, 185(3), 220–226.

Bécares, L., Shaw, R., Nazroo, J., Stafford, M., Albor, C., Atkin, K., ... Pickett, K. (2012). Ethnic density effects on physical morbidity, mortality, and health behaviors: A systematic review of the literature. *American Journal of Public Health*, 102(12), e33-e66.

Beck, R. (2015). *We Believe the Children: A Moral Panic in the 1980s*. Hachette UK.

Begby, E. (2021). *Prejudice: A Study in Non-Ideal Epistemology*. Oxford University Press.

Bell, V., Raihani, N., & Wilkinson, S. (2021). Derationalizing delusions. *Clinical Psychological Science*, 9(1), 24–37.

Bendixen, T., Lightner, A. D., Apicella, C., Atkinson, Q., Bolyanatz, A., Cohen, E., ... Purzycki, B. G. (2023). Gods are watching and so what? Moralistic supernatural punishment across 15 cultures. *Evolutionary Human Sciences*, 5, e18.

Bentall, R. P. (2004). *Madness Explained: Psychosis and Human Nature*. Penguin UK.

Bentall, R. P. (2018). Delusions and other beliefs. In L. Bortolotti (Ed.), *Delusions in Context* (pp. 67–95). Springer International Publishing.

Bentall, R. P. (2024). Delusion and unrealistic comparator. In E. Sullivan-Bissett (Ed.), *The Routledge Handbook of the Philosophy of Delusion* (pp. 557–572). Routledge.

Bentall, R. P., Kaney, S., & Dewey, M. E. (1991). Paranoia and social reasoning: An attribution theory analysis. *British Journal of Clinical Psychology*, 30(1), 13–23.

Bermúdez, J. L. (2022). Rational framing effects: A multidisciplinary case. *Behavioral and Brain Sciences*, 45, e220.

Berrios, G. E., & Luque, R. (1995). Cotard's syndrome: Analysis of 100 cases. *Acta Psychiatrica Scandinavica*, 91(3), 185–188.

Bhui, R., Chudek, M., & Henrich, J. (2019). How exploitation launched human cooperation. *Behavioral Ecology and Sociobiology*, 73(6), 78.

Bialecki, J. (2017). *A Diagram for Fire: Miracles and Variation in an American Charismatic Movement*. University of California Press.

Billon, A. (2016). Making sense of the Cotard syndrome: Insights from the study of depersonalisation. *Mind & Language*, 31(3), 356–391.

Birch, S. A., & Bloom, P. (2007). The curse of knowledge in reasoning about false beliefs. *Psychological Science*, 18(5), 382–386.

Blakemore, S. J., Smith, J., Steel, R., Johnstone, E. C., & Frith, C. D. (2000). The perception of self-produced sensory stimuli in patients with auditory hallucinations and passivity experiences: Evidence for a breakdown in self-monitoring. *Psychological Medicine*, 30(5), 1131–1139.

Blanchard, J. L., Horan, W. P., & Brown, S. A. (2001). Diagnostic differences in social anhedonia: A longitudinal study of schizophrenia and major depressive disorder. *Journal of Abnormal Psychology*, 110(3), 363.

Boehm, C. (2012). *Moral Origins: The Evolution of Virtue, Altruism, and Shame*. Hachette UK.

Bongiorno, F. (2022). Spinozan doxasticism about delusions. *Pacific Philosophical Quarterly*, 103(4), 720–752.

Borsboom, D., & Cramer, A. O. J. (2013). Network analysis: An integrative approach to the structure of psychopathology. *Annual Review of Clinical Psychology*, 9, 91–121.

Bortolotti, L. (2009). *Delusions and Other Irrational Beliefs*. Oxford University Press.

Bortolotti, L. (2015). *Irrationality*. Polity Press.

Bortolotti, L. (2016). Epistemic benefits of elaborated and systematized delusions in schizophrenia. *The British Journal for the Philosophy of Science*, 67(3), 879–900.

Bortolotti, L. (2020). *The Epistemic Innocence of Irrational Beliefs*. Oxford University Press.

Bortolotti, L. (2022). Delusion. In E. N. Zalta (Ed.), *The Stanford Encyclopedia of Philosophy* (Summer 2022 ed.). https://plato.stanford.edu/archives/sum2022/entries/delusion/

Bortolotti, L. (2023). *Why Delusions Matter*. Bloomsbury Publishing.

Bortolotti, L., & Miyazono, K. (2015). Recent work on the nature and development of delusions. *Philosophy Compass*, 10(9), 636–645.

Boyd, R. (1991). Realism, anti-foundationalism and the enthusiasm for natural kinds. *Philosophical Studies*, 61(1), 127–148.

Boyd, R. (2017). *A Different Kind of Animal*. Princeton University Press.

Boyer, P. (2001). *Religion Explained*. Basic Books.

Boyer, P. (2018). *Minds Make Societies: How Cognition Explains the World Humans Create*. Yale University Press.

Boyer, P. (2022). Why we blame victims, accuse witches, invent taboos, and invoke spirits: A model of strategic responses to misfortune. *Journal of the Royal Anthropological Institute*, 28(4), 1345–1364.

Bratman, M. E. (1992). Practical reasoning and acceptance in a context. *Mind*, 101(401), 1–15.

Brennan, G., & Pettit, P. (2004). *The Economy of Esteem: An Essay on Civil and Political Society*. Oxford University Press.

Brennan, J. (2016). *Against Democracy*. Princeton University Press.

Brewer, M. B. (1991). The social self: On being the same and different at the same time. *Personality and Social Psychology Bulletin*, 17(5), 475–482.

Brewer, M. B. (1999). The psychology of prejudice: Ingroup love or outgroup hate? *Journal of Social Issues*, 55(3), 429–444.

Brewer, M. B., & Gardner, W. (1996). Who is this "We"? Levels of collective identity and self representations. *Journal of Personality and Social Psychology*, 71(1), 83.

Brotherton, R. (2015). *Suspicious Minds: Why We Believe Conspiracy Theories*. Bloomsbury Publishing.

Bulbulia, J., & Sosis, R. (2011). Signalling theory and the evolution of religious cooperation. *Religion*, 41(3), 363–388.

Buller, D. J. (2006). *Adapting Minds: Evolutionary Psychology and the Persistent Quest for Human Nature*. MIT Press.

Bunyan, J. (1980). *The Miscellaneous Works of John Bunyan: Vol. I: Some Gospel-truths Opened, A Vindication of Some Gospel-truths Opened, A Few Sighs from Hell*. Edited by T. L. Underwood. Clarendon Press. (Original work published in 1656)

Butler, P. V. (2000). Reverse Othello syndrome subsequent to traumatic brain injury. *Psychiatry*, 63(1), 85–92.

Butterworth, J., Trivers, R., & von Hippel, W. (2022). The better to fool you with: Deception and self-deception. *Current Opinion in Psychology*, 47, 101385.

Cameron, N. (1959). The paranoid pseudo-community revisited. *American Journal of Sociology*, 65(1), 52–58.

Campbell, J. (2001). Rationality, meaning, and the analysis of delusion. *Philosophy, Psychiatry, & Psychology*, 8(2), 89–100.

Cantlon, J. F., & Piantadosi, S. T. (2024). Uniquely human intelligence arose from expanded information capacity. *Nature Reviews Psychology*, 3(4), 275–293.

Capps, D. (2004). John Nash's delusional decade: A case of paranoid schizophrenia. *Pastoral Psychology*, 52(3), 193–218

Carruthers, P. (2011). *The Opacity of Mind: An Integrative Theory of Self-Knowledge*. Oxford University Press.

Cassam, Q. (2016). Vice epistemology. *The Monist*, 99(2), 159–180.

Cassam, Q. (2019). *Conspiracy Theories*. Polity Press.

Castillejos, M. D. C., Martín-Pérez, C., & Moreno-Küstner, B. (2018). A systematic review and meta-analysis of the incidence of psychotic disorders: The distribution of rates and the influence of gender, urbanicity, immigration and socio-economic level. *Psychological Medicine*, 48(13), 2101–2115.

Cermolacce, M., Sass, L., & Parnas, J. (2010). What is bizarre in bizarre delusions? A critical review. *Schizophrenia Bulletin*, 36(4), 667–679.

Černis, E., Evans, R., Ehlers, A., & Freeman, D. (2021). Dissociation in relation to other mental health conditions: An exploration using network analysis. *Journal of Psychiatric Research*, 136, 460–467.

Chagnon, N. A. (2013). *Noble Savages: My Life Among Two Dangerous Tribes—the Yanomamo and the Anthropologists*. Simon and Schuster.

Chanes, L., Wormwood, J. B., Betz, N., & Barrett, L. F. (2018). Facial expression predictions as drivers of social perception. *Journal of Personality and Social Psychology*, 114(3), 380–396.

Chen Zeng, T., Cheng, J. T., & Henrich, J. (2022). Dominance in humans. *Philosophical Transactions of the Royal Society B: Biological Sciences*, 377(1845), 20200451.

Cheng, J. T., Tracy, J. L., Foulsham, T., Kingstone, A., & Henrich, J. (2013). Two ways to the top: Evidence that dominance and prestige are distinct yet viable avenues to social rank and influence. *Journal of Personality and Social Psychology*, 104(1), 103–125.

Chudek, M., & Henrich, J. (2011). Culture–gene coevolution, norm-psychology and the emergence of human prosociality. *Trends in Cognitive Sciences*, 15(5), 218–226.

Clark, A. (2013). Whatever next? Predictive brains, situated agents, and the future of cognitive science. *Behavioral and Brain Sciences*, 36(3), 181–204.

Clark, A. (2015). *Surfing Uncertainty: Prediction, Action, and the Embodied Mind*. Oxford University Press.

Cohen, S. (2001). *States of Denial: Knowing About Atrocities and Suffering*. John Wiley & Sons.

Cohen, S. (2011). *Folk Devils and Moral Panics*. Routledge.

Collin, S., Rowse, G., Martinez, A. P., & Bentall, R. P. (2023). Delusions and the dilemmas of life: A systematic review and meta-analyses of the global literature on the prevalence of delusional themes in clinical groups. *Clinical Psychology Review*, 104, 102303.

Coltheart, M. (2007). Cognitive neuropsychiatry and delusional belief. *Quarterly Journal of Experimental Psychology* (2006), 60(8), 1041–1062.

Coltheart, M. (2013). On the distinction between monothematic and polythematic delusions. *Mind & Language*, 28(1), 103–112.

Coltheart, M., & Davies, M. (2024a). Delusional belief about location ("reduplicative paramnesia"). *Cognitive Neuropsychiatry*, 29(4–5), 268–285.

Coltheart, M., & Davies, M. (2024b). Koro: A socially-transmitted delusional belief. *Cognitive Neuropsychiatry*, 29(1), 10–28.

Coltheart, M., Langdon, R., & McKay, R. (2007). Schizophrenia and monothematic delusions. *Schizophrenia Bulletin*, 33(3), 642–647.

Coltheart, M., Langdon, R., & McKay, R. (2011). Delusional belief. *Annual Review of Psychology*, 62, 271–298.

Coltheart, M., Menzies, P., & Sutton, J. (2010). Abductive inference and delusional belief. *Cognitive Neuropsychiatry*, 15(1–3), 261–287.
Conner, C. T., & MacMurray, N. (2022). The perfect storm: A subcultural analysis of the QAnon movement. *Critical Sociology*, 48(6), 1049–1071.
Cooper, R. (2007). *Psychiatry and Philosophy of Science*. Routledge.
Corlett, P. R. (2019). Factor one, familiarity and frontal cortex: A challenge to the two-factor theory of delusions. *Cognitive Neuropsychiatry*, 24(3), 165–177.
Corlett, P. R., Murray, G. K., Honey, G. D., Aitken, M. R., Shanks, D. R., Robbins, T. W., ... Fletcher, P. C. (2007). Disrupted prediction-error signal in psychosis: Evidence for an associative account of delusions. *Brain*, 130(9), 2387–2400.
Corlett, P. R., Taylor, J. R., Wang, X. J., Fletcher, P. C., & Krystal, J. H. (2010). Toward a neurobiology of delusions. *Progress in Neurobiology*, 92(3), 345–369.
Corlett, P., Rossi-Goldthorpe, R., Suthaharan, P., Sheffield, J. M., de Obeso, S. C., & Heyes, C. (2025). Pseudosocial cognition and paranoia. *Trends in Cognitive Sciences*, 29(11), 997–1006
Craig, E. (1990). *Knowledge and the State of Nature: An Essay in Conceptual Synthesis*. Clarendon Press.
Craver, C. F. (2009). Mechanisms and natural kinds. *Philosophical Psychology*, 22(5), 575–594.
Crichton, P., Carel, H., & Kidd, I. J. (2017). Epistemic injustice in psychiatry. *BJPsych Bulletin*, 41(2), 65–70.
Curley, E. (1975). Descartes, Spinoza, and the ethics of belief. In E. Freeman (Ed.), *Spinoza: Essays in Interpretation* (pp. 159–189). Open Court.
Cutajar, M. C., Mullen, P. E., Ogloff, J. R., Thomas, S. D., Wells, D. L., & Spataro, J. (2010). Schizophrenia and other psychotic disorders in a cohort of sexually abused children. *Archives of General Psychiatry*, 67(11), 1114–1119.
David, A. S. (1999). On the impossibility of defining delusions. *Philosophy, Psychiatry, & Psychology*, 6(1), 17–20.
Davies, M., & Coltheart, M. (2022). Cotard delusion, emotional experience and depersonalisation. *Cognitive Neuropsychiatry*, 27(6), 430–446.
Davies, M., & Coltheart, M. (2024). The two-factor theory. In E. Sullivan-Bissett (Ed.), *The Routledge Handbook of Philosophy of Delusion* (pp. 430–449). Routledge.
Coltheart, M., & Davies, M. (2024). Koro: A socially-transmitted delusional belief. *Cognitive Neuropsychiatry*, 29(1), 10–28.
Davies, M., & Egan, A. (2013). Delusion: Cognitive approaches, Bayesian inference and compartmentalisation. In K. W. M. Fulford, M. Davies, R. G. T. Gipps, & G. Graham (Eds.), *Oxford Handbook of Philosophy and Psychiatry* (pp. 689–727). Oxford University Press.
Davies, M., Coltheart, M., Langdon, R., & Breen, N. (2001). Monothematic delusions: Towards a two-factor account. *Philosophy, Psychiatry, & Psychology*, 8(2), 133–158.
Davis, W. (2000). Heaven's Gate: A study of religious obedience. *Nova Religio*, 3(2), 241–267.
Dawkins, R. (2007). *The God Delusion*. Random House.
de Pauw, K. W., & Szulecka, T. K. (1988). Dangerous delusions: Violence and the misidentification syndromes. *British Journal of Psychiatry*, 152(1), 91–97.
Del Giudice, M. (2018). *Evolutionary Psychopathology: A Unified Approach*. Oxford University Press.
Dennett, D. C. (2006). *Breaking the Spell: Religion as a Natural Phenomenon*. Viking.
Descartes, R. (1984). *The Philosophical Writings of Descartes* (Vol. 2). Cambridge University Press.
Dessalles, J.-L. (2007). *Why We Talk: The Evolutionary Origins of Language*. Oxford University Press.
Diamond, J. M. (1997). *Guns, Germs, and Steel: The Fates of Human Societies*. W. W. Norton & Company.
Diehl, M. (1990). The minimal group paradigm: Theoretical explanations and empirical findings. *European Review of Social Psychology*, 1(1), 263–292.
DiResta, R. (2024). *Invisible Rulers: The People Who Turn Lies into Reality*. Hachette UK.
Dorst, K. (2023). Rational polarization. *The Philosophical Review*, 132(3), 355–458.

Douglas, K. M., Sutton, R. M., & Cichocka, A. (2017). The psychology of conspiracy theories. *Current Directions in Psychological Science*, 26(6), 538–542.

Dudley, R., Taylor, P., Wickham, S., & Hutton, P. (2016). Psychosis, delusions and the 'jumping to conclusions' reasoning bias: A systematic review and meta-analysis. *Schizophrenia Bulletin*, 42(3), 652–665.

Dunbar, R. I. M. (2004). Gossip in evolutionary perspective. *Review of General Psychology*, 8(2), 100–110.

Durkheim, É. (2001). *The Elementary Forms of Religious Life*. Oxford University Press. (Original work published in 1912)

Eagleton, T. (1991). *Ideology: An Introduction*. Verso.

Edsall, T. (2021, February 3). Opinion | The QAnon delusion has not loosened its grip. *The New York Times*. https://www.nytimes.com/2021/02/03/opinion/qanon-conspiracy-theories.html

Egan, A. (2008). Seeing and believing: Perception, belief formation and the divided mind. *Philosophical Studies*, 140, 47–63.

Eisenacher, S., & Zink, M. (2017). Holding on to false beliefs: The bias against disconfirmatory evidence over the course of psychosis. *Journal of Behavior Therapy and Experimental Psychiatry*, 56, 79–89.

Eisenberger, N. I., Moieni, M., Inagaki, T. K., Muscatell, K. A., & Irwin, M. R. (2017). In sickness and in health: The co-regulation of inflammation and social behavior. *Neuropsychopharmacology*, 42(1), 242–253.

El Sendiony, M. F. M. (1976). Cultural aspects of delusions: A psychiatric study of Egypt. *Australian & New Zealand Journal of Psychiatry*, 10(2), 201–207.

Ellis, H. D., & Young, A. W. (1990). Accounting for delusional misidentifications. *The British Journal of Psychiatry*, 157(2), 239–248.

Ellis, H. D., Young, A. W., Quayle, A. H., & De Pauw, K. W. (1997). Reduced autonomic responses to faces in Capgras delusion. *Proceedings of the Royal Society of London. Series B: Biological Sciences*, 264(1384), 1085–1092.

Enders, A. M., Uscinski, J. E., Klofstad, C. A., Wuchty, S., Seelig, M. I., Funchion, J. R., ... Stoler, J. (2022). Who supports QAnon? A case study in political extremism. *The Journal of Politics*, 84(3), 1844–1849.

Endo, Y., Heine, S. J., & Lehman, D. R. (2000). Culture and positive illusions in close relationships: How my relationships are better than yours. *Personality and Social Psychology Bulletin*, 26(12), 1571–1586.

Epley, N., & Gilovich, T. (2016). The mechanics of motivated reasoning. *Journal of Economic Perspectives*, 30(3), 133–140.

Faunce, A. F., & Tennant, W. B. (2024). Exploring Cotard's delusion within the context of major depressive disorder with psychotic features: A case report. *Cureus*, 16(8), e68047.

Fenigstein, A. (1984). Self-consciousness and the overperception of self as a target. *Journal of Personality and Social Psychology*, 47(4), 860–870.

Festinger, L., Riecken, H. W., & Schachter, S. (1956). *When Prophecy Fails*. University of Minnesota Press.

Feyaerts, J., Henriksen, M. G., Vanheule, S., Myin-Germeys, I., & Sass, L. A. (2021). Delusions beyond beliefs: A critical overview of diagnostic, aetiological, and therapeutic schizophrenia research from a clinical-phenomenological perspective. *The Lancet Psychiatry*, 8(3), 237–249.

Fichera, A., & Kelety, J. (2022, January 8). FACT FOCUS: Unfounded theory used to dismiss COVID measures. *The Associated Press*. https://apnews.com/article/coronavirus-pandemic-science-health-joe-rogan-ap-fact-check-a87b1044c6256968dcc33886a36c949f

Firestone, C., & Scholl, B. J. (2016). Cognition does not affect perception: Evaluating the evidence for "top-down" effects. *Behavioral and Brain Sciences*, 39, e229.

Fitouchi, L., & Singh, M. (2022). Supernatural punishment beliefs as cognitively compelling tools of social control. *Current Opinion in Psychology*, 44, 252–257.

Fitouchi, L., Singh, M., André, J.-B., & Baumard, N. (2023). Prosocial Religions as Folk-Technologies of Mutual Policing. OSF. https://doi.org/10.31234/osf.io/qdhka

Fletcher, P. C., & Frith, C. D. (2009). Perceiving is believing: A Bayesian approach to explaining the positive symptoms of schizophrenia. *Nature Reviews Neuroscience*, 10(1), 48–58.
Fletcher, P. C., & Frith, C. D. (2009). Perceiving is believing: A Bayesian approach to explaining the positive symptoms of schizophrenia. *Nature Reviews Neuroscience*, 10(1), 48–58.
Fodor, J. A. (1975). *The Language of Thought*. Harvard University Press.
Fodor, J. A. (1983). *The Modularity of Mind: An Essay on Faculty Psychology*. MIT Press. 2
Fontaine, J. S. L. (1998). *Speak of the Devil: Tales of Satanic Abuse in Contemporary England*. Cambridge University Press.
Ford, J. M., & Mathalon, D. H. (2004). Electrophysiological evidence of corollary discharge dysfunction in schizophrenia during talking and thinking. *Journal of Psychiatric Research*, 38(1), 37–46.
Foucault, M. (1961). *Histoire de la folie à l'âge classique*. Plon.
Foucault, M. (1963). *Naissance de la clinique: Une archéologie du regard médical*. Presses Universitaires de France.
Foucault, M. (1975). *Surveiller et punir: Naissance de la prison*. Gallimard.
Frankish, K. (2010). Dual-process and dual-system theories of reasoning. *Philosophy Compass*, 5(10), 914–926.
Freeman, D. (2007). Suspicious minds: The psychology of persecutory delusions. *Clinical Psychology Review*, 27(4), 425–457.
Freeman, D. (2016). Persecutory delusions: A cognitive perspective on understanding and treatment. *The Lancet Psychiatry*, 3(7), 685–692.
Freeman, D. (2024). Understanding and treating persecutory delusions. *Schizophrenia Bulletin*, 50(2), 233–235.
Freeman D. (Director). (2018). BBC Radio 4—A history of delusions [Broadcast]. *BBC*. https://www.bbc.co.uk/programmes/m0001d95
Freeman, D., & Garety, P. A. (1999). Worry, worry processes and dimensions of delusions: An exploratory investigation of a role for anxiety processes in the maintenance of delusional distress. *Behavioural and Cognitive Psychotherapy*, 27(1), 47–62.
Freeman, D., & Garety, P. (2006). Helping patients with paranoid and suspicious thoughts: a cognitive–behavioural approach. *Advances in Psychiatric Treatment*, 12(6), 404–415. https://doi.org/10.1192/apt.12.6.404
Freeman, D., & Loe, B. S. (2023). Explaining paranoia: Cognitive and social processes in the occurrence of extreme mistrust. *BMJ Mental Health*, 26(1), 1–8.
Freeman, D., Dunn, G., Murray, R. M., Evans, N., Lister, R., Antley, A., ... Morrison, P. D. (2015a). How cannabis causes paranoia: Using the intravenous administration of Δ9-Tetrahydrocannabinol (THC) to identify key cognitive mechanisms leading to paranoia. *Schizophrenia Bulletin*, 41(2), 391–399.
Freeman, D., Dunn, G., Startup, H., Pugh, K., Cordwell, J., Mander, H., ... Kingdon, D. (2015b). Effects of cognitive behaviour therapy for worry on persecutory delusions in patients with psychosis (WIT): A parallel, single-blind, randomised controlled trial with a mediation analysis. *The Lancet Psychiatry*, 2(4), 305–313.
Freeman, D., Emsley, R., Diamond, R., Collett, N., Bold, E., Chadwick, E., ... Twivy, E. (2021). Comparison of a theoretically driven cognitive therapy (the Feeling Safe Programme) with befriending for the treatment of persistent persecutory delusions: A parallel, single-blind, randomised controlled trial. *The Lancet Psychiatry*, 8(8), 696–707.
Freeman, D., Garety, P. A., Bebbington, P. E., Smith, B., Rollinson, R., Fowler, D., ... Dunn, G. (2005). Psychological investigation of the structure of paranoia in a non-clinical population. *The British Journal of Psychiatry*, 186(5), 427–435.
Freeman, D., Garety, P. A., Fowler, D., Kuipers, E., Bebbington, P. E., & Dunn, G. (2004). Why do people with delusions fail to choose more realistic explanations for their experiences? An empirical investigation. *Journal of Consulting and Clinical Psychology*, 72(4), 671–680.
Freeman, D., Garety, P. A., Kuipers, E., Fowler, D., & Bebbington, P. E. (2002). A cognitive model of persecutory delusions. *British Journal of Clinical Psychology*, 41(4), 331–347.

Freeman, D., Garety, P. A., Kuipers, E., Fowler, D., Bebbington, P. E., & Dunn, G. (2007). Acting on persecutory delusions: The importance of safety seeking. *Behaviour Research and Therapy*, 45(1), 89–99.
Freeman, D., Lister, R., & Evans, N. (2014). The use of intuitive and analytic reasoning styles by patients with persecutory delusions. *Journal of Behavior Therapy and Experimental Psychiatry*, 45(4), 454–458.
Freeman, D., Pugh, K., Antley, A., Slater, M., Bebbington, P., Gittins, M., ... Garety, P. (2008). Virtual reality study of paranoid thinking in the general population. *The British Journal of Psychiatry*, 192(4), 258–263.
Freeman, D., Pugh, K., Vorontsova, N., Antley, A., & Slater, M. (2010). Testing the continuum of delusional beliefs. *Journal of Abnormal Psychology*, 119(1), 83–92.
Freeman, D., Startup, H., Dunn, G., Černis, E., Wingham, G., Pugh, K., ... Kingdon, D. (2013). The interaction of affective with psychotic processes: A test of the effects of worrying on working memory, jumping to conclusions, and anomalies of experience in patients with persecutory delusions. *Journal of Psychiatric Research*, 47(12), 1837–1842.
Freud, S. (1958). Psycho-analytic notes on an autobiographical account of a case of paranoia (dementia paranoides). In J. Strachey (Ed. & Trans.), *The Standard Edition of the Complete Psychological Works of Sigmund Freud* (Vol. 12, pp. 1–82). Hogarth Press. (Original work published 1911)
Freud, S. (1989). *The Future of an Illusion*. Norton. (Original work published in 1927)
Fricker, M. (2007). *Epistemic Injustice: Power and the Ethics of Knowing*. Oxford University Press.
Friston, K. (2005). A theory of cortical responses. *Philosophical Transactions of the Royal Society B: Biological Sciences*, 360(1456), 815–836.
Frith, C. (2005). The self in action: Lessons from delusions of control. *Consciousness and Cognition*, 14(4), 752–770.
Frith, C. D. (1992). *The Neuropsychology of Schizophrenia*. Lawrence Erlbaum Associates.
Frith, C. D. (2004). Schizophrenia and theory of mind. *Psychological Medicine*, 34(3), 385–389.
Frith, C. D. (2014). *The Cognitive Neuropsychology of Schizophrenia*. Psychology Press.
Frith, C. D., & Frith, U. (2021). Mapping mentalising in the brain. In M. Gilead & K. N. Ochsner (Eds.), *The Neural Basis of Mentalizing* (pp. 17–45). Springer International Publishing.
Fuchs, T. (2015). The intersubjectivity of delusions. *World Psychiatry*, 14(2), 178.
Fuhrmann, D., Knoll, L. J., & Blakemore, S.-J. (2015). Adolescence as a sensitive period of brain development. *Trends in Cognitive Sciences*, 19(10), 558–566.
Funkhouser, E. (2017). Beliefs as signals: A new function for belief. *Philosophical Psychology*, 30(6), 809–831.
Funkhouser, E. (2019). *Self-Deception*. Routledge.
Funkhouser, E. (2022). A tribal mind: Beliefs that signal group identity or commitment. *Mind & Language*, 37(3), 444–464.
Furl, N., Coltheart, M., & McKay, R. (2024). The paradox of delusions: Are deluded individuals resistant to evidence? In E. Sullivan-Bissett (Ed.), *Belief, Imagination, and Delusion* (pp. 240–265). Oxford University Press.
Fusar-Poli, P., Howes, O., Valmaggia, L., & McGuire, P. (2008). 'Truman' signs and vulnerability to psychosis. *The British Journal of Psychiatry*, 193(2), 168–168.
Gadsby, S. (2024). Delusions in anorexia nervosa. In E. Sullivan-Bissett (Ed.), *The Routledge Handbook of the Philosophy of Delusion* (pp. 115–126). Routledge.
Garety, P. (1991). Reasoning and delusions. *The British Journal of Psychiatry*, 159(S14), 14–18.
Garety, P. A., & Freeman, D. (2013). The past and future of delusions research: From the inexplicable to the treatable. *The British Journal of Psychiatry*, 203(5), 327–333.
Garety, P. A., & Hemsley, D. R. (1997). *Delusions: Investigations Into the Psychology of Delusional Reasoning*. Psychology Press.
Garety, P. A., Gittins, M., Jolley, S., Bebbington, P., Dunn, G., Kuipers, E., ... Freeman, D. (2013). Differences in cognitive and emotional processes between persecutory and grandiose delusions. *Schizophrenia Bulletin*, 39(3), 629–639.

Gerrans, P. (2002). A one-stage explanation of the Cotard delusion. *Philosophy, Psychiatry, & Psychology*, 9(1), 47–53.
Gervais, W. M., Shariff, A. F., & Norenzayan, A. (2011). Do you believe in atheists? Distrust is central to anti-atheist prejudice. *Journal of Personality and Social Psychology*, 101(6), 1189–1206.
Gilbert, D. T. (1991). How mental systems believe. *American Psychologist*, 46(2), 107.
Gilbert, D. T., Tafarodi, R. W., & Malone, P. S. (1993). You can't not believe everything you read. *Journal of Personality and Social Psychology*, 65(2), 221–233.
Gilovich, T., Medvec, V. H., & Savitsky, K. (2000). The spotlight effect in social judgment: An egocentric bias in estimates of the salience of one's own actions and appearance. *Journal of Personality and Social Psychology*, 78(2), 211–222.
Gluckman, M. (1973). *The Judicial Process Among the Barotse of Northern Rhodesia*. Manchester University Press.
Gold, I. (2017). Outline of a theory of delusion: Irrationality and pathological belief. In T. -W. Hung & T. J. Lane (Eds.), *Rationality: Constraints and Contexts* (pp. 95–119). Academic Press.
Gold, J., & Gold, I. (2015). *Suspicious Minds: How Culture Shapes Madness*. Simon and Schuster.
Goldman, A. I. (1999a). *Knowledge in a Social World*. Oxford University Press.
Goldman, A. I. (1999b). Social epistemology. *Crítica: Revista Hispanoamericana de Filosofía*, 31(93), 3–19.
Goleman, D. (1994, October 31). Proof lacking for ritual abuse by Satanists. *The New York Times*. https://www.nytimes.com/1994/10/31/us/proof-lacking-for-ritual-abuse-by-satanists.html
Gopnik, A., & Meltzoff, A. N. (1997). *Words, Thoughts, and Theories*. MIT Press.
Gould, S. J. (1996). *Mismeasure of Man*. W. W. Norton.
Gould, S. J., & Lewontin, R. C. (1979). The spandrels of San Marco and the Panglossian paradigm: A critique of the adaptationist programme. *Proceedings of the Royal Society of London*, B(205), 581–598.
Gralnick, A. (1942). Folie a deux-the psychosis of association: A review of 103 cases and the entire English literature: with case presentations. *The Psychiatric Quarterly*, 16, 491–520.
Green, M. J., & Phillips, M. L. (2004). Social threat perception and the evolution of paranoia. *Neuroscience and Biobehavioral Reviews*, 28(3), 333–342.
Greenburgh, A., Zamperetti, L., Bell, V., & Raihani, N. (2024). Social identification and paranoia. *Royal Society Open Science*, 11(6), 231961.
Griffin, J. D., & Fletcher, P. C. (2017). Predictive Processing, Source Monitoring, and Psychosis. *Annual Review of Clinical Psychology*, 13, 265–289.
Gufler, H. (1999). Witchcraft beliefs among the Yamba (Cameroon). *Anthropos*, 94(1/3), 181–198.
Haidt, J. (2013). *The Righteous Mind*. Penguin.
Hamilton, W. D. (1964). The genetical evolution of social behaviour. I. *Journal of Theoretical Biology*, 7(1), 1–16.
Hannon, M. (2019). *What's the Point of Knowledge? A Function-First Epistemology*. Oxford University Press.
Harding, J. N., Wolpe, N., Brugger, S. P., Navarro, V., Teufel, C., & Fletcher, P. C. (2024). A new predictive coding model for a more comprehensive account of delusions. *The Lancet Psychiatry*, 11(4), 295–302.
Hare, R. M. (1952). *The Language of Morals*. Oxford University Press.
Haselton, M. G., & Nettle, D. (2006). The paranoid optimist: An integrative evolutionary model of cognitive biases. *Personality and Social Psychology Review*, 10(1), 47–66.
Hayden, B. (2018). *The Power of Ritual in Prehistory: Secret Societies and Origins of Social Complexity*. Cambridge University Press.
Heath, J. (2022). *Cooperation and Social Justice*. University of Toronto Press.
Heider, F., & Simmel, M. (1944). An experimental study of apparent behavior. *The American Journal of Psychology*, 57(2), 243–259.
Henrich, J. (2006). Cooperation, punishment, and the evolution of human institutions. *Science*, 312(5770), 60–61.

Henrich, J. (2009). The evolution of costly displays, cooperation and religion: Credibility enhancing displays and their implications for cultural evolution. *Evolution and Human Behavior*, 30(4), 244–260.

Henrich, J. (2015). *The Secret of Our Success: How Culture Is Driving Human Evolution, Domesticating Our Species, and Making Us Smarter*. Princeton University Press.

Henrich, J. (2020). *The WEIRDest People in the World: How the West Became Psychologically Peculiar and Particularly Prosperous*. Farrar, Straus and Giroux.

Henrich, J., & Gil-White, F. J. (2001). The evolution of prestige: Freely conferred deference as a mechanism for enhancing the benefits of cultural transmission. *Evolution and Human Behavior*, 22(3), 165–196.

Henrich, J., & McElreath, R. (2007). Dual-inheritance theory: The evolution of human cultural capacities and cultural evolution. In L. Barrett & R. Dunbar (Eds.), *Oxford Handbook of Evolutionary Psychology* (pp. 555–564). Oxford University Press.

Henrich, J., & Muthukrishna, M. (2021). The origins and psychology of human cooperation. *Annual Review of Psychology*, 72, 207–240.

Heyes, C. (2018). *Cognitive Gadgets: The Cultural Evolution of Thinking*. Harvard University Press.

Hirstein, W., & Ramachandran, V. S. (1997). Capgras syndrome: A novel probe for understanding the neural representation of the identity and familiarity of persons. *Proceedings of the Royal Society of London. Series B: Biological Sciences*, 264(1380), 437–444.

Hoffer, E. (1951). *The True Believer*. Harper and Brothers.

Hoffman, M., & Yoeli, E. (2021). *Hidden Games*. Basic Books.

Hofmann, S. G. (2014). Toward a cognitive-behavioral classification system for mental disorders. *Behavior Therapy*, 45(4), 576–587.

Hohwy, J. (2004). Top-down and bottom-up in delusion formation. *Philosophy, Psychiatry, & Psychology*, 11(1), 65–70.

Hohwy, J. (2013). *The Predictive Mind*. Oxford University Press.

Hollander, A. C., Dal, H., Lewis, G., Magnusson, C., Kirkbride, J. B., & Dalman, C. (2016). Refugee migration and risk of schizophrenia and other non-affective psychoses: Cohort study of 1.3 million people in Sweden. *BMJ*, 352, i1030.

Holt-Lunstad, J., Smith, T. B., & Layton, J. B. (2010). Social relationships and mortality risk: A meta-analytic review. *PLOS Medicine*, 7(7), e1000316.

Holt-Lunstad, J., Smith, T. B., Baker, M., Harris, T., & Stephenson, D. (2015). Loneliness and social isolation as risk factors for mortality: A meta-analytic review. *Perspectives on Psychological Science*, 10(2), 227–237.

Honey, G. D., Corlett, P. R., Absalom, A. R., Lee, M., Pomarol-Clotet, E., Murray, G. K., ... Fletcher, P. C. (2008). Individual differences in psychotic effects of ketamine are predicted by brain function measured under placebo. *Journal of Neuroscience*, 28(25), 6295–6303.

Horowitz, D. L. (2001). *The Deadly Ethnic Riot* (1st ed.). University of California Press.

Hrdy, S. B. (2009). *Mothers and Others: The Evolutionary Origins of Mutual Understanding*. Harvard University Press.

Hughes, K., Bellis, M. A., Hardcastle, K. A., Sethi, D., Butchart, A., Mikton, C., ... Dunne, M. P. (2017). The effect of multiple adverse childhood experiences on health: A systematic review and meta-analysis. *The Lancet Public Health*, 2(8), e356–e366.

Huq, S. F., Garety, P. A., & Hemsley, D. R. (1988). Probabilistic judgements in deluded and non-deluded subjects. *The Quarterly Journal of Experimental Psychology Section A*, 40(4), 801–812.

Hutton, R. (2017). *The Witch: A History of Fear, From Ancient Times to the Present*. Yale University Press.

Iannaccone, L. R. (1992). Sacrifice and stigma: Reducing free-riding in cults, communes, and other collectives. *Journal of Political Economy*, 100(2), 271–291.

Iannaccone, L. R., & Berman, E. (2006). Religious extremism: The good, the bad, and the deadly. *Public Choice*, 128(1), 109–129.

Isham, L., Griffith, L., Boylan, A.-M., Hicks, A., Wilson, N., Byrne, R., ... Freeman, D. (2021). Understanding, treating, and renaming grandiose delusions: A qualitative study. *Psychology and Psychotherapy: Theory, Research and Practice*, 94(1), 119–140.

Jackson, J. C., Caluori, N., Abrams, S., Beckman, E., Gelfand, M., & Gray, K. (2021). Tight cultures and vengeful gods: How culture shapes religious belief. *Journal of Experimental Psychology. General*, 150(10), 2057–2077.

James, W. (2000). *Pragmatism and Other Writings* (G. Gunn, Ed.). Penguin Books. (Original work published 1907)

Janis, I. L. (1982). *Groupthink: Psychological Studies of Policy Decisions and Fiascoes*. Houghton Mifflin.

Jaspers, K. (1963). *General Psychopathology*. Manchester University Press. (Original work published in 1913)

Johnson, D. D. P., Blumstein, D. T., Fowler, J. H., & Haselton, M. G. (2013). The evolution of error: Error management, cognitive constraints, and adaptive decision-making biases. *Trends in Ecology & Evolution*, 28(8), 474–481.

Jongsma, H. E., Karlsen, S., Kirkbride, J. B., & Jones, P. B. (2021). Understanding the excess psychosis risk in ethnic minorities: The impact of structure and identity. *Social Psychiatry and Psychiatric Epidemiology*, 56(11), 1913–1921.

Joshi, K. G., Frierson, R. L., and Gunter, T. D. (2006). Shared psychotic disorder and criminal responsibility: A review and case report of folie à trois. *Journal of the American Academy of Psychiatry and the Law Online*, 34(4), : 511–517.

Kahan, D. (2017). Misconceptions, misinformation, and the logic of identity-protective cognition. *SSRN Electronic Journal*. https://doi.org/10.2139/ssrn.2973067.

Kahan, D. M. (2015). The Politically Motivated Reasoning Paradigm (SSRN Scholarly Paper 2703011). https://papers.ssrn.com/abstract=2703011

Kahneman, D. (2003). Maps of bounded rationality: Psychology for behavioral economics. *American Economic Review*, 93, 1449–1475.

Kapur, S. (2003). Psychosis as a state of aberrant salience: A framework linking biology, phenomenology, and pharmacology in schizophrenia. *American Journal of Psychiatry*, 160(1), 13–23.

Karabegovic, M., Wang, L., Boyer, P., & Mercier, H. (2024). Epistemic gratitude and the provision of information. *Evolution and Human Behavior*, 45(3), 252–260.

Kay, J. (2011). *Among the Truthers: A Journey Through America's Growing Conspiracist Underground*. HarperCollins.

Keefe, R. S., Arnold, M. C., Bayen, U. J., & Harvey, P. D. (1999). Source monitoring deficits in patients with schizophrenia; a multinomial modelling analysis. *Psychological Medicine*, 29(4), 903–914.

Kendi, I. X. (2016). *Stamped From the Beginning: The Definitive History of Racist Ideas in America*. PublicAffairs.

Keynes, J. M. (1936). *The General Theory of Employment, Interest and Money*. Macmillan.

Kiran, C., & Chaudhury, S. (2009). Understanding delusions. *Industrial Psychiatry Journal*, 18(1), 3.

Kirkbride, J. B., Anglin, D. M., Colman, I., Dykxhoorn, J., Jones, P. B., Patalay, P., ... Griffiths, S. L. (2024). The social determinants of mental health and disorder: Evidence, prevention and recommendations. *World Psychiatry*, 23(1), 58–90.

Kluckhohn, C. (1944). *Navaho Witchcraft*. Beacon Press.

Kornblith, H. (2002). *Knowledge and its Place in Nature*. Oxford University Press.

Korver-Nieberg, N., Fett, A.-K. J., Meijer, C. J., Koeter, M. W., Shergill, S. S., de Haan, L., & Krabbendam, L. (2013). Theory of mind, insecure attachment and paranoia in adolescents with early psychosis and healthy controls. *Australian & New Zealand Journal of Psychiatry*, 47(8), 737–745.

Kotov, R., Krueger, R. F., Watson, D., Achenbach, T. M., Althoff, R. R., Bagby, R. M., ... Zimmerman, M. (2017). The Hierarchical Taxonomy of Psychopathology (HiTOP): A dimensional alternative to traditional nosologies. *Journal of Abnormal Psychology*, 126(4), 454–467.

Kraepelin, E. (1921). *Manic-Depressive Insanity and Paranoia* (R. M. Barclay, Trans.; G. M. Robertson, Ed.). E. & S. Livingstone.
Kraus, M. W., Horberg, E. J., Goetz, J. L., & Keltner, D. (2011). Social class rank, threat vigilance, and hostile reactivity. *Personality & Social Psychology Bulletin*, 37(10), 1376–1388.
Krueger, R. F., & Eaton, N. R. (2015). Transdiagnostic factors of mental disorders. *World Psychiatry*, 14(1), 27–29.
Kunda, Z. (1990). The case for motivated reasoning. *Psychological Bulletin*, 108, 480–498.
Kuran, T. (1997). *Private Truths, Public Lies: The Social Consequences of Preference Falsification*. Harvard University Press.
Kurzban, R. (2011). *Why Everyone (Else) Is a Hypocrite: Evolution and the Modular Mind*. Princeton University Press.
Kurzban, R., & Christner, J. (2011). Are supernatural beliefs commitment devices for intergroup conflict? In J. P. Forgas, A. W. Kruglanski, & K. D. Williams (Eds.), *The Psychology of Social Conflict and Aggression* (pp. 209–224). Psychology Press.
Lake, B. M., Ullman, T. D., Tenenbaum, J. B., & Gershman, S. J. (2017). Building machines that learn and think like people. *Behavioral and Brain Sciences*, 40, e253.
Lake, C. R. (2008). Hypothesis: Grandiosity and guilt cause paranoia; paranoid schizophrenia is a psychotic mood disorder; a review. *Schizophrenia Bulletin*, 34(6), 1151–1162.
Langdon, R., Connaughton, E., & Coltheart, M. (2014). The Fregoli delusion: A disorder of person identification and tracking. *Topics in Cognitive Science*, 6(4), 615–631.
Leary, M. R., & Baumeister, R. F. (2000). The nature and function of self-esteem: Sociometer theory. *Advances in Experimental Social Psychology*, 32, 1–62.
Leary, M. R., & Kowalski, R. M. (1990). Impression management: A literature review and two-component model. *Psychological Bulletin*, 107(1), 34–47.
Leary, M. R., Jongman-Sereno, K. P., & Diebels, K. J. (2014). The pursuit of status: A self-presentational perspective on the quest for social value. In J. T. Cheng, J. L. Tracy, & C. Anderson (Eds.), *The Psychology of Social Status* (pp. 159–178). Springer.
Leaune, E., Dealberto, M. J., Luck, D., Grot, S., Zeroug-Vial, H., Poulet, E., & Brunelin, J. (2019). Ethnic minority position and migrant status as risk factors for psychotic symptoms in the general population: A meta-analysis. *Psychological Medicine*, 49(4), 545–558.
Lee, R. J. (2017). Mistrustful and misunderstood: A review of paranoid personality disorder. *Current Behavioral Neuroscience Reports*, 4(2), 151–165.
Leuenberger, M. (2021). What is the point of being your true self? A genealogy of essentialist authenticity. *Philosophy*, 96(3), 409–431.
Levy, N. (2021). *Bad Beliefs: Why They Happen to Good People*. Oxford University Press.
Lewandowsky, S., Ecker, U. K. H., Seifert, C. M., Schwarz, N., & Cook, J. (2012). Misinformation and its correction: Continued influence and successful debiasing. *Psychological Science in the Public Interest*, 13(3), 106–131.
Lewandowsky, S., Oberauer, K., & Gignac, G. E. (2013). NASA faked the moon landing—therefore, (climate) science is a hoax: An anatomy of the motivated rejection of science. *Psychological Science*, 24(5), 622–633.
Li, J. (2010). Koro endemic among school children in Guangdong, China. *World Cultural Psychiatry Research Review*, 5, 102–105.
Lieder, F., & Griffiths, T. L. (2020). Resource-rational analysis: Understanding human cognition as the optimal use of limited computational resources. *Behavioral and Brain Sciences*, 43, e1.
Liekefett, L., Christ, O., & Becker, J. C. (2023). Can conspiracy beliefs be beneficial? longitudinal linkages between conspiracy beliefs, anxiety, uncertainty aversion, and existential threat. *Personality and Social Psychology Bulletin*, 49(2), 167–179.
Litwack, L. F. (1998). *Trouble in Mind: Black Southerners in the Age of Jim Crow*. Knopf.
Longino, H. E. (1990). *Science as Social Knowledge: Values and Objectivity in Scientific Inquiry*. Princeton University Press.
Longino, H. E. (2002). *The Fate of Knowledge*. Princeton University Press.
Loury, G. C. (1994). Self-censorship in public discourse: A theory of "political correctness" and related phenomena. *Rationality and Society*, 6(4), 428–461.

Luhrmann, T. M. (2007). Social defeat and the culture of chronicity: Or, why schizophrenia does so well over there and so badly here. *Culture, Medicine and Psychiatry*, 31(2), 135–172.
Luhrmann, T. M. (2020). *How God Becomes Real: Kindling the Presence of Invisible Others*. Princeton University Press.
MacKay, C. (1841). *Extraordinary Popular Delusions and the Madness of Crowds*. Richard Bentley.
Mackie, J. L. (1974). *The Cement of the Universe: A Study of Causation*. Oxford University Press.
Maher, B. A. (1974). Delusional thinking and perceptual disorder. *Journal of Individual Psychology*, 30(1), 98.
Maher, B. A. (1999). Anomalous experience in everyday life: Its significance for psychopathology. *The Monist*, 82(4), 547–570.
Mair, L. (1969). *Witchcraft*. McGraw-Hill.
Mandelbaum, E. (2014). Thinking is believing. *Inquiry*, 57(1), 55–96.
Manning, J. (2020). *Suicide: The Social Causes of Self-Destruction*. University of Virginia Press.
Marcotte, A. (2016, September 27). It's science, stupid: Why do Trump supporters believe so many things that are crazy and wrong? *Salon*. https://www.salon.com/2016/09/26/its-science-stupid-why-do-trump-supporters-believe-so-many-things-that-are-crazy-and-wrong/
Marcus, R. B. (1990). Some revisionary proposals about belief and believing. *Philosophy and Phenomenological Research*, 50, 133–153.
Marie, A., Altay, S., & Strickland, B. (2023). Moralization and extremism robustly amplify myside sharing. *PNAS Nexus*, 2(4), pgad078.
Marmot, M. (2005). *Status Syndrome: How Your Social Standing Directly Affects Your Health*. A&C Black.
Mars, R. B., Neubert, F.-X., Noonan, M. P., Sallet, J., Toni, I., & Rushworth, M. F. S. (2012). On the relationship between the "default mode network" and the "social brain". *Frontiers in Human Neuroscience*, 6, 189.
Marwick, A. E., & Partin, W. C. (2022). Constructing alternative facts: Populist expertise and the QAnon conspiracy. *New Media & Society*, 26(5), 2535–2555.
Marx, K., & Engels, F. (1970). *The German Ideology*. International Publishers Co. (Original work published in 1845–1846)
Mayer-Gross, W., Slater, E., & Roth, M. (1954). *Clinical Psychiatry*. Cassel.
McCutcheon, R. A., Reis Marques, T., & Howes, O. D. (2020). Schizophrenia—An overview. *JAMA Psychiatry*, 77(2), 201–210.
McKay, R. (2012). Delusional inference. *Mind & Language*, 27(3), 330–355.
McKay, R. T., & Dennett, D. C. (2009). The evolution of misbelief. *Behavioral and Brain Sciences*, 32(6), 493–561.
McKay, R., & Mercier, H. (2023). Delusions as epistemic hypervigilance. *Current Directions in Psychological Science*, 32(2), 125–130.
McLean, B. F., Mattiske, J. K., & Balzan, R. P. (2017). Association of the jumping to conclusions and evidence integration biases with delusions in psychosis: A detailed meta-analysis. *Schizophrenia Bulletin*, 43(2), 344–354.
Melnikoff, D. E., & Strohminger, N. (2020). The automatic influence of advocacy on lawyers and novices. *Nature Human Behaviour*, 4(12), 12.
Mercier, H. (2017). How gullible are we? A review of the evidence from psychology and social science. *Review of General Psychology*, 21(2), 103–122.
Mercier, H. (2020). *Not Born Yesterday*. Princeton University Press.
Mercier, H. (2022). Reputation management and cultural evolution. *Journal of Cognition and Culture*, 22(5), 485–498.
Mercier, H., & Morin, O. (2019). Majority rules: How good are we at aggregating convergent opinions? *Evolutionary Human Sciences*, 1, e6.
Mercier, H., & Sperber, D. (2011). Why do humans reason? Arguments for an argumentative theory. *Behavioral and Brain Sciences*, 34(2), 57–74; discussion 74–111.
Mercier, H., & Sperber, D. (2017). *The Enigma of Reason*. Harvard University Press.

Merton, R. K. (1957). Priorities in scientific discovery: A chapter in the sociology of science. *American Sociological Review*, 22(6), 635–659.

Mill, J. S. (1869). *On Liberty* (4th ed.). Longmans, Green, Reader, and Dyer.

Millikan, R. G. (1984). *Language, Thought, and Other Biological Categories: New Foundations for Realism*. MIT Press.

Millikan, R. G. (1995). Pushmi-pullyu representations. *Philosophical Perspectives*, 9, 185–200.

Millikan, R. G. (2004). *Varieties of Meaning: The 2002 Jean Nicod Lectures*. MIT Press.

Mills, C. W. (1997). *The Racial Contract*. Cornell University Press.

Mills, C. W. (2007). White ignorance. In S. Sullivan & N. Tuana (Eds.), *Race and Epistemologies of Ignorance* (pp. 11–38). State University of New York Press.

Mills, C. W. (2017). *Black Rights/White Wrongs: The Critique of Racial Liberalism*. Oxford University Press.

Miyazono, K. (2015). Delusions as harmful malfunctioning beliefs. *Consciousness and Cognition*, 33, 561–573.

Miyazono, K. (2018). *Delusions and Beliefs: A Philosophical Inquiry*. Routledge.

Miyazono, K., & Inarimori, K. (2021). Empathy, altruism, and group identification. *Frontiers in Psychology*, 12, 749315.

Miyazono, K., & McKay, R. (2019). Explaining delusional beliefs: A hybrid model. *Cognitive Neuropsychiatry*, 24(5), 335–346.

Miyazono, K., & Salice, A. (2021). Social epistemological conception of delusion. *Synthese*, 199(1), 1831–1851.

Morgan, C., & Gayer-Anderson, C. (2016). Childhood adversities and psychosis: Evidence, challenges, implications. *World Psychiatry*, 15(2), 93–102.

Morgan, C., Reininghaus, U., Fearon, P., Hutchinson, G., Morgan, K., Dazzan, P., ... Craig, T. (2014). Modelling the interplay between childhood and adult adversity in pathways to psychosis: Initial evidence from the AESOP study. *Psychological Medicine*, 44(2), 407–419.

Morin, O. (2016). *How Traditions Live and Die*. Oxford University Press.

Morin, O., Jacquet, P. O., Vaesen, K., & Acerbi, A. (2021). Social information use and social information waste. *Philosophical Transactions of the Royal Society B: Biological Sciences*, 376(1828), 20200052.

Moritz, S., & Woodward, T. S. (2006). A generalized bias against disconfirmatory evidence in schizophrenia. *Psychiatry Research*, 142(2–3), 157–165.

Moritz, S., Veckenstedt, R., Randjbar, S., Vitzthum, F., Karow, A., & Lincoln, T. M. (2010). Course and determinants of self-esteem in people diagnosed with schizophrenia during psychiatric treatment. *Psychosis*, 2(2), 144–153.

Mueser, K. T., Bellack, A. S., Douglas, M. S., & Morrison, R. L. (1991). Prevalence and stability of social skill deficits in schizophrenia. *Schizophrenia Research*, 5(2), 167–176.

Munro, A. (1999). *Delusional Disorder: Paranoia and Related Illnesses*. Cambridge Univesity Press.

Murphy, D. (2012). The folk epistemology of delusions. *Neuroethics*, 5(1), 19–22.

Murphy, D. (2013). Delusions, modernist epistemology and irrational belief. *Mind & Language*, 28(1), 113–124.

Murray, G. K., Corlett, P. R., Clark, L., Pessiglione, M., Blackwell, A. D., Honey, G., ... Fletcher, P. C. (2008). Substantia nigra/ventral tegmental reward prediction error disruption in psychosis. *Molecular Psychiatry*, 13(3), 267–276.

Myers, E., Startup, H., & Freeman, D. (2011). Cognitive behavioural treatment of insomnia in individuals with persistent persecutory delusions: A pilot trial. *Journal of Behavior Therapy and Experimental Psychiatry*, 42(3), 330–336.

Napolitano, M. G., & Reuter, K. (2023). What is a conspiracy theory? *Erkenntnis*, 88(5), 2035–2062.

Nasar, S. (1998). *The Beautiful Mind: The Life of Mathematical Genius and Nobel Laureate John Nash*. Touchstone.

Nathan, D., & Snedeker, M. (2001). *Satan's Silence: Ritual Abuse and the Making of a Modern American Witch Hunt*. iUniverse.

Nesse, R. M. (2023). Evolutionary psychiatry: Foundations, progress and challenges. *World Psychiatry: Official Journal of the World Psychiatric Association (WPA)*, 22(2), 177–202.
Nettle, D., & Scott-Phillips, T. (2023). Is a non-evolutionary psychology possible? In A. Du Crest, M. Valković, A. Ariew, H. Desmond, P. Huneman, & T. A. C. Reydon (Eds.), *Evolutionary Thinking Across Disciplines: Problems and Perspectives in Generalized Darwinism* (pp. 231–250). Springer.
Nietzsche, F. W. (2008). *On the Genealogy of Morals: A Polemic.* Oxford University Press. Edited by Douglas Translator: Smith. (Original work published in 1887)
Nietzsche, F. W. (1996). *Human, All Too Human.* Cambridge University Press. (Original work published in 1878)
Nietzsche, F. W. (2002). *Beyond Good and Evil: Prelude to a Philosophy of the Future.* Cambridge University Press. (Original work published in 1886)
Noelle-Neumann, E. (1974). The spiral of silence a theory of public opinion. *Journal of Communication*, 24(2), 43–51.
Noordhof, P., & Sullivan-Bissett, E. (2021). The clinical significance of anomalous experience in the explanation of monothematic delusions. *Synthese*, 199(3), 10277–10309.
Norris, P., & Inglehart, R. (2011). *Sacred and Secular: Religion and Politics Worldwide.* Cambridge University Press.
Nowak, M. A. (2006). Five rules for the evolution of cooperation. *Science*, 314(5805), 1560–1563.
Nozick, R. (1993). *The Nature of Rationality.* Princeton University Press.
O'Connor, C., & Weatherall, J. O. (2019). *The Misinformation Age: How False Beliefs Spread.* Yale University Press.
Olson, M. (1965). *The Logic of Collective Action.* Harvard University Press.
Orchinik et al., 2025). Orchinik, R., Rand, D., & Bhui, R. (2024). The not so illusory truth effect: A rational foundation for repetition effects. PsyArXiv. https://osf.io/preprints/psyarxiv/qvwdy_v3
Orchinik, R., Bhui, R., & Rand, D. G. (2024). Repetition does not increase belief in claims from distrusted politicians. PsyArXiv. https://osf.io/preprints/psyarxiv/y7pn5
Origgi, G. (2017). *Reputation: What It Is and Why It Matters.* Princeton University Press.
Pacherie, E. (2013). Intentional joint agency: Shared intention lite. *Synthese*, 190(10), 1817–1839.
Pan, X., Hsiao, V., Nau, D. S., & Gelfand, M. J. (2024). Explaining the evolution of gossip. *Proceedings of the National Academy of Sciences*, 121(9), e2214160121.
Papineau, D. (1984). Representation and explanation. *Philosophy of Science*, 51(4), 550–572.
Parsons, T. (1951). *The Social System.* Routledge.
Pedersen, C. B., & Mortensen, P. B. (2001). Evidence of a dose-response relationship between urbanicity during upbringing and schizophrenia risk. *Archives of General Psychiatry*, 58(11), 1039–1044.
Penn, D. L., Sanna, L. J., & Roberts, D. L. (2008). Social cognition in schizophrenia: An overview. *Schizophrenia Bulletin*, 34(3), 408–411.
Pickard, H. (2021). Addiction and the self. *Noûs*, 55(4), 737–761.
Pinker, S. (2003). *The Blank Slate: The Modern Denial of Human Nature.* Penguin UK.
Pinker, S. (2010). The cognitive niche: Coevolution of intelligence, sociality, and language. *Proceedings of the National Academy of Sciences*, 107(supplement_2), 8993–8999.
Pinker, S. (2011). *The Better Angels of Our Nature: The Decline of Violence in History And Its Causes.* Penguin UK.
Pinker, S. (2021). *Rationality: What It Is, Why It Seems Scarce, Why It Matters.* Penguin UK.
Pinsof, D., Sears, D. O., & Haselton, M. G. (2023). *Strange Bedfellows: The Alliance Theory of Political Belief Systems.* Psychological Inquiry.
Prinz, J. J. (2014). *Beyond Human Nature: How Culture and Experience Shape the Human Mind.* W. W. Norton & Company.
Putnam, H. (1975). The meaning of 'meaning'. *Minnesota Studies in the Philosophy of Science*, 7, 131–193.
Queloz, M. (2021). *The Practical Origins of Ideas: Genealogy as Conceptual Reverse-Engineering* (Open Access). Oxford University Press.

Radden, J. (2010). *On Delusion*. Routledge.
Raihani, N. (2021). *The Social Instinct*. Penguin UK.
Raihani, N. J., & Bell, V. (2019). An evolutionary perspective on paranoia. *Nature Human Behaviour*, 3(2), 2. https://doi.org/10.1038/s41562-018-0495-0
Ramachandran, V. S., & Blakeslee, S. (1999). *Phantoms in the Brain: Probing the Mysteries of the Human Mind*. HarperCollins.
Ramsey, F. P. (1990). *Philosophical Papers*. Cambridge University Press.
Rappe, S., & Wilkinson, S. (2023). Counterfactual cognition and psychosis: Adding complexity to predictive processing accounts. *Philosophical Psychology*, 36(2), 356–379.
Rauch, J. (2021). *The Constitution of Knowledge: A Defense of Truth*. Brookings Institution Press.
Read, J., van Os, J., Morrison, A. P., & Ross, C. A. (2005). Childhood trauma, psychosis and schizophrenia: A literature review with theoretical and clinical implications. *Acta Psychiatrica Scandinavica*, 112(5), 330–350.
Reed, E. J., Uddenberg, S., Suthaharan, P., Mathys, C. D., Taylor, J. R., Groman, S. M., & Corlett, P. R. (2020). Paranoia as a deficit in non-social belief updating. *eLife*, 9, e56345.
Reeve, S., Sheaves, B., & Freeman, D. (2015). The role of sleep dysfunction in the occurrence of delusions and hallucinations: A systematic review. *Clinical Psychology Review*, 42, 96–115.reference items
Rey, G. (2007). Meta-atheism: Religious avowal as self-deception. In L. M. Antony (Ed.), *Philosophers Without Gods: Meditations on Atheism and the Secular Life* (pp. 173–196). Oxford University Press.
Richerson, P. J., & Boyd, R. (2005). *Not By Genes Alone: How Culture Transformed Human Evolution*. University of Chicago Press.
Ridgeway, C. (2019). *Status*. Russel Sage Foundation. https://www.russellsage.org/publications/status
Ritunnano, R., Kleinman, J., Whyte Oshodi, D., Michail, M., Nelson, B., Humpston, C. S., & Broome, M. R. (2022). Subjective experience and meaning of delusions in psychosis: A systematic review and qualitative evidence synthesis. *The Lancet. Psychiatry*, 9(6), 458–476.
Romano, A. (2016, October 30). Demonic rituals, false confessions, ruined lives: Satanic Panic is still alive and well. *Vox*. https://www.vox.com/culture/22358153/satanic-panic-ritual-abuse-history-conspiracy-theories-explained
Rorty, A. O. (1994). User-friendly self-deception. *Philosophy*, 69(268), 211–228.
Rose, D., Buckwalter, W., & Turri, J. (2014). When words speak louder than actions: Delusion, belief, and the power of assertion. *Australasian Journal of Philosophy*, 92(4), 683–700.
Ruddick, W. (1988). 17. Social self-deceptions. In B. P. McLaughlin & A. O. Rorty (Eds.), *Perspectives on Self-Deception* (pp. 380–389). University of California Press.
Salice, A., & Henriksen, M. G. (2015). The disrupted 'we': Schizophrenia and collective intentionality. *Journal of Consciousness Studies*, 22(7-8), 145–171.
Salice, A., & Henriksen, M. G. (2021). Disturbances of shared intentionality in schizophrenia and autism. *Frontiers in Psychiatry*, 11, 570597.
Salice, A., & Miyazono, K. (2019). Being one of us. Group identification, joint actions, and collective intentionality. *Philosophical Psychology*, 33, 42–63.
Salice, A., & Montes Sánchez, A. (2016). Pride, shame, and group identification. *Frontiers in Psychology*, 7, 557.
Samuels, R. (2009). Delusions as a natural kind. In M. Broome & L. Bortolotti (Eds.), *Psychiatry as Cognitive Neuroscience: Philosophical Perspectives* (pp. 49–79). Oxford University Press.
Samuels, R. (2025). Delusion and natural kinds. In E. Sullivan-Bissett (Ed.), *The Routledge Handbook of the Philosophy of Delusion* (pp. 87–101). Routledge.
Sani, F. (2012). Group identification, social relationships, and health. In J. Jetten, C. Haslam, & S. A. Haslam (Eds.), *The Social Cure: Identity, Health and Well-Being* (pp. 21–37). Psychology Press.
Sapolsky, R. M. (2004). Social status and health in humans and other animals. *Annual Review of Anthropology*, 33(Volume 33, 2004), 393–418.
Sapolsky, R. M. (2005). The influence of social hierarchy on primate health. *Science*, 308(5722), 648–652. https://doi.org/10.1126/science.1106477

Sass, L. A., & Pienkos, E. (2013). Delusions: The phenomenological approach. In K. W. M. Fulford, M. Davies, R. Gipps, G. Graham, J. Sadler, G. Stanghellini, & T. Thornton (Eds.), *The Oxford Handbook of Philosophy and Psychiatry* (pp. 632–657). Oxford University Press.

Schliesser, E. (2019). Synthetic philosophy. *Biology & Philosophy*, 34(2), 1–9.

Schmid, L., Chatterjee, K., Hilbe, C., & Nowak, M. A. (2021). A unified framework of direct and indirect reciprocity. *Nature Human Behaviour*, 5(10), 1292–1302.

Schwardmann, P., & van der Weele, J. (2019). Deception and self-deception. *Nature Human Behaviour*, 3(10), Article 10.

Schwardmann, P., Tripodi, E., & van der Weele, J. J. (2022). Self-persuasion: Evidence from field experiments at international debating competitions. *American Economic Review*, 112(4), 1118–1146.

Sedikides, C., & Gebauer, J. E. (2010). Religiosity as self-enhancement: A meta-analysis of the relation between socially desirable responding and religiosity. *Personality and Social Psychology Review: An Official Journal of the Society for Personality and Social Psychology, Inc*, 14(1), 17–36.

Sellars, W. (1956). Empiricism and the philosophy of mind. *Minnesota Studies in the Philosophy of Science*, 1(19), 253–329.

Selten, J.-P., van der Ven, E., Rutten, B. P. F., & Cantor-Graae, E. (2013). The social defeat hypothesis of schizophrenia: An update. *Schizophrenia Bulletin*, 39(6), 1180–1186.

Sheffield, J. M., Brinen, A. P., & Freeman, D. (2021). Paranoia and grandiosity in the general population: Differential associations with putative causal factors. *Frontiers in Psychiatry*, 12, 668152.

Sheffield, J. M., Suthaharan, P., Leptourgos, P., & Corlett, P. R. (2022). Belief updating and paranoia in individuals with schizophrenia. *Biological Psychiatry: Cognitive Neuroscience and Neuroimaging*, 7(11), 1149–1157.

Shergill, S. S., Samson, G., Bays, P. M., Frith, C. D., & Wolpert, D. M. (2005). Evidence for sensory prediction deficits in schizophrenia. *American Journal of Psychiatry*, 162(12), 2384–2386.

Shevlin, M., Houston, J. E., Dorahy, M. J., & Adamson, G. (2008). Cumulative traumas and psychosis: An analysis of the national comorbidity survey and the British Psychiatric Morbidity Survey. *Schizophrenia Bulletin*, 34(1), 193–199.

Shimizu, M., Kubota, Y., Toichi, M., & Baba, H. (2007). Folie à deux and shared psychotic disorder. *Current Psychiatry Reports*, 9(3), 200–205.

Sidanius, J., & Pratto, F. (2001). *Social Dominance: An Intergroup Theory of Social Hierarchy and Oppression*. Cambridge University Press.

Sijilmassi, A., Safra, L., & Baumard, N. (2024). 'Our roots run deep': Historical myths as culturally evolved technologies for coalitional recruitment. *Behavioral and Brain Sciences*, 47, e171.

Simler, K., & Hanson, R. (2016). *The Elephant in the Brain: Hidden Motives in Everyday Life*. Oxford University Press.

Simonsen, A., Fusaroli, R., Petersen, M. L., Vermillet, A. Q., Bliksted, V., Mors, O., ... Campbell-Meiklejohn, D. (2021). Taking others into account: Combining directly experienced and indirect information in schizophrenia. *Brain*, 144(5), 1603–1614.

Singh, M. (2021). Magic, explanations, and evil: The origins and design of witches and sorcerers. *Current Anthropology*, 62(1), 2–29.

Singh, M. (2022). The idea of primitive communism is as seductive as it is wrong. *Aeon*. https://aeon.co/essays/the-idea-of-primitive-communism-is-as-seductive-as-it-is-wrong

Singh, M., Kaptchuk, T. J., & Henrich, J. (2021). Small gods, rituals, and cooperation: The Mentawai water spirit Sikameinan. *Evolution and Human Behavior*, 42(1), 61–72.

Slavich, G. M. (2020). Social safety theory: A biologically based evolutionary perspective on life stress, health, and behavior. *Annual Review of Clinical Psychology*, 16(Volume 16, 2020), 265–295.

Sloan, A. F., Kittleson, A. R., Torregrossa, L. J., Feola, B., Rossi-Goldthorpe, R., Corlett, P. R., & Sheffield, J. M. (2025). Belief updating, childhood maltreatment, and paranoia in schizophrenia-spectrum disorders. *Schizophrenia Bulletin*, 51(3), 646–657.

Sloman, S. (2005). *Causal Models: How People Think About the World and Its Alternatives*. Oxford University Press.

Smith, B., Fowler, D. G., Freeman, D., Bebbington, P., Bashforth, H., Garety, P., Dunn, G., & Kuipers, E. (2006). Emotion and psychosis: Links between depression, self-esteem, negative schematic beliefs and delusions and hallucinations. *Schizophrenia Research*, 86(1), 181–188.
Smith, J. M., & Harper, D. D. (2003). *Animal Signals*. Oxford University Press.
Smith, M. K., Trivers, R., & von Hippel, W. (2017). Self-deception facilitates interpersonal persuasion. *Journal of Economic Psychology*, 63, 93–101.
Snyder-Mackler, N., Burger, J. R., Gaydosh, L., Belsky, D. W., Noppert, G. A., Campos, F. A., ... Tung, J. (2020). Social determinants of health and survival in humans and other animals. *Science*, 368(6493), eaax9553.
So, S. H. W., Siu, N. Y. F., Wong, H. L., Chan, W., & Garety, P. A. (2016). 'Jumping to conclusions' data-gathering bias in psychosis and other psychiatric disorders—Two meta-analyses of comparisons between patients and healthy individuals. *Clinical Psychology Review*, 46, 151–167.
So, S. H.-W., Chau, A. K. C., Peters, E. R., Swendsen, J., Garety, P. A., & Kapur, S. (2018). Moment-to-moment associations between negative affect, aberrant salience, and paranoia. *Cognitive Neuropsychiatry*, 23(5), 299–306.
Sommer, J., Musolino, J., & Hemmer, P. (2024). Updating, evidence evaluation, and operator availability: A theoretical framework for understanding belief. *Psychological Review*, 131(2), 373–401.
Sosa, E. (1991). *Knowledge in Perspective: Selected Essays in Epistemology*. Cambridge University Press.
Sosis, R., & Alcorta, C. (2003). Signaling, solidarity, and the sacred: The evolution of religious behavior. Evolutionary anthropology: Issues, *News, and Reviews*, 12(6), 264–274.
Sperber, D. (1985). Anthropology and psychology: Towards an epidemiology of representations. *Man*, 20(1), 73–89.
Sperber, D. (1996). *Explaining Culture: A Naturalistic Approach*. Basil Blackwell.
Sperber, D. (1997). Intuitive and reflective beliefs. *Mind & Language*, 12(1), 67–83.
Sperber, D., & Baumard, N. (2012). Moral reputation: An evolutionary and cognitive perspective. *Mind & Language*, 27(5), 495–518.
Sperber, D., Clément, F., Heintz, C., Mascaro, O., Mercier, H., Origgi, G., & Wilson, D. (2010). Epistemic vigilance. *Mind & Language*, 25, 359–393.
Stark, R., & Finke, R. (2000). *Acts of Faith: Explaining the Human Side of Religion*. University of California Press.
Startup, H., Freeman, D., & Garety, P. A. (2007). Persecutory delusions and catastrophic worry in psychosis: Developing the understanding of delusion distress and persistence. *Behaviour Research and Therapy*, 45(3), 523–537.
Startup, M., & Startup, S. (2005). On two kinds of delusion of reference. *Psychiatry Research*, 137(1), 87–92.
Sterelny, K. (2012). *The Evolved Apprentice*. MIT Press.
Sterelny, K. (2018). Why reason? Hugo Mercier's and Dan Sperber's the enigma of reason: A new theory of human understanding. *Mind & Language*, 33(5), 502–512.
Sterelny, K. (2020). Religion: Costs, signals, and the Neolithic transition. *Religion, Brain & Behavior*, 10(3), 303–320.
Sterelny, K. (2021). *The Pleistocene Social Contract: Culture and Cooperation in Human Evolution*. Oxford University Press.
Sterzer, P., Adams, R. A., Fletcher, P., Frith, C., Lawrie, S. M., Muckli, L., ... Corlett, P. R. (2018). The predictive coding account of psychosis. *Biological Psychiatry*, 84(9), 634–643.
Stich, S. P. (1990). *The Fragmentation of Reason: Preface to a Pragmatic Theory of Cognitive Evaluation*. MIT Press.
Stokes, D., & Bergeron, V. (2015). Modular architectures and informational encapsulation: A dilemma. *European Journal for Philosophy of Science*, 5(3), 315–338.
Stone, T., & Young, A. W. (1997). Delusions and brain injury: The philosophy and psychology of belief. *Mind & Language*, 12(3-4), 327–364.

Storr, W. (2021). *The Status Game*. HarperCollinsPublishers.
Strevens, M. (2008). *Depth: An Account of Scientific Explanation*. Harvard University Press.
Stuart, K. (1999). *Defiled Trades and Social Outcasts: Honor and Ritual Pollution in Early Modern Germany*. Cambridge University Press.
Sullivan-Bissett, E. (2020). Unimpaired abduction to alien abduction: Lessons on delusion formation. *Philosophical Psychology*, 33(5), 679–704.
Sullivan-Bissett, E. (2022). Against a second factor. *Asian Journal of Philosophy*, 1(1), 33.
Sullivan-Bissett, E. (2024a). Monothematic delusions are misfunctioning beliefs. *Synthese*, 204(6), 157.
Sullivan-Bissett, E. (2024b). The one-factor theory. In E. Sullivan-Bissett (Ed.), *The Routledge Handbook of the Philosophy of Delusion* (pp. 414–429). Routledge.
Sullivan-Bissett, E. (Ed.). (2024c). *The Routledge Handbook of Philosophy of Delusion*. Routledge.
Sunstein, C. R. (2019). *Conformity: The Power of Social Influences*. New York University Press.
Sunstein, C. R., & Vermeule, A. (2009). Conspiracy theories: Causes and cures. *Journal of Political Philosophy*, 17(2), 202–227.
Tajfel, H. (1970). Experiments in intergroup discrimination. *Scientific American*, 223(5), 96–103.
Tajfel, H., Billig, M. G., Bundy, R. P., & Flament, C. (1971). Social categorization and intergroup behaviour. *European Journal of Social Psychology*, 1(2), 149–178.
Tappin, B. M., Pennycook, G., & Rand, D. G. (2020). Thinking clearly about causal inferences of politically motivated reasoning: Why paradigmatic study designs often undermine causal inference. *Current Opinion in Behavioral Sciences*, 34, 81–87.
Tavris, C., & Aronson, E. (2008). *Mistakes Were Made (but Not by Me): Why We Justify Foolish Beliefs, Bad Decisions, and Hurtful Acts*. Harcourt.
Taylor, S. E., & Brown, J. D. (1988). Illusion and well-being: A social psychological perspective on mental health. *Psychological Bulletin*, 103(2), 193–210.
Tetlock, P. E. (2002). Social functionalist frameworks for judgment and choice: Intuitive politicians, theologians, and prosecutors. *Psychological Review*, 109(3), 451–471.
Tetlock, P. E. (2017). *Expert Political Judgment: How Good Is It? How Can We Know?* (New edn). Princeton University Press.
Thiel, C. M., Studte, S., Hildebrandt, H., Huster, R., & Weerda, R. (2014). When a loved one feels unfamiliar: A case study on the neural basis of Capgras delusion. *Cortex*, 52, 75–85.
Tibbetts, E. A., Pardo-Sanchez, J., & Weise, C. (2022). The establishment and maintenance of dominance hierarchies. *Philosophical Transactions of the Royal Society B: Biological Sciences*, 377(1845), 20200450.
Tomasello, M. (2014a). *A Natural History of Human Thinking*. Harvard University Press.
Tomasello, M. (2014b). The ultra-social animal. *European Journal of Social Psychology*, 44(3), 187–194.
Tomasello, M. (2016). *A Natural History of Human Morality*. Harvard University Press.
Tooby, J. (2017). Coalitional instincts. *Edge*. https://www.edge.org/response-detail/27168
Tooby, J., & Cosmides, L. (1992). The psychological foundations of culture. In J. H. Barkow, L. Cosmides, & J. Tooby (Eds.), *The Adapted Mind: Evolutionary Psychology and the Generation of Culture* (pp. 19–136). Oxford University Press.
Tooby, J., & Cosmides, L. (2010). Groups in mind: The coalitional roots of war and morality. In H. Høgh-Olesen (Ed.), *Human Morality and Sociality: Evolutionary and Comparative Perspectives* (pp. 91–234). Palgrave-Macmillan.
Townsend, C., Aktipis, A., Balliet, D., & Cronk, L. (2020). Generosity among the Ik of Uganda. *Evolutionary Human Sciences*, 2, e23.
Trivers, R. (2011). *Deceit and Self-Deception: Fooling Yourself the Better to Fool Others*. Penguin UK.
Trivers, R. L. (1971). The evolution of reciprocal altruism. *The Quarterly Review of Biology*, 46(1), 35–57.
Turner, B. S., Abercrombie, N., & Hill, S. (1980). *The Dominant Ideology Thesis*. Routledge.
Turner, J. C. (1982). Towards a cognitive redefinition of the social group. In H. Tajfel (Ed.), *Social Identity and Intergroup Relations* (pp. 15–40). Cambridge University Press.

Tversky, A., & Kahneman, D. (1973). Availability: A heuristic for judging frequency and probability. *Cognitive Psychology*, 5(2), 207–232.
Uexküll, J. von. (1992). A stroll through the worlds of animals and men: A picture book of invisible worlds. *Semiotica*, 89(4), 319–391.
Van Leeuwen, N. (2014). Religious credence is not factual belief. *Cognition*, 133(3), 698–715.
Van Leeuwen, N. (2023). *Religion as Make-Believe: A Theory of Belief, Imagination, and Group Identity*. Harvard University Press.
van Os, J., Hanssen, M., Bijl, R. V., & Ravelli, A. (2000). Strauss (1969) revisited: A psychosis continuum in the general population? *Schizophrenia Research*, 45(1–2), 11–20.
van Os, J., Kenis, G., & Rutten, B. P. (2010). The environment and schizophrenia. *Nature*, 468(7321), 203–212.
van Prooijen, J.-W., & Acker, M. (2015). The influence of control on belief in conspiracy theories: Conceptual and applied extensions. *Applied Cognitive Psychology*, 29(5), 753–761.
van Prooijen, J.-W., & van Vugt, M. (2018). Conspiracy theories: Evolved functions and psychological mechanisms. *Perspectives on Psychological Science*, 13(6), 770–788.
Varese, F., Smeets, F., Drukker, M., Lieverse, R., Lataster, T., Viechtbauer, W., ... Bentall, R. P. (2012). Childhood adversities increase the risk of psychosis: A meta-analysis of patient-control, prospective- and cross-sectional cohort studies. *Schizophrenia Bulletin*, 38(4), 661–671.
Vassos, E., Pedersen, C. B., Murray, R. M., Collier, D. A., & Lewis, C. M. (2012). Meta-analysis of the association of urbanicity with schizophrenia. *Schizophrenia Bulletin*, 38(6), 1118–1123.
Veblen, T. (1912). *The Theory of the Leisure Class*. Transaction Publishers. (Original work published in 1899)
Von Domarus, E. (1944). The specific laws of logic in schizophrenia. In J. S. Kasanin (Ed.), *Language and Thought in Schizophrenia* (pp. 104–114). University of California Press.
von Hippel, W., & Trivers, R. (2011). The evolution and psychology of self-deception. *Behavioral and Brain Sciences*, 34(1), 1–16.
Vonasch, A. J., Reynolds, T., Winegard, B. M., & Baumeister, R. F. (2018). Death before dishonor: Incurring costs to protect moral reputation. *Social Psychological and Personality Science*, 9(5), 604–613.
Wakefield, Jerome C. (1992). Disorder as harmful dysfunction: A conceptual critique of DSM-III-R's definition of mental disorder. *Psychological Review*, 99(2), 232–247.
Watson, C. G., & Wold, J. (1981). Logical reasoning deficits in schizophrenia and brain damage. *Journal of Clinical Psychology*, 37(3), 466–471.
Wendling, M. (2020, July 22). QAnon: What is it and where did it come from? *BBC News*. https://www.bbc.com/news/53498434
Westen, D., Blagov, P. S., Harenski, K., Kilts, C., & Hamann, S. (2006). Neural bases of motivated reasoning: An fMRI Study of emotional constraints on partisan political judgment in the 2004 U.S. presidential election. *Journal of Cognitive Neuroscience*, 18(11), 1947–1958.
White, S. C., Ruiz, J. M., Allison, M., Uchino, B. N., Smith, T. W., Taylor, D. J., ... Smyth, J. M. (2024). Cardiovascular risk, social vigilance, and stress profiles of male law enforcement officers versus civilians. *Health Psychology Open*, 11, 20551029241244723.
Wilkinson, R. G. (1999). Health, hierarchy, and social anxiety. *Annals of the New York Academy of Sciences*, 896(1), 48–63.
Wilkinson, S. (2014). Accounting for the phenomenology and varieties of auditory verbal hallucination within a predictive processing framework. *Consciousness and Cognition*, 30, 142–155.
Wilkinson, S. (2016). A mental files approach to delusional misidentification. *Review of Philosophy and Psychology*, 7, 389–404.
Wilkinson, S. (2020). Expressivism about delusion attribution. *European Journal of Analytic Philosophy*, 16(2), 59–77.
Wilkinson, S. (2021). What can predictive processing tell us about the content of perceptual experience? In *Heather Logue & Louise Richardson, Purpose and Procedure in Philosophy of Perception* (pp. 174–190). Oxford University Press.

Wilkinson, S. (2025). Delusion attribution. In E. Sullivan-Bissett (Ed.), *The Routledge Handbook of Philosophy of Delusion* (pp. 228–244). Routledge.

Wilkinson, S., Dodgson, G., & Meares, K. (2017). Predictive processing and the varieties of psychological trauma. *Frontiers in Psychology*, 8, 1840.

Willer, R. (2009). Groups reward individual sacrifice: The status solution to the collective action problem. *American Sociological Review*, 74(1), 23–43.

Willer, R., Kuwabara, K., & Macy, M. W. (2009). The false enforcement of unpopular norms. *American Journal of Sociology*, 115(2), 451–490.

Williams, D. (2018). Hierarchical Bayesian models of delusion. *Consciousness and Cognition*, 61, 129–147.

Williams, D. (2021a). Signalling, commitment, and strategic absurdities. *Mind & Language*, 37(5), 1011–1029.

Williams, D. (2021b). Socially adaptive belief. *Mind & Language*, 36(3), 333–354.

Williams, D. (2022a). Identity-defining beliefs on social media. *Philosophical Topics*, 50(2), 41–64.

Williams, D. (2022b). The marketplace of rationalizations. *Economics & Philosophy*, 39(1), 99–123.

Williams, D. (2023a). Scaffolding Motivated Cognition. OSF. https://doi.org/10.31234/osf.io/7m4r3

Williams, D. (2023b). The case for partisan motivated reasoning. *Synthese*, 202(3), 89. https://doi.org/10.1007/s11229-023-04223-1

Williams, D. (2024a). The social turn in delusions research. In E. Sullivan-Bissett (Ed.), *The Routledge Handbook of Philosophy of Delusion* (pp. 520–532). Routledge.

Williams, D. (2024b). Why do people believe true things? *Conspicuous Cognition*. https://www.conspicuouscognition.com/p/why-do-people-believe-true-things

Williams, D., & Miyazono, K. (2023). Culture, partisanship, and signaling: The social nature of political belief systems. *Psychological Inquiry*, 34(3), 217–220.

Williams, D., & Montagnese, M. (2023). Bayesian psychiatry and the social focus of delusions. In T. Cheng, R. Sato, & J. Hohwy (Eds.), *Expected Experiences: The Predictive Mind in an Uncertain World* (pp. 257–282). Routledge.

Woodward, T. S., Moritz, S., Cuttler, C., & Whitman, J. C. (2006). The contribution of a cognitive bias against disconfirmatory evidence (BADE) to delusions in schizophrenia. *Journal of Clinical and Experimental Neuropsychology*, 28(4), 605–617.

Wrangham, R. (2019). *The Goodness Paradox: How Evolution Made Us Both More and Less Violent*. Profile Books.

Wright, E. C., Hostinar, C. E., & Trainor, B. C. (2020). Anxious to see you: Neuroendocrine mechanisms of social vigilance and anxiety during adolescence. *The European Journal of Neuroscience*, 52(1), 2516–2529.

Wright, L. (2013). *Going Clear: Scientology, Hollywood, and the Prison of Belief*. Knopf Doubleday Publishing Group.

Wu, V., Carey, J., Guess, A., Nyhan, B., & Reifler, J. (2022). Legislator criticism of a candidate's conspiracy beliefs reduces support for the conspiracy but not the candidate: Evidence from Marjorie Taylor Greene and QAnon. *HKS Misinformation Review*, 3(5), 500602.

Xygalatas, D. (2022). *Ritual: How Seemingly Senseless Acts Make Life Worth Living*. Little, Brown Spark.

Yap, P. M. (1965). Koro—a culture-bound depersonalization syndrome. *The British Journal of Psychiatry*, 111(470), 43–50.

Young, H. P. (2015). The evolution of social norms. *Annual Review of Economics*, 7, 359–387.

Zerilli, J. (2020). *The Adaptable Mind: What Neuroplasticity and Neural Reuse Tell Us about Language and Cognition*. Oxford University Press.

Index

For the benefit of digital users, indexed terms that span two pages (e.g., 52–53) may, on occasion, appear on only one of those pages.